CU00406705

# A History of Fra

## PALGRAVE ESSENTIAL HISTORIES

**General Editor: Jeremy Black**

This series of compact, readable and informative national histories is designed to appeal to anyone wishing to gain a broad understanding of a country's history.

*Published*

**A History of the Low Countries (2nd edn)** *Paul Arblaster*
**A History of Italy** *Claudia Baldoli*
**A History of Russia** *Roger Bartlett*
**A History of Spain (2nd edn)** *Simon Barton*
**A History of the British Isles (3rd edn)** *Jeremy Black*
**A History of France** *Joseph Bergin*
**A History of Israel** *Ahron Bregman*
**A History of Ireland (2nd edn)** *Mike Cronin & Liam O'Callaghan*
**A History of Greece** *Nicholas Doumanis*
**A History of the Pacific Islands (2nd edn)** *Steven Roger Fischer*
**A History of Korea** *Kyung Moon Hwang*
**A History of the United States (4th edn)** *Philip Jenkins*
**A History of Denmark (2nd edn)** *Knud J. V. Jespersen*
**A History of the Baltic States** *Andres Kasekamp*
**A History of Australia** *Mark Peel and Christina Twomey*
**A History of Poland (2nd edn)** *Anita J. Prazmowska*
**A History of India (2nd edn)** *Peter Robb*
**A History of China (3rd edn)** *J. A. G. Roberts*
**A History of Germany** *Peter Wende*

**Series Standing Order**
**ISBN 978-1-4039-3811-4 hardback**
**ISBN 978-1-4039-3812-1 paperback**

If you would like to receive future titles in this series as they are published, you can make use of our standing order facility. To place a standing order please contact your bookseller or, in case of difficulty, write to us at the address below with your name and address and the name of the series. Please state with which title you wish to begin your standing order. (If you live outside the United Kingdom we may not have the rights for your area, in which case we will forward your order to the publisher concerned.) Customer Services Department, Macmillan Distribution Ltd, Houndmills, Basingstoke, Hampshire, RG21 6XS, UK

# A HISTORY OF FRANCE

Joseph Bergin

 macmillan education    palgrave

First published 2015 by
PALGRAVE

Palgrave in the UK is an imprint of Macmillan Publishers Limited, registered in England, company number 785998, of 4 Crinan Street, London, N1 9XW.

Palgrave Macmillan in the US is a division of St Martin's Press LLC, 175 Fifth Avenue, New York, NY 10010.

Palgrave is a global imprint of the above companies and is represented throughout the world.

Palgrave® and Macmillan® are registered trademarks in the United States, the United Kingdom, Europe and other countries.

ISBN 978-1-137-33904-1    ISBN 978-1-137-33906-5 (eBook)

DOI 10.1007/978-1-137-33906-5

A catalogue record for this book is available from the British Library.

A catalog record for this book is available from the Library of Congress.

Typeset by MPS Limited, Chennai, India.

*For Edward and Olivia*
*That they may continue to love France*

# Contents

# List of Maps

# Preface

France has unfailingly challenged historians to write both general and specialised scholarly works on its past. The international reputation of its own historians has led historians elsewhere not merely to emulate their efforts but also to research and write on French history itself, especially since the 1950s. The resulting bibliography in English alone is impressive in both its range and volume. Translations into English, in full or in part, of some French-language series of general histories, further attest to the subject's enduring interest for English-language readers. But while single-volume accounts of France's history abound in French, English-language counterparts are remarkably few, despite the numbers of English-language historians of France being greater than ever before. Perhaps it has become more difficult than in the past to identify the potential readers of such books, especially that great will o' the wisp, the 'intelligent lay reader'. Such uncertainty has scarcely encouraged either historians or publishers to undertake a venture whose purpose and audience seem so elusive.

Yet the continuing attraction of French history to a non-French public, Anglo-Saxon or other, is undeniable. It may seem trivial to relate it to the huge numbers of tourists who visit France every year. Even if the majority of them have no burning desire to familiarise themselves with the detail of its history, they 'consume' French history in their choice of itineraries and destinations, as anyone who has joined the endless queues to visit its great cultural patrimony will concede. More than most of its neighbours, France still personifies some of the key developments of European history, from its largely unproblematic relations of state and nation to its experience of enlightenment, revolution, or secularisation, to mention just a few. The connections between the frequency of political upheaval and the continuity of social formations must rate among the most difficult challenges for an outsider historian of France to grasp and convey to readers. The echos of the Revolution of 1789 may have weakened in recent generations, but the changes that it unleashed, inside and outside of France, remain foundational in many respects. That heritage is another reason why France still attracts the curiosity of outsiders, even at a time when its major artists, writers, and intellectuals appear less pre-eminent than in earlier generations.

This book's centre of gravity lies, broadly speaking, in the connections, sometimes visible but often subterranean, between political power, social change, and cultural forces over time. Its brevity necessarily limits the scope for extended analysis of numerous topics. If it offers a framework for further reading and reflection on the essential features of French history, as the title of the series to which it belongs promises, it will have served its purpose.

In writing this book, I have accumulated several debts that I am happy to avow here. Firstly, I am grateful to several friends and colleagues for assistance and guidance in those areas of French history that are far removed from my habitual 'comfort zone'. I have an additional debt towards those among them who, despite the other calls upon their time, accepted the thankless task of reading my chapters in draft. Paul Fouracre, Mark Greengrass, Malcolm Crook, and Stuart Jones were especially generous with their time, offering both sound advice and shrewd comments on my early efforts. At Palgrave Macmillan, I would like to thank Jenna Steventon and especially Rachel Bridgewater for smoothing the path towards publication with unfussy efficiency.

# Abbreviations

| | |
|---|---|
| ATTAC | Association pour la taxation des transactions financières et pour l'action citoyenne |
| CAP | Common Agricultural Policy |
| CDD | Contrat de durée déterminée |
| CFDT | Conféderation française démocratique du travail |
| CFTC | Conféderation française de travailleurs chrétiens |
| CGT | Conféderation générale du travail |
| CPE | Contrat première embauche |
| ECSC | European Coal and Steel Community |
| EDC | European Defence Community |
| EEC | European Economic Community |
| EMS | European Monetary System |
| ENA | École nationale d'administration |
| FLN | Front de libération nationale |
| FN | Front National |
| GDP | Gross Domestic Product |
| HEC | Hautes études commerciales |
| MRP | Mouvement républicain populaire |
| NATO | North Atlantic Treaty Organization |
| OAS | Organisation de l'armée secrète |
| OECD | Organisation for Economic Co-operation and Development |
| OPEC | Organization of the Petroleum Exporting Countries |
| ORTF | Office de radiodiffusion-télévision française |
| PACS | Pacte civil de solidarité |
| PCF | Parti communiste français |
| PS | Parti socialiste |
| RER | Réseau express régional |
| RMI | Revenu minimum d'insertion |
| RPF | Rassemblement du peuple français |
| RPR | Rassemblement pour la République |
| SFIO | Section française de l'Internationale ouvrière |
| SMIC | Salaire minimum inter-professionnel de croissance |
| SMIG | Salaire minimum inter-professionnel garanti |
| SNCF | Société nationale des chemins de fer |
| STO | Service du travail obligatoire |

TGV     Train à grande vitesse
UDF     Union pour la démocratie française
UDR     Union des démocrates pour la République
UMP     Union pour un movement populaire

# Introduction

If the past is a foreign country where things are done differently, then what is it that makes a country 'foreign' except its past? Neither isolation nor distance alone can explain it, as the numerous differences between those nearest of neighbours, England and France, suggest. Endlessly commented upon, yet never quite clarified, the centuries-old friction between them has notoriously been a breeding ground for xenophobic or nationalist sentiments on both sides of the Channel. The presence of France has been so familiar on the map of Europe for the past millennium that it can feel like a simple fact of nature. Its shape – a subject to which we shall return later – seems no less 'obvious', but on examination it proves a far more complex question. Of course, it helped that, apart from England (or Britain), France did not have enduringly 'noisy', let alone dangerous, neighbours until the mid-nineteenth century. The Habsburg empire of the early modern period is often considered as such. But formidable as it was in its time, that empire's loose, composite structure and its internal problems ensured that its efforts to 'encircle' France, which were much exaggerated at the time, never produced invasions remotely like those of 1870, 1914, or 1940.

By the same token, few European countries can boast of a history as long and distinctive as that of France. That history is not merely something 'objective', based on measurable territory or shape, but is a 'subjective' chronicle of an 'imagined community', of a people and a nation conscious of its own existence over a very long period of time. As this suggests, the most visible dimension of that history is, in the widest sense of the term, political. By European standards, France reached an effective level of such self-awareness by the later Middle Ages, when it was buttressed by a well-honed historical narrative whose earliest chronicles dated from the seventh century. At that point, its monarchy was both the focus and the vehicle of these early forms of pre- or proto-national sentiment. Such sentiment was mainly confined to France's elites, clerical and lay, until the experiences of the Revolution of 1789 rewrote the script and diffused it throughout the population. Underpinning the earlier mix of political attitudes was a very powerful religious charge, one which closely associated the king with God's designs and which also made him 'the eldest son of the church'. However focussed on the monarchy they might usually be, such sentiments could survive and thrive on adversity, as was demonstrated by the extraordinary

1

saga of a peasant girl, Joan of Arc, galvanising that same monarchy into action during the crucial years of the Hundred Years' War with England and its French (or Burgundian) allies. In modern times, the disaster of defeat in 1870 and 1940 (prolonged by the 'Vichy' years until 1944) represented another such moment. The state and the political elites of the day were so thoroughly discredited as guardians of French-ness that alternatives were desperately sought. The nearest France got to having a second Joan of Arc was Charles de Gaulle.

Such shocks were all the greater as they cut across a history covering several proud centuries, from at least the end of the Hundred Years' War onwards, during which France was Europe's single most powerful country. Its prolonged conflicts with neighbours like England, Spain, or (later) Germany shaped it not merely territorially, but also institutionally. French hegemony of the kind that Louis XIV and Napoleon embodied was only buried by the outcome of the Revolutionary and Napoleonic wars respectively. Since then, the steep decrease in French power has been a constant challenge – and, at times, a genuine obsession about wider national decline. It has involved a continuous search for a 'grandeur' that corresponds to its imagined, glorious past. In pre-modern times, the size of a country like France was not decisive in determining its power. Indeed, Europe's larger states – Poland is the best example – were more likely to be vulnerable unless they had a correspondingly effective infrastructure of institutions and communications to mobilise resources. France potentially faced similar problems, but for centuries after the Hundred Years' War, its population density and its network of internal communications were sufficient to deter would-be invaders.

Above all, France could also draw on a long culture and framework of governance extending back to Roman times in some respects. Well-known and extended periods of serious internal disorder and political weakness – the Hundred Years' War, the wars of religion, successive royal minorities, and so on – make it easy to forget that France had by far the most continuous and stable form of dynastic monarchy of any European country before 1789. Of course, dynastic monarchy inevitably had its own weaknesses, with failure to produce heirs leading to a search for successors that might precipitate either civil war or the well-known European phenomenon of 'wars of succession' – or both. The Hundred Years' War was one such conflict, whose dynastic lessons were learned in the rejection of royal succession in the female line (the Salic law). Less well known but equally vital was another 'fundamental' law of this period that declared the integrity and inalienability of the royal domain. This denied monarchs the right permanently to sub-divide or give away any part of the kingdom in the form of dowries or apanages to sons or daughters on marrying. The Franks, Carolingians, and their successors had regularly practised sub-division, as did European neighbours like the Habsburgs and German princes until the eighteenth century, with territorial fragmentation as its inevitable consequence. France's handful of fundamental laws may not have prevented disruptive internal conflicts, but they were, in their time, a kind of constitution, which jurists and other commentators defended and systematically expounded. This is not to deny that the contours of France were primarily determined by dynastic expansion based on military strength, yet the maxims enshrined in its fundamental laws helped to copper-fasten concepts of the territorial integrity of a stable state, without which a basic sense of 'French-ness' would have been both less precocious and certainly more precarious. France's historical experiences were singular in many ways, but they did not prevent it from being widely seen as the model of the modern nation-state.

Some years ago, the eminent French medievalist, Jacques Le Goff, wrote that 'France took shape between the middle of the ninth and the end of the thirteenth century'. This assertion was made in relation to France's monarchy, but it sidestepped the question of whether there was – or indeed could be – an entity recognisable as 'France', as distinct from the 'monarchy of the Franks', at that time. With its northern, western, southern, and south-eastern boundaries determined primarily by seas and mountains, it was from (roughly) Geneva to the English Channel that there was no 'natural' demarcation line. Throughout the Middle Ages, this eastern 'march' was considered to be defined by the 'four rivers' – the Rhône, the Saône, the Meuse, and the Scheldt – which corresponded to the sub-division of Charlemagne's empire in 843. French interest in these eastern borderlands varied considerably over the centuries. Of the four rivers, the Rhône offered the least resistance to an expanding French monarchy, which acquired Lyon (and its region), but also the Dauphiné and Provence on its left bank, by the later Middle Ages. Other smaller neighbouring entities (Gex, Bresse) would duly follow around 1600, with the acquisition of Savoy and Nice completing the process as recently as 1859.

The other three rivers proved far more problematic, especially with the sudden emergence in the early sixteenth century of a Europe-wide Hapsburg empire, which acquired formerly French Burgundian lands spreading from the Franche-Comté to northern Flanders. The resulting wars saw French gains, especially in the north-east (around Lille and Cambrai) and the Franche-Comté, which finally became French under Louis XIV in 1679. With the subsequent decline of Spanish Habsburg power, the Rhine was increasingly seen France's new 'natural' eastern frontier. But the absence of a major state on either side of the Rhine until the emergence of Bismarckian Germany in 1870, made such a need somewhat less than urgent. It should be realised that for centuries, the modern concept of fixed or 'natural' frontiers (such as the Rhine) was simply not dominant, but was subordinated to the possession of strategic sites that would both prevent invasion or facilitate military action beyond France's normal frontiers. Territory alone – and thus frontiers – was not decisive until the national unifications of the nineteenth century. It was only after 1945 and the tentative steps towards a European union that it became possible to think of France in more politically neutral ways. The term hexagon is now widely used to describe France, but most of those who employ that term are oblivious of how recent it is.

Around 1000 AD, a full millennium after Julius Caesar famously but erroneously declared that 'all Gaul is divided into three parts', there was still no name to describe the area governed by the early Capetians other than 'the kingdom', while the term *Francia* itself still applied only to the modern Ile-de-France region around Paris. In 1083, Philip I was described in an official document as the king 'reigning in Francia'. Educated clerics employed a vocabulary inherited from Rome, so they referred to *Gallia* rather than to *Francia*, which belonged to 'profane' parlance. On the other hand, certain Latin terms, such as the highly charged *patria*, had lost their Roman resonance by then. Although the word *pays* served as a French equivalent of *patria*, until the Revolution it almost always signified one's own locality, adopted or otherwise, and far less the kingdom as a whole. Not until the heady days of the Revolution would *la patrie* would become sacred again and, literally, to die for. It was now a nation owning a claim on all citizens. Long before then, however, the gradual increase of royal power in northern France from around 1100, which was partly driven by conflicts with the English kings over possession of the duchy of Normandy, had stimulated the desire to move beyond the earlier imprecision. It was in 1204–5, soon after capturing Rouen from the English, that for the first time Philip Augustus described himself as 'king of Francia' rather than, as hitherto, simply 'of the Franks'. His realm began to be officially styled the 'kingdom of Francia', and from the 1250s onwards Louis IX was the first to consistently identify himself as 'king of France'. Thereafter, with the gradual replacement of clerics and Latin by lay officials and the French vernacular in royal service, such terminology became increasingly common in official documents, inscriptions, and seals; from there it spread outwards to literary texts generally. For centuries the 'France' to which they referred remained a shifting patchwork of often-unconnected territories ruled by the monarch of the day, and not necessarily some ideal construct, whether gallic or hexagonal.

The identity of the 'French' themselves was no less heatedly debated for centuries. In our time, the nostalgia for reassuringly ancient origins has enabled phrases such as 'our ancestors, the Gauls' to become a staple of French popular culture; packaged in humorous cartoons, the Gauls remain infinitely more appealing to the age of *Asterix* than the Barbarians (with or without more specific tribal names) who swarmed across the Roman imperial provinces. By the end of the fifth century, it was the least disliked and most assimilated of these successive invaders, the Franks, who came to control the largest portion of north-eastern Gaul, thanks mainly to the conquests of their king, Clovis. The Franks were themselves keen to retain Gallo-Roman institutions in order to facilitate their rule, not least because like earlier Germanic invaders, they were simply too few in number to replace the older Celtic-Gallic population. Clovis's conversion to Christianity around 500 voided a major objection among the already christianised Gallo-Roman elites towards the previously pagan Franks, and seriously facilitated their efforts to absorb the Gallo-Roman elites. But it would be several centuries before the rest of the non-Frankish subject population was included in references to the 'Franks'.

From the seventh century onwards, the literate elite began describing the Franks as 'really' descendants of the Trojans – like the Romans before them. Moreover, the legend had it that they had merely 'migrated' to France and had emphatically not conquered it, which in turn meant that their right to rule there was not based on the laws of conquest. It was not until the Renaissance of the sixteenth century that this myth was seriously challenged, as a result of which there was a return of the Gauls as the ancestors of preference among the educated classes. The very first printed map of France (1525) was actually a map of Gaul as understood by Renaissance humanists! It would be easy, from a twenty-first century perspective, to deride such shifts of identification as pure fantasy, but they were regularly mobilised to support successive causes, social and political, down to the Revolution. Indeed, with the rise of nineteenth-century Romantic and nationalist histories, there was more scope than ever for constructing political parables based on the history of France before it became known as France. These waters having now receded, it has become easier to argue, as many historians do, that France was not an eternal nation with a corresponding territorial extension, but a historical product with its own changing characteristics.

A major reason why France was long considered the epitome of a nation-state was the French language itself. Of course, not all French-speakers are French, and France itself continues to have its own non-French languages, such as Breton, Provençal, or Occitan. Despite rejecting a Protestant reformation in the sixteenth century that might have made French even more dominant within France, the use of the vernacular grew substantially, and French Catholicism was far less averse to using the vernacular than its European counterparts. The monarchy also became a key promoter of such linguistic diffusion by insisting on French as the language of the courts and the administration. The Renaissance and post-Renaissance flowering of French as a literary, even philosophical and scientific language, was vital in widening its appeal beyond France to Europe's social and intellectual elites by the eighteenth century; it was culture as much as language per se which subsequently sustained that appeal. Yet within pre-nineteenth-century France itself, the use of French was not as uniform as is sometimes imagined. In many, especially southern or western regions, speaking and writing French signified belonging to a wider national elite, but without necessarily cutting oneself off from the local *patois* spoken by the majority. The Revolution's rejection of old-regime provinces was duly extended to local languages, but it was the Third Republic's drive for universal education a century later that did most to discredit them for their supposed backwardness. This may well overestimate the impact of schooling on local societies, and justify the view that it was the trenches of 1914–18 that did most – and not just linguistically – to make Frenchmen of provincials.

France's particular trajectory, seen from a wider European perspective, requires that attention be paid to a wide range of factors that may help to explain both its differences and similarities to other countries. When foreign observers or travellers tried to explain France's power from about 1500 onwards, many, like the Italian Machiavelli, drew attention to its 'populousness'. They were clearly awed by its demographic superiority, which made France virtually three times more populous than its greatest rival of the time, Habsburg Spain. France's own proto-economists regularly repeated the maxim of the great sixteenth-century political theorist, Jean Bodin, that without an 'abundance of men' there could be neither power nor wealth. That perceived advantage was only lost to its emerging rival, the increasingly populous Germany, during the nineteenth century. Anxious debate on the subject, and its wider social features, by economists, sociologists, and politicians ensued for a century until the 1960s.

Despite its demographic 'abundance', French society had a comparatively low proportion of town-dwellers to peasants, a long-term characteristic that lasted well into the twentieth century. This contrasts sharply with the neighbouring territories running from Lombardy via the Rhineland to Flanders, where precocious urbanisation during the Middle Ages produced a geo-political map that was seriously hostile to the development of extensive territorial states. Within France, towns and *bourgs*, many of them of

Roman origin (especially in the Midi), were numerous but unevenly distributed across its many regions, and for centuries the bigger they were the more heavily they depended on continuing rural immigration to sustain their often modest population levels. These factors had a considerable impact on France's long-term social structures. Like most of their counterparts, in western Europe at least, France's peasants gradually shed the shackles of serfdom by the fourteenth and fifteenth centuries, although in some provinces, such as Burgundy and Brittany, strong traces of serfdom remained until the Revolution. Elsewhere, the peasantry was still mostly bound to attenuated forms of lordship which involved a mixture of financial obligations and subjection to numerous symbolic forms of social domination down to August 1789. France's nobility was numerically superior to England's – because based on different principles – but far inferior to those of Spain or Poland. It was constantly renewing itself, however, especially from the sixteenth century onwards, thanks to the influx of newly ennobled office-holders of bourgeois origin whose service to the monarchy gradually won them the formal right to noble status. These new nobles often slipped, via intermarriage, into the shoes of older noble families in decline.

Such developments were of major consequence for the bourgeoisie, to whom Karl Marx assigned the role of the motor of modern historical change. Some historians have turned Marx on his head, asserting either that there was no distinctive middle-class in pre-Revolutionary France or, if there was one, it was a middle-class intent on class treason, given that its principal ambition was to enter the ranks of the nobility. Regardless of which verdict is the most credible, it provides clear evidence of how closely connected the social and political were under the pre-1789 *ancien régime*. The monarchy could not (re-) shape society 'from above' singlehandedly, but its alliances with social or economic groups gave it considerable 'leverage' in the process of social change. The scale of the dismantling of the *ancien régime* that commenced in 1789 was testimony to that past.

No account of French history could underestimate the long-term significance of the Revolution, which was both a key slice of history and an 'idea' that would divide future generations, horrifying some while inspiring others to repeat it for their own time. One after another, the Revolution's attempts, for example, to devise a formal constitution or to re-create France's institutions – indeed to re-make society and human beings – involved scrapping historical precedents and taking 'nature' and 'reason', as understood by Enlightenment thinkers and their disciples, as their rationale. From the outset, the Revolution sought to define and defend universal values, which transcended mere historical precedents. It created the notion of an 'ancien régime' that was consigned to the dustbin of history, as the colossal destruction of archives, titles, and monuments during the years after 1789 attests. The Revolution's first major source of enduring conflict concerned Catholicism, whose transformation into a national – but not 'established' – church and religion at the hands of a parliamentary assembly was itself a huge shock in 1790. This was the beginning of a major divide that would produce civil war in the short term and deep political hostility in the long term. Pitting clericals against anti-clericals, and conservatives against republicans (or radicals), these divisions would long be associated with particular regions of France. The regicide of 1793 had similar repercussions, ones which often overlapped, socially and geographically, with those concerning religion. These are only a few examples of the kinds of mobilisation and polarisation that the Revolution stood for until recent times. For Socialists and Communists who identified themselves as heirs of the Revolution, it was unfinished work that needed to be completed by a new social and economic revolution. Thus, where one stood on one or other legacy of the Revolution sufficed to situate individual French people, politically and culturally, for generations. Because of its enormous impact, it introduced an un-erasable caesura into French history – a 'before' and an 'after' that was unrivalled elsewhere in Europe. The Revolution's first centenary was celebrated in 1889 as an indivisible 'block' – the term used at the time. Decoded, this meant that its less savoury aspects (e.g. the reign of Terror 1793–4) were considered intrinsic to its legacy. The 1989 bicentenary studiously avoided evoking the 'blood and guts' years of Robespierre and the accompanying Terror by focussing on 1789 itself and its universalist legacy, namely the rights of man and civil society. The simultaneous transfer in late 1989 to the Pantheon of the remains of the philosopher Condorcet, the abbé Grégoire, and the mathematician Monge – a noble, clergyman, and commoner respectively who had lived through the Revolution – was another gesture symbolising compromise and consensus which would have been virtually unthinkable only a few decades earlier. As the Revolution recedes into an older historical timescale, its contentiousness and capacity to serve as a guide for the present seems likely to decline even further.

At this point, it may be worth saying the obvious: historians make bad prophets of future developments. Like good cobblers, they should stick to their lasts. Such advice probably applies even more to a book like the present one.

# 1 Capetian Beginnings

Anyone searching for an unarguable birth-date for the entity that would become known as France in the centuries following the collapse of the Roman empire is likely to be severely frustrated. During the half-millennium or more after the invasion and settlement of Germanic peoples across Roman Gaul, successive kingdoms rose and fell, partly because their rulers all shared an imperative habit of sub-dividing their territories among their surviving sons. The numerous partitions of these lands show scarcely any wider logic or continuity beyond dynastic considerations. The tripartite division of Charlemagne's vast empire in 843, which many have seen as a key moment precisely because its western kingdom came close to resembling the France of later centuries, was no exception. If anything, notions of territorial continuity weakened even further because of the numerous partitions made and unmade *after* 843.

By comparison, the election as king of the Franks of Hugh Capet (c. 940–96) by an assembly of magnates (lay and clerical) near Paris in 987, may seem a rather unspectacular event in what was then just west *Francia*. Nobody thought of it then as an attempt to guarantee a stable Frankish monarchy. Indeed, the choice of Hugh was prompted by the new-style Holy Roman Emperor, Otto III, king of Germany, supported by his current ally, the 'middle' kingdom of *Lotharingia* ('Lorraine'), both of whom wished to keep the western kingdom in a dependent position. On that occasion, the eloquence of Archbishop Adalberon of Reims was apparently crucial in persuading the electors to choose Hugh. The enduring connection between the future French monarchy and Reims was direct and intimate from the outset. The biggest challenge to Hugh and his successors was how to exert their notional primacy in dealing with these major political figures who, like Hugh himself before his election, personified the real power that resided in the kingdom's principalities. By then, Charlemagne's great imperial monarchy had shrivelled into a congeries of such principalities. Yet their rulers had been partners rather than mortal enemies of the Carolingians, and they continued Carolingian forms of rule within their lands. Their growing autonomy was a consequence of royal inadequacy rather than mutual incompatibility. Although the principalities lay mainly between the Loire and the Rhine, easily the largest of them were 'Aquitaine' and 'Burgundy', both far bigger than their later incarnations.

The electors of 987 merely envisaged choosing one of their own – one to whom most of them were connected by ties of marriage – as a *primus inter pares*. There was no intention, let alone guarantee, that the new Capetian monarchy after 987 would be more coherent or successful than its predecessors. But in due course, by avoiding dynastic partition as much as possible and solidifying their grip on their existing lands, the Capetians did restore the boundaries agreed in 843. One important result of this was the emergence of a linguistic border running through the middle kingdom of Lotharingia, on the western side of which 'French' emerged as the dominant language. The significance of such developments would only become clear with hindsight, which explains why they remain such a fixture in France's pantheon of myth and memory.

# I

The founder of the new dynasty only survived his election by less than ten years, but thereafter the reigns of virtually all the Capetians until their disappearance in 1328 were, with the exception mainly of the last three kings, remarkably lengthy for any age. Such regnal longevity (over forty years was not uncommon) guaranteed, if nothing else, substantial – and novel – continuity for the post-Carolingian monarchy. Biological good fortune played its part, too, as successive Capetian monarchs regularly produced legitimate male heirs – a much bigger challenge than might be imagined at a time when the church was increasingly hostile towards the rights of bastards. But good luck alone would not have sufficed for the Capetians to escape the fate of earlier powerless, 'seat-warming' rulers. Henceforth, the kings routinely 'inducted' their heirs as co-rulers and had them formally crowned *before* their actual succession, a tactic that had precedents under both the Merovingians and the Carolingians, but which now imperceptibly transformed a theoretically elective monarchy into a *de facto* hereditary one. The royal coronation at Reims duly registered this shift, by introducing an 'acclamation' of the new king by those present that effectively replaced the previous elections. This tactic also helped to stave off the familiar political upheavals that so often accompanied a transition to a new reign. The Capetians were anxious to identify their rule with that of Charlemagne and to use the same icons of power, such as the *oriflamme* (the royal military banner), to symbolise that continuity. But as in other European monarchies, there was no escaping factional in-fighting involving different combinations of queen-mothers, uncles and younger brothers seeking to either regain or obtain political influence. Such conflicts often became violent, leading to civil wars, prolonged hostilities, and vendettas between major political figures.

The early Capetians of the 1000s and 1100s had to survive within a constantly shifting world of regional principalities (see Map 1). What has often been called the 'feudal anarchy' saw power drain away from large-scale, and downwards to regional and local political units. In their efforts to deal with them, it helped that the Capetians were themselves the product of such a process. Hugh Capet and his father, Hugh 'the Great', had gradually built up

**Map 1** *The Frankish kingdom and its principalities, c. 1000*

during the 900s the largest political entity in west Francia after Aquitaine and Flanders, which enabled them to become dukes of the Franks. But attaining kingship was no sure protection against future sorcerer's apprentices with ambitions to undermine their new suzerains; ultimately, royal titles and emblems were of only limited use unless buttressed by extensive lands and lordship. The early Capetians were realists enough to avoid direct confrontation with the major princes; like a typical landholder, they focussed on consolidating their own still quite limited royal domain in the wider Paris region – scattered through the Seine-Oise-Marne-Essonne river valleys from Soissons to Orléans, roughly – by recovering lands previously granted out and then tightening their grip on them. Hugh Capet's reign began with only one 'city', Orléans, within his domain. He and his successors decided to 'retain' under direct control a number of key counties, which included Paris, rather than confer them, as was expected of Frankish kings, on *vicomtes* to administer and, most likely, to make their own in due course. The Capetians also acquired full patronage rights to bishoprics and the major abbeys in the same region (and to some well outside of it), which was of considerable benefit, given the church's enormous landed wealth and influence in the region. Archbishop Hincmar of Reims (806–82), a former monk of Saint-Denis, had already embellished the story of Clovis's baptism at Reims as a royal anointment, one that each new coronation at Reims repeated and amplified. The foundations of the myth of a monarchy enjoying divine origins already existed, and further elements would be added in the following centuries. These abbeys, famously led by Saint-Denis, the historical burial-place of French monarchs just outside of Paris, played a major role in devising and disseminating propaganda (lives, chronicles, genealogies, etc.) for the successive dynasties. The connexion between the two proved invaluable in establishing – and inflating – the monarchy's claims to rule and, by extension, its superiority to other forms of authority and legitimacy.

The early Capetians were probably fortunate in that for some time the greatest principalities developed primarily on the peripheries of west Francia; that trend only later affected the centre of the kingdom. The duchy of Aquitaine (which stretched from Poitou almost to the Pyrenees) was probably the least threatening towards the early Capetians, since its mainly Gallo-Roman population, legal customs, and culture rendered it unreceptive to Frankish ways, and especially to the so-called feudal institution of vassalage. Consequently, with a greater affinity towards Catalonia, Aquitaine largely ignored the Franks until its incorporation into the Plantagenet 'empire' in the 1150s rendered that impossible. Other southern principalities – Gascony, Catalonia-Provence and, to a lesser extent, 'Burgundy' – were primarily concerned with developments in the Mediterranean region, and notably the Saracen and Moorish incursions of the ninth and tenth centuries.

This was just as well, since north of the Loire several formidable principalities – the counties of Flanders and Champagne to the east, and Normandy and Anjou-Maine in the west – hemmed in the Capetians. Such political geography meant that they were for long completely landlocked. Normandy is the best known of the principalities, for the obvious reason that in 1066 its duke was powerful and confident enough to invade and conquer England. The formidable Norman duchy owed its origin to the Viking sea-borne expeditions, whose incursions far inland both revealed and exacerbated the weakness of the later Carolingians – and indeed of other principalities already mentioned from Flanders to Guyenne. Paris was sacked several times in the 840s and 850s, and the Carolingians were eventually forced, in 911, to concede to the Viking-Normans the county of Rouen, with its extensive allodial lands (i.e. not subject to feudal lordship) and the attached rights of church patronage in the surrounding lower Seine valley. The future duchy soon became co-terminous with the church province of Rouen, which gave it far greater institutional density than the more artificially constructed territorial entities of the time; it also facilitated its expansion westwards towards Brittany. Thus, without being typical, Normandy was probably the strongest principality by the time of Hugh Capet's election in 987; its strength made it an effective defence against the newest wave of Viking expansion in the next century. Closer still to the Capetian heartlands were the ambitious counts of Vermandois-Vexin and, especially, those of Champagne. In 1023, Champagne acquired, via dynastic inheritance, the older, 'composite' principality that included the Loire valley counties of Blois, Chartres and Tours. Further north again, the county of Flanders, stretching southwards almost to the Ile-de-France, was the most powerful vassal and neighbour of the Capetians. Its famed wealth, based on its textile production and its trade with England and Germany, made it a desirable acquisition for any neighbour, but also made it a formidable adversary.

All of these 'princes' were seeking to expand their lands, often through marriage alliances, which placed enormous pressure on the Capetians trapped at the heart of this immense patchwork of lands, jurisdictions and patronage rights which defy easy or legible mapping, since they did not express or require territorial exclusiveness. Rivals as much as allies, each of these princes sought their individual advantage. That in turn meant the Capetians' strategy had to be one of exploiting differences among them and taking advantage of their own royal 'superiority' and good fortune, most of all by recovering lands from princes without heirs. The territorial patch-work of these centuries would have been infinitely more complicated if the bishops of northern France had sought, like their German counterparts, to turn their extensive landholdings into territorial principalities.

If dynastic solidity and longevity gave the Capetians an advantage over their rivals, it still had to be actively exploited. As king, Hugh Capet and his successors were suzerains and lords to most of the dukes and counts encountered above, but without a firm power base within their own lands formal royal or imperial titles made little difference. During the reigns of Hugh Capet's four immediate successors, who totalled 140 years between them (996–1137), such consolidation seems to have been their primary focus; their efforts understandably remain rather obscure in comparison with the exploits of their better-known successors. Philip I (1060–1108) is a good example here: his role as king over almost fifty years is largely invis-ible apart from his assiduity as lord of his domain, which he rounded out by a mixture of unspectacular local purchases and conquests; he also reorgan-ised the administration of his household and estates, strengthened royal authority within the towns, and increased the number of royal strongholds. He actively used the bishops of the region, conferring the status of counts on them. His successors Louis VI (r. 1108–37) and Louis VII (r. 1137–80) appear to have done largely the same, but more anonymously still. Louis VI 'the Fat' is known primarily for his increased recourse to 'new men', rather than the more independent aristocrats, in running his affairs, a lead that many of his successors would follow.

## II

For centuries the Frankish monarchy was also an itinerant one, since the royal ability to move around the kingdom, and especially in the form of encounters with vassals, was a critical indicator of a king's authority. Without such surveillance, local officials usually found it much easier to pri-vatise the royal authority delegated to them; the immobility practised later by Louis XIV and his successors at Versailles was unthinkable because it sig-nified powerlessness. But the more the Capetians strengthened their grip on their core lands, the more sedentary they – or rather certain elements of their as-yet rudimentary administration – could indeed become, which in turn made possible the emergence of Paris, thanks to its convenient loca-tion along or near the main rivers of the Ile-de-France, as a quasi-capital. It was not until around 1200, thanks to new fortifications, which included the Louvre, built by Philip II Augustus (1180–1223), that such a status would have become apparent. In the longer term, however, the expansion of royal power beyond that historic nucleus made it imperative that the kings engage in yet more extensive progresses. However, even when confined within their Paris-centred domain, the Capetians were not disconnected from the wider world of European politics, from England to Aragon and Sicily; the web of dynastic interests alone made sure of that. Participation in the Crusades from 1147 onwards expanded their horizons further afield, as is well illustrated by possibly the first grand royal 'progress' which Louis IX conducted on his return from the crusade in 1254; such expeditions became familiar, and were still felt to be necessary as late as the 1560s and 1570s.

Although the powerful duchy of Normandy was a potentially danger-ous neighbour by the mid-1000s, the most consistently antagonistic one was the extensive Blois-Champagne dynasty whose lands, as its geography suggests, hemmed in the Capetians far more tightly. It was not until the reign of Louis VII (1137–80) that this roadblock to Capetian expansion eastwards finally began to be lifted, commencing with a three-way parti-tion (1152) of the lands in question and, thanks to intermarriage, the onset of better relations between the Capetians and the counts of Champagne themselves. However, almost simultaneously, another set of dynastic events that would spell a different kind of trouble for the Capetians, was in train. In 1152, Louis VII, just returned from the Second Crusade, divorced his wife Eleanor, who duly recovered her enormous Aquitaine inheritance in the west and south-west. Within two months she had married Henry of Plantagenet, duke of Normandy, as he then was, a union that on its own represented a major geo-political transformation. But this already enor-mous conglomerate soon grew even further, with her husband's accession as King Henry II of England in 1154. A Plantagenet 'empire' – also labelled 'Angevin' because Anjou was its historic nucleus – was suddenly born, one which dwarfed the Capetians' still modest lands; and it had active designs on neighbouring areas such as Brittany (which it annexed for a time), Auvergne and Toulouse county. Admittedly, Henry II consented to pay homage to the king of France for his French lands, in addition to Normandy, possibly because up to then such formalities had little real sig-nificance. But when the two royal dynasties began seriously to lock horns either side of 1200, the political capital incrementally accumulated by the successive Capetians, especially in enforcing their conception of royal suze-rainty over vassals, great as well as small, was capable of paying substan-tial dividends. It also helped that they were by now extracting substantial revenues from the areas under their direct control.

It was the challenge represented by the Plantagenets' composite mon-archy which gradually obliged the Capetian monarchy to look beyond its usual ken, especially south of the Loire. During the long reign of Philip II, a mediocre Crusader but the only French monarch to have the sobriquet (Augustus) of the Caesars routinely attached to his name, 'internal' and 'external' challenges, as well as royal responses to them, dovetailed. These years were to prove decisive for the monarchy's future. Only fourteen on his accession, Philip needed a regent, his god-father the count of Flanders, to govern for several years; the days when French kings came of age at thirteen rather than twenty-one only came much later, in 1374. Regencies were and would remain moments of uncertainty and danger: the solidity of the Capetian polity was not yet indisputable, and the neighbouring principalities remained potentially as predatory as before. But Philip Augustus enjoyed some good fortune, as virtually all his major rivals died in quick succession – several during the Third Crusade (1190–2) – while his careful deployment of his own numerous siblings from his father's successive marriages proved invaluable, not least via marriage alliances, which duly brought further lands into the royal domain. During his forty-three years of rule, Philip Augustus capitalised on his predecessors' work, mainly through family inheritance or the growing invocation of his rights as feudal overlord. Most of the gains occurred in the two final decades of his reign, after 1202. In the process, he increased the royal domain threefold and took possession areas that had historically been the most problematic – the Vexin, Vermandois (which included much of Artois and Picardy) and, above all, Normandy and several other Plantagenet lands in the Loire-Anjou region. Likewise, he almost doubled the number of bishoprics to which he could provide to over forty.

Not all of these gains were peacefully made. Normandy was the major problem either side of 1200, with Philip Augustus exploiting the hostility between the English royal brothers Richard II and John from the 1190s onwards. In dealing with John, now king of England, after 1202, Philip used another familiar tactic: John's 'failure' to attend a court of Philip's barons allowed him to declare John's French fiefs forfeit and his vassals free to recognise another suzerain. After ten years of campaigning, Philip occupied most of the Plantagenet lands in northern and western France. No less significant was his victory at Bouvines (1214) over the German Emperor and his Flemish allies. Bouvines was a landmark in several ways. Perhaps its greatest value was to enhance the military prowess (hitherto rather mediocre) of the Capetians, thus making the king the natural commander of his aristocracy. It also secured Philip's annexation of Normandy, Anjou (with Maine and Touraine), Brittany and large parts of Aquitaine over the previous decade, at the expense of the Plantagenets. It established Capetian dominance across the kingdom as it then was for the first time, whereas a

Capetian defeat would almost certainly have unravelled the process of territorial aggregation. In a largely forgotten coda to these campaigns, Philip's son, the future Louis VIII (r. 1223–6), defeated King John before conducting the last French invasion of England on the invitation of its barons, then in revolt against King John. Although Louis failed in this by no means preposterous attempt of 1217 to repeat the Norman conquest, the Capetian kingdom had, for the first time, not one but three windows onto the sea, in Normandy, western Poitou (La Rochelle and its environs), and the county of Toulouse by the 1220s.

That change was partly a consequence of the Plantagenet empire compelling the Capetians to turn their attention, to an unprecedented degree, to southern France. Despite the north-south differences already mentioned, the world south of the Loire was not wholly *terra incognita* to the Capetians before 1200: they already had a foothold in certain areas south of the Loire (Berry, Burgundy), and were increasingly careful not to allow their regalian prerogatives over their great vassals there to lapse by default. In addition, the more powerful the Capetians became, the more their assistance or intervention was solicited by southern 'parties', especially when disputed dynastic successions occurred. Consequently, the southwards expansion of the Capetian monarchy was always likely to be haphazard, the fruit of opportunities offered and taken and, by the same token, potentially reversible. It began with the Albigensian crusades of 1209 and 1226 which brought northern armies for the first time to the Toulouse-Carcassonne region, where fighting, characterised by numerous massacres, mass executions and pillaging, continued into the 1240s. But the northern aristocratic crusaders, initially led by the Montforts, proved unable to survive there without royal assistance, which was slow in coming; when it did finally show, in 1226–9, the Montforts had effectively to surrender their claims on the huge county of Toulouse to the monarchy via a marriage alliance. This pact brought a huge windfall in 1271, when Poitou and Saintonge, as well as the counties and *sénéchaussées* that constituted the future province of Languedoc, reverted to the crown on the death of Louis IX's brother, Philip, whose marriage to the southern heiress Jeanne de Toulouse, had been childless.

Dynastic fortune was still evidently smiling on the Capetians, the shape of whose crazy-paving kingdom defies modern geographical logic, but which evidently only sharpened their appetite for more. By marrying another heiress, Jeanne de Navarre, Philip IV (r. 1284–1314) was behaving as contemporaries would have expected him, since he could expect to acquire not just distant Navarre, but above all Champagne, which was by now in Navarre hands and which opened the doors towards Lorraine. Philip left Mediterranean ambitions, especially in southern Italy, to his Angevin relatives, preferring to focus his attention on reducing English power in the large duchy of Guyenne. He also incorporated Lyon and its *pays* in 1312, and where the acquisition of borderland principalities from Hainaut to Savoy seemed beyond reach, he actively sought to expand his feudal lordship over the princes who ruled there.

At the same time, Philip IV's reign witnessed major efforts to increase royal control of the lands he governed. The *baillis* introduced by Philip Augustus were by now the lynchpin of royal administration, especially in the more distant areas; their southern equivalents, the *sénéchaux*, presided over an administration that was often considered oppressive because of its military character. The celebrated crusading king, Saint Louis IX (1226–70), had already tried to regulate the behaviour of both types of official and, more broadly, to remedy perceived weaknesses in government during the mid-1250s; the legend of Saint Louis giving justice in person to his subjects was often invoked by disgruntled later generations to criticise bad government. The Paris parlement, which would remain the highest law court in France until the Revolution, became a permanent, sedentary institution of considerable authority under Louis IX's grandson, Philip IV. A new Chamber of Accounts was also created to supervise the expanding royal fiscal machinery, whose enviable ability to invent new taxes was badly needed at a time when soaring royal expenditure (particularly on war) made traditional domain revenues a shrinking proportion of its receipts. Already, the monarchy had asserted its right to control the currency; it regulated markets and trade and, above all, began developing a long-lasting relationship with the principal towns (the *bonnes villes*) of the kingdom.

Despite its importance, the role of the stern and diligent Philip IV (1284–1314) in internal affairs has often been underestimated. It suited him to allow the increasingly ubiquitous legists and his other councillors, imbued with a precociously advanced creed of royal authority, to appear on-stage. He regularly insisted that as monarch his ultimate power was that of final and supreme judge in all but specifically ecclesiastical affairs. Although a claim rather than a statement of fact, the ensuing authoritarianism began to raise hackles in the last years of the reign, especially in the expulsion of the Jews (1306) and the brutal destruction of the order of the Templars (1307), in both of which financial appetites were foremost. Not for the last time, manipulation of the coinage to the treasury's advantage drew stinging criticism, while damaging commercial activity. The shrillest confrontation of Philip IV's reign, with Pope Boniface VIII, proved to be a defining moment in church-state relations in France for centuries; it was only possible because of Philip's conviction, which he did not invent, that his lineage and established rights entitled him to defend the church against an unworthy pope. It says much about the continuing bonds between monarchy and church that Philip had little difficulty in securing the support of the kingdom's clergy against the pope.

Yet within just over a generation after Philip the Fair's death (1314), there began a major and long-lasting conflict with England – the Hundred Years' War – that nearly tore France apart. No more than their contemporaries, the Capetians were not politically infallible – or secure. In his final year, Philip IV himself was forced to back down in the face of resistance from the nobility against the levy of a feudal 'aid' for war-making purposes. Judging the charge excessive – the campaign was cancelled, but not the levy! – several noble leagues, seeking a return to the days of 'the good king Saint Louis', had to be pacified by Philip's short-lived successor; it was the king's chief extorter of funds who paid the ultimate price of execution promptly after his master's death. Such behaviour, often involving open revolt over taxation, would become a familiar feature of later French history. Above all, Philip IV's succession caused trouble. His son, Louis X, only lasted eighteen months, after which the throne was effectively 'usurped' by Philip IV's own brother, the childless Philip V 'the Tall' (r. 1316–22), who was then followed, equally briefly, by the last of the Capetians, Charles the Fair (r. 1322–8). The Capetians' prolonged good luck was running out, and its major consequence was the Hundred Years' War.

In a context of such unusual dynastic fragility, and unresolved differences about succession rights, another recent departure from the normal Capetian practice of preserving the royal domain intact is noteworthy. A century earlier, in 1225, Louis VIII (r. 1223–6) willed his father's patrimony to his eldest son, the future Louis IX, and simultaneously endowed his three younger sons with individual apanages consisting mainly of recently acquired provinces as large as Artois, Anjou-Maine, Auvergne and Poitou. His intention, he asserted, was to prevent discord among his sons. The aristocracy had long practised such division of their estates, but it was new for the Capetians to follow their example. The long 'age of the apanage', which would endure until the seventeenth century, would cause much trouble for reigning monarchs, but this may not have been evident in the 1220s. Its endurance over the following centuries shows how formidable, even irresistible, the pressures to share one's patrimony could be at the highest level; by 1225 and later, the Capetians' successes in acquiring new lands seem to have persuaded them to reverse their previous parsimony towards younger sons. In any event, Louis IX, Philip III and Philip IV all imitated the example of Louis VIII, but tried to 'circulate' roughly the same territories and ensure that they would revert to the crown in due course. Such caution indicates their awareness of the need to obviate the problems that might otherwise arise, but it did not persuade them to drop the practice altogether. Substituting members of the royal dynasty for the previous princes of recently acquired principalities made good sense, and was designed to facilitate the process of absorbing such territories, especially distant ones, into the royal domain. But the meaning of such gestures could be read in ways other than those intended, as was to become evident in due course. Despite the proper emphasis laid by historians on the precocious development of a concept of the state – or the 'crown' – as a distinct, abstract entity during the twelfth and thirteenth centuries, political practice was only partially governed by such lofty, self-denying principles.

## III

This cursory exploration of the French monarchy – its unstable territory and its fluctuating but gradually developing capacity to rule it – only scratches the surface of a world characterised by a bewildering complexity of interests and motivations, where 'modern' distinctions between 'public' and 'private', 'monarchy' (or the 'state') and 'aristocracy' were not yet familiar, let alone lived by. Personal bonds that were based on blood, on oaths taken and accepted, and on lord-vassal relations, were the strongest of all, but were far from sacrosanct when hard political decisions had to be made. In a world where the question 'who made you a count?' could be answered by another – 'who made you king?' – power essentially belonged, for a long time still, to the landed aristocracy who, from the early Germans to the Vikings, eagerly stepped into the shoes of their Gallo-Roman predecessors. Gradually the Roman practices – and language – of patronage and clientage within the political elites were adapted to the *mores* of Frankish society. Rule increasingly revolved around land and attached forms of local power and jurisdiction held 'in fief' by dependent vassals, both clerical and lay, who in return owed fidelity and service (primarily military) to their lords. Varying substantially from region to region, such practices and their consequences were central to a highly complex and endlessly discussed feature of medieval society – feudalism, a modern construct whose various meanings still divide historians.

The eleventh and twelfth centuries can be labelled as 'seigneurial' (literally, 'lord-ly') as much as 'feudal'. With the decline of the Carolingian empire, the oaths of fidelity to emperors and kings lost their substance, and in any case they now ranked below fidelity to one's immediate lord; as clienteles of vassals became more regional, even local in character, the result was that power migrated downwards. It was around such smaller fry that different forms of lordship began to emerge, in which a new class of knights, the *milites*, were the most visible and problematic. These shifts were closely connected to another contemporary phenomenon, the extensive nucleation of the hitherto thin and scattered rural populations into 'villages' near a local lord's fortified castle. This process was often violent. Local lords fought brutally to exert control over 'their' villages and peasants, whose legal status was fast becoming that of un-free serfs rather than Roman-style slaves, from whom no doubt many were descended. To impose their authority, lords often employed the knights, 'maintaining' them either as household retainers or, as gradually became the norm, conferring fiefs on them in return for military service or cash payment.

The social background of these knights is not easy to determine, but some were from lesser branches of existing aristocratic families, others of free peasant status. In any event, these *milites* duly entered the lower ranks of the nobility by the thirteenth century. Forged in violence, such lordship was a complex and locally variable mixture of rights to extract rents (in kind or in money) and labour services from the peasantry, administer justice and impose economic monopolies on the population of each lordship. This combination of rights and obligations explains the use of the term 'banal' lordship (deriving from 'ban', a lord's monopoly on powers that were originally royal rather than private) to describe the outcome. The extensive expropriation and subsequent partition of former peasant land into often-tiny fiefs and the proliferation of 'castles' – initially no more than earth-mounds with rudimentary defences – signalled an age of increased local disruption and violence; it was to counter the latter, at least as far as church lands and peasants were concerned, that the 'peace of God' movement came into existence by the late tenth century. Inadequately documented, the building of towers does not seem to have been a *Francia*-wide development, and it may have been most fully developed in the parts of Burgundy (especially the Mâcon area), Catalonia and other parts of southern France; in parts of western France, such as Saintonge, it produced a forest of fortified sites and extensive local feuding. But elsewhere, particularly in those regions, such as Normandy or Flanders, where princely power was strong enough to resist fragmentation and lawlessness, it was contained.

All of this produced a more complex noble-aristocratic landed society than previously, where land and the terms on which it was held determined the status and obligations, political and military, of the social elite. It was also one in which the church, especially through its monasteries, bishoprics, cathedral and other chapters, was fully involved, since its estates and peasant dependents grew hugely in size and number under the Capetians.

Dominated by sons and daughters of the aristocracy, the church's behaviour was not consistently different from that of society's masters. However, the violence generated by the seizures of local power was not discriminating, so that clergy and church property became as vulnerable as were pilgrims, livestock and other targets. From the 970s to the 1050s in southern and later in northern France, church authorities attempted to protect the vulnerable and impose sanctions under 'the Peace of God', for which they obtained royal support. But their achievements were probably modest, as the challenge at issue could only be dealt with by exerting more direct, downward pressure on the lords most involved in such violence. This is where the unspectacular growth of Capetian power within its domain, and indeed beyond, began to pay off during the twelfth century and after; gradually the monarchy began 'joining up' the ties of lordship-vassalage into a single pyramid, in which all vassals were ultimately royal vassals, however indirect or 'mediate'; none could hide behind the fiction that that was true only of its minority of 'direct' vassals. From the latters' perspective, this approach was a two-edged sword: while it brought the prospect of royal support to major vassals having trouble with *their* recalcitrant vassals, it also enabled sub-vassals to seek royal protection against *them*. Of course, realising such an aspiration long remained a pipe dream. But once it became common for the great lords to do homage to twelfth-century kings like Louis VI (1108–37) and once royal law-courts and jurisdiction became more familiar throughout the royal domain, it grew increasingly feasible. This was an important first step towards a hierarchical 'feudal system', in which the monarchy would duly become the grand ringmaster. In later centuries, French jurists would claim that the monarchy alone made nobles, but of course that was only formally true. As the sixteenth-century quip – 'the king can make nobles, but not gentlemen' – suggested, French kings were not considered to be social alchemists.

By the early 1300s, relations between monarchy and nobility generally had changed significantly. The increasing insistence by the monarchy that its major vassals pay homage to the king, as well as the absorption of substantial territories, especially in central and southern France, into the royal domain, hugely boosted the numbers of such royal vassals. The rapid territorial expansion of the monarchy in the 1200s increasingly made it a 'neighbour' rather than a distant phantom, as in the past, to ever more of them. The growing military reputation of the Capetians, thanks in part to the Crusades, naturally attracted many younger ambitious nobles into royal service. Nobles of particular regions were not infrequently assembled to offer advice to the monarchy, and Philip IV effectively used such assemblies to support and implement his demands for additional financial support.

At the same time, a kind of hierarchy emerged within the nobility, aided, in ways that we shall examine later, by the demographic and economic changes of the Capetian centuries. At the highest level, there stood a small group of great princely figures, like the dukes of Burgundy and Brittany or the count of Flanders, who developed powers over their lands not dissimilar to those of the king, whose direct vassals they were; in doing so, they frequently appropriated fiefs held by their own vassals or obliged the latter to convert free (allodial) lands into fiefs for which they henceforth owed homage. Below them, we find aristocrats with estates scattered across more than one province, extensive rights of 'high' justice within their lordships, numerous retainers and wide influence, due in part to matrimonial alliances with similar families. The 'middling sort' of nobles possessed fiefs and a castle, increasingly of stone, but such castles were expensive to build and, above all, to maintain; some of these nobles probably served as officials under different headings in managing the royal domain. At the bottom of the hierarchy were the poor nobles, who were still knights; heavily dependent on patrons, they typically possessed few of the typical symbols of nobility – such as administering justice. A survey conducted around 1250 on behalf of the powerful count of Champagne gives an unusual snap-shot of what that could mean. The county was divided into thirty-seven *châtellenies*, in twenty-three of which the count had a total of 1,182 direct vassals, four out of five of whom were men holding just a single fief; over half of them were described as 'lords' or 'knights' with limited revenues. At the apex of this pyramid, just below the count, stood a dozen or so major families. An extrapolation suggests that in Champagne as a whole, the count's direct vassals numbered about 1,800. But he also had 1,519 sub-vassals, the great majority of whom had fewer means and lower status. Such substantial differences were acceptable because of the centrality of personal relations between those involved; they were also made possible because by the thirteenth century an ideology that revolved around socially differentiating notions of nobility, lineage, chivalry and gentility, to which the great and small could subscribe, were constructed. The second estate of the realm was acquiring more explicit contours, while remaining a house of many mansions, with rooms for genealogies, emblems, coats of arms and other accoutrements that cumulatively became a distinctive chivalric culture.

## IV

One of the myths about Clovis's conversion was that it triggered the conversion of west Francia to christianity, when in fact its elites had been christians for generations. Clovis only brought his own Frankish people of the Tournai area into the orthodox fold with him, as would the Viking dukes of Normandy after 911. The church had already spread rapidly northwards via Gaul's main river arteries and spawned a dense network of dioceses and monasteries, with parishes coming later. Dioceses were most numerous and thus smallest in the urbanised Roman south, but increasingly vast in the more rural central and northern provinces, which were converted later. The Gallo-Roman churches and clergy were primarily town-based communities. The process of turning the peasantry – the *pagani* living in the countryside – into christians was a much longer one, especially among the Frankish and related populations. From Martin of Tours and Saint Denis onwards, the successive evangelisers of Gaul and Francia were revered as saints, intercessors and protectors, especially if they had been bishops. This cult of the saints, which included few martyrs, and of the relics associated with them, took hold among populations seeking effective mediators with a new kind of divinity. The seventh-century Irish missionaries, who promoted monasticism among the Franks in north-eastern France, added further ingredients, such as newer, more 'flexible' forms of penitence, which the Franks welcomed.

But the network of parishes, which played so many vital roles in medieval society, only really came into being on the ground with Charlemagne and took over three centuries to develop. Despite being promoted since the early sixth century, this sub-division of Christianity into tiny territorial cells helped to bring together elements which had been separate in Roman society – namely, places of settlement, worship, and burial grounds. The village, the cemetery, and the parish church became virtually inseparable henceforth, so that parishes continued to proliferate wherever new villages appeared. Thus in Normandy, Picardy, the Ile-de-France, for example, a compact village network produced an equally dense parochial structure, in which parishes were small in size. In many western and southern provinces, the opposite – large and more thinly populated parishes – was the norm, which led to the creation of local chapels and alternative burial-places where distances from the parochial 'mother-church' were considered too great. Around 1000, an enthusiastic chronicler of the Loire valley spoke of the 'white mantle of the churches' that he observed everywhere.

Charlemagne had supported the efforts to christianise his subjects by requiring weekly attendance at church, but principally by establishing a universal church tithe (tenth) on agricultural produce for the upkeep of the parish clergy. For nearly a thousand years thereafter, tithe and trouble would be synonymous: its appropriation, reform, and proper use provoked inextricable conflicts involving locals against outsiders, clergy against laypeople, to mention only a few. The subsequent 'secularisation' of the tithe by powerful interests, clerical as much as lay, was facilitated by the fact that for a long time the lower, parish clergy were little better than serfs, dependent on landowners or other 'patrons' of the parish benefice and unsupported by their 'natural' but distant superiors, the bishops. For centuries many of these clergymen lived and worked as farmers in rural areas, and were scarcely distinguishable in attitudes and behaviour from the local populations. If this did not make them capable of 'christianising' their flocks, as reformers of every generation would insist they should, it probably made for better relations between the local clergy and their parishioners. With the arrival of the 'mendicant' religious orders – the Dominicans and Franciscans in particular – in the thirteenth century, cities and towns would be exposed to a new kind of clergy and new techniques of evangelisation; with some exceptions, the countryside would have to wait much longer.

We have seen more than once how the Capetian monarchy developed close ties to the Frankish church and its leaders, given the wealth and authority that it already possessed. In that, it was only imitating its Merovingian and Carolingian predecessors because, like the Gallo-Romans before them, the converted Franks moved swiftly to occupy the major positions within the church. Bishoprics were particularly desirable, since the papacy was as yet neither determined nor capable of asserting any right to select and appoint bishops. For centuries, monarchs, lay princes, and local families fought for control over them, promoting their own close kin most of the time. Bishops were expected to be – and were – politically and militarily active; the deposition and murder of bishops was commonplace in Merovingian times; many of them were not ordained as priests or bishops at all. The numerous monasteries, male and female, founded across *Francia* long before the great monastic orders began to appear with Cluny (910), were not radically different. They were usually founded and controlled by aristocratic families, who used them to preserve their patronage and wealth, and to place family members and other dependents in them. The monasteries' wealth increased thanks to legacies and gifts, despite occasional bouts of spoliation. To take just one example: under the Carolingians, the great Parisian abbey of Saint-Germain-des-Prés held some 80,000 acres of land, half of it directly managed, the other half leased to peasant tenants. Such vast resources enabled Saint-Germain and many other abbeys, from Vézelay to Cluny and Saint-Denis, to build or upgrade some of Europe's finest churches and other monastic buildings in the successive Romanesque and especially the flamboyant Gothic styles of the period. Even when the French monarchy subsequently became the single most prestigious patron of artists, it could never match the church's country-wide resources which ensured it would remain the principal attraction for architects, builders, and sculptors.

Aristocratic and partially laicised in its higher echelons, the Frankish church was ill equipped to offer the kind of leadership or initiate the religious reform that surfaced during the early Capetian period. Instead, such reform came mainly from two unexpected players, the papacy and the new monastic orders. The papacy had experienced its own long eclipse after the Carolingian age, becoming the plaything of local Roman factions or the Holy Roman Emperor who between them made and unmade popes until the 1040s, when a reformist reaction set in. Gregory VII (1073–85) and his successors were hostile to the form of lay control of the church that existed across most of Europe, and not just in *Francia*. The celebrated 'investiture conflict' of the 1060s–1180s was an attempt, led by Rome, to revive church autonomy, starting at the top, by refusing to recognize bishops or abbots who were 'invested' with their spiritual authority by laymen, whose competence, Rome claimed, simply did not include the spiritual. In fact, this was only the beginning of a papal claim to far wider authority within the church, which was exemplified by the excommunication of Philip I (r. 1060–1108) and other princes for flouting the church's discipline over marriage and divorce. More controversial still was the subsequent papal claim to superiority over lay princes of every rank, a challenge which came to a head during the 1290s and early 1300s in the reign of Philip IV. In the French rejection of papal ambitions, as Christ's vicar on earth, to make or unmake princes, lay the first shoots of 'gallicanism', a fiery defence of France's politico-religious autonomy based on ancient customs and liberties that would remain in service in successive guises until the nineteenth century. In the longer term, the Gregorian movement was simply too radical to be sustained, although it did succeed in distinguishing spiritual from temporal investiture. The Frankish monarchy's historic closeness to its bishops was simply too valuable to *both* sides, and from Philip I to Philip IV, it had little difficulty in rallying them to its cause during spats with Rome. Yet the monarchy benefited in numerous ways from the Gregorian reforms of church governance which were conceivable in, and transferable to the secular sphere.

The Gregorian movement was not confined to high politics: beyond the separation of the spiritual and non-spiritual, it sought an extensive reform of the church. Having obtained the release of huge numbers of parishes from lay investiture, it insisted on clerical celibacy so as to avoid other conflicts of interest based on family ambition. Its pastoral reforms, many of them focussed on the use of the sacraments by the laity, were less controversial but not necessarily easy options; set in train by general church councils (some of which met in Lyon and Vienne) between 1123 and 1312, they were followed up, often in considerable detail, by church synods held across France. In addition to a gradual harmonisation of existing religious practices across the kingdom, such councils and synods contributed to the genesis of a reformist mind-set that crossed over into the political sphere with calls for the 'reform of the realm' in the following centuries.

The new religious orders of the central Middle Ages actually preceded the Gregorian movement. Their 'newness' lay partly in the fact that the monks concerned were separated from the 'world', and the abbeys were henceforth placed under direct papal rather than local, princely protection. Most of them were French in origin, beginning with that of Cluny in Burgundy founded in 910 by Duke William of Aquitaine, one of the most powerful Frankish princes of his time. William's motivation was that of numerous other aristocrats seeking safe passage to the next life thanks to the prayers of the monks, but who were also anxious to 'place' their own younger children there. Governed very loosely by a succession of able abbots, especially during the eleventh century, Cluny expanded across Europe to become by far the largest single group of monasteries (over 1,000 by 1120 approximately) living under the rule of St Benedict; many older monasteries, too, were drawn into its embrace in a process strikingly similar to the dominant lord-vassal relationship of the age. Admired and courted by kings and prelates alike, Cluny even produced the pope, Urban II, who issued the call (1095) that launched the Crusades. Cluny's soaring reputation meant that it prospered mightily, which enabled it, among other things, to build, by the early 1100s, the largest church in the world, which would only be overtaken by St Peter's in Rome four centuries later.

But Cluny itself was not immune to the reformist mind-set already encountered; by the later eleventh century, criticisms of its worldliness, political involvements, and 'mitigated' observance of the Benedictine rule were circulating. A new breakaway order of 'white' monks, the Cistercians, was founded near Dijon in 1098 and spread rapidly, mimicking in some ways Cluny's previous success, and aided mightily from the 1110s onwards by the prodigious energy and charisma of St Bernard (1090–1153), abbot of Clairvaux. By 1250 approximately, the Cistercians had around 650 houses, many of which pioneered new forms of agricultural production on farms usually carved out of previously uncultivated tracts of land. A three-step sequence of reform-decadence-revival was thus emerging, although within France or Europe generally no monastic order thereafter would surpass Cluny and Cîteaux in either numbers or extension. Moreover, the monastic community living under one roof was not the only formula tried during these creative years – life as a hermit also appealed to many during the twelfth century, and it had the sanction of the early church tradition. The scale of this phenomenon, best illustrated by the Carthusians, is more elusive, but should not be underestimated.

With some exceptions, most of these new orders were for *both* men and women; substantial numbers of female houses, usually following the Benedictine rule and no less dominated by the aristocracy, either joined them or were founded from scratch around this time. Only Fontevrault in western France had a woman at its head who enjoyed the right to govern male monks; but despite its royal connections – it was the favourite burial-place of the Plantagenets – it remained a tiny congregation.

Built in rural surroundings for the most part, these monasteries, with their often-huge endowments of land, enjoyed extensive authority over their tenants and rural populations generally. Despite figures like Bernard of Clairvaux, who preached and travelled widely, they were contemplative and liturgical rather than pastoral communities, although many did perform religious services for local villages and sometimes sent their monks to serve in parishes in their patronage. The next wave of orders would be radically different, taking the now familiar conviction of the decadence of the older monastic orders in unfamiliar directions. The Dominicans were founded as the Order of Preachers during the Albigensian crusade (1215), with a mission to oppose heresy and instruct people in orthodox doctrine. In their renunciation of key features of the monastic model and their imitation of the apostles, the Dominicans were overtaken by their exact contemporaries, the more turbulent and demotic Franciscans, who rejected formal endowments, practised collective as well as individual poverty and, like their founder, Francis of Assisi, begged for alms (hence the term 'mendicant' used to describe the new orders).

Most importantly, the houses of these new-style orders were located in towns, where they developed their pastoral activities, preaching, confessing, and administering the sacraments in their own chapels. Over time, they also devised new devotions, such as processions and pilgrimages, topping them out with confraternities and other forms of common life for the more devout. Female houses of Dominican and Franciscan nuns were also founded and spread widely. The orders' direct subordination to the papacy, perhaps Cluny's greatest legacy, enabled the mendicants to escape if not ignore episcopal supervision of their activities, despite such exemption producing much conflict, then and later. Above all, the mendicants appeared at a time when towns were growing beyond the capacity of the existing church structures to cope, and when there were increasing fears about the spread of urban dissent, even heresy, as evidenced by the Albigensians, the

Waldensians, and other movements before them. Such fears were inflated by the active participation in these movements of laypeople, male and female, who evinced a virulent hostility to the wealthy and, in their eyes, corrupt clergy. Thus, the more 'intellectual' Dominicans became prominent theologians and defenders of orthodoxy, and the Franciscans the 'popular' preachers of their age, even though such contrasts should not be exaggerated. The 'encounter' between the new mendicant orders and urban society, especially in the southern provinces where dissent was more widespread, was successful insofar as the orders filled a major hole in the church's pastoral arsenal; yet another pattern was set that would endure for centuries.

The arrival of the intellectual Dominicans is a reminder that for centuries the church was the principal custodian of learning and letters. Since Merovingian times, some of the great monasteries, like Saint-Denis or Saint-Germain, had libraries and *scriptoria* where their monks composed, copied and circulated texts, both sacred and profane; monastic schools may have also educated a few laypeople, but no more than that. Before the twelfth century clerics were, thus, far better educated than any of their lay counterparts, which made it only natural for them to gravitate towards princely courts and government; the Carolingian renaissance either side of 800 was a consequence of such an encounter between clerical learning and lay patronage. Much later, the famous abbot Suger (1081–1151) of Saint-Denis was for many years the closest advisor of Louis VI, and even became regent of the realm while Louis VII was on crusade in the late 1140s. Suger's younger contemporary, Bernard of Clairvaux (1090–1153), was perhaps the most complete product of monastic education and culture. He and those shaped by him wrote extensively on theological questions, while Bernard himself maintained extensive relations with the great and good of Christendom.

By the 1140s approximately, newer influences were emerging within an intellectual world that was still almost wholly clerical. By then, cathedral 'schools' like those of Chartres or Paris (based in Notre-Dame and the city's abbeys) were already flourishing, having gradually eclipsed their monastic predecessors. With royal and papal support, the schools of Paris gained university status in 1215, as did several others, notably Angers, Orléans, Toulouse, Bourges, and Montpellier. While some specialised in law (e.g. Orléans, Bourges) or medicine (Montpellier, Paris), it was theology, where the dominance of Paris was soon Europe-wide, that was considered the 'queen of the sciences'. Roman law and church ('canon') law faculties educated clerics and laymen who would serve both secular and ecclesiastical masters indiscriminately; the major religious orders, such as the Dominicans, were soon sending their brightest recruits to be educated, as well as to teach theology, at universities. The rediscovery and translation of Aristotle's lost writings triggered a huge effort to rethink Christian theology within a rationalist Aristotelian framework. However, the early attempts of Peter Abelard (1079–1142) and Peter Lombard (1096–1160) encountered much opposition from opponents like Bernard of Clairvaux, whose monastic idiom, built around charity and the personal love of God, had markedly different priorities to the ambitious system-building enterprises of the new intellectuals. A century later, in the 1270s, Thomas Aquinas, the greatest Paris 'doctor' of all, found his monumental effort at such a synthesis being sharply challenged by some church authorities. Despite such high-level reservations, the new university 'system' had become firmly established by then, and its teaching methods, based on lectures and disputation, likewise. Paris university became the oracle of Christendom on theological matters, attracting students and masters from across the 'nations' of Europe. Law and theology may have been different disciplines, but the church was their common denominator, since the *ecclesia* could be theorised from both perspectives. Given such an environment, it is hardly surprising that the most influential ideas on power and authority, political as well as ecclesiastical, emanated from the universities by the thirteenth century.

From Abelard to Aquinas, the fear of intellectual deviation mirrored that concerning popular heresy, and the outcome has been labelled 'the persecuting society', which was quick to see subversive influences at work. Popular 'superstitions' that had been hitherto tolerated were increasingly seen as threatening; church teaching and legislation produced an arsenal of counter-measures, educational as well as punitive, to deal with them. Even lepers were executed in 1321. The experience of the Crusades also produced a hardening of the arteries towards the Jews, who were expelled more than once from the royal domain and the kingdom itself in 1306. It is highly symbolic that the Dominicans – the Order of Preachers, to give them their proper name – were put in charge of Europe's first inquisition.

## V

A striking cartoon of 1789 depicts a sturdy, if also somewhat emaciated peasant carrying on his back a well-fed noble and a cleric. The image was designed to convey the parasitic character of the two principal bloodsuckers who exploited the largest group in French society; it subverted the centuries-old rhetoric of a 'society of orders' which had been invented around 1000 by clerical intellectuals seeking to formulate an image of society divided into three distinct orders – those who prayed, fought and worked. This tripartite framework endured despite the considerable degree of social change during the intervening centuries. Like the 1789 image, no account of France's early history would make sense without exploring the wider socio-economic foundations of the Capetian era, some of which are implicit in the themes already covered in this chapter.

The corralling of the peasantry into village settlements that began in the tenth century was connected to factors not yet encountered. The first is, simply, population change. It seems that the collapse of the Roman Empire and the invasions that followed – up to and especially those of the ninth century – caused significant declines in population levels, which the Germanic tribes or Vikings were simply not numerous enough to repair. The Carolingian church and monarchy also made their own contribution towards reshaping family structures by elaborating and imposing the christian precepts concerning marriage – monogamy and exogamy – while rejecting divorce, abortion, and infanticide; as subsequent censures and excommunications suggest, these rules were probably less readily accepted by kings and aristocrats than their subjects. Figures for any pre-nineteenth century population are subject to caution, but demographic historians seem to agree that the population of France within its present borders was in the region of 6 million around 1000. They also argue that it rose to about 18–19 million around 1340, after which the Black Death decimated it; the biggest surge in numbers occurred, it seems, during the twelfth century. Such a growth-rate may sound modest by our contemporary standards, but it was nothing less than spectacular, and would not be finally overtaken until around 1720! The obstacles to sustained growth were numerous and sometimes severe – famines, epidemics, warfare (especially civil wars), low levels of agricultural productivity, poor diet, and so on. These factors, which often struck in combination, kept life-expectancy rates correspondingly low; critically, they affected child-bearing women and newborn children most. If not always nasty or brutal, life could be very short indeed, and re-marriage was common. Scarcely anything is known about the age of marriage, particularly of women, or fertility rates, for the early or central medieval period. Towns and cities were, for centuries, subject to higher mortality rates than rural areas, so that continuing immigration was necessary simply to sustain their population levels. Such immigration, if continuous, would in turn indicate relatively high population density in the immigrants' rural places of origin. Despite such inhibiters, by 1328 Paris was the largest city in Europe bar Constantinople, with around 200,000 inhabitants. Its nearest internal competitors, Lyon, Rouen, Bordeaux, or Marseille, ranged between 30,000 and 40,000 – a ratio that has not changed much over the centuries! Indeed, the relatively high population density of northern France, and the Ile-de-France in particular, ultimately had major political consequences: it was here that the Capetians found plentiful resources, human and otherwise, whereas much of central and southern France was thinly or unevenly populated. The Capetian kingdom was already Europe's most populous monarchy by the 1320s.

Such demographic patterns were at least partially determined by economic circumstances. That affected the clearing of forests (when not owned by nobles or the church), moors (usually quite poor-quality land), and marshes (the most difficult to reclaim) that lay close to the most populated regions, as well as the migration of the demographic 'surplus' into those new and often empty spaces. As a result of such expansion, French historians have often referred to a 'full world' (*monde plein*) – the moment around 1320 when demographic pressure reached its peak and the new, less fertile marginal lands could no longer sustain further growth without making the population vulnerable to crop failure.

The early phase of this demographic expansion coincided with the 'feudal revolution' of the eleventh century in which, as already indicated, knights and castellans grabbed for themselves both local power and control of the peasantry, whose lands they 'returned' to their previously independent owners under conditional tenure. Where men were more valuable than land, many free peasants surrendered, under conditions of widespread violence, their lands and rights in return for security and protection. This reduced much of the rural population to various degrees of un-freedom, making it subject to both seigneurial jurisdiction – which replaced the previously public courts – and an equally bewildering range of labour services on their lords' manor, rents, dues, and other forms of tribute, such as inheritance or transfer taxes. The application of the northern French adage of 'no land without a lord' meant that peasants were assumed to be *naturally* subject to a lord, unless they could prove otherwise; in southern France this was much less true, since the Roman law that dominated the region held there could be 'no lord without a title'. But there was no return of the Roman villa-estate worked by a slave population. The newly enserfed peasants of the eleventh century were housed together in village communities next to the lord's often makeshift 'castle', from where they worked on both their own holdings and the lord's demesne; such physical proximity facilitated the enforcement of lords' rights by the manor courts and village custom. It was usually lords, lay or ecclesiastical, who were behind the development of the new villages – and with them, new parishes – in those northern uninhabited areas where clearances were made; in this process, the Cistercian abbeys were the ablest pioneers, especially in the twelfth century. Moreover, most lords imposed a monopoly on owning grain mills or wine presses – for the use of which the peasants had to pay – but also on hunting, fishing, and timber felling. Bishops, monasteries and other churches owned huge, and frequently dispersed estates of this kind, with a correspondingly dependent peasant population for which they were also spiritually responsible. In such a myriad of ways did those who worked support those who fought or prayed, as the three-estates creed required.

In a country as diverse climatically, topographically and agriculturally as France, this slowly evolving rural landscape could not but vary significantly from place to place. In the core regions of northern France (the Ile-de-France, the Beauce and Upper Loire valley, Picardy, and much of Normandy) an open-field system followed from extensive clearance of woodland, in which strip cultivation was the norm; here village communities were best suited to managing the complexities of the 'three-field' crop-rotation system that was widespread. In the less populated areas of western and central France, heath and moors were cleared, though more slowly and more partially, giving rise to a more individualistic landscape of enclosed fields that still bears the name of *bocage*. In the southern regions, with their often-inhospitable uplands, clearances were more haphazard, determined mainly by the possibility of irrigating dry soils subject to a hot climate. Population pressure, as already suggested, did much to determine these trends, and the stronger it became the more the land-hungry peasants of northern France found it hard to resist clearing the surviving woodlands around them, despite the fact many of their other activities, from raising animals to producing building materials, depended on the preservation of, and access to such resources. But such constraints did not have serious consequences before the early 1300s.

Meanwhile the changes just discussed produced a certain loosening of peasant dependency over time. The pressure of numbers and migration to towns or new villages forced lords to adjust, at least in part, their expectations and behaviour. Serfdom in the strict sense declined considerably, but did not fully disappear. Around 1270, about one-fifth of the rural population of the Paris region were still serfs. But legally free tenants were still subject to heavy surplus-extraction by their lords. Obligations in kind were often commuted to monetary payments, effectively legalising what many had previously regarded as exactions. The gradual abandonment of direct farming by lords of their reserves, which were henceforth leased out to peasants, both recognised and encouraged the growth of a wealthy peasant elite, who in turn needed and employed poorer, even landless peasants, to work such lands. In the process, some successful peasants became richer than the local nobility. A distinct peasant hierarchy of rich and poor developed, especially during the thirteenth century and across the great northern plains, with the poor heavily dependent on the resources of common lands, rivers, and woodlands to support their families.

## VI

Long before 1300, an urban revival had occurred across much of western Europe, facilitated by the end of the raids and invasions after the 950s, and by the gradual reprise of trade, both inland and maritime. It overlapped with the feudal revolution and economic-demographic revival already discussed, and was shaped by features of both. It is often said, especially in the wake of Karl Marx, that towns were the radical opposite and the 'outsiders' of feudal society, but they could not have grown or flourished had that been more than partially true. Yet the long-term relationship of town and country, which did involve much antagonism and snobbery, is far too complex to be reduced to any one dimension, however important. A few key features of the origins and early growth of urban France may be discussed here, with other aspects figuring in later chapters.

Roman Gaul, and especially its southern regions, had, like Italy and Mediterranean Spain, been heavily urbanised; after the Empire's fall, those towns shrivelled in size and vigour, but did not disappear. Subsequently, it was those which were seats of bishoprics which fared best, benefiting from the wealth of the church and the presence in their midst of local elites, but in the longer term that heritage limited their scope for expansion. When it came, the urban revival began, paradoxically, in the northern areas, along and inland from the English Channel, where Roman towns had been relatively few. It was along the north-south axis linking northern Italy and Flanders, an area that substantially overlapped with the 'four-rivers' façade of the Frankish kingdom, that urban growth was strongest. Elsewhere in the kingdom, towns with good communication routes, maritime, or fluvial (the Garonne, Loire and Seine river-valleys), grew fastest, while whole regions, such as Brittany and the Cevennes, had relatively few towns. Across many provinces, *bourgs* grew up close to fortified castles, abbeys, and other sites. In the south-west, hill-top towns known as *bastides*, grew like mushrooms during the 1200s, but not as a result of any demographic or economic pressure. For their own political or fiscal reasons, local lords but also the counts of Toulouse, and later the kings of England and France, wished to re-group scattered rural populations. That exception apart, the urban map of France's later centuries was virtually complete by 1150, but within it individual towns would rise or fall depending on circumstances (e.g. war, trade-route changes, etc.) and opportunities. By the time of the 1328 survey of the royal domain, the kingdom had approximately twenty well-scattered towns with a population of 10,000 or over; but the vast majority fell far below such figures.

At the bottom end of the scale, that of the smallest towns, much depended on the mutual needs of town and country. Peasant surpluses fed urban populations, but town dwellers were often farmers, too; peasants needed textiles and some other goods, but sometimes produced such items themselves. For a long time, artisans and pedlars were characteristic of *both* urban and rural society, but once the scale of production grew, artisans tended to congregate in workshops in local towns. Regular markets were another marker of urban status, however limited the wares on offer. At this level, town and country were a continuum, not separate worlds, not least because lords were keen to maintain control over both and impose tolls and other taxes. Salt, wine, and some other goods moved across provinces and overseas, since their producers, like other artisans, needed to sell them in order to support themselves and their families. Vineyards were far more widely spread than in subsequent centuries: the 'northern limit of the vine' still included most of northern France.

At the top end of the scale we find the great northern textile towns, which were concentrated by the thirteenth century in Flanders; they made the county of Flanders a major political neighbour of the Capetians and an attractive focus of their dynastic acquisitiveness until the French army was trounced by rebel artisans at Courtrai in 1302. But towns like Beauvais, Amiens, and Reims were by then active textile centres, too, and belonged, as did smaller towns like St-Quentin or Abbeville, to a trading confederation (the 'Hansa of the seventeen cities') by the thirteenth century. Long before then, the prospects of urban prosperity in northern France had been seriously boosted when the Flanders textile merchants encountered their Italian counterparts seeking to sell their exotic Mediterranean and Near-Eastern wares. The outcome was the famous fairs of Champagne, whose heyday ran approximately from 1180 to 1320. They actually began in Lagny, close to Paris, before expanding south-eastwards into the towns of Champagne (Provins, Troyes and Bar-sur-Aube), where they lasted virtually all-year round. The Capetians' great rivals, the powerful counts of Champagne, encouraged, protected, and regulated the fairs – indirectly drawing financial benefits from them – and that nurturing, which included tax exemptions on sales, was crucial to the fairs' development. When they reached their zenith, around 1250, the Italian merchants had mutated into bankers and the fairs became Europe's premier money exchange, where accounts and exchange rates were settled, and debts were paid off.

By then, the Italian bankers – the Mouche and Biche of the age – were also lending money to Europe's monarchs, and the Capetians in particular, in return for which they gained considerable control over the royal finances. The Champagne fairs did not disappear altogether after 1300, but the great merchants and bankers gravitated towards 'the Europe of warehouses' (i.e. major cities like Bruges, Avignon or Paris), while also moving southwards into Burgundy and the Lyon region. The Rhône valley and the Midi stood to gain considerably from the installation at Avignon, in 1316, of the papacy, with its enormous financial resources and high levels of elite consumption. The fairs at neighbouring Beaucaire flourished and were still operating four centuries later. Elsewhere, hundreds, if not thousands, of small-scale markets or fairs, lubricated the micro-economies of the kingdom.

As might be expected, the urban development of France's three maritime façades was dictated by commercial opportunities. Norman towns, led by Rouen, maintained close contacts with English markets, even after the province was lost to Philip Augustus in 1204. The ports of La Rochelle, Bordeaux and Bayonne grew because the main products of their extensive hinterlands – principally salt and wine – had considerable overseas and inland markets. Further south, the growth of Marseille and Montpellier (which was only French after 1349) benefited from being the main points of contact with the Mediterranean commercial world.

The vast majority of France's towns, whether Roman survivors or newcomers, operated somewhere between these two extremes. In an economy with a serious shortage of specie, barter-exchange dominated at the lower end, where the innovations of the Champagne fairs remained largely unknown. But the demographic growth of the early Capetian centuries did enable small to medium-sized towns, from 3,000 to 6,000 in population, to multiply as centres of local exchange for rural and urban products. And the larger cities, beginning with Paris, had ever-growing needs for food, which could only be supplied by an ever-expanding hinterland.

A range and hierarchy of towns gradually developed from the eleventh century onwards, and was in turn mimicked by the trades and professions that emerged within their walls. Butchers and bakers were everywhere, but where demand for goods was socially differentiated – e.g. textiles of various qualities and functions – specialisation soon appeared. The names of many streets or urban districts still recall such long-forgotten skills. As the trades expanded, their practitioners banded together into guilds that devised sometimes extraordinarily detailed regulations governing membership as well as the production of goods; their ability to enforce them made 'closed shops' of the guilds in question. These guild structures were usually reinforced by the confraternities, which were social as much as religious bodies, which the crafts also adapted for their members and their families. Living cheek by jowl within towns and intermarrying to a high degree, guild members developed an uncommonly powerful *esprit de corps* which made them formidable social and political forces in the towns. Where they were strong enough, they obtained representation on town councils; where that was denied them, they remained potentially dangerous sources of revolt.

A German dictum had it that 'city air makes people free' (*Stadtluft macht frei*), but the degrees of urban liberty that obtained during the Capetian centuries varied hugely across time and place. It was the status of towns and their inhabitants that was at stake, not merely who should participate in their governance. Nineteenth-century liberal historians idolised the bourgeois of an earlier age for fighting so heroically to escape the arbitrariness of lordship, old or new, and to secure the rule of law, in civilian as in business life, as well as legal freedom for townspeople. But the Europe-wide 'communal' moment that personified such demands was relatively confined within France, first appearing across northern areas after 1060. Compared to other parts of Europe, it produced relatively few full-scale communes despite – or perhaps because of – violent urban revolts in Le Mans (1070), Laon (1112) and elsewhere. Until this juncture, and as part of their policy of strengthening their domain, the early Capetians had, if anything, been increasing the number of urban lordships that they possessed; the growth of towns meant rising revenues from markets and tolls. In several towns, they imposed themselves as co-lords alongside the previous holders, lay or clerical. By contrast, the Norman-Plantagenets were powerful enough to effectively combine a high degree of 'retained' ducal authority with substantial legal uniformity in the urban 'customs' of Normandy itself, before extending them, from the 1160s onwards, across their other domains. The outcome was different again in southern France: towns here were socially and culturally distinctive, and Capetian influence only came much later. Many were under episcopal lordship since late Roman times, but they habitually housed noble families within their walls. These nobles frequently exploited lay dislike of church power to obtain concessions, primarily for themselves, but which they had subsequently to share with the local bourgeois and artisans. The ruling counts of Toulouse and other regional princes were not averse to such changes, which were mostly peaceful in character. Consequently, most southern towns were governed by a *consulat* of councillors, each of whom represented a specific social or professional 'constituency' (nobles, clergy, merchants, artisans and legists) from the twelfth century onwards.

For their part, the Capetians proved increasingly willing, from the 1150s onwards, to concede – often for cash – particular 'franchises' (privileges) and charters to towns, and especially to those located outside their domain, as a means of extending royal influence there. Thus Philip Augustus (1180–1223) granted many such charters, but with specific conditions attached (e.g. military obligations). Often determined by financial needs or other short-term considerations, this approach enabled him and other princes elsewhere to decide which powers to 'retain' rather than concede to the towns. Paris is one example of this compromise: its provost of merchants was not really its mayor for, as his title indicates, he was entitled to deal primarily with commercial and related matters; it was the royal provost, usually a ranking noble, who held the real power within the walls. Philip's successors seem to have been less generous with concessions, while the overall effect of the Capetians' pragmatism was a landscape of urban liberties that was nearly as chaotic as was that of the lordships that we have already seen. However, so long as the monarchy was intent on, and capable of maintaining its oversight of these liberties, the renewals of urban 'customs', usually at the outset of a new reign, allowed for some measure of revision and 'codification' of urban status over the following centuries.

Thus, across the kingdom as a whole, the acquisition of substantial self-governing status and freedom from servitude for the inhabitants of towns was an incremental and 'stop-go' rather than a once-for-all achievement. It was very unevenly spread, even in the regions most affected by it; at times, towns without charters could be more genuinely 'autonomous' than those with one; important and prosperous towns like Reims or Beauvais remained firmly under episcopal lordship. The increasing grip of the merchant bourgeoisie and, to a lesser extent, of the artisan guilds on municipal authority was its major outcome. That would in due course lead to another round of conflicts, this time *within* the towns themselves, conflicts to which the monarchy would also be party.

A shifting combination of factors enabled the Capetians to pull together by 1320 a kingdom whose territorial contours and resources, especially demographic, were impressive for their time. Across the generations, dynastic biological continuity and political astuteness helped to keep the wheels of territorial consolidation and expansion turning. The emergence of a hierarchy of nobility and of towns seeking their corporate liberty made for a more fluid and differentiated society, one whose internal stratification was increasingly emphasised. In both cases, the Capetian monarchy gained considerable social ballast: it gradually turned the institutions and culture of vassalage to its advantage, and it played a key role as arbiter and protector of urban 'liberties'. Monarchical rule seemed wholly natural in a polity whose advocates emphasised its descent from Carolingian and Roman ancestors. Such propaganda itself drew on the intimate ties between the monarchy and the church, whose resources, intellectual as much as material, were decisive in forging a royal cult. Of course, the Capetians were not unique, since both the resources and techniques of rule they deployed were familiar in the Europe of their time. There was nothing irreversible about the 'France' of the early 1300s.

# CHRONOLOGY

| | |
|---|---|
| 987 | End of Carolingians, Hugh Capet elected king of the Franks |
| 996 | Hugh Capet succeeded by son Robert II |
| 1020s | Romanesque cathedral building (Chartres, Auxerre, Orleans, Poitiers, Angers) |
| 1027 | Truce of God proclaimed |
| 1033 | Burgundy incorporated into Holy Roman Empire |
| 1066 | William the Conqueror king of England |
| 1095 | Pope Urban II preaches first Crusade at Clermont |
| 1098 | Foundation of Cistercian order |
| 1112 | Urban rebellion at Laon, movement of 'communes' |
| 1120 | Order of Templars founded |
| 1132–44 | Building of Saint-Denis abbey |
| 1140s | Gothic cathedrals spread (Sens, Senlis, Noyon, Paris Notre-Dame, Saint-Malo) |
| 1140s | Cathar heresy denounced |
| 1145 | Second Crusade |
| 1152 | Eleanor of Aquitaine marries Henry II of England; new Plantagenet 'empire' |
| 1180s | Philip Augustus acquires Arras, Vermandois, and Berry |
| 1187 | Third Crusade |
| 1202–04 | Philip Augustus captures English lands in France |
| 1209–13 | Anti-Cathar/Albigensian crusade |
| 1211–18 | Mont-Saint-Michel built |
| 1214 | Decisive battle of Bouvines consolidates kingdom |
| 1215 | Paris 'schools' become university, confirmed by pope (1231) |
| 1220s | Several southern fiefs enter royal domain |
| 1226 | New crusade against Cathars |
| 1248–54 | Louis IX on crusade |
| 1257 | Robert de Sorbon founds Paris university college ('la Sorbonne') |
| 1268–73 | Thomas Aquinas teaches in Paris, completes *Summa Theologica* |
| 1270 | Louis IX dies at Tunis, returning from crusade |

| | |
|---|---|
| 1271 | County of Toulouse incorporated into royal domain |
| 1294 | Philip IV annexes Gascony |
| 1303 | Philip IV conflict with Pope Boniface VIII |
| 1306 | Jews expelled from kingdom |
| 1309 | Avignon papacy (to 1376) |
| 1312 | Suppression of Templars |
| 1314–17 | Political unrest, series of famines |
| 1328 | End of direct Capetian dynasty, accession of Philip VI of Valois |

# 2 A Society and Polity in Crisis and Recovery

Around 1320, few could have foreseen that Philip the Fair's formidable kingdom, which had recently faced down the papacy and brought it submissively to reside in Avignon, would shortly be plunged into an apparently interminable war that was both 'civil' and 'external', or that epidemics and their associates would prove no less destructive (see Map 2). Crucially, these deadly horsemen of the Apocalypse often struck simultaneously, thus multiplying each other's individual effects. Not until the 1450s approximately would they be sufficiently overcome to inaugurate a long century of renaissance. This rebirth should not be seen in a narrow artistic or literary perspective, important as that was. The challenges of the 1300s and 1400s led to social and political changes that would only become fully visible by the early 1500s. France's revival was such that in 1519, its king, Francis I, only narrowly failed in his attempt to become Holy Roman Emperor and thus a new Charlemagne. That failure may have been a blessing in disguise, as it sparked a considerable effort to elevate the monarchy and nation of France above its European neighbours.

## I

The notorious Black Death made its first appearance across Europe in late 1347 and wherever it struck during the following years – from Messina (Sicily), its point of entry into Europe, to the British Isles and Scandinavia – it rapidly scythed down up to two-fifths of the population. Local populations had virtually no immunity to, and certainly no effective medical defences against this devastating and mostly rat-borne bubonic plague. Vulnerable southern towns like Aix and Albi swiftly lost up the three-quarters of their inhabitants; towns generally were death-traps whereas, thanks to the hit-and-miss trajectory of the epidemic, many rural areas escaped more lightly, at least in subsequent years. But in the villages where it did strike, the results were just as savage, given its exceptional contagiousness. One Burgundian village lost 649 people – half its population – in 1349

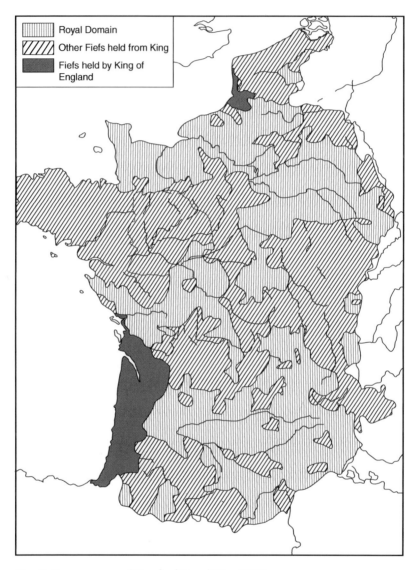

**Map 2**  *France on eve of Hundred Years' War, 1328*

alone, as against 30 deaths in an average year. Although a 'national' figure for population loss during the years around 1350 would make little sense, it seems that up to 40% of the population had disappeared by 1352 alone, when the plague temporarily disappeared. But it – and other pulmonary or intestinal epidemics – soon returned, albeit more regionally or locally, in virtually every decade thereafter down to 1403, after which it struck more randomly until the 1450s, when it vanished again for several decades.

The effect of such erratic recurrences was to thwart sustained demographic recovery for well over a century; they also weakened the overall resistance of populations to normally less deadly diseases. Worse still, warfare and the particularly destructive forms of scorched-earth banditry that accompanied it, especially in the wake of the peace of 1360, 'surfed' atop the continuing mortality crisis. In areas particularly exposed to military activity, the opportunities for recovery that abandoned lands might have otherwise provided the surviving population went a-begging. The Hundred Years' War could hardly have come at a worse time, as it ensured that France would suffer proportionately far more, demographically and economically, than its European neighbours. Thus, 'Hiroshima in Normandy', in one historian's words, meant that this rich and densely populated province lost around 56% of its population by 1390; measured by the decline of numbers of households, such heavy losses were matched in Provence and the Dauphiné, neither of which yet belonged to France. Paris itself lost perhaps around two-thirds of its inhabitants between 1328 and 1425, and many other towns probably fared as badly. Such a prolonged blight could not but heighten the sense of social dislocation and helplessness in the face of such divine – as it seemed – retribution. The fears it produced, especially during the 'smallpox' epidemic that decimated children in the early 1360s, were unparalleled. Images such as the dance of death remain one of the period's most enduring visual legacies, the leitmotifs of which also pervaded contemporary spiritual and other writings. Resignation was not the only response, though, as the period was strewn with rebellions, urban and rural.

For all its unique ferocity, the 1348 epidemic was neither the first nor the only harbinger of social crisis; its timing exacerbated its effects. The demographic and economic expansion of the previous centuries had, in fact, already run out of steam sometime before 1300, especially in the northern regions. Workable land was by now scarce and expensive, holdings were smaller owing to sub-division arising from partible inheritance practices, and crop-yields from over-worked fields were scarcely higher than under the Carolingians. Thus, up to two-thirds of peasant holdings may have been unable – because too small or marginal – to produce enough to feed their families. This meant that anything contributing to survival came first for the majority of the population; the ensuing vicious circle, which would last for centuries, of over-population, intensive agriculture, low or declining crop yields, and malnutrition left rural and urban populations fragile, especially in 'bad' years. For many historians, France was already rubbing up against a Malthusian ceiling, where further population growth would outstrip the food-supply and trigger disaster. Such developments were quite independent of the contemporary epidemics. Harvest failures and high mortality rates without epidemics, and vice versa, became frequent occurrences then and later; there was no single causal factor. Combinations of poor crops, food scarcity, and rising grain prices had appeared in the early 1300s; the first major famines occurred in 1315–17, mainly in central and northern provinces, and in 1339–41 and 1343–6 in the south. Peasants with land had at least some resources to fall back on, and could borrow money if necessary, but those already indebted often had to surrender their tenures altogether and join the increasingly numerous landless labourers who, in times of crisis, were far more vulnerable to grain shortages, high prices, and loss of employment. For centuries thereafter, one of the prime responsibilities of urban authorities was to police the supply and price of grain, and to take action whenever scarcity or hoarding might lead to price-hikes and, worse still, bread-riots. But the peasantry, who constituted 90% of the population, had no such cushion to depend on.

Demographic collapse on such a scale, especially as it was prolonged, was bound to have much wider social and economic consequences. It could also be a cloud with a silver lining for those lucky enough to survive the demise of their neighbours and relatives. Falling population levels reversed 'normal' economic logic in important respects. Serfdom had already declined significantly before 1300, partly because the more prosperous peasants bought themselves out of it and other seigneurial dues, as lords cashed in on favourable conditions. The monarchy encouraged – and practised – the freeing of serfs; it also legalised peasant gains by recognising local 'customs' that embodied such success against seigneurial exactions. But now, after 1348, acute labour shortages and empty peasant holdings compelled lords to entice new tenants with better conditions and labourers with higher wages than previously. This trend, which continued into the mid-fifteenth century, made more and more French peasants the de facto owners of their holdings and, with seigneurial dues gradually declining in real value, made lordship less burdensome.

Lordship was far from dead, however. As economic conditions began to change again around 1450–70, the judicial functions and monopolies of lordship (mills, wine-presses, etc.) enabled it to recover lost ground; its capacity to adapt to different challenges meant that robust forms of both lordship and peasant tenure would characterise rural France until the Revolution. Meanwhile, the internal stratification of the peasantry was such as to enable the *coqs de village* increasingly to dominate village communities. By now, these 'big' farmers owned relatively large amounts of land, plough teams, and other assets; they usually rented, or managed, the *seigneurs'* own lands and mills, and employed landless or land-hungry peasants; intermarriage between similar families groups set them even further apart, gradually creating almost as much scope for antagonism between rich and poor peasants as between lords and peasants.

French towns, from Paris downwards, suffered no less, as we have seen, from the grim reaper's recurring visitations. Urban households might have remained fewer until the fifteenth century had not the successive influxes of peasants escaping the ravages of war helped to staunch population losses in towns. But whenever the neighbouring countryside was devastated by warfare or brigandage, its adverse effects soon hit the local towns, too. In addition, towns were under growing pressure from the monarchy by the 1350s to modernise their fortifications; such expense was invariably heavy, and the sums levied to pay for it were all the more burdensome as royal taxation had already risen sharply under Philip IV. By then, a further effect of prolonged warfare was the diminution of France's place in Europe-wide trade, which made these costs even harder for towns to bear. The fairs of Champagne were losing their attraction to Europe's merchants, a decline to which the monarchy's frequent manipulations of the coinage, especially under Philip IV, contributed substantially. The consequent fall in commercial activities reduced the scope within towns for both artisan activities and work for rural immigrants.

These multiple entanglements help to explain France's vulnerability, for well over a century, to setbacks of different origins but similar consequences. Town and country were not worlds apart, despite their growing differences, and in the face of common hardships, both engaged in revolt throughout the period, as they did in neighbouring Flanders, northern Italy, and Catalonia. Extensive rural revolts like the *Jacquerie* (1358) in the Paris region and the *Tuchinat* across Languedoc (1382) were directed against a cluster of 'enemies' of the peasantry – war, high taxes, and especially 'bad' landlords – and they had the support of certain towns. *Jacquerie* would become a generic name for a peasant revolt in subsequent centuries, and in 1358 it was triggered by the northern Estates-General's demand for taxes to fortify the châteaux of the Paris region against mercenary freebooters. The timing of such demands was poor, since the military reputation of the French nobility, and therefore, their right to act as lords, had been badly damaged in the eyes of the rebels by humiliating defeats against the English.

Urban revolts with not dissimilar grievances occurred in Paris (1358), and then in Rouen, Paris and neighbouring towns in the early 1380s. Towns where wealthy patrician elites held power were the most susceptible to revolt by artisans and craft guilds still excluded from municipal politics;

relations between these groups were less frayed in towns where political participation was more accessible. Some of these revolts were later hailed as precursors of class war, but sustained revolt rather than 'mere' riot could only be the work of artisans or merchants and not of poor, unorganised labourers. Although many revolts were triggered by royal fiscal demands, opposition to them 'on the ground' was often directed against the local elites who benefited substantially from them. Frequently characterised by murders and atrocities on both sides, the revolts were brutally repressed. A new round of them returned from the 1410s onwards, and were increasingly connected to wider 'national' factions.

## II

After Philip IV's death, the Capetians' biological good luck quickly ran out, as his three sons reigned for a mere 14 years (1314–28) and left no direct male heirs. This opened the way for their closely related junior branch, the Valois, under the ambitious Philip VI (r. 1328–50) to claim the crown, with the support of an assembly of nobles, in 1328. A reaction against Philip IV's grasping and authoritarian methods of rule had, as we have seen, surfaced during his last years, one of the first results of which was a series of charters (among them the famous 'charter of the Normans') granting the right to consent, in assembly, to future taxation (1314–16). Philip VI's own accession was contested – and contestable – at a time when the Salic law banning female rule or inheritance through the female line did not yet formally exist. An evident reluctance to accept such female inheritance rights was strengthened by an adultery scandal of 1312 involving Philip IV's three daughters-in-law, which raised doubts about the legitimacy of *their* children. Not surprisingly, Edward III of England, whose claim to the French throne was actually stronger than Philip VI's but which had been ignored in 1328, finally declared that his homage for his lands in France (Guyenne and Ponthieu) to Philip VI was null and void and that he was the true king of France. Philip VI riposted like his predecessors, confiscating Guyenne from his 'rebel' vassal.

Two years later, in 1339, Edward III led the first of several English military campaigns across France, thus starting a stop-go war between Europe's two most powerful monarchies that would only end with a French victory at Castillon near Toulouse in 1453. But that little-known victory proved no more definitive than any of its celebrated predecessors, from Crécy and Poitiers to Agincourt, as England retained a dangerous foothold in France until it finally lost Calais in 1557. Between these book-end dates, France's political fortunes wobbled dramatically, as epitomised by the contrast between the effective Charles V 'the Wise' (r. 1360–82) and the long agony of his son Charles VI 'the Mad' (r. 1382–1422). To regard the Hundred Years' War as an Anglo-French conflict lasting approximately a century is doubly misleading: firstly, most of the clashes were 'Franco-French' and dominated by the 'great' princes, in which the English were actively involved from time to time; secondly – and for that reason – they lasted much longer than usually imagined, from around 1340 to the 1480s.

With these caveats in mind, it is possible to divide the century or so after 1339 into distinct phases. Edward III's intentions in 1337 are still debated – did he really wish to become king of France, or was he just using his claim in order to obtain significant territorial concessions from France, especially over English Guyenne? His subsequent failure, in 1359, to take Reims, which would have enabled him to be crowned king of France in full solemnity, meant that he did not answer the question. Despite that setback, the first phase of the war, from 1339 to 1360, saw the French nobility routed at Crécy (1346) and Poitiers (1356), when John II was taken captive and had to be ransomed for a colossal sum of three million crowns, about 15 times the crown's annual income. Raising the money in question proved to be a critical moment in French history: it was the origin of permanent taxation, even in peacetime, which proved a major break with the established medieval precedent that taxation should cease when its cause did. But the feudal concept of subjects' duty to come to the aid of their lord was not yet dead, and it seriously muddied the waters of political debate over taxation. This confusion enabled the monarchy to evade recognising the right of subjects to consent to taxation per se, an outcome that would leave a defining mark on French socio-political evolution for centuries.

The treaty of Brétigny of 1360, which followed the recent military disasters, made enormous concessions to Edward III – tenure in full sovereignty of 'Aquitaine' (from Poitou to the Pyrenees, and eastwards almost to the southern Rhône valley in places) as well as the bridgeheads around Calais and along the Channel coast. In return, Edward renounced his claim to the throne of France. However, since other terms of the treaty soon proved unworkable, their non-implementation effectively voided Brétigny within a few years. During this second phase, Edward III began by resuming his title of 'king of France' in 1369. Frequent expeditions to defend English Guyenne followed during the next decades, because Charles V re-took most of the English possessions during the early 1370s, and was threatening what now remained of English Guyenne. No English king set foot on French soil again until 1415, when the flamboyant Henry V launched the final phase of the Franco-English conflict.

Meanwhile, the shock of massive military defeat on 'home' soil allowed pent-up antagonisms to explode within France during the late 1350s; the urban and rural revolts of 1358 and later were, as we have already seen, a rude reminder that the 'mere' commons held the governing classes in low esteem because of their military failures. The increasing recourse, from as early as 1316, to ad hoc assemblies of the three estates, separately or together, was one sign that the crown, its back to the wall, could be persuaded to convene assemblies and allow them to propose measures to reform the tax system, justice and administration generally. War did not suspend the monarchy's efforts to sustain its authority, but facilitated its use of previously under-used instruments to confront both internal faction and war with England. This was epitomised by John II's successor, Charles V 'the Wise' (r. 1364–80), whose political ability was matched by his wide intellectual interests, which focussed on embellishing the monarchy's 'liturgy' and the sources of its authority. For later scholars and monarchs, such a programme was an inspiration. However, much of what he did to reinforce the monarchy 'on the ground' was undone during his turbulent last years (1380–2) and especially during the chaotic 30 final years of the reign of his unfortunate son, Charles VI 'the Mad' (r. 1380–1422).

Despite truces and treaties, war became a virtually permanent presence on French soil in the later fourteenth and early fifteenth century. These wars overlapped with other conflicts along France's borders, from Flanders to Aragon, in which France, England and other states participated, making and breaking alliances that often directly influenced the conflicts within France itself. Along with English Guyenne, Flanders and Burgundy were the biggest principalities owing homage to the king of France at this juncture. So too was the duchy of Brittany, which had been increasingly dominated by France under Philip IV. But in 1341 it too descended into a bitter, destructive war of succession, in which England and France fought a proxy war of their own; by the time the succession was resolved in 1381, Breton independence had been restored and French influence seriously weakened there. Smaller principalities, such as those of Albret, Foix, and Armagnac in the south, were also scattered across the kingdom, but most of their rulers were simultaneously powerful figures in French court politics, and thus doubly capable of independent political action.

The Valois monarchy had also accumulated its share of over-mighty subjects, many of them of its own making. At the top of this political tree, immediately below the king, stood the grandees of the royal blood. More systematically than their Capetian predecessors, the Valois distributed apanages to younger sons, who in due course might become uncles to the succeeding generation of *apanagistes*, but also mentors or regents to under-age kings and power-brokers in council and at court. Successive monarchs from Philip VI and John II onwards elevated particular individuals among these princes to favour and influence, often via attractive marriages, with a view to sustaining royal power. Thus, the experienced Charles V endowed his two brothers with substantial apanages, but they remained fully supportive of him and his policies, which enabled him to recover in the early 1370s most of the lands ceded to England in 1360. It was these same men, the dukes of Burgundy and Berry (along with the duke of Anjou), who then dominated the regency of his son, Charles VI, in the 1380s, until he finally 'rebelled' against their dominance in 1388. When Charles succumbed to mental illness in 1392, his uncles returned in force, reinstating the spoils system they had presided over during the 1380s. But they soon faced a determined opponent in Charles VI's younger brother, Louis of Orleans. Orleans' murder in 1407 on the orders of his first cousin and main rival, the formidable John 'the Fearless', duke of Burgundy, unleashed a vicious civil war between the two evenly balanced factions, the Armagnacs (or Orleanists) and Burgundians; the tit-for-tat murder of the duke of Burgundy himself in 1419 only perpetuated these murderous rivalries. Paris and several other towns changed masters and experienced brutal purges several times during these years.

It was this context, in which rival factions pursued foreign alliances with promises of territorial concessions, that rekindled English interest in the lost Plantagenet empire and the French crown itself. In August 1414, Henry V summoned Charles VI to restore the kingdom to him and give him his youngest daughter in marriage; unlike Edward III, Henry V clearly *did* want the crown of France. A year later, he crossed the Channel, destroying the French army at Agincourt in October 1415. Together, English military successes such as the conquest of Normandy (1417–19) and Burgundian support, squeezed Charles VI's freedom of choice, eventually forcing him into signing the draconian treaty of Troyes (1420). Henry V would marry Charles VI's daughter, the dauphin Charles would be debarred from the succession, and Henry V would succeed Charles VI. But just two years later, both kings died almost simultaneously, and a nine-month old infant, Henry VI, was theoretically king of both England and France! In fact, France was divided three ways by 1422. The Paris region was Anglo-Burgundian; Guyenne, Normandy and the Channel coastal areas were in English hands; the much-mocked 'kingdom of Bourges' south of the Loire was the residual, makeshift refuge of the future Charles VII and his Orleanist-Armagnac supporters. Ejected from its historic heartlands for the first time, the French monarchy, as personified by the 'king of Bourges', seemed destined to disappear for good.

An English regency had to be installed after 1422 because the infant king Henry VI could obviously not be crowned until his majority. But by the time it arrived, in late 1431, it was too late. Instead, Charles VI's disinherited dauphin had been crowned as Charles VII at Reims, which he had captured in 1429. Precisely because it occurred at Reims, this coronation was a critical gesture of defiance that helped to turn the tide. The French monarchy was still a long way from having a 'fundamental' law of automatic succession that would make the coronation itself legally irrelevant, regardless of its propaganda value. That an initially hesitant Charles VII went on the offensive at the persistent urging of a young peasant girl, Joan of Arc, who was to be executed by the English in 1431 for heresy, only rendered France's recovery all the more providential and miraculous. Within a few years major writers like Jean Gerson and Christine de Pizan would write accounts of these events in such a vein, singularly enhancing the religious aura of both monarchy and country.

The reality was more mundane, but Charles VII made further military gains by the mid-1430s before securing the decisive alliance of the powerful duke of Burgundy (1435). Bereft of princely allies within France, the English were henceforth isolated and gradually forced out of Normandy during the 1440s; the simultaneous re-conquest of Guyenne was duly completed in 1453, though not without considerable local resistance from its leading towns, led by Bordeaux and Bayonne, which had enjoyed considerable autonomy under English rule. Henceforth, England retained only Calais, while its own civil war, the war of the Roses, which coincidentally began in 1453, would keep it distracted for over a generation (see Map 3).

By 1453, victory over the English was mainly symbolic. The major obstacle to a restoration of political unity under royal control remained the grandees, who were as problematic as ever, especially during the 1440s, when Charles VII's own son, the future Louis XI (r. 1461–83), was frequently in cahoots with them! But when his time came to succeed his father, Louis XI proved an even more authoritarian taskmaster whose harsh methods quickly provoked a brief and successful 'war of the public good' (1465), led by disgruntled nobles who forced him to make concessions and even a promise to govern with their support. He promptly reneged on those commitments, and thereafter his efforts focussed on rebuilding royal authority by bringing the 'great' fiefs back into the royal domain. Brittany would have to wait a generation longer, although he laid the dynastic foundations for its eventual union with France. In several major cases – Burgundy, Berry, and Anjou-Provence – luck was on his side: the death without male heirs of the reigning princes was the common factor, but even here there was resistance to the tactics adopted by the 'universal spider', as Louis XI was called.

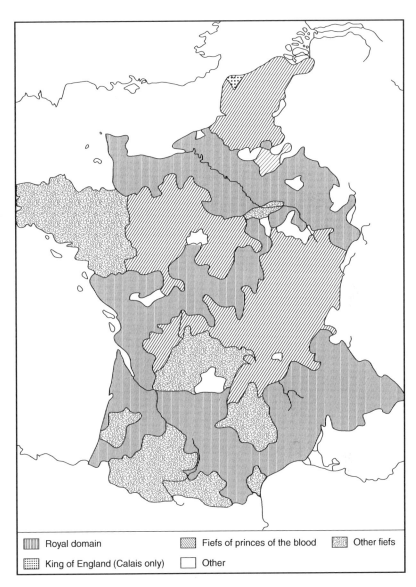

**Map 3** *France at end of Hundred Years' War, 1461*

Burgundy had resumed its earlier role of implacable enemy in the early 1460s, but Louis XI's tactics there backfired, prompting one of Europe's most momentous dynastic marriages, that of the Burgundian heiress, Mary, to Maximilian of Habsburg. Their grandson, the emperor Charles V (1500–59), would inherit the largest territorial conglomerate seen in Europe since the Roman Empire, one which was contiguous with France on all sides. Louis XI did gain the duchy of Burgundy for France, but the Burgundian dynasty's most important lands, from the county of Franche-Comté northwards to the Netherlands, escaped his grasp. The loss of Flanders-Artois-Hainaut, in particular, which had figured so prominently in French politics for centuries, posed major problems until Louis XIV's time.

Dynasticism of this kind was no respecter of notions of stable political geography. When Louis XI or his successors recovered principalities like Burgundy or Anjou they inevitably inherited their rights or claims to lands outside France. Thus regaining Anjou actually brought him Provence (1480) and, theoretically, the kingdom of Naples and Sicily; the Orleans claim to the duchy of Milan was inherited by Louis XII (r. 1498–1515). The dynastic and territorial bases for the protracted Italian – in reality, European – wars against the Habsburgs were already complete, and it was French initiative that kicked them off.

The problems posed by great principalities before and during the Hundred Years' War were familiar to France's neighbours, England and Castile, among others. They did not disappear overnight. Given the socio-economic structures on which political power had been based for centuries, the grandees 'naturally' inhabited all the key political spaces, even if names and faces changed at different times. Using the same dynastic tactics as the monarchy, their relative influence could change quickly, especially when comparable dynastic 'accidents' (early deaths, minorities, absence of heirs) could multiply the extent of their lands. The size and resources of the larger French principalities – from Champagne to Gascony – made them formidable, as they possessed some of the key powers of a state, such as issuing coinage, making laws, and collecting taxes. Individual grandees, especially those possessing military prestige, also attracted wider clienteles of ambitious and needy lesser nobles, for whom they sought preferment – offices, military commands, land, and advantageous marriages. If the monarchy was to obtain the support of the nobility at provincial and local level, it needed both to sustain and tap into such power. Equally, great nobles like the dukes of Burgundy drew much of their financial resources from their positions within the *French* monarchy, especially at times when their loyalty was crucial. When the age of the great principalities finally ended, the monarchy would continue to use the leading aristocrats as provincial governors

**Map 4**  *The principal fiefs and apanages of medieval France*

and intermediaries, but in unstable times, that recipe, too, could prove dangerous. Coined to describe English experience, the term 'over-mighty subjects' fits late medieval France perfectly (see Map 4).

In such a world, there was little room for the voices of other social groups, even when the impact of war and natural disasters prompted widespread rebellion. Peasant revolts were, as later history would attest, the easiest to repress, especially when they failed to gain a foothold in towns; mercy was rarely shown to them in open battle. Far fewer in France than in

Flanders, urban revolts were more difficult to handle because of the political framework into which they fitted, especially when their leaders were patricians like the Parisian Étienne Marcel with connections to princely factions.

## III

In view of the seigneurial-aristocratic political 'establishment' and the relative haphazardness with which legal and other institutions developed throughout France's provinces, it should be easier to comprehend the continuing importance of the only 'universal' institution of the age, the church. It was critical for the monarchy itself, as the close links between the two since Merovingian times attests. Senior clergy continued to serve as confidants and councillors, and until Philip IV's reign the chancellor was always a cleric. Large numbers of clerics, especially cathedral canons, served the crown in numerous capacities – financial included – until the sixteenth century, while drawing a comfortable income from their church benefices; rarely were senior clergy so numerous in political, diplomatic, and other positions than in the years 1500–50. The presence of the papacy in Avignon from 1306 to 1378 only encouraged such high-level political activity by French clerics, who dominated its administration, which was probably the most advanced in Europe. Such close, enduring co-habitation cemented bonds that became most visible during moments of crisis, especially in disputes with the post-Gregorian papacy. The most famous of them, during the 1290s and 1300s, between Philip IV and Boniface VIII, escalated into a conflict about papal supremacy over temporal rulers, echoes of which still resonated three centuries later. In this conflict, Philip IV, thanks to the effective use of assemblies of French prelates, had little difficulty rallying church leadership to his defence. That conflict did much to stimulate the idea of the French church as enjoying a large measure of autonomy, given its apostolic origins and long history of self-government; for this reason, the idea would later be labelled 'gallicanism', which firmly rejected papal claims to universal jurisdiction over the church in favour of a form of 'collegial' governance. For their part, the wider French responses to papal claims around 1300 became key elements in a slowly evolving doctrine of royal authority, elaborated by theologians as much as by lawyers, which duly became the foundations of absolute monarchy.

But like other princes, French kings made other more everyday demands of the church, especially financial. In his conflict with Rome, Philip IV, thanks to the effective use of assemblies of French prelates, had little difficulty rallying church leadership to his side, forbidding the payment of 'annates' to Rome by French clerics or obtaining church 'tenths' at regular intervals. Such financial resources would prove precious to successive monarchs, especially during the Hundred Years' War, when much of the realm was not in trustworthy hands and ordinary taxes might not materialise. Not surprisingly, French church leaders became wary of royal appetites and struck hard bargains, which could lead later kings to prefer to cut deals over their heads with the papacy in order to raise monies from them without their formal consent!

For these and other reasons the monarchy increasingly sought to regain the patronage rights that it had lost since the Gregorian attack on the lay investiture of bishoprics and major abbeys; subsequently, the papacy's own claims to appoint to major church positions reached their apex during its residence in Avignon (1306–78), but the 'great' schism that followed (1378–1418) enabled France, and other monarchies, to recover much of their control of church patronage, something that a badly weakened post-schism papacy had little choice but to accept. In 1439, Charles VII proclaimed the restoration of elections of bishops, but on condition that his suggestions ('friendly and well intentioned') would receive preferential consideration by the cathedral chapters; and the 'elected' bishops no longer needed to seek papal confirmation. This scarcely disguised restoration of royal patronage was further consolidated in 1516 by the famous concordat of Bologna, which explicitly recognised royal nomination rights to bishoprics as well as to hundreds of abbeys and priories, but also brought the pope back into the process of appointment. More prescriptive and extensive than any other such agreement, Bologna consolidated the notion of a ring-fenced gallican church under obvious royal tutelage. Apart from the monarchy itself, which henceforth controlled an unparalleled portfolio of major church titles, the beneficiaries were the sons of the nobility or of court and government officials with close ties to the crown; the losers were the cathedral chapters and local clerics, whose search for preferment now obliged them to look towards crown and court. Such a metamorphosis enabled many high-ranking if not always well-born clerics to dominate France's political and diplomatic-administrative elite by the sixteenth century; it waned thereafter, but the rise to prime-ministerial power of later cardinals like Lorraine, Richelieu, Mazarin, or Fleury would have been unthinkable without the persistence of what has been labelled an 'ecclesial' monarchy.

With its upper ranks so anchored in France's governing structures, it was only natural for critics and reformers to insist, as did the Gregorian reformers of an earlier age, that the entire edifice was worldly and neglectful of its religious duties. Such a polemical view has been criticised as misleading. It is true that by the thirteenth century, the major innovations of the medieval church – schools, universities, mendicant religious orders, confraternities – were in place, making the following two centuries seem rather sterile by comparison. The church had largely contained the earlier dissenting movements, and the religious orders were more densely settled by 1500; their preaching and other pastoral efforts were appreciated by laypeople, if we can judge from legacies and the numbers of those joining the orders. Their impact on the mass of the rural population was far more limited, but the parish-based, secular clergy were never more numerous, with increasing numbers of 'chantry' priests whose primary duty was to say masses for the dead in an age of mass death. Never, it seems, did families have more sons and daughters who 'joined the church', so that by around 1520 the clericalisation of French society had reached record levels. What the church did not yet try to do was to formally educate or train the clergy as a whole, which accounts for the radical differences in their capacity and reputation. A small minority of university graduates were favoured when it came to seeking positions (benefices) such as those of parish priests in towns, but they were often accused of pocketing the income while hiring hard-up vicars to replace them as they themselves sought better opportunities elsewhere. It would take the shock of the Protestant reformation as well as the impact of its Catholic counterpart from the mid-seventeenth century onwards to reshape and redirect the Catholic clergy towards a different sort of pastoral activity.

The religious culture of the late medieval population has also had its detractors, especially the humanist and Protestant reformers, who denounced it as superstitious and superficial. Historians have attempted to take account of the wider socio-cultural environment of the age, dominated by epidemic and sudden mass-death. Such a prospect left its mark firmly on religious practices, especially in the widespread obsession with death and dying, and how best to prepare for a 'good' death. Confraternities of 'intercession' were generally the most attractive to vulnerable populations seeking protectors against evil and misfortune; they may have focussed on death, but the confraternities were as much concerned with actually burying the dead and assisting the survivors, especially widows and children, as they were with devotion in the narrow sense. The social and the religious spheres were far too intertwined for such (later) distinctions to make sense during the later medieval period. In fact, confraternities are themselves strong evidence of a widening laicisation of religious life during the period, given how much their members organised their own religious activities and employed their own chaplains. Moreover, the churchwardens, drawn mainly from the better-off parishioners, controlled the parochial finances and hired clergy in some cases. With the end of the Hundred Years' War in the 1450s, they gradually began the reconstruction of damaged or abandoned churches, often with considerable embellishments; they also organised the increasingly elaborate festive days such as *Corpus Christi*. The same slow shift to lay control over hospices and works of charity generally is also evident by the late fifteenth century. It is more difficult to generalise about forms of lay piety, but it seems that the traditional saints, led by the Virgin Mary, remained popular as ever, with Francis of Assisi the only new face in the gallery. The surviving iconography, especially of the *pietà*, shows that the figure of the suffering Christ was central, but within the wider kinship of the Holy Family. In southern regions, new devotional confraternities of 'penitents', modelled on those of Italy, began to appear in the 1490s; in northern towns, older confraternities remained dominant, but groups of pious women called *beguines* were also numerous. Attendance at Mass on Sundays and (numerous) feast-days was nearly universal, as was the practice of confession and communion at least once a year. But the latter duty was often performed perfunctorily, as most people were not sufficiently instructed by their clergy to treat it as they would in later centuries. As practised by most of the population, even among the urban minority, religion was still firmly grounded in parish-centred social obligation ('friendship') rather than inward-looking, personal piety.

## IV

The medieval church's power derived in part, as we have already seen, from its virtual monopoly on educational institutions and its continuing ability to define the framework of knowledge and enquiry. Latin was its language, the only one capable of expressing the elevated truths of philosophy and theology, but also of law (with *its* prestigious Roman ancestry) and medicine; the medieval university was no haven for poetic or imaginative literary creations expressed in the vernacular. Having survived early fears and attacks, the scholastic synthesis of Greek philosophy and Christian theology dominated university teaching for the following centuries, despite the often-strident rivalry between the different 'schools' of thought. The Paris theology faculty retained its leading position, although it did suffer from the city's political turbulence during the Hundred Years' War. Moreover, the late medieval crises of the church – from the Philip IV-Boniface VIII conflict to the great schism (1378–1418/39) – made universities and their 'masters' anything but ivory-towered egg-heads, contrary to what their humanist critics claimed later. French theologians, in particular, were increasingly drawn into disputes over fundamental questions of spiritual and political power.

Papal attempts since the twelfth century to create a machinery of government that would faithfully mirror its claims to sovereignty over temporal rulers involved borrowing Roman and canon-law concepts; and these reworked ideas were central to efforts to resolve the intractable problem of rival popes during the great schism. Generations of French academics, from Pierre d'Ailly to Jean Gerson, took a leading role in these debates, one major effect of which was to bolster the hitherto rather vague notions of a gallican church and its liberties. But, not surprisingly, such debates and concepts were eminently transferable, not least because of their increasingly juridical content, so that they became central to the theories advanced, even in times of adversity, about the nature of monarchy itself. Having viscerally refused any subordination to the papacy and declared that 'the king is emperor in his own realm' – a powerful Roman-law assertion – the French monarchy was well placed to take advantage of the papacy's discomfiture after 1378. This was partly because its councillors and legists had also been busy re-casting earlier notions of vassalage to the king's advantage and ultimately in the direction of sovereignty, a term that did not yet exist but which owed much to the medieval papacy's notion of 'full power' (*plena potestas*). These increasingly successful efforts were one reason why Edward III sought the trade in his claim to the French throne for 'full power' over Guyenne. In subsequent years, similar notions of royal authority were deployed to deny that taxation required prior consent by subjects.

The French monarchy was still some way from claiming that its king was absolute, but some of the key ingredients for such an assertion were already present. The more the monarchy expanded its judicial and administrative structures, and the more graduates and practitioners of law monopolised them, the more ideas of a uniquely superior royal power acquired a social and professional foundation. Finally, the majority of French church leaders with a university education had studied law rather than theology – which was still largely the preserve of the religious orders – a choice that makes it easier to understand the common culture of the secular and ecclesiastical elites who served the monarchy.

By the fifteenth century, the intellectual landscape, too, was beginning to change, as part of a Europe-wide movement, the Renaissance. Such 'rebirths' had happened in the Carolingian period and the twelfth century, characterised by the recovery and reworking of certain elements of classical, especially Roman, culture. That of the fifteenth century, centred in Italy, was far more comprehensive, and the invention of printing was perfectly timed to diffuse and perpetuate its enthusiasm for everything classical – from poetry to architecture. That enthusiasm was driven partly by hostility towards contemporary academic-university learning, something that would later be shared by Erasmus, Luther, and other religious reformers, who rejected the scholastic synthesis as imprisoning Christian thought in a rationalist straitjacket. 'Renaissance' promised the return of a golden age, thus ending the barbarism of the 'Middle Ages' – a term the humanists invented – as epitomised by the uncouth Latin, in both style and vocabulary, used by medieval writers. Instead, Renaissance humanists cultivated 'humane letters' (the original meaning of the term 'humanist'), among which the works of the great masters of rhetoric, from Demosthenes to Cicero and Quintilian, were especially prized. For humanists seeking religious reform, the early church Fathers belonged fully to that classical past, and thus became models to follow, at the expense of the more recent Scholastics. By encouraging new methods of teaching, writing, and argument, the 'new learning' appealed to a potentially wider audience, lay as much as clerical.

French exposure to new intellectual currents was relatively limited – compared to Germany and the Netherlands – before the 1470s–1480s approximately. In fact, the most brilliant court of the age, that of Burgundy, proved more attractive to artists and scholars than any other, and it would be some time before the French monarchy would successfully emulate it. Robert Gaguin (1433–1501) is often considered to be the first French humanist. A mentor and friend of the Dutch humanist, Erasmus (1469–1536), he vigorously defended the new learning from the 1470s within the university of Paris itself, but he evinced only limited enthusiasm among his contemporaries there – or beyond. It was the next generation of humanists like Erasmus and his French contemporaries (Jacques Lefèvre d'Étaples, Gillaume Budé, and many others) who began making up for the delay from the 1490s onwards, adapting the techniques of humanist scholarship to law, theology, and the study of the Bible in its original language; the commentaries and glosses of the intervening centuries were discarded in favour of the original texts, which in some cases they re-translated to meet the new humanist scholarly exigencies. Such achievements led them to claim by the 1520s that Paris, the Sorbonne notwithstanding, had regained its place as the principal seat of European learning.

The next two generations witnessed an explosion of scholarly and literary talent, beginning with that of Marguerite de Navarre (sister of Francis I), Clément Marot, François Rabelais, Maurice Scève, and Louise Labé, 'la belle cordière'. They were followed in the 1540s–1550s by a galaxy of younger writers (they actually called themselves by that term, the *pléiade*) that included Pierre Ronsard, Joachim du Bellay, and Jean Dorat, and who urged the combination of the French language with classical genres (odes, elegies, epigrams). Taken together, their works definitively established the credentials of French as a full-blown literary language. Latin and Greek retained their prestige, but the narrow linguistic banks of the earlier (Italian) Renaissance had been spectacularly burst. The spread, after the 1520s, of France's equivalent of grammar schools, and the eagerness of towns to have such schools and the humanist schoolteachers who ran them, is perhaps the best evidence of the wider – a relative term here – impact of, and demand for the Renaissance.

Long before that point was reached, French culture had responded to the other challenges posed by the Italian Renaissance in ways that were both predictable and novel. Charles VIII's invasion of Italy in 1494 undoubtedly had a significant impact, but the claim that 'once the French nobility had seen Italy, France would never be the same' should not be taken too literally. Until the seventeenth century, France's elites, and not just the military nobility, would continue to see in Italy a source for models to follow. But they emphatically sought to harmonise them with their own artistic and architectural traditions, about which they had no inferiority complex; the same stance was, as we saw above, increasingly true of French humanist scholars. While the Italians dubbed the French 'barbarians' in, and long after 1494, there was soon a growing traffic northwards of Italian artists, engineers, builders – all lured by French patronage that was royal, aristocratic, and clerical. The Loire-valley monarchy of Louis XII (r. 1498–1515) and his successors did not always lead the way, since the earliest *châteaux* built in the Italianate style were those of the crown's principal financiers (Chenonceaux, Azay-le-Rideau, Villandry) or of leading aristocrats and cardinals like Georges d'Amboise (Gaillon) and the Guises and Montmorencys (Joinville, Écouen).

The absorption of Italian artistic canons by France was a gradual, cumulative process in which diplomatic missions, improved relations with the papacy, dynastic marriages with the Medici or the Este families, and other encounters provided renewed opportunities for cultural and artistic transfer. This was not confined to painting or architecture, but included the various arts (music, emblems, and poetry) needed to embellish the festivals, banquets, royal entries, and other ceremonies that characterised the elite society of the time. Music, as is well known, ceased to be a virtually exclusive church preserve and 'invaded' secular society during the Renaissance. Yet it was not Italy, but northern France and Flanders – essentially 'Burgundy' – which dominated European music in this period, beginning with Guillaume Dufay (1400–74) and Johann Ockeghem (?–1497). Indeed, their disciples and successors, Josquin des Prés (1440–1521), Clément

Jannequin (1485–1558), and others, were nowhere in higher demand than in Italy. Unlike their predecessors, they wrote secular as well as church music. Similarly, northern European painters like van Eyck, van der Weyden, and Jean Fouquet flourished, and it was not until the early 1500s that high Renaissance classical art came to dominate Europe. For all his fondness of Italian art, Francis I remained faithful to Jean Clouet and his son as royal portraitists. If the Italian 'mannerist' style became so prominent in French painting after 1530, it was thanks mainly to Francis I's decision to employ Primaticcio and Rosso Fiorentino to decorate Fontainebleau. His personal aesthetic tastes apart, it was his grasp of the political value of artistic capital that distinguished Francis from most of his successors before Louis XIV.

One reason for this gradual but diffused acceptance of Italian models was that there were smaller princely centres that attracted French (and other) writers, musicians, and artists. The most prominent one, Burgundy, was not the only such court; others existed at Tours, Blois, and Aix. Under Francis I and Henry II, the royal court increasingly came to set the tone for cultural festivities, ones in which monarchical 'perfection' itself found new forms of expression and communication; the capacity of the monarchy to out-spend every other patron became decisive in imposing its version of the culture–power nexus. The scholars and artists who obtained such employment proclaimed, in return, the glory and reputation of their patrons. Meanwhile, urban provincial elites, especially in towns like Toulouse, Lyon, or Poitiers, adapted their own cultural pursuits, from poetry competitions to informal 'academies'. The growing presence of educated magistrates and royal officials in the major towns gradually nudged learned culture there towards philological, historical (broadly conceived), geographical, and legal themes. Printing presses, wherever they existed, invariably served as lively places of intellectual exchange, given how many humanists were printers and editors as well as authors. With neither a university nor a parlement, Lyon nevertheless became one of Europe's major printing and intellectual centres.

# V

There are good reasons for applying the notion of re-birth to France, viewed from a social angle, during the century after 1450 approximately. It was no revolution, however, but a recovery substantial enough to sustain some of the other 'renaissances' of the day. Indeed, it was in the mid-sixteenth century that European observers – diplomats and travellers – began to comment on the sheer wealth of France, one they measured primarily in human terms. It seems that by the 1470s, at the latest, almost every area of France was experiencing population recovery, thanks to the lull in epidemics and the disappearance of the ravages of war; couples, it seems, could marry younger because of the availability of unworked land, while the more benign economic and pathogenic conditions meant higher survival rates among young children, historically the most vulnerable cohort but vital for population increase. This revival may have slowed somewhat by 1500–20, depending on the region, but overall it continued until the 1550s. Most estimates equate the population of 1560 to that of 1347, the eve of the Black Death, with around 18 million inhabitants within France's present frontiers. These figures and 'chronology' are only indicative, given the continuing absence of reliable national or even regional sources. Local epidemics still flared up, notably in towns, while new ones, like typhus and syphilis, appeared for the first time, but leprosy virtually disappeared for good. Cities and towns expanded considerably, housing about two of the 18 million inhabitants, a recovery which could only have happened via continuous immigration from rural areas.

This population recovery seems to have stalled nearly everywhere by the 1560s. Even without the massively damaging wars of religion that followed, it was probably unsustainable because conditions were worsening. The peasantry, who had benefited earlier from lower population levels, had only partially loosened the seigneurial corset. Between them, population growth and land-hunger eventually played into the hands of landlords, who no longer needed to make the same concessions as previously to the peasantry; competition arising from population growth meant that rents could now be raised and conditions of tenancy be made tougher. In many areas, landlords re-structured abandoned lands into more onerous share-cropping tenancies; they were short-term and the lords usually took half of the crop in kind, which enabled them to benefit substantially from the rising prices of agricultural produce. No significant improvements in French agricultural practices or technology occurred that would have raised crop-yields proportionately. The same logic led to wages for rural and urban workers gradually falling in real terms, as measured against the rising prices of basic necessities.

The *seigneurs* of Renaissance France had themselves experienced upheaval. From one province to another, the density of noble settlement varied hugely, but the combination of epidemics (which they may have escaped better than other social groups) and especially protracted warfare seems to have frequently wiped out the majority of local lineages. Some of them were replaced by lords newly ennobled for their military service to the crown, but by the early 1500s, 'new' families were also filling their shoes, buying land (especially with seigneurial attributes) and, like the English gentry, 'living nobly' in the expectation of gradual recognition from local society. Some of these aspiring 'nobles' included rich peasants, but increasingly they were merchants and royal officials in search of the social esteem which the 'vile' professions, such as trade generally, denied them. Such social osmosis raised few eyebrows before 1560, possibly because it was less frequent than is often assumed, but also because it was a gradual process spread over two to three generations and was essentially local in nature. Things only began to change when tax burdens on local communities increased and, crucially, when the nobility, old and new, claimed to be exempt from paying them. At that point, both the monarchy and local communities started to react in order to limit the access of new families to noble status. Ironically, it was the taxes which nobles did *not* pay that did more than anything else to define their status and privileges as nobles.

Urban recovery was equally notable during the century after 1460. By the 1550s, Paris was again Europe's largest city, with approximately 300,000 inhabitants, while Lyon emerged as its nearest rival with about 80,000; Rouen, Bordeaux, Marseille, Toulouse doubled or even tripled their previously maxima to between 40,000 and 60,000 people. Some 30 cities had populations of 10,000 or more by 1560, despite the urban 'deserts' of regions like Brittany and the Auvergne. The larger cities, and especially Paris, needed substantial quantities of foodstuffs, which only an ever-widening hinterland could adequately supply. Such town-country inter-dependence was to remain a major economic stimulus for centuries. A different kind of link, one detrimental to urban prosperity, was already appearing by 1500 with the 'putting-out' system, in which urban merchants removed the production of textiles (serges, linen, hemp) to the countryside, where costs were far lower than in guild-dominated towns.

At the same time, the internal 'constitution' of French towns was changing. Most French towns only formally became municipalities during the later medieval period, an outcome of pressure to build defensive walls and to raise the finances that that required. But as their 'general assemblies' of *bourgeois* subsequently declined, the prestige of those holding municipal office rose accordingly; tenure of municipal office enabled patricians and merchants to advertise the process of their separation from 'trade', great or small. These emerging urban 'notables' widely dominated urban politics during the period 1470–1560, having side-lined the artisans and lesser legal practitioners; subsequently, their own power would be challenged by local royal officials who 'invaded' the town councils, great and small, despite both local and royal objections; their divided loyalties muddied the waters of urban politics thereafter. On the one hand, they belonged to families with essentially local interests; on the other, service to the monarchy, which might involve acting against local interests, was a more certain road to higher status (ennoblement included) than anything available from other sources. But such tensions remained latent during the century after the Hundred Years' War, especially as financial relations between the towns and the crown were to the towns' advantage. The monarchy and its 'loyal towns', the 300 or so *bonnes villes*, enjoyed an *entente cordiale*, which it would take the experiences of the wars of religion to transform into one reminiscent of the urban revolts of the 1350s, 1380s, and 1410s.

The prolonged disruption and insecurity caused by wartime conditions since the 1340s had, as already noted, gradually marginalised France within Europe's commercial networks to the benefit of Italian, German, and Flemish rivals. Louis XI tried to develop an economic policy, but it proved to be more political than economic. Wishing to revive the great fairs which had long since declined, he was obliged to 'adopt' those of Lyon, where the Italian merchant-bankers were already dominant; he also sought to create French 'draperies' capable of rivalling those of Flanders, and slapped tariffs on imported Flemish textiles, but with only limited and probably negative results. Further west, France's Atlantic-Channel ports and hinterlands continued to trade with their Spanish and English-Flemish neighbours, especially for products like wine and salt, and later textiles, but it seems that it was foreign merchants residing in the ports themselves – some of whom settled permanently and later became French – who dominated these exchanges. Native Breton or Norman merchants were active enough in the age of Columbus to fit out expeditions from 1503 onwards to the Americas, north and south, and Africa. Jacques Cartier discovered what would be called henceforth 'new France', but in the absence of sustained royal interest in such ventures, the results were decidedly patchy, and no French colonial empire would appear for a long time. This can be explained in part by the acquisition of Provence in 1481 and especially the Italian wars after 1494, in which the monarchy sought to acquire Milan and Naples, and which duly led to alliances with the Ottoman empire. The price of such intense, sustained focus on the Mediterranean for over 60 years was relative neglect of the wider world overseas.

# VI

The French monarchy's recovery from its nadir of the 1420s, when the prospect of incorporation into an expanded English empire seemed inescapable to many, may also be considered a rebirth. Historians disagree about how much the notion of a 'Renaissance monarchy' – a term denoting rule that was 'popular and consultative' rather than authoritarian or absolutist in character – fits France. What follows takes its cue from an epigram that seems well suited to late medieval France – 'states make wars and wars make states' – but without implying that a conscious agenda of 'state-building' was part of it. Within only a generation after the ending of the brief civil war of the mid-1460s, France precipitated an international conflict on a grand scale – the so-called Italian wars (1494–1559) that would last over 60 years. The major difference, of course, was that, with one or two brief exceptions, French armies now fought on foreign soil; for that reason, the impact of war was bound to be different. Changes introduced by war were improvised rather than part of any long-meditated programme of state-building. For example, reconquering certain territories, especially in the south and west during the 1450s, offered opportunities to modify local institutions, such as municipal privileges, customs or tax exemptions, in order to strengthen royal control, but a healthy realism ruled out wholesale changes lest they create further, unnecessary conflict.

The failure of Charles V's attempts in the 1370s to form the nucleus of a standing army meant that French forces throughout the Hundred Years' War consisted, with the exception of mercenary companies, of the 'host' of the king's vassals and their men; it was feudal military service rendered by those required to serve personally. Towards the end of the war, in 1449 and 1445, Charles VII ordered the creation of permanent ordinance companies of approximately 12,000 men, even in peacetime; above all, he wished to make them more 'royal' than the existing forces were. Such ambitions were only partially realised until Louis XIV's time, despite the gradual emergence of an administrative and financial infrastructure of royal officials for that purpose. The effective recruitment and leadership of military forces remained firmly in the grip of the nobility, who would buy and sell regiments as a matter of course. When provincial governors became the norm across France by the early 1500s, their primary functions were, as befitted their high status, military – to command royal troops and recruit new ones. By the onset of the Italian wars in 1494, the French army was considered the most powerful in Europe.

Charles VII's efforts to create a standing army followed rather than preceded the emergence of a new fiscal dispensation cobbled together in some desperation and political uproar in 1360. Up to then, the royal finances came overwhelmingly from the royal domain, judicial fees, excises, church 'tenths' and the like; ad hoc taxes were voted by assemblies of estates here and there, but were not guaranteed from year to year. Military disaster at

Poitiers (1356) and the enormous ransom demanded for John II heralded a new age, one in which 'extraordinary' revenues (i.e. taxes) would come to swamp the 'ordinary' ones just itemised. Vassals and subjects were obliged to ransom their lord, but in 1360 this 'evident necessity' could no longer be met from classic 'feudal' methods or resources. Similarly, the discredit of the ruling feudal elite led to the convening of a 'northern' Estates-General, but it proved unable to deal with the challenge, alienating both the government and the local assemblies and towns; the Estates-General thus lost a vital key to its continuing political relevance, while the monarchy reached out over its head to the regional or town assemblies to distribute and levy the new taxes. The latter, different in principle from feudal levies, included a generic tax, the *aides*, on sales as well as the notorious *gabelle* on salt; only later, in 1384, did the royal *taille*, which was based on a seigneurial levy of that name, join the other two as the core of the crown's 'extraordinary' revenue; all three fell primarily on the lower classes in town and country. In nearly every case, there had to be a separate arrangement for Languedoc, owing to the vitality of its estates and the need to ensure co-operation over the new taxes; that in turn introduced a long-standing fiscal boundary within France; other such 'frontiers' would follow, especially for the salt tax, dividing several regions almost arbitrarily from each other.

In the century after 1356–60, war and government needs rendered taxes permanent de facto, in the raising of which provincial estates gradually became key players, especially in the more distant and often newly acquired provinces. Because of their capacity efficiently to assess, raise, and deliver taxes, their assistance was invaluable to a monarchy that simply lacked such a capacity. Their financial credit grew accordingly, which of course made them an invaluable source of short-term funds for a frequently impecunious monarchy. In due course, the estates of Languedoc, Burgundy, Normandy, and Brittany developed different taxes that corresponded more closely to their socio-economic structures than 'national' ones ever could.

A similar common denominator brought the monarchy and the *bonnes villes* ever closer. The towns would raise loans for the crown, the interest of which was paid out of local taxes. But the towns then gradually off-loaded, especially under Louis XI, the taxes onto the rural communities which could not compete with the towns in framing the emerging fiscal nexus. Successive monarchs like Charles VII and Louis XI made sure that these taxes did not disappear in peacetime, and that royal revenues would continue to grow. Nevertheless, it is generally agreed that such steep tax rises were bearable, thanks to the economic recovery since 1460.

The remaking of the realm during and after the Hundred Years' War witnessed the multiplication of existing institutions, as well as other innovations. The growth of assemblies of estates in many provinces, especially in those recently acquired or regained, was designed to solidify centre–periphery relationships. Other parallel initiatives were taken. The parlement of Paris, an emanation of the royal council that gradually became the highest court of justice during the 1200s, was for a long time the only body of its kind. But with the re-composition of the royal domain under Charles VII, 'provincial' equivalents were created at Poitiers (1418, suppressed in 1436), Toulouse (1443), Grenoble (1453), Bordeaux (1456), Dijon (1477), Rouen (1499), Aix (1501), and Rennes (1554). With a few exceptions, the dates of foundation came soon after the provinces' return, or entry into the royal domain. Covering nearly half of the realm, the Paris parlement's immense area of jurisdiction remained unchanged, while the others were confined to their respective provinces. The parlements were not just courts of appeal in the narrow modern sense: their principal responsibility was, as it was for the lower courts, to maintain 'la bonne police' – good order – a much wider duty than administering civil and criminal justice. A lower and nation-wide tier of *présidial* courts was added in one swoop in 1551, partly because of urgent royal need for money, but also with a view to bridging the wide gap separating the parlements from the local courts (*bailliages* and *sénéchaussés*). The parlements in particular were staffed by professional magistrates with law degrees, who were usually the offspring of upwardly mobile urban bourgeois families; by the early to mid-1500s these magistrates were, de facto, purchasing and owning their offices. They formed the educated 'governing' elite of the major law-courts, which also attracted an expanding population of barristers, solicitors, process-servers, and other clerks from further down the social scale. Many a provincial town's prosperity derived from the presence of such figures and their households within its walls, especially if it was the seat of more than one court or administrative institution.

Not surprisingly, the invention of new taxes in the 1350s led, within a generation or two, to a parallel machinery of financial administration, for which France was initially divided into four massive units known as 'generalities'; further sub-division saw their number rise to ten by 1523 and to sixteen by 1542. Each generality consisted of 'elections', whose numbers also increased through sub-division over the same period. As with other sub-divisions, the need to raise money by creating and selling new offices was their principal driver. Chambers of accounts and courts of 'aides' were created, first in Paris, and then spread haphazardly to the different provinces, gradually expanding in remit and personnel, especially in the royal heartlands where there were no provincial assemblies to handle financial affairs. In the 'peripheral' provinces, which included major sources of revenue like Normandy, Burgundy, and Languedoc, financial administration was cheaply and efficiently conducted by the local estates rather than by royal officials. The fiscal system's *ad hoc* origins and organisation made it virtually impossible to harmonise, since the selling of offices, which became indispensable in wartime, constantly added powerful counterweights to structural reform. There were, for example, internal boundaries for certain key taxes, like the *gabelle*, which meant that extending particular taxes to areas previously exempt could easily provoke local rebellions. Governing an enlarged kingdom with a turbulent recent history was primarily a political question of securing obedience, in which institutional homogeneity was a lesser consideration.

## VII

This was the monarchy that confidently launched the Italian wars in 1494 when Charles VIII asserted his claim, as heir of the Anjou dynasty, to the kingdom of Naples. The expedition initially encouraged other crusading-*reconquista* hopes, as Charles VIII also had titles to the kingdom of Jerusalem and the Byzantine empire! Although older, the claim to Milan was only taken up by Louis XII, grandson of a Visconti, in 1498. Meanwhile, Charles VIII had led the first French army to cross the Alps for several centuries; this invasion smashed the equilibrium of the Italian state-system as comprehensively as the fearsome French artillery smashed the walls of recalcitrant Italian cities on their triumphant promenade to Naples. The French had not been in southern Italy since 1282, when the Angevins were bloodily chased out of Palermo during the celebrated Sicilian Vespers, while the claim to *both* Naples and Milan soon suggested an ambition to dominate the entire peninsula. The initial shock of the unopposed French return quickly wore off, and an anti-French coalition of Italian powers, in which Venice and the papacy were important players, began to form. Above all, the Aragonese, who had dominated southern Italy and the western Mediterranean for generations, were determined to resist French expansion, and thanks to successive dynastic alliances with Castile (1469) and Habsburg (1500), their power would grow substantially during the early 1500s. As a result, Charles VIII had to retreat hastily to France as early as 1495, the first of many such occurrences up to 1557, when the last inconsequential Italian adventure had to be hastily curtailed in order to confront a more dangerous Spanish threat from Flanders.

These dates – 1494 to 1557 – book-end the French dalliance with Renaissance Italy, which never lost its allure for the imagination of poets, painters, and musicians, but also for military captains, like the horribly disfigured Jean de Monluc, whose memoirs evoked a powerful nostalgia for the years he spent there. During those years, Italy proved to be both a quagmire where France could never convert initial military triumphs into a durable political toehold, and a snake-pit whose suddenly shifting alliances it was unable to control. The outcome was there were no territories left in French hands by 1515, when Francis I had to start all over again; this scenario would recur in subsequent decades.

Above all, the stakes of the Italian wars quickly became European. The sense that France was now in a stranglehold created by the Habsburgs since Charles V had become king of Spain (1516) and Holy Roman emperor (1519), may have been self-induced, but it had significant consequences. Franco-Habsburg rivalry became the fulcrum around which most other European disputes revolved for over a century. Thus the sixth of the Italian wars (1521–6) counts as the first of an equally long series of Europe-wide wars between Francis I and his successor Henry II against Charles V. French victories, even the most celebrated such as Marignano (1515), were too rare to modify the map of Italy for long, and they were more than negated by their biggest military disasters since Agincourt, such as La Bicocca (1522) and then Pavia (1525), where Francis I was himself taken prisoner. He spent the following year in Madrid, while the peace of that name was negotiated and in which he renounced French suzerainty over Burgundy, Artois, and Flanders, as well as his claims to Milan and Naples; he managed to recover Burgundy almost immediately after his release, but not the others. These lands indicate clearly where and what the main sources of Franco-Habsburg rivalry were. In fact, as soon as Francis I returned to France in 1526, he renounced the treaty of Madrid as signed under duress, but France never quite succeeded thereafter in imposing its leadership of an anti-Habsburg coalition, especially in Italy. The following decades were ones of inconclusive diplomacy and expensive military campaigning. Henry II (r. 1547–59) inherited his father's ambitions, but was more successful on France's northern and eastern borders – the recovery of Calais, the acquisition of Metz, Toul, and Verdun – than in Italy, where all was comprehensively lost by 1559.

These wars were markedly different to those of the two previous centuries. Francis I's captivity did not produce the upheavals that accompanied John II's in 1356, and the substantial ransom was rapidly and (relatively) painlessly raised and paid. The wars were inevitably expensive, particularly the expeditions to Italy, but as they were mostly fought on foreign soil, their costs could be partially recouped on the ground. However, the wider the conflicts became, after 1520, and the more allies were involved, the more the costs of diplomacy and alliances climbed and needed to be funded from crown revenues; the hiring of mercenary regiments, especially the Swiss, added substantially to these outlays. As early as 1522–3, two historically durable financial institutions were born. The first was the creation, during a re-configuration of the central financial administration, of a separate treasury for 'occasional income' (*parties casuelles*), an unlikely name for the receipts of the sale of, and other transactions concerning, offices in the king's service. Acquiring, conveying, and inheriting offices via 'loans' or 'gifts' was already common but highly unregulated, so this measure put it on a public, institutional footing for the first time, and made possible the take-off of the venality of office on a huge scale; a second initiative, in 1604, offered a mechanism for ennoblement to the holders of such offices. The second innovation of 1522 was the institutionalisation of government borrowing in the form of *rentes* (annuities). Investors in *rentes* were offered attractively high interest rates – around 8% to begin with. Channelling the administration of the *rentes* through the Paris municipality reassured people that their capital and income were in safe hands.

Both innovations were designed to raise funds at relatively short notice, which was simply not possible with established taxes. Both were to have a profound impact on the evolution of *ancien-régime* society itself, and particularly its characteristic clusters of *rentiers*, living off their investments, and their alter ego, the office-holding nobility 'of the robe'. Meanwhile, paying the annuities seemed to pose few difficulties around 1520, since royal revenues were already rising, and would so continue into the reign of Henry II. In 1460, the 'new' taxes produced around 1.8 million *livres* a year, but the royal domain only a paltry 50,000 *livres*. By 1515, thanks to the abstemious Louis XII, total revenues stood at approximately 4.9 million *livres*, of which 231,000 *livres* came from the domain. Thereafter, a combination of more extensive wars and a more prodigal monarchy pushed those totals much higher, especially under Henry II, when total revenues reached 13.5 million *livres* by 1555; by then half of them was provided by the *taille*. In fact, this was only part of the story, as royal borrowing also ballooned during these years. By the late 1550s, debts of nearly 10 million *livres* were owed to the merchant-bankers of the 'great syndicate' of Lyon, then Europe's largest money-market; they were rolled over so often that by 1557 Henry II's credit was virtually exhausted. Fortunately for France, that was also true of his new rival, Philip II of Spain, with the result that both monarchies were soon forced into effective bankruptcy. But with Spain now dominant in Italy, France faced the more difficult future when Henry II died prematurely, in mid-1559, from a wound suffered during a tournament celebrating the peace with Spain!

Within France itself, the reigns of Francis I and Henry II continue to evoke a royal splendour associated with the Renaissance and proto-absolutist methods of government. The exuberant young Francis I led the flower of the French nobility into Italy within months of his accession, and brought Leonardo da Vinci back to France with him the next year (1516). But it was later, from the 1530s onwards, and less in the Loire valley than in the Paris region – especially at Fontainebleau and Saint-Germain-en-Laye – that his artistic patronage, mainly in painting and architecture, expressed itself the most fully. He was also keenly interested in literature and ideas, seeing himself as the embodiment of the educated, humanist prince proposed by Erasmus. His older sister Marguerite (1492–1549), queen of Navarre, was herself a humanist whose literary talents and patronage of poets and writers expanded the scale of royal patronage of letters and religious reform. With a lavish and expensive court, Francis I strove to outshine his contemporary rivals, Henry VIII and Charles V. On the advice of his royal librarian, the great scholar Guillaume Budé, he founded in 1530 the *Collège royal*, a humanist rival to the Sorbonne. Erasmus's refusal to join the new institution came as a major shock to a king utterly unfamiliar with rejection. Henry II was far less interested in such matters, but by then the cultural magnetism of the royal court was such that personal characteristics mattered rather less. In any case, the influx of pro-French exiles from 'Spanish' Italy familiarised those French elites who had never set foot in the peninsula with its latest artistic and cultural trends.

As for the style of royal government, temperament mattered more than principle. France remained highly de-centralised in major respects, but there was a powerful nucleus of royal authority at the centre that, though hard to quantify, should not be underestimated. Within such a context, Francis I was in his element; he does not seem to have had a consistent political 'philosophy' beyond maxims of the 'I-shall-be-obeyed' variety. This approach is evident in his dealings with the great aristocracy, who collectively continued to dominate his court and government but who, individually, were often exposed to a potentially dangerous loss of favour. The immense estates of the constable of Bourbon across central France were confiscated in 1523, as punishment for a revolt that Francis I himself contrived in the first place. This augmentation of the royal domain continued with the entry of other lands – mostly via marriage or the lack of male heirs – such as Brittany and the widely scattered Albret-Navarre estates, while Charles V finally renounced his attempts to recover the duchy of Burgundy in 1529.

Other targets of royal repression included the leading financiers who first experienced the rigours of royal political justice in 1527. Royal debts were conveniently wiped out and their holders evicted from their positions or, more rarely, executed. Francis I famously clashed with the parlement of Paris on returning from imprisonment in Spain, when he publicly chastised it in a special 'royal session' for overstepping the mark in relation to royal authority. This dressing-down came closer than anything else to a 'declaration' of royal absolutism for its time. Francis I and Henry II both had able ministers and councillors who, with the assistance of magistrates, sought to 'rationalise' some of the institutions of a still highly ramshackle realm, especially its complex conciliar and legal structures. Wide-ranging and sustained efforts were made to record and stabilise the customary laws of northern and central France, but a full legal unification remained several centuries off. Such 'unifying' ambitions extended beyond government in the narrow sense. Around 1500, and for centuries afterwards, France was a linguistic patchwork, but scholars and administrators under Francis I were increasingly keen to take the emergence of French as a literary language a step further, and to make it the *lingua franca* of the kingdom. One such step was taken in 1539, when French became the language of government, law, and formal record. This politically inspired decision in practice concerned the educated elites, whose mastery of French became yet another mark of their difference from *le peuple*. Ironically, this initiative coincided with the Protestant Reformation, whose use of the vernacular would pose greater headaches than anyone had imagined. Finally, during these same decades, judicial and financial administration drilled further down into provincial society, lengthening the arm of monarchy considerably. But the real incentive for much of this expansion was frequently financial: new courts and offices signified more 'casual' receipts for the monarchy's often depleted coffers, and both Francis I and Henry II readily resorted to such fixes.

The last years of Francis I's reign were almost paralysed by faction, with both king and government indecisive and slow, even on foreign issues. The less extrovert Henry II was more viscerally anti-Habsburg, losing few opportunities to oppose them, in Flanders and Germany as much as in Italy. The upshot of such continuous but widely dispersed efforts was, as we have just seen, financial overstretch and, ultimately, severe military defeat in 1557. By the late 1550s, times were changing: royal financial demands were now hurting taxpayers, as the economic growth of previous generations was stalling in many regions. Francis I and Henry II were both strong enough politically to keep the concomitant 'malcontent' factor under control. It would resurface sooner than imagined, but nobody peering into France's looking glass around 1559 could have predicted how or what form it would take.

# CHRONOLOGY

| | |
|---|---|
| 1337 | Philip VI confiscates Guyenne from England; Edward III claims French crown, invades France (1339); Hundred Years' War begins |
| 1346 | French army routed at Crécy |
| 1348 | Beginning of Black Death |
| 1349 | Dauphiné and county of Montpellier added to kingdom |
| 1356–62 | Major French defeat at Poitiers, John II captured, ransomed, released, returned to prison |
| 1357–60 | Political crisis, popular revolt; Estates-General vote taxes and demand reforms; English military campaigns in France; treaty of Brétigny, Edward III renounces French crown, acquires sovereignty over Aquitaine |
| 1364 | Death of John II in captivity, London, succession of Charles V; *franc* minted for first time |
| 1377–82 | War resumes with England; revolts provoked by taxes and war devastation |
| 1380 | Charles VI (aged 12) king, suffers from insanity from 1392, uncles rule in his name, provoking opposition, leagues, and unrest |
| 1394 | Jews expelled |
| 1401–13 | Major feuds between pro-English Burgundians and Armagnacs, with some popular involvement (Paris); Estates General |
| 1404 | Christine de Pizan, *Livre de la cité des dames* |
| 1410–16 | Creation of the *Très riches heures de Jean de Berry* |
| 1415 | Henry V of England invades France, defeats French army at Agincourt, marries daughter of Charles VI, claims French throne, recognised by duke of Burgundy |
| 1420 | Treaty of Troyes provides for Henry V's son to succeed Charles VI as king |
| 1422 | Accession of Charles VII, with limited grip on kingdom |
| 1429 | Charles VII, aided by Joan of Arc, begins to reclaim kingdom from English and their Burgundian allies (down to 1453) |
| 1449–53 | Conquest of Normandy and Guyenne, end of Hundred Years' War |
| 1456 | Joan of Arc rehabilitated |
| 1461–83 | Reign of Louis XI 'the spider', revolt and repression |
| 1461–2 | François Villon, *Le grand testament* |
| 1470 | Printing press in Sorbonne |
| 1477–82 | Duchy of Burgundy incorporated into France |

| | |
|---|---|
| 1482 | Provence escheats to France |
| 1486–8 | *Guerre folle* civil war |
| 1491 | Franco-Breton dynastic marriage and 'personal' union |
| 1494 | Beginning of Italian wars |
| 1515 | Accession of Francis I |
| 1516 | Concordat of Bologna with Pope |
| 1523 | Confiscation of Constable of Bourbon's lands |
| 1524 | Francis I defeated at Pavia, prisoner in Madrid |
| 1532 | Brittany incorporated into France; Rabelais publishes *Gargantua* |
| 1534 | Affair of placards, persecution of religious dissent begins; Jacques Cartier's first voyage to Newfoundland |
| 1539 | Ordinance of Villers-Cotterêts enjoining use of French in public documents |
| 1549 | Joachim du Bellay *Défense et illustration de la langue française* launches *Pléiade* group of poets |
| 1555 | Calvinist churches spread within France |
| 1559 | Treaty of Cateau-Cambrésis ends Franco-Habsburg wars; death of Henry II |

# 3  The *Ancien Régime*
   in the Making

Until the late 1550s, it seemed that France and the Spanish lands (the Netherlands included) had avoided the upheavals of the Protestant reformations in neighbouring countries. Since the 1520s, France had its own circles of active humanist reformers, led by disciples of the cosmopolitan Erasmus, who sought orderly reform 'from above'. By contrast, Lutheran ideas made little headway, and their adherents were easily contained. By the 1550s, however, the landscape had changed. A younger generation of determined reformers was increasingly inspired by John Calvin, who fled during the 1530s from Paris to Strasbourg and Geneva, where he had painfully established a reformed church that was deeply hostile to Catholicism, and even to Lutheranism. From 1534 to 1557, royal legislation to root out heresy and to identify it with political sedition grew ever more draconian, forcing many 'heretics' into exile. Despite the risks of being executed if caught, many returned clandestinely to France as itinerant preachers and, once the new 'Genevan' churches had been established there, as their pastors. The impetus seemed increasingly with the reformers, though, who by 1561 claimed to have 2,000 churches (more than double the real number) and, by 1565, perhaps two million adherents, the great majority of whom were town-dwellers. Repression had failed, as the royal law-courts proved either unwilling or incapable of containing the growing threat of religious 'sedition'. The political crisis triggered by Henry II's unexpected death in 1559 seemed to open the floodgates, as court factions, dominated by the Bourbon, Guise-Lorraine, and Montmorency clans, fought for control of royal patronage, finances, and military resources, under a much-weakened and financially desperate monarchy.

Religious differences soon became entangled with these conventional political affiliations. Some members of the extended royal family and leading aristocrats became Protestants, and persuaded many of their clients and tenants to follow their example. If this ensured powerful protection for the Protestant cause, in subsequent years grandee leadership often had the affect of subordinating the cause of religion to the vagaries of aristocratic politics. Meanwhile the anti-heresy laws were suspended, but high-level conferences in 1560–1 failed to find common ground for a negotiated religious settlement that was acceptable to all sides. The first edict of 'toleration' followed in January 1562; it granted France's Protestants – already nicknamed 'Huguenots' – limited religious rights but, with their numbers still increasing steadily, it aimed at a moving, elusive target. As with the seven similar edicts that followed it down to 1598, that of 1562 was designed to permit temporary co-existence pending full confessional reunification with the 'true' church. Scarcely any contemporaries – the Huguenots included – approved of religious freedom in itself; it was emphatically never royal policy, despite the frequent criticisms made by Catholics, for whom even limited toleration (in the contemporary sense of 'to put up with') of 'heresy' was itself an abomination. In the short term, from 1563 to 1598, the principal consequence was a series of wars of greater or lesser duration in which religious and, increasingly, political issues became inextricably bound together. The terms of each successive edict of pacification varied depending on the politico-military balance of power at the end of each war, and did not represent any logical progression of ideas on religious unity or plurality. Those who were discontented with an edict usually bided their time before triggering the next conflict, in the hope that it would rectify the balance of power in their favour.

The French wars of religion owe their notoriety less to their duration than to their brutality, especially in the early years. The first spark flew in 1562 with the massacre of Protestant worshippers at Vassy by soldiers led by the Catholic duke of Guise. It set the tone for repeated tit-for-tat atrocities during the next decade, in which widespread Protestant iconoclasm elicited Catholic retribution, which included equally gruesome murders. This violence culminated in early modern Europe's most infamous bloodbath, St Bartholomew's Day Massacre (22 August 1572) in Paris and, during subsequent weeks, in other French cities. Triggered by a botched attempt to assassinate the leading Protestant figure, Admiral Coligny, a chain-reaction followed in which up to 10,000 Huguenots were hunted down and massacred by Catholic militants intent on ridding France of the pollution of heresy. This and earlier operations effectively halted the growth of French Protestantism, many of whose adherents abjured in sheer panic, especially in the northern provinces where they were more thinly spread and thus more vulnerable. By contrast, in the distant southern provinces, the bulging Protestant 'crescent' stretched from La Rochelle through Montauban and Nîmes to Geneva. This evolving geography enabled Protestantism to survive in the provinces most remote from the centre of royal power, but there were significant exceptions, since important outlying provinces like Burgundy, Brittany, Provence, and much of Guyenne remained overwhelmingly Catholic. From the mid-1570s onwards, local inter-confessional violence actually declined, but not the deep distrust or language of mutual demonisation, the evidence of which is inescapable. The best hope for the Protestant churches by the 1570s was a stable regime of toleration. Then, in 1584, the sudden death of Henry III's younger brother and heir-apparent gave Henry of Bourbon, then king of Navarre and Protestant leader, the strongest claim to be France's next king. The Huguenots began again to believe that providence destined France to become Protestant after all. With Henry III's assassination in 1589, that wish seemed accomplished. For Catholics, a Protestant monarchy meant a Protestant France – a nightmare to be prevented at all costs.

This prospect prompted the emergence of the most widespread opposition movement for a long time. Earlier attempts, in 1576–7, to form a Catholic League to defend the true church had been de-railed by Henry III. After 1584, however, a far more extensive second League took shape, including major aristocrats like the Guises and their allies, but also many of the towns, the *bonnes villes*, whose late-medieval idyll with the monarchy was now emphatically over, owing to the fiscal exploitation that had actually worsened since the end of the Italian wars in 1559. Building on fears of pollution and revenge by the Huguenots, the loosely federated Catholic League spread rapidly from 1585 onwards. In May 1588, it engineered a successful insurrection in Paris against Henry III, the first of many times that barricades were used on a grand scale. When an exasperated and cornered king retaliated in December 1588 by having the League's leaders, the Guise brothers, assassinated, the insurrection spread further, forcing Henry III to team up with Henry of Navarre, whom he recognised as his heir when he was himself dying from an assassin's cut in August 1589.

By this juncture, the wars of religion were also a potentially international war of dynastic succession, but that might have been easier to resolve were it not for the issue of Henry IV's religion. Needing all the Protestant support he could get, he delayed the inevitable – conversion to Catholicism – for as long as he judged possible. His military successes proving less than decisive, he took 'the perilous leap' to convert in mid-1593. His reported quip 'Paris is worth a Mass' was invented by his enemies to discredit him as an opportunist, but by 1593–4 many of the Catholic League's supporters were war-weary and ready to end the conflict; Henry IV's willingness to meet some of their key demands enabled them to make terms without feeling defeated. Ironically, he proved far less responsive to the demands of his former co-religionists, and it took an unmistakable Protestant threat of renewed civil war to nudge him into making the concessions contained in the celebrated edict of Nantes of 1598. In fact, it was not radically different, albeit more generous, than several previous edicts of pacification. It created a separate legal framework to resolve Catholic–Protestant disputes and allowed the Huguenots to hold a large number of garrisoned towns as 'places of security'. As on previous occasions, a Catholic backlash against the edict was expected, but it proved quite subdued this time, almost certainly because the Catholics had already obtained reassuring settlements of their own in the wake of the royal conversion. The immediate future of the new Bourbon dynasty was secured thanks to Henry IV's re-marriage in 1600 to the Florentine Marie de Medici, who soon bore him two sons. The edict of Nantes itself remained in force until 1685, but it had been effectively hollowed out well before then.

Needless to say, the impact of such interminable conflict was comparable to those of earlier centuries. Royal control of the kingdom shrank considerably in peripheral provinces and especially in the south generally. Increasingly, high-ranking aristocratic governors or military commanders of both religions played the over-mighty subject's role with renewed vigour. In the wake of the 1572 Massacre, a non-confessional 'party' of aristocratic malcontents headed by the king's own brother – not an unfamiliar combination – caused real trouble for both Charles IX and Henry III. The latter's efforts, especially during the 1580s, to rebuild royal authority by relying on, and promoting second-rank nobles made some sense in such a context, but his efforts failed, while further alienating the existing aristocracy. One of the major challenges of Henry IV's reign was how to regain the loyalty of the serving nobility and wean them from the temptation of conspiracy and foreign alliances.

Not surprisingly, the royal finances, already shattered by the costs of the Italian wars, were never flush enough to sustain military campaigns for long, thus rendering a negotiated (and often very costly) settlement in the form of an edict of pacification the normal outcome of the successive religious wars. Nor could the crown prevent hostile military commanders from seizing badly needed revenues at crucial moments. Its virtuoso efforts to raise money by all imaginable means led to record tax burdens under Henry III, all of which badly soured relations with the *bonnes villes* and provoked peasant rebellions by the 1580s. Inevitably, the return of civil war brought much material destruction in its wake, the worst of which seems to have occurred between 1585 and 1598. The wars certainly exacerbated the slowdown of the pre-1560 demographic and economic expansion noted in the previous chapter by disrupting commercial and even agricultural activities. In many southern regions, and perhaps elsewhere, the wars were characterised by the formation of durable local leagues and militias, whose raids and exactions often became endemic because quite independent of any 'national' agenda. Equally, however, the damage done by such methods often prompted fixed-term local truces by the 1580s, if not earlier, so as to enable peasants and merchants to work without fear of plunder or harassment. In towns that joined the Catholic League, hitherto excluded social groups seized office, both municipal and royal. Such 'coups' were rarely undone after their return to obedience to Henry IV, who judged it better to bury – or ignore – such factional rivalries in his efforts to rebuild relations with the towns.

The wars of religion also prompted severe attacks on the late Valois monarchy's political foundations. The succession of three young monarchs enabled their mother Catherine de Medici to become a major political figure, even when she was not formally acting as regent for them. Her Florentine origins enabled critics to lump together two contemporary pet-hatreds – of Italians fleecing France and of women wielding political power. But there were more serious problems. Catholics blamed the monarchy for failing to defend the true faith, even when individual monarchs, like Henry III, openly advertised their own religious commitment; but when Catholic militants took matters into their own hands, it led to massacres like those of 1572 or insurrections like those of 1588–9. For Calvinist-Genevan Protestants, certain key features of France's royal ideology were simply too 'Catholic' to swallow, even though Calvin denied, somewhat ambiguously, the right to rebel against rulers inflicting religious persecution on their subjects. The 1572 massacres unleashed a series of radical attacks on the monarchy's actual tyranny and excessive claims to 'absolute' authority. These attacks implied rather than explicitly defended the right to kill tyrants; 'mixed' monarchy was best, as it was tempered by a combination of 'aristocracy' and political assemblies. Indeed, an assembly of southern Protestants in 1573 drafted a 'constitution' for a 'United Provinces of the Midi'; but no such 'republic' came into being, possibly because it was too urban-based for the nobility to swallow. However, when Henry of Navarre became heir apparent in 1584, the Protestants promptly dumped such inconvenient ideological baggage, henceforth preaching full obedience to royal authority. It was now the Catholic League which dusted off and recycled ideas of limited monarchy in its revolt against both Henry III and IV. The League's ultimate political failure ensured that, more by default than by sheer force of persuasion, ideas of absolute monarchy prevailed, in which the king, as God's anointed, could not be subject to judgement by his subjects and, as the maker of laws, could not be bound by those laws. As in the past, the monarchy managed to hold the centre of the ring, whence it arbitrated and resolved conflicts, not because it was all-powerful, but because no other force(s) seemed capable of preserving the unity of the French polity.

The religious wars opened up unprecedented divisions, so it is hardly surprising that the most celebrated defence of sovereignty as the key attribute of a state was published in 1576, a year of major political crisis, by Jean Bodin, a jurist and royal official. Unlike its English and other counterparts, the French monarchy had always resisted conceding formal powers, such as voting taxation or making laws, to political assemblies, and only convened them when it had no other options or when they could be useful. For those reasons, the Estates-General met several times during the religious wars – notably in 1576 when Bodin himself was a deputy – but differences between lords, clergy, and commons played into the hands of the monarchy, even when it was not especially strong. Where most of France's European neighbours found governing with the participation of more or less 'representative' assemblies both necessary and useful, the French monarchy insisted that there was no room for others to share its authority; the result, its champions argued, would be faction and chaos. During the 1580s and early 1590s, the question of whether the Protestant Henry IV was obliged to convert to Catholicism in order to be a legitimate king, produced a torrent of political argument. The Catholic League refused to obey a heretic king under any conditions, but moderate Catholics, nicknamed derogatorily the 'politiques', defended the right of a Protestant king to rule a country so overwhelmingly Catholic as France. But it would be mistaken to view this argument as a beacon of modernity: it was a brief parenthesis that everyone hoped would not last and was happy to forget, given its unforeseeable implications.

Despite the emphasis successively placed by modern historians on the political, social, and economic factors, the question of how religious were the wars of religion remains a pertinent one. The accounts subsequently compiled of the St Bartholomew's Day Massacre suggested that Protestants of different backgrounds understood and accepted the prospect of martyrdom for the truth; then and later, they 'read' adversity in biblical terms, while Protestant religiosity in general was defined in stark contrast to Catholicism. Unlike their Dutch counterparts who were urged to turn to self-examination and reformation, French Catholics were mobilised by clerical and other activists, who from the 1560s onwards preached open confrontation with a view to annihilating Satan's proxies, the Protestants. Even in the 1580s, when the earlier Catholic exhortations to physically exterminate Protestants gave way to penitential discipline for their own sins, Catholic rhetoric remained no less strident. And, of course, the prospect of a Protestant king kept those fires burning, as the fierce assaults on Henry IV, even after his conversion in 1593, demonstrate. The enormous processions and pilgrimages of these years, and their various offshoots, such as militant confraternities and new devotions, re-energised the religious commitment on which the Catholic reformation of the next century drew heavily.

## II

The relatively short reign of Henry IV (r. 1589–1610) was mainly one of pacification and reconstruction, which extended well beyond the edict of Nantes (1598). He once complained that his subjects had sold rather than given their loyalty to him, but the alternatives were far worse! Keeping France out of foreign wars once a brief conflict with Spain (1595–8) was settled made a difference, as did the simultaneous ending of other conflicts in western Europe generally. The 'treaties' that Henry IV had negotiated with numerous towns and leading aristocrats were especially valuable in restoring political stability, despite some of his aristocratic allies of earlier years, among them Huguenots, being tempted by conspiracy. Meanwhile, Sully, Henry's finance minister, restored the health of the royal finances, partly by sharp dealings with the crown's creditors, domestic and foreign. Tax arrears from large numbers of local communities were effectively written off, encouraging economic recovery, which continued into the 1620s or 1630s. Crucial for the longer term was the realisation that the already inflated class of royal officials – the religious wars had added substantial numbers of them – should not be tempted, as they had been during the recent conflicts, into political opposition. The result was an arrangement, introduced in 1604, that made them de facto proprietors of their offices, with the right to sell or bequeath them without prior royal consent; above all, the measure ensured that tenure of royal office by three generations would guarantee hereditary nobility to their holders' lineage. This concession was technically for nine years only, but whenever the crown was tempted, as in 1614 and later, to scrap it under pressure from the older nobility, the counter-pressure proved irresistible. Indeed, the crown quickly learned to exploit that counter-pressure and extract further funds from its office-holders by agreeing, after loud ritualistic noises to the contrary, to prolong what became known as the 'paulette'. Unlike Spain, France never discovered gold mines in conquered lands, but its variant of the venality of office came a close second, especially during war, when the *parties cas-uelles* treasury worked overtime. Its social and political consequences were equally profound, creating bonds that were not always harmonious between France's upwardly mobile elites, while also siphoning ambitions for status and power into the service of the monarchy in a manner that trounced other alternatives.

Such long-term outcomes would take many years and conflicts to become clear. Henri IV's efforts to pacify the realm and consolidate royal power were thrown into disarray when he was assassinated in May 1610 by François Ravaillac, a deranged Catholic convinced that he was still 'really' a Protestant bent on destroying the true faith. It would take half a century before the relative stability of Henri's final years would return. His assassination, like that of his predecessor Henry III, created a mighty shock which further strengthened the argument for, but not the reality of, a divine-right monarchy whose actions were beyond audit by subjects. As Louis XIII (r. 1610–43) was only nine years old, his mother, Marie de Medici, became regent. She was often attacked, then and later, for being an Italian *dévote* in hock to the papacy and Spain, but that was mostly character assassination. She did roll back her husband's imminent confrontation with the Habsburgs, successfully negotiated two Franco-Spanish dynastic marriages, and used Sully's famous cash surplus to buy domestic peace by bribing potentially wilful aristocrats. The last Estates-General before 1789 met in 1614, just as Louis XIII came of age, but as on previous occasions its internal divisions allowed the crown to exploit its weaknesses and dissolve it without making any serious concessions or, more importantly, allowing the aristocracy to hijack it for its purposes. However, the regent's increasingly reliance on the Concinis, a fellow-Italian favourite and her husband, compromised these achievements and re-ignited noble revolts for several years to come. Indeed, Louis XIII had to engineer a *coup d'état* in 1617 to oust the Concinis and Marie de Medici herself, who had continued to act as if her regency was not over. It soon emerged that the inexperienced Louis depended even more heavily on own his personal favourite, the duke of Luynes, who held all the reins of power until his death in 1621. By then, the successive noble revolts of the 1610s had ceased, with Louis XIII's final reconciliation with Marie de Medici in 1620 pulling the plank from under them. It was the last of these revolts, in 1620, which unexpectedly – and despite Huguenot professions of blind obedience to the crown – revived the wars of religion. Louis XIII's military intervention in the far-away, Huguenot-dominated principality of Béarn in mid-1620 suddenly re-lit the fires of religious revolt, which would dominate the rest of the decade. The high point came with the fall of the hitherto impregnable La Rochelle after a 15-month siege in October 1628. Several southern towns still remained defiant, but they accepted a negotiated peace in mid-1629. Huguenot military and political power was effectively undermined, but nobody could rule out the prospect of further revolts in the more inaccessible southern regions.

Coinciding with the first decade of the great European conflict, the Thirty Years' War, these revolts, aristocratic and religious, kept France on the side lines, unsure of when or how the next revolt, especially if supported by a foreign power (England or Spain), might supervene. They did not preclude some important political changes at the top. Marie de Medici's return to favour enabled her to usher some of her leading advisors into high office – and none higher than that Cardinal Richelieu, who recovered, against all expectations, from the disgrace of serving as a minister under Concini. Promoted a cardinal in 1622, he returned to the royal council in 1624 and soon became the king's leading minister, in fact if not in name. He nearly came unstuck a second time in dealing with the Huguenots, and took full advantage of their defeat in 1629 to strengthen his position. By then, however, he was at loggerheads with his patron, Marie de Medici, and some of her other protégés, who argued that France stay out of the Thirty Years' War, given the need to resolve the Protestant problem and for France to undertake internal reform. However, both Louis XIII and Richelieu leaned in the opposite direction, seeing the Habsburg threat as the biggest problem of all. It was not until November 1630 that the political abscess finally burst, and Marie de Medici and her Catholic *dévot* supporters were removed from office. Only from then on did Richelieu have a firm grip on the agenda of government and on royal ministers who depended entirely on his favour. He remained vulnerable, however, as he never obtained the full trust of Louis XIII, a monarch whose well-known desire to rule was not matched by the necessary ability to do so.

The 1630 political crisis did not precipitate immediate or full-scale war against the Habsburgs. Richelieu preferred limited confrontation with the Habsburgs, especially in northern Italy, or by allies and proxies – mostly Protestant – that he was prepared to subsidise. But by 1635 these choices had all failed, leaving France no other option but openly to enter the war itself. Early expectations of quick success at relatively limited cost proved seriously misguided. Instead, the next 24 years (1635–59) were dominated by the grind of war that, as it did across Europe, wreaked havoc on both government and society. With only limited experience of 'European' warfare since the 1550s, France was fighting simultaneously in too many campaign theatres to deploy its resources effectively, thereby rendering cumulative military success problematic. When military victories materialised, even that of Rocroi (June 1643), they were never decisive, and their impact was quickly blunted by sometimes unspectacular failures elsewhere. When Richelieu and Louis XIII died within six months of each other (December 1642 and May 1643 respectively), and the five-year old Louis XIV came to the throne, renewed political instability seemed inevitable. As so often in the past, a long regency spelled trouble, especially as the incoming regent, Anne of Austria, was a sister of Philip IV of Spain and a bitter enemy of Richelieu and his policies. The continuation of the war was far from certain. But since she took on – and then kept – Richelieu's protégé, the Italian Cardinal Mazarin, as her chief minister, Anne effectively dashed hopes that a quick peace might end the hardship caused by military and financial exactions at a time of economic difficulties and the return of epidemics. Nor was Mazarin's tortuous diplomacy not quite as superior as it is usually depicted. While the rest of Europe made peace with the treaties of Westphalia in 1648, Mazarin failed to clinch a peace treaty with Spain; he overplayed his hand, and Spain was not so weak as to make peace at any price. It would take another decade for French arms and diplomacy to prevail, an outcome that was nearly rendered impossible by one of the most complex revolts of the century.

The Fronde – so-called after a sling used by children – is often viewed as frivolous because its chief actors, male and female, were usually depicted as intriguing, aristocratic *gallants* with few political principles or objectives other than their own self-aggrandisement. Certainly, the outcome was a victory for Mazarin and his policies, but that took six years (1648–53) and two successive periods of exile to finally achieve, during which time the regime was largely paralysed. Unlike Richelieu, Mazarin was chief minister to an under-age king until his majority in 1651. If that made him even more hated for his monopoly of royal patronage and power, it meant that Louis XIV, unlike Charles I in England, could not be held responsible for the political upheaval. Mazarin's decision after his accession in 1643 to go for broke in the war against the Habsburgs added hugely to the existing fiscal burden, and the continuing lack of decisive military success only worsened future prospects. Worst of all, it began to hurt those groups that possessed political clout. The Fronde was actually sparked by the grievances of royal officials, led by the parlements, complaining of being dispossessed of their historic role in administering France, as well as being ruthlessly exploited financially. Only when Mazarin was cornered in early 1649 when he tried to repudiate concessions made to the office-holders did the aristocracy begin to participate on both sides of the conflict. By late 1649–50, a political crisis within the regime broadened into a civil war in which the initial griev-ances did not disappear but were largely superseded by aristocratic revolt. The aristocracy divided into factions, as it had during the various attempts to oust Richelieu, from 1626 to 1642, with leading members of the royal family also playing a leading role. By 1650, a new generation of aristocratic military commanders, like the prince of Condé, Turenne, and others, turned politicians, using their armies to topple or defend Mazarin. Their mutual rivalry and distrust ultimately played into Mazarin's hands, and here at least he played a brilliant hand – and from exile near Cologne – in buying them off one by one. The spectre of other revolts across Europe, and especially the execution of Charles I in England (1649), helped to limit the scope of the Fronde, as nobody wanted such a radical outcome in France. As a result, it was only during the post-Fronde years (1653–61) that Mazarin really had a relatively free hand to pursue his foreign policies and establish his grip on French government. By the time he died in early 1661, France was again at peace; the young Louis XIV had, like his father, married a Spanish princess; and Mazarin himself was, like Richelieu before him, the richest man in Europe.

The age of the chief ministers (1617/1624–61) was almost as turbulent as the wars of religion, albeit in different ways and for different reasons. Luynes, Richelieu, and Mazarin were widely detested because there was in principle no place for a chief minister-cum-favourite in the political catechism of the French monarchy. Mazarin was so closely identified with Richelieu that his position as minister to an under-age king has attracted little notice. Like Henry IV, adult monarchs should rule as well as reign, and keep ministers and confidants in their rightful place. Anything that made kings prisoners of their favourites was an aberration against which it was legitimate for royal subjects, especially members of the great nobility, to revolt. Against Richelieu conspiracy was the preferred tactic of his opponents: there was always a chance that, since he was not the royal favourite, Louis XIII would dump him. In contrast, Mazarin's favour with Anne of Austria and then Louis XIV was rock-solid, so that rebellion 'from the outside' seemed the only way to oust him.

The age of the chief ministers was also critical for the evolution of royal absolutism. It added relatively little to the arsenal of arguments inherited from the previous century, but it significantly bolstered and extended the machinery of government, less because of any putative grand design for absolute monarchy than in response to the dictates of war. Like Olivares in Spain, Richelieu deferred his early plans to reform government until the war against the Habsburgs was over, an outcome that he did not live to see, while Mazarin simply had no such plans. Instead, the changes made to provincial government in the financial, judicial, and administrative spheres were determined by military necessity and its logistical ramifications, but also by the kinds of opposition to such measures, especially from the monarchy's own officials. Most enduringly, provincial 'intendants' were used in increasing numbers by the late 1620s to supervise local administration. They gradually took over so many functions hitherto discharged by office-holders that when the political crisis of the Fronde broke in 1648, the office-holders, led by the parlements, demanded that such 'extraordinary' forms of government be scrapped and the 'ordinary' ones reinstated; that demand included the suppression of the intendants, who disappeared from almost every province until the Fronde ended in 1653. By then, it was clear that the ever-expanding sale of office over the previous century had created vested interests within government itself that were too massive and entrenched to remove by royal decree. With its back to the wall, the monarchy found that it needed to use new methods, personified by the special and short-term commissioner rather than the proprietary office-holder, to ensure that its most urgent tasks of raising funds and troops, as well as suppressing revolt, were carried out. Ironically, these commissioner-intendants, who were in some respects the ancestors of the Napoleonic prefects, were themselves drawn from the higher ranks of the same office-holding elites.

These years also witnessed more revolt by the lower social groups, urban and rural, than in any century before the Revolution. Such revolt was endemic and sometimes prolonged. The economic recovery facilitated by Henry IV's reign continued into the 1620s and, in some regions, the 1630s, when it was halted by a combination of poor harvests and the return of epidemics originating in northern Italy. In addition, Europe generally experienced commercial stagnation from the 1620s onwards. In many places, misery, poverty, and vagabondage of rural provenance spread to towns, whose authorities tried to prevent the influx of destitute peasants, rounding them up and expelling them, or placing them in poorhouses. *Dévot* groups like the Daughters of Charity improvised forms of poor relief. However, the 'popular' rebellions of the 1620s to the 1650s and beyond were not the work of the uprooted and the destitute, but rather of those further up the social ladder, like rural small-holders, village artisans, or shopkeepers, who feared that newer and higher taxes were undermining their livelihoods altogether. If there were elements of class hostility at times, it was not the driving force behind the revolts, which were occasionally led by rural clergy or impoverished nobles down on their luck but with some military experience. The Richelieu-Mazarin governments were also perceived as attacking local privileges – fiscal or otherwise – for which communities were prepared to fight. The biggest cluster of revolts coincided with France's early participation in the Thirty Years' War (1636–40), as groups condescendingly nicknamed the *Croquants* (the 'Latecomers') or the *Nu-Pieds* (the 'Barefeet'), took up arms in regions as far apart as Quercy and Normandy. The 'Barefeet' revolt was provoked by widespread rumours across lower Normandy of new taxes on leather goods and salt; the rebels knew their history well enough to demand that the fourteenth-century 'charter of the Normans' over consent to taxation be respected! Wherever they managed to gain control of local towns, rebels could hold out for a time against hastily organised militias or royal forces diverted from other operations, but that opportunity was often denied them owing to town-dwellers' own fears of peasant excesses once inside their walls.

The disruption that rebellions caused, notably the non-payment of taxes, was something the government could ill afford in wartime. It was a major reason for the increased deployment of intendant-commissioners in the provinces, where they were instructed to combat corruption in tax assessment and collection, in which existing local officials were complicit, but also to investigate the causes of individual revolts. None of that signalled a diminished determination to put down rebellion in bloodshed, as the Barefoot rebels would discover. The Fronde years saw a pause in popular revolts, since a weakened government simply had to loosen its fiscal pressure, whose reduction the original Frondeurs of 1648 had openly demanded. But post-Fronde, such revolts became almost endemic in certain parts of France and tended to migrate from the peripheral provinces towards the older central provinces in the Loire valley. The last great peasant revolt before 1789, that of the Breton 'Red Hats' in 1675, was also sparked by the prospect and rumours of new taxes; the last great urban revolt occurred the same year in Bordeaux. Louis XIV's government punished these rebels, especially the Bretons, even more severely than Richelieu or Mazarin had, in order to dissuade them from rising again. One consequence of the disappearance of such revolts over the following century was that the French monarchy had no memory or experience of dealing with large-scale popular protest, especially by peasants, and was unexpectedly vulnerable to its sudden revival in the 'great fear' of 1789.

## III

In the *Memoires for the instruction of the Dauphin*, ghost-written around 1670, Louis XIV noted that 'disorder reigned everywhere' in 1661, an indictment that he applied to all the social orders. Involving attitudes and forms of behaviour widely shared across society, French traditions of rebellion make clear distinctions between elite and popular culture difficult to sustain for this period. But under growing pressure from the churches, municipal authorities, and the monarchy itself, such distinctions did gradually take root during the seventeenth century. An increasingly broad definition of disorder, embracing witchcraft, vagabondage, blasphemy, insult, and so on, was at work, demanding different types of response, from repressive measures to 'education' in the broad sense. The impressive spread of

schools and colleges, led by the Jesuits but imitated by many other teaching orders and congregations, female as well as male, responded to the
demands of urban elites. The more the latter were royal rather than 'merely'
municipal in profession and outlook, the more they sought an education
that combined Renaissance rhetoric and reformed Catholic piety, one that
the increasingly dormant university colleges could not satisfactorily offer.
Enjoying wealth, offices, and social distinction, the same elites engaged
increasingly in 'high-brow' cultural activities revolved around salons and
learned circles, in which women were often the moving spirits; Madame de
Maintenon, Louis XIV's second wife, became known primarily for hosting
such a salon in the 1660s, but she was only one of many. Some of those
learned circles, particularly in Paris, were co-opted for political purposes by
the monarchy from Richelieu onwards, and formed the basis of the various
'chartered' academies beginning with the French Academy in 1635. From Caen
to Toulouse and Dijon, provincial equivalents gradually followed, obtaining
royal approval and statutes, in due course. These, and other related practices, resulted in a gradual withdrawal by the still-expanding elites from the
common urban culture of previous generations; it was only partial, since
so much of that common culture remained religious and thus socially universal. But in abandoning the festive and sometimes subversive contents
of that common culture the elites pigeonholed it, by default at least, as a
'popular' culture characteristic of the lower classes. That perspective was
reinforced by the actions of both monarchy and urban authorities in introducing more intrusive forms of policing that went far beyond occasionally
chasing vagabonds and pickpockets. The dissemination of behavioural
norms from the royal court also played a part in changing existing habits.
For all that, 'popular' culture was not a mere residue, and it continued to
evolve, especially within towns, where the impact of the Catholic reform
was, as we shall see presently, the most marked.

It would, however, be a travesty to reduce the high-brow culture of
Bourbon France to an agent of social discipline. From Descartes and Pascal
to Corneille, Molière, and Fénelon, seventeenth-century French writers
remain among the best known in the country's literary Pantheon; few
letter-writers have ever bettered Mme de Sévigné. Only some of these figures were 'insiders' belonging to the recognised academies or the church.
Descartes was son of a magistrate and spent many years pursuing a military career. Pascal, who was from a more modest but similar background,
abandoned his early scientific work for religious and philosophical questions. The great mathematician, Fermat, was a modest magistrate in the
Toulouse parlement, a position which gave him – and so many others – the
leisure needed to follow their intellectual pursuits. From Montaigne to La

Rochefoucauld, the combination of reflection, often in a pessimistic light, on the human condition and the use of French rather than Latin to communicate those reflections became a distinctive feature of French culture. Long before the Enlightenment, the cultural supremacy of the French language had been actively pursued by a combination of 'style-setters' for both poetry and prose (Malherbe and Guez de Balzac respectively) and the French academy (1635), whose primary purpose was to 'purify and perfect' the French language. The increase in periodicals, especially post-1660, proved another vehicle for the diffusion of French culture.

It would, of course, be misleading to say that such traffic was one-way. It is most evident in the fact that despite the well-known political enmity between France and Spain, no cultural iron curtain appeared between the two countries; the power and achievements of the Spanish monarchy went beyond mere politics, and elicited considerable enthusiasm for Spanish literary and artistic influences in France after 1600. For Corneille and his contemporaries, the leading writers of Spain's 'golden age' were models to follow and re-work. This unexpected hispanophilia was reinforced by the activity of French religious reformers, who read and translated numerous works of Spanish spirituality, before embarking on their own compositions. With Italy, there were no such political rivalries to obstruct cultural interaction, which remained as intense as ever during the seventeenth century. In one form or another, Italy was part of the education of France's elites, even if they never set foot there. The continuing lure of Italy and its historical Roman past explains why Richelieu and Mazarin still sent agents there to collect antiquities and commission new works from its great master painters, architects, and musicians.

However, as during the Renaissance, French art and architecture refused unquestioning imitation of the mannerist or baroque styles of Italy. As the seventeenth century wore on, they fixed upon a neo-classical form that signalled a search for order and harmony, while avoiding the passions and the irrational. The monarchy again acted, as it had under Francis I, as the principal patron and focus of much literary and artistic activity, with the new academies, as well as the salons, increasingly intent on defining what was 'good taste'. These traditions enabled Richelieu, Mazarin, and Louis XIV to attract the most ambitious – and usually the most talented – artists into royal service. Political thought may have been uninspired during the same period, but the visual glorification of benevolent royal rule reached spectacular heights after 1660. Indeed, by the later seventeenth century, French learned culture was increasingly regarded as superior to that of Italy – a view that Italian observers themselves shared. This 'silent revolution' within the republic of letters owed much to the patronage of major French writers and artists by Europe's most prestigious monarchy, a combination that made France, as Voltaire would later claim, the rightful successor to Greece and Rome. Some Italians did protest against the invasion of their own language by French terms, an early intuition of the 'empire' of the French language as the obligatory *lingua franca* of Europe's elites.

## IV

In his review of the disorders that 'reigned everywhere' in 1661, Louis XIV included the church, whose 'ordinary ills', he opined, were exacerbated by pointless doctrinal disputes. This was a reference to Jansenism, a recent phenomenon that he detested, but which was a by-product of the intense renewal within French Catholicism since the wars of religion. The latter had mobilised France's Catholics, especially in the major cities, in defence of their faith, and the return of peace after 1598 made it possible to catch up with the rest of Europe in adapting the reforms of the Council of Trent. The same mobilisation ensured that spiritual, mystical, and devotional practices were imported, primarily from Spain and Italy. But as with the Renaissance a century earlier, French Catholicism soon found ways of deploying its pent-up religious energies to add distinctive elements of its own to the process of reform. Much of this energy was supplied by successive generations of *dévots*, female and male, some of whom were heirs of the Catholic League and its pro-Spanish affiliations, political and religious. Albeit very different in style and methods, religious writers as different as François de Sales (1567–1621) and Pierre de Bérulle (1575–1629) exerted a profound influence on their (educated) readers, and spawned a generation of younger disciples. New religious orders, such as the Carmelites and Capuchins, not to mention the Jesuits, were introduced – or re-introduced in the case of the Jesuits, whose schools spread rapidly across France after 1603. Until the 1760s, the Jesuits were the premier educators of France's social elites, and that education was often prolonged by active membership of devotional confraternities for their alumni. The Jesuits' activities as preachers, confessors, and missionaries were equally extensive. By the 1630s, new and more pared-down types of religious 'orders', male and female, were emerging within France – from the male congregations of the Oratory and the Mission to the female Daughters of Charity – all of which enjoyed strong support from high-ranking families. There was no shortage of objects of their attention, especially preaching and religious instruction; where they could not found schools, they often encouraged local confraternities to perpetuate the work initiated by brief preaching 'missions'. In an age of widespread destitution, many of the congregations – and their local offshoots – engaged in poor relief, working in the existing hospices and, after the 1660s, in the new 'general' hospitals, which were places of confinement and work-houses. The militant confraternities of the previous century also directed their energies towards spiritual objectives, and new offshoots focused their attention on 'christianising' the behaviour of France's notoriously licentious nobility and, especially, its recent 'addiction' to duelling. At this level, moral, social, and religious reforms were ultimately inseparable.

Such a profusion of religious energy was even more valuable, as the ordinary 'parish' clergy remained for long poorly prepared for their duties. It was really only well into Louis XIV's reign that new-style seminaries to train them began to appear. Initially small and poorly funded, their ambition and impact were seriously limited until the next century. By then, at least, the drive for a better-trained parish clergy was led by an upper clergy which, thanks to more careful choices of bishops by Louis XIV, increasingly conformed to the model of an active, resident bishop. In turn, their effectiveness owed much to the development of a diocesan administration that was capable of acting autonomously if and when, as aristocratic *grands seigneurs*, they were absent from their dioceses. By the later 1600s, 'petites écoles' (primary schools), teaching religious doctrine (catechism) and the three 'Rs', were appearing in many parts of France, especially north of the Saint-Malo-Geneva line. In southern France, similar schools were required to compete with those of the Huguenots in areas where the latter were numerous before the revocation of the edict of Nantes in 1685; after 1685, such schools were needed to educate and indoctrinate the younger generation of 'new' Catholics.

French Catholicism was not immune to the internal intellectual controversies of the post-Trent church, among which figured the un-named dispute derided by Louis XIV's *Memoires*. In fact, the Jansenist conflict was to have a wide-ranging and long-lasting impact on France's religious and intellectual, not to mention political life, one that Louis XIV's own incomprehension boosted rather than diluted. Disparaged by many as 're-heated Calvinism' – itself a threatening accusation in the age of Louis XIV – Jansenism emphasised the devastating effects of original sin on mankind. It meant that Christians, despite the church's sacraments, were saved by God's grace rather than by their own 'good works'; this position implied, in turn, some form of predestination, which usually meant that only an elite would be saved and the mass would be damned. The Jansenist dispute did not begin in France but, despite the existence there of only a handful of 'theological' Jansenists, it was where Jansenism became most enduring. Above all, French Jansenism quickly escaped, during the early 1640s, from the conventional domain of theological system-building, largely because it became entangled with existing disputes – between the Jesuits and their opponents, gallicans and pro-Romans, rigorists and laxists in the field of morality. This embedded Jansenism in contemporary social and political debates that attracted a much wider audience, which was aided by the publication of the major writings on the subject in French. Thus, Jansenist thinking had unintended affinities with the stoicism and ethical strands of much seventeenth-century French thought and literature, in which a persistently pessimistic view of human nature undermined the pretensions to grandeur or virtue not just of kings and aristocrats, but also of lesser mortals. Such pretensions were openly pilloried in Molière plays, but also by the literary giants of the day such as Corneille, Pascal, La Rochefoucauld, and La Bruyère. In 1653 and 1715, Jansenism was formally condemned by two popes, and at Louis XIV's explicit request on both occasions. But his efforts to nail such an elusive target drew surprisingly effective resistance, even though he faced a relatively small number of opponents, female as well as male, clerical as well as lay. Against all expectations, that particular legacy of Louis XIV would prove an increasingly poisoned one.

The experiences of France's Protestants were even more painful. Having adopted a stance of absolute obedience, they benefited from relative protection by Richelieu and Mazarin, a policy that Louis XIV seemed quite ready to continue after 1661. But it was based heavily on 'reason of state' calculations rather than any principled argument for religious toleration. Since the 1630s, Catholic *dévots*, lawyers, and local magistrates gradually began turning the screws on the Protestants through a systematically 'minimalist' interpretation of the edict of Nantes; and the accumulating pressure ultimately began to steer, albeit haphazardly, government policy towards repression. Increasingly, the Huguenots were accused of 'rebellion' for refusing to adopt the religion of the king. By the time the edict of Nantes was revoked in 1685, restrictions on Protestants were stifling – their temples demolished, schools closed, access to the professions virtually all closed off, and their children liable to sequestration if they wished to become Catholics. What such methods had not achieved, the notorious *dragonnades* (the billeting of soldiers on Protestant families with instructions to brutalise them into converting to Catholicism) completed. Indeed, the revocation of 1685 was justified on the ground that, as virtually no Protestants remained in France, the edict of Nantes was redundant. This delusion was soon shattered, but it produced no change of heart. At least 150,000 Protestants defied the law and emigrated to (mainly) central and northern Europe, from where the intellectuals of the Protestant diaspora, especially in the Netherlands, launched innumerable attacks on the 'enslavement' of France under the 'tyranny' of Louis XIV. They failed to persuade him to undo the revocation, but inflicted considerable reputational damage on France among neighbouring states, which subtly contributed to diminishing its aura abroad, not to mention fuelling the Enlightenment's later critique of religious persecution. Active Protestant resistance, such as that of the prophets (some of them young girls) and preaching assemblies of the late 1680s and the violent revolt of the Camisards (1702–04), was limited and brutally repressed. It was from 1715 onwards that a younger generation of intrepid Protestant pastors began to clandestinely re-build the Protestant churches 'of the desert'.

## V

Louis XIV's grasp of 'normal' politics, especially internal, was for the most part sounder than these examples suggest. The age of the chief ministers ended with Mazarin's death in 1661, when Louis XIV declared, to widespread approval, that he would rule as well as reign; he confounded those sceptics, like his mother, who doubted whether he possessed the discipline that this required. Sometimes described as 'the revolution of 1661', this was in reality a return to a widely accepted norm. By keeping his promise over the next half-century, he removed a major source of political polarisation within the ruling elites. Furthermore, he refused to have high-ranking dignitaries, aristocratic or clerical, as ministers, preferring men of robe-nobility background who, towards the end of the reign, were increasingly connected, especially by marriage, to leading aristocratic families. Under Louis XIV ministerial longevity was the rule, and disgrace or dismissal the exception; that ensured stability, if not always out-and-out competence within the higher spheres of government. Royal favour towards individual ministers was expressed mainly by their accumulation of additional responsibilities and offices. This in turn enabled the Colbert and Le Tellier ministerial families – complete with brothers, sons, nephews, in-laws, and other clients – to colonise and dominate much of central government for virtually the entire half century. Jean-Baptiste Colbert, Le Tellier de Louvois, and Pontchartrain, the three most prominent of these ministers, were so overburdened that the first two died of exhaustion, a fate that Pontchartrain avoided only by becoming chancellor of France. Under Louis XIV, government was thus 'personal' in many more ways than is usually realised.

The age of rebellion, by nobles, towns, and peasants, was almost over by 1660; even the Protestants remained stoically peaceful in the face of growing repression during the following decades. As we have seen, rebellion and the need to ensure men and money for a long war-effort had already begun tilting the balance within government away from the office-holding magistrates and lawcourts, with their tendency to resist innovations they disliked. The beneficiaries of this shift were initially improvised commissioner-intendants specially despatched to the provinces. That arrangement was still fragile around 1660, but it gave the royal council closer oversight of provincial government. It continued under Louis XIV, with provincial governors of aristocratic rank retaining their overall position as the king's representative and exercising control of military affairs and substantial patronage powers within their 'governments'. The provincial intendants thus became increasingly important at the administrative level, and henceforth served much longer terms in 'their' regions. This suited the finance minister Colbert (1661–83), who was also a de facto minister of the interior, not to mention his successors. Colbert reorganised rather than genuinely reformed the tax system, making sure his clients were in control of its key levers, but the return of war in the early 1670s halted his efforts. His attempts to codify existing laws – on forests and rivers, civil and criminal law, commerce, the navy, slavery, and so on – dominated the 1660s and 1670s. Interestingly, whereas previous royal ordinances often originated from deliberations in assemblies of notables or the Estates-General, Colbert put his faith overwhelmingly in 'experts' of a new type; relying on the provincial intendants to supply the essential information, he believed that government should be based on information, reports, and statistics, especially of the country's resources, natural and human. As a mercantilist, he viewed international trade as a zero-sum game in which France must compete, especially with the Dutch and the English. That in turn required enterprises like the East or West 'India' chartered trading companies, a mercantile fleet, and a navy, in order to acquire a colonial empire like its major rivals. With the onset of the major wars of Louis XIV's reign, such plans were subordinated, as had occurred during the Richelieu-Mazarin years, to other, 'continental' imperatives nearer to home, but without ever quite disappearing from view. Indeed, ports like Saint-Malo, Nantes, La Rochelle, and Marseille offset the normal restrictions of war on trade by privateering and interloping in trade with Spanish possessions overseas either side of 1700. 'Colbertism' survived Colbert and has remained synonymous with detailed regulation supervised by inspectors of manufactures, ports, and commerce, but similar methods were applied to other spheres of government – frontiers, fortifications, and so on.

The sense of a governmental system more dominant and coherent than previously was enhanced by the most enduring image of Louis XIV's reign: Versailles. Transformed from the residence of 'a majestic gentleman' into

Europe's most imposing palace, by 1683 it housed the greatly enlarged royal government to a degree that the Louvre, Saint-Germain-en-Laye, or Fontainebleau had not previously done. But Versailles was much more than a functional administrative centre: it was an elaborate temple to royal power, whose iconography bordered on idolatry towards the person of Louis XIV. The royal triumphs, military and otherwise, dominated its walls and ceilings; France's best artists and its academies were mobilised to depict, via paintings, tapestries, and medals, the insatiable royal quest for glory. Elements of such display later migrated to provincial cities, many of which erected their own imposing equestrian statues of Louis XIV. Contributing to the diffusion of French culture and language across Europe, the court set the standard by which other European monarchies set out their symbolic stalls thereafter.

Versailles' reputation has also been that of a gilded cage in which the French nobility were kept in political impotence and under close supervision. Such a vision derives largely from Louis XIV's ghost-written *Mémoires*, whose leitmotif was the 'reducing' of the recalcitrant elements of French society to obedience. Despite a century of turmoil, relations between monarchy and nobility were not so one-dimensional that they can be reduced to the daily rituals of Versailles and its vigilant master. Only a relatively small number of nobles could afford to live in Versailles at any time, and many of them were there essentially because they held court office, high or low; intermarriage with ministers brought the highest nobility close to political office again by the early 1700s. The extensive enquiry into titles to nobility during the 1660s is often seen as evidence of the nobility's wider descent into dependence. However, genuine nobles, happy to see newcomers or imposters excluded from their ranks, welcomed it. Above all, Mazarin had already begun weaning the aristocracy away from factional politics, in which they either led or tacitly supported revolt by their clients. With such hitherto 'natural' bonds weakened or dissolved, revolt by lower nobles – or even their complicity with 'popular' rebellion – would henceforth lack the oxygen of high-level support. Beyond that, Louis XIV's regime sought co-operation rather than confrontation with the nobility. The vast expansion of France's armies and military operations, especially from 1689 onwards, guaranteed the nobility the role they desired most under the leadership of a king eager to play the part of a *roi de guerre*. Of course, military activity, starting with the purchase of officerships, was simply too expensive for poorer nobles; those who could afford it often found themselves seriously out of pocket during campaigns. But the very high ratio of officers to serving soldiers in French armies suggests that institutionalised military careers were increasingly the norm for the nobility. Despite frequent complaints of absenteeism

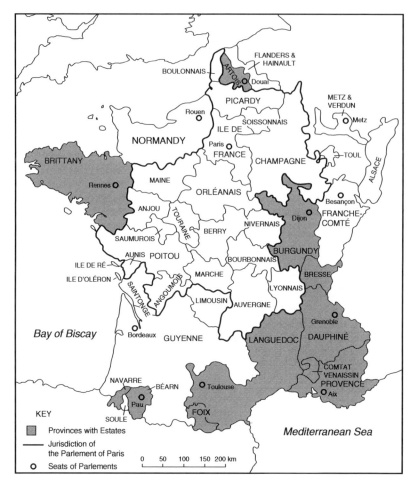

**Map 5**  *France under Louis XIV*

among French officers, military activity proved a more effective disciplinary instrument over far more nobles than the unyielding etiquette of court life ever could.

## VI

On his deathbed, Louis XIV famously regretted that he had loved war too much. It certainly dominated his reign, especially the decades after 1689, and left a heavy legacy to his successors. Conscious of the military superiority that France had obtained by 1660, Louis XIV was not averse to using it, even where minor slights to his grandeur were perceived. An old ally of France, the Dutch, bore the initial brunt of French resentment of its commercial success and upstart republican status, but Louis XIV also entertained the ambition, inherited from Mazarin, to add the Spanish Netherlands to France, in the hope of extending and fortifying France's vulnerable northern frontier. Fénelon (and many others after him) would later claim that the war against the Dutch (1672–8) was a decisive turning point, orienting Louis XIV's reign towards military confrontation with the rest of Europe. Tellingly, Louis XIV himself later brushed it off as an 'error of youth'. In 1672, overwhelming force led to rapid military success for France, which promptly overplayed its hand by making excessive territorial demands, which the Dutch rejected; thereafter the French gains were gradually neutralised by a growing anti-French coalition of European powers. French diplomacy rescued the day, as it would more than once, by exploiting the mutual suspicions of the allies in the treaty of Nijmegen in 1678. France gained the previously Spanish France-Comté, along with a series of towns along the frontier with the Spanish Netherlands. Although it was much less than might have been obtained in 1672–3, even this outcome made Louis XIV, as was said at the time, the 'arbiter of Europe'. During the relatively peaceful 1680s that followed, France strengthened its grip on Alsace by taking Strasbourg in 1681 and then by 'reuniting' to the royal domain numerous eastern lands and lordships to which it could establish a historical claim, however contrived or artificial. This was also the age of Vauban (1633–1707), the great military engineer who made the notion of a linear military frontier, replete with new-style fortresses, a reality; its corollary was no less historic, namely the dismantling of the walled fortress cities of France's interior provinces. The 'policy of reunions' was not war, but it was not peace either; as a form of creeping defence, it increasingly alarmed France's neighbours, especially now that the upper Rhine was part of its eastern frontier, and it sowed mistrust that formed the basis of the subsequent alliances against Louis XIV. The next great conflict was the accurately named War of the League of Augsburg (1689–97) – it was the most 'German' of Louis XIV's wars, as his most numerous opponents were German princes, led by Emperor Leopold I. But this 'grand alliance' also included the implacable William of Orange, now king of England as well as Stadtholder of the Dutch republic. Increasingly France had difficulty finding substantial allies, a task that its treatment of its Protestants before and after 1685 made more arduous still. Even the pope kept well clear of Louis XIV during the 1680s. But France was probably unique at this time in being the

European power most capable of operating without allies. The ensuing war from 1689 to 1697 was on a far greater scale than that of the 1670s, as is evident from its naval operations. Colbert's navy held its own for a time, but gradually France was forced to abandon 'normal' operations for more lucrative forms of privateering by 1694. Diplomacy continued during the war years, but this time it was the allies' demands which France found disproportionate, which delayed peace until 1697. French diplomacy was still effective in dividing its enemies, even if it had to give up important strategic possessions like Luxembourg, Lorraine, Casale, and Pinerolo.

Despite its name, the peace of Ryswick (1697) was a truce rather than a peace, one in which France's concessions were calculated with the next major challenge in mind. By the late 1690s, European power politics were dominated by a prospect that was already 30 years old, but whose timing nobody could predict – the Spanish succession once the childless and sickly Carlos II finally died. The major rivals were the Vienna Habsburgs and the French Bourbons, but their previous attempts to agree on how to divide up Carlos II's lands were no longer valid when Carlos finally died in 1700. In his will he chose Louis XIV's grandson, Philip of Anjou, as his successor. After much discussion, the legacy was accepted by Versailles, despite every-one knowing the likelihood that France would again be facing a European coalition, determined to prevent it from becoming the continental – and overseas – hegemon, given the extent of the Spanish Habsburg empire. But it was only after Louis XIV gave to understand that Spain and its overseas possessions would fall under French control ('there are now no Pyrenees') that open war began in 1702. What followed was the most extensive con-flict in Europe since the Thirty Years' War, but one with substantial naval and overseas dimensions largely missing from that earlier conflict. The 12 years of fluctuating continent-wide warfare involved enormous armies that often suffered huge casualties, accompanied by the familiar diplomatic near-misses, misunderstandings, and miscalculations. If the Bourbon suc-cession in Spain was finally accepted, it was on condition that there would be no union of the French and Spanish monarchies. The transfer of Spain's Italian and 'Belgian' lands to the Vienna Habsburgs confirmed the steady rise of 'Austrian' power since the 1680s, thus clipping France's wings further. As in the 1690s, France fought virtually singlehanded, which is testimony to its remarkable military, organisational, and financial capacities. Beyond the conventional dynastic issues, the stakes could scarcely have been higher, as control of Spain's huge empire would have made France a major global power overnight, with access to vast resources that had previously eluded it. Not surprisingly, the opposition of the English and Dutch, Europe's dominant trading and colonial powers, was fundamental in preventing such an outcome.

The congress and treaties of Utrecht (1713) and Rastatt (1714), which restored peace to Europe, brought the curtain down on two decades of attritional warfare on an unprecedented scale. The wars had piled enormous pressures on French society, the effects of which would in some cases endure until the Revolution. Taxes, new as well as old, rocketed, as did the multiplication and sale of superfluous offices, the exploitation of privileges, the manipulation of the coinage, and recourse to forms of paper money which made things much worse. By 1715, the stratospheric royal debts were somewhere in the region of 2,000 million *livres*, the mere servicing of which alone devoured much of the crown's annual revenues! Such a financial nightmare came during a generation when France had suffered other setbacks. The 'Colbert years' (1660–85 approximately) had seen financial restraint alongside demographic and economic recovery, despite the loss of the Protestant émigrés in the 1680s. A severe subsistence crisis in 1693–4 sparked famine and epidemics that reduced the population by around 1.5 million inhabitants. Remarkably, the losses seem to have been made good by the time the 'terrible winter' of 1709–10 arrived, which was followed by widespread crop-failure and famine. The actual demographic losses were perhaps only half of those of 1693–4, but a proportionately weakened society took longer to recover this time. Nevertheless, France easily remained Europe's most populous country, and during these 'years of misery' its demographic system showed its capacity to loosen some established structural restraints (e.g. late marriage) in the cause of regeneration, which would accelerate substantially with the return of peace in 1713. Unlike past generations, France suffered little war-damage apart from the high casualty rates among its armies, which operated mostly beyond its frontiers. With a population that was not substantially higher in 1715 than in 1610 (about 21.5 against 19.5 million), it is clear that the horsemen of the apocalypse, either separately or in tandem, had not been idle.

## VII

After a reign of 72 years, Louis XIV was succeeded his only surviving, five-year old great-grandson, Louis XV, whose uncle, Philip V of Spain, was debarred from the succession by the treaty of Utrecht. As in 1643, a long regency was in prospect, but in 1715 France was at least at peace. The first male regent since 1380, Philippe d'Orléans, the king's great-uncle, had a reputation as a libertine and opportunist that had made Louis XIV deeply distrust him. Ambitious and authoritarian, he was shrewd enough to see the need to break with the stifling late years of Louis XIV and to cultivate groups (the court aristocracy) and institutions (the parlements) that Louis XIV had kept on a tight leash. The early return of the court from Versailles to Paris was another early signal of change. Plans for changes in government had circulated for years at court – some were emanations of earlier criticisms of Louis XIV's regime, and some were more radical than others. Anxious to secure political elbow-room for himself, Orléans adopted individual elements of them, downgrading or eliminating ministers and secretaries of state and replacing them with councils presided over by senior aristocrats; he restored to the parlement the precious right to 'remonstrate' against royal decrees that it had lost under Louis XIV. Such politically astute changes bought Orléans time and support, but did not all work in practice; by 1718, he returned to the ministerial *status quo ante*. It proved the last attempt at restructuring the core of central government before the Revolution.

Meanwhile, Orleans could not afford merely to 'mind the shop' until Louis XV came of age. Reversing Louis XIV's diplomacy, he secured alliances in 1718 with former adversaries, Holland and England, which solidified the Utrecht settlement – something badly needed by the new Bourbon Spain and Hanoverian England – and which bought peace for over 20 years. But the greatest problem facing the regency was, of course, the massive royal debt-mountain. Some voices proposed outright bankruptcy and the convening of the Estates-General in 1715, but that was rejected as too radical. More conventional measures were approved, such as re-minting the coinage and an early-modern anticipation of the 'haircut' to holders of government bonds; a special tribunal was convened to pursue profiteering military suppliers and financiers of the war years. But such measures could only partially plug the gaping hole in the finances, which in turn opened the door to a Scots exile, John Law, who offered more novel and ambitious solutions. Having created a general bank in 1716 (which became 'royal' in 1718) and then re-founded the overseas trading companies, Law sought to combine monetary abundance and commercial activity. Early success in attracting investors catapulted him into formal charge of the royal finances in early 1720, but his various schemes, especially the use of paper money, simply proved too daring and complex for his contemporaries; the result was a speculative frenzy (a contemporary of the London South Sea Bubble) that ended France's brief experiment with non-metallic money for generations to come. Law had managed to reduce the debt by perhaps one-third to around 1.5 billion *livres*, but his resignation in late 1720 saw the return of the tax-farmers and other old-style financiers who had bitterly opposed him. Many people lost out, while others gained during the short life of 'the system', as it was called. For its part, the monarchy rode rough shod over its creditors to reduce its debts towards them, but the Law experience probably increased rather than decreased the difficulty of dealing with what remained unredeemed. Numerous peasant communities paid off their debts using Law's paper money, while others, such as convents, which held bonds (*rentes*) often saw them redeemed with increasingly worthless paper money. As a warning against innovation, Law's failure left painful memories – and especially of banks. His schemes, which were frequently opposed by a re-invigorated parlement of Paris, in turn fed emerging critiques of the 'despotism' – a term that would become increasingly common during the eighteenth century – of a monarchy which, as in its treatment of the Protestants, respected neither the rights nor the property of its subjects.

By the time Louis XV came of age in 1723, several options for reforming the state had been tried and closed off. Not that he was desperate to seize control of government, either then or later. For the next 20 years, until 1743, effective power would rest with a new generation of chief ministers, especially with the king's elderly former tutor, Cardinal Fleury (1653– 1743). Thereafter, no minister-favourite emerged, but the leading minister was mostly, as under Louis XIV, the controller-general of the finances, a sign of where both the power and the problems of government resided. Louis XV's reluctance to govern personally left individual ministers and ministries vulnerable to factional attack. One of these short-lived ministers even bore the name of Silhouette. During the successive political crises of these years, royal support was rarely guaranteed or reliable when it was most needed. The middle decades of the reign were characterised by drift and indecision, which only changed in the last few years of the reign (1770–4).

Despite the outcome of Louis XIV's wars, France after 1714 remained Europe's strongest state, with no intention of disappearing from the inter-state stage. It finally acquired Lorraine in 1766, followed by Corsica in 1768. It took part in the successive wars of Polish (1733–8) and Austrian succession (1740–8) as well as the Seven Years' War (1756–63) – all of which, but especially the last, further aggravated the unreformed finances of the monarchy. That damage was relatively lighter, however, as these decades witnessed a recovery of France's economy and the beginnings of a certain level of prosperity. The last great plague decimated the population of Marseille in 1720, but effective quarantining prevented it from spreading beyond the city itself. The last great subsistence crisis of the age occurred in 1739–41, although numerous harvest failures and localised food shortages continued until the 1780s. Overall, the more peaceful eighteenth century witnessed a steady, if at times staccato-like population increase from 21 to approximately 28.5 million between 1715 and 1789; the growth-rate was modest by comparison with other parts of Europe, but France started from a much higher base-line.

In the past, such demographic growth would have been reversed by combinations of famine and 'plague', which has led some historians to posit the effects of an 'agricultural revolution' by 1789. But in a country with so many micro-economies, localised markets, and poor inland communications, that seems improbable. France experienced nothing resembling England's enclosures, merely the age-old, haphazard concentration of land arising from the dispossession of smaller peasants fallen into debt; royal taxes and seigneurial-ecclesiastical dues remained a significant burden for many peasants, preventing all but modest improvements. The pull of city markets, particularly that of Paris, continued to offer real incentives to more productive and more diversified farming as, of course, did the significant rises in food prices; feeding a growing population was made possible by more extensive agriculture rather than by supposed technological improvements. However, wages lagged behind prices, which was bound to cause trouble in due course.

Eighteenth-century France also became a far more significant colonial power than previously. A latecomer to European expansion, its meagre overseas possessions, such as New France (Canada and the Mississippi valley), a handful of Caribbean islands, and a few trading posts on the African and Indian coasts (Senegal, Madagascar, and Pondicherry) were slow to bring benefits, commercial and political. The efforts of Colbert and his successors to develop a more active policy – with its inevitable crown-sponsored trading companies – in order to rival the English or Dutch, yielded relatively few new colonies, but did generate self-sustaining trading links in the process. Viewed from this angle, the prospect for France of a Spanish succession as an 'El Dorado' moment is understandable, as is the opposition from France's overseas rivals to such a vast windfall; in both 1713 and 1763 most of its first colonies were lost to England as a result of European wars. Such losses elicited little regret, as French settler populations were always tiny apart from New France, and they were drawn mostly from its Atlantic provinces, with which commercial ties were also strongest. During the eighteenth century, the small Caribbean islands (Martinique, Guadaloupe, and especially the future Haiti, then Saint-Domingue) led the world in sugar and, later, coffee production which, alongside the slave-trading that such a plantation-based economy implied, laid the foundations of the new prosperity of Marseille, Bordeaux, La Rochelle, and Nantes. Surviving the final loss in 1763 of New France and other toeholds in Senegal and India, which French naval forces were unable to defend against superior English sea power, 'Atlantic' France came into its own under Louis XV. Along with the rest of the French mainland economy, it benefited from the stability of the currency after 1726 and the efforts to expand internal trade by improving river navigation and roads and building canals. The events of the Revolution would provoke drastic transformations.

## VIII

Among the most surprising losers of France's colonial expansion figured its Jesuits, whose business activities (including slave-trading!) in Martinique put them in substantial debt by the late 1750s. But the Jesuits' vulnerability had scarcely anything to do with business itself. It was the return of the Jansenist affair in 1713 and its subsequent permutations that were their real nemesis – just as it was the most persistent political thorn in the monarchy's side until the 1760s. Voltaire and the *philosophes* claimed the credit for the final expulsion of the Jesuits from France in 1762, but the real damage was done by the Jansenists and their allies, opportunist or principled, who capitalised on other grievances and effectively yoked them to their cause. After 1715, the Regent suspended the measures taken or planned against the Jansenists by Louis XIV, but the Jesuits inevitably came under fire as the Jansenists defended themselves in subsequent years. In 1730, Cardinal Fleury finally decided to have *Unigenitus* registered as a state law (and not merely a papal bull) as a prelude to a massive purge of Jansenists across the French church. He succeeded in part because the Jansenist cause was badly weakened by the excesses of the 'convulsionary' events (and their attendant 'miracles') in Saint-Médard parish in Paris during 1731–3, which were mocked by the *philosophes* and which dismayed many Jansenists themselves. Fleury won a pyrrhic victory, however, since his purge left behind hundreds of disgruntled and unemployed clerics, while the elusiveness of Jansenism and its capacity to attract other forms of dissidence remained largely intact. The parlement of Paris, which contained only a small number of Jansenists, was silenced by Fleury, but it continued to strike down anti-Jansenist instructions and other such actions by pro-*Unigenitus* French bishops. In 1752, the archbishop of Paris handed it an unlikely cause – that of defending Jansenists who were being denied the sacraments because they failed to produce a certificate (*billet*) of absolution from a priest who accepted the bull *Unigenitus*.

The ensuing conflict was anything but obscure. It pitted the parlement against the king's council for several years, during which the parlement argued it was acting in the public interest and as guardian of the fundamental laws of the kingdom; it also denounced *Unigenitus* as having 'neither the character nor the effect of a rule of faith'. It also did what it enjoyed most – humbling church jurisdiction by considering the refusal of absolution a matter of social order rather than of religious conscience. The 1750s were punctuated by such tussles, in which strikes by, and even the exile of the Paris parlement, helped tip opinion against the government and its supporters. In such a context, in which almost any incident could mutate into a clash of principles, it is not hard to see how a lawsuit concerning Jesuit debts in Martinique quickly became grist to the Jansenist-parlementaire mill. Other parlements, such as Rennes and Rouen, played their part in hastening the expulsion (1762) and formal abolition of the Jesuits in France (1765). That outcome was not a foregone conclusion, until Louis XV's leading minister, Choiseul, who was desperate to regain the support of the parlements, sacrificed the Jesuits. Having destroyed its prime enemy, the Jansenist cause was now largely redundant. By then, however, it had produced an oppositionist mind-set, a 'party' with its own financial resources ('Perette's chest'), and a clandestine periodical (the *Nouvelles Ecclésiastiques*). It had also developed an elaborate idiom derived from the Bible that could be translated to the secular and political spheres. The combativeness of the parlements and their magistrates – and the wider world to which they belonged – had also returned; while stopping short of claiming to possess powers independent of the monarchy itself, they formulated historical-constitutional arguments to checkmate royal decisions down to 1789. Under a detached and inactive Louis XV, who by the late 1740s had squandered his personal capital as the 'well beloved king', absolute monarchy was accused not merely of abandoning France's gallican traditions but of descending into a form of 'despotism'.

To contemporaries such political infighting hardly seemed earth-shattering, let alone capable of undermining the *ancien régime*. The fundamental structures of both the regime and the society that anchored it seemed more solid than ever. By then, the governmental and social hierarchies were clearly defined, and disputes over status and authority within them were much less worrisome than a century earlier. Above all, the habit of rebellion among the higher and lower echelons of society had died out, and was by now a distant memory. The ensuing stability seemed to promise better conditions for France's population, now that the previous century's great wars were in the past. Only in retrospect would certain decisions, such as the return of the royal court to Versailles in 1722, seem symbolic of a widening gap between two increasingly different worlds.

## CHRONOLOGY

1559   Francis II under-age, regency of Catherine de Medici
1561   Failure of inter-confessional colloquy of Poissy

| | |
|---|---|
| 1562–97 | Eight wars of religion |
| 1562 | First attempt to legalise Protestant churches, civil war follows; Jesuits open college of Clermont (Paris) |
| 1564 | New Year begins 1 January (previously 25 March) |
| 1572 | Saint Bartholomew's Day Massacre of Protestants in Paris (and later in provinces) |
| 1576 | First Catholic League; Estates-General at Blois; Jean Bodin, *Six Books of the Republic* |
| 1580 | Montaigne, *Essays* |
| 1584–9 | Second Catholic League, with Spanish support; war against Protestants |
| 1588 | Day of Barricades, Parisian revolt against Henry III |
| 1589 | Assassination of Henry III, end of Valois dynasty; succeeded by Protestant Henry of Bourbon, king of Navarre (Henry IV) |
| 1593–6 | Henry IV converts to Catholicism, obtains papal absolution, gradually gains Catholics' allegiance |
| 1598 | Edict of Nantes attempts to organise Catholic-Protestant co-existence; peace with Spain |
| 1608 | François de Sales, *Introduction to the devout life*; Samuel Champlain founds Quebec |
| 1610 | Assassination of Henry IV, succeeded by under-age Louis XIII, regency of Marie de Medici |
| 1614 | Last meeting of Estates-General before 1789 |
| 1614–20 | Royal minority ends, revolts by leading nobles |
| 1620–9 | Wars against Protestant rebels, capture of La Rochelle and southern strongholds. Edict of Nantes retained |
| 1624 | Cardinal Richelieu returns to ministerial office |
| 1630–1 | Political crisis ('day of the dupes'), Richelieu survives, Marie de Medici goes into exile |
| 1635 | France declares war on Spain, joins Thirty Years' War; Richelieu founds French Academy |
| 1635–58 | Popular revolts versus taxes across France |
| 1636 | Corneille, *Le Cid* |
| 1637 | Descartes, *Discours de la méthode* |
| 1642–3 | Deaths of Louis XIII and Richelieu; succession of under-age Louis XIV; regency of Anne of Austria (to 1651), Cardinal Mazarin chief minister; Antoine Arnauld, *Frequent communion*; first papal condemnation of Jansenism |
| 1648 | Treaty of Westphalia (no peace between France and Spain); beginnings of revolt (the *Fronde*) by royal magistrates and nobility (until 1653) |

| | |
|---|---|
| 1656–7 | Pascal, *Provincial Letters* |
| 1659 | Treaty of Pyrenees ends Franco-Spanish war |
| 1661 | Death of Mazarin, Louis XIV's personal rule begins |
| 1664 | Molière, *Tartuffe* |
| 1667–8 | War of Devolution with Spain; Franche-Comté ceded by Spain to France; Racine, *Andromaque*; La Fontaine, *Fables* |
| 1672–8 | War with Dutch, French territorial gains |
| 1675 | Revolts in Bordeaux and Brittany |
| 1681 | Strasbourg becomes French; first *dragonnades* versus Protestants |
| 1682 | Four gallican articles adopted; royal court moves to Versailles |
| 1685 | Revocation of the Edict of Nantes |
| 1688–97 | War of the League of Augsburg, French territorial losses, keeps Alsace |
| 1693–4 | Major famine, over 1.3 million dead |
| 1699 | French settlement in Louisiana |
| 1702–4 | Revolt of Protestant Camisards in Cévennes |
| 1702–13 | War of Spanish succession |
| 1709–10 | Famine, ca 800,000 dead |
| 1713 | *Unigenitus*, papal condemnation of Jansenism |
| 1715 | Death of Louis XIV; succession of under-age great-grandson, Louis XV; regency led by Philip of Orleans (to 1722); first Protestant synod of 'the desert' |
| 1718–20 | John Law's 'system' of finance |
| 1725 | First French lodge of freemasons |
| 1740–8 | War of Austrian succession |
| 1748 | Montesquieu's *Spirit of the Laws* |
| 1751 | Publication of *Encyclopédie* begins; Voltaire, *Le Siècle de Louis XIV* |
| 1756–63 | Seven Years' War; France loses major colonies |

# 4 From Enlightenment to Empire

## I

For generations the Enlightenment was considered a French phenomenon that naturally migrated across Europe as part of France's continent-wide cultural and intellectual dominance. As proof, it sufficed to cite the names of a handful of its best-known *philosophes* – Voltaire and Diderot – and their extensive connections and influence, especially among 'enlightened' rulers across Europe. It was no less firmly believed that the French Revolution and the wider modernity that it engendered were the direct offspring of the same intellectual explosion; the quip that 'the Revolution was Voltaire's fault' itself dates from the early 1790s. Such a causal construction has been questioned, even rejected, in more recent times, with several accounts of the Enlightenment finding its origins and main inspirations elsewhere – in Scotland, England, or the Dutch republic. In these accounts, France's 'lights' appear alongside other 'national' ones, but not as the originators of radically new ideas. However, the French Enlightenment and its impact has never been a purely intellectual matter. Endlessly scrutinised, celebrated, or denounced, its precise role in the most radical upheaval of the age, the Revolution, remains as intriguing as ever. If more radical ideas circulated elsewhere before 1789, there is little evidence that they produced proportionately radical change. Rather than 'causing' the Revolution, the Enlightenment proved invaluable to revolutionaries searching for ideas to legitimate their innovations.

There was no radical break between the intellectual life of the seventeenth and eighteenth centuries. The earlier Republic of Letters that included figures like Descartes, Pascal, Pierre Bayle, and many others continued to flourish and even to grow with the rising interest in the new sciences. Both the French monarchy and church continued to patronise scholarly work in the widest sense, while academies and other societies multiplied (from 13 around 1715 to 33 by 1760) in the provinces; their debates and, above all, their essay-prize competitions provoked some of the best-known reflexions of the French Enlightenment on questions of public interest. Voltaire, the presiding genius of the French Enlightenment from the 1730s onwards, explicitly recognised this continuity with the earlier Republic of Letters and its traditions; in his view, it had culminated in the reign of Louis XIV, which he regarded as one of the four great ages in western civilisation. The fact that the eighteenth-century *philosophes* shared essentially the same backgrounds as these predecessors and engaged in similar forms of exchange (academies, salons, and the newer masonic lodges), makes it virtually impossible to date the beginnings of the Enlightenment.

Yet there were differences and additions. Perhaps the most difficult problem of all is to grasp how or why the cultural-intellectual climate altered after Louis XIV's reign. The changed political landscape of the regency helped, releasing pent-up intellectual energies long kept under wraps under Louis XIV. As we saw, the reopening of the Jansenist controversy brought key political issues in relation to religion under intense scrutiny. This emboldened many of the *philosophes*, as disciples of the scientific revolution, to propose forms of deism or 'natural' religion, in which virtue and natural sentiments would replace dogmatic overkill and its futile controversies. But even in France, where criticism of existing churches and religion could be more virulent than anywhere in Europe, there was only a tiny number of atheists who publicised their views; vigilant state censorship compelled even the best-known writers to resort to satire or descriptions of imaginary worlds in order to convey their ideas. This and the contemporary evolution of moral and economic thought, especially with the so-called Physiocrats, made the *philosophes* increasingly focus their attention on the notion of 'society'. The term itself was relatively new, and increasingly distinct from the (political) 'republic'. Thus, while political regimes and religions might be transitory, society's priorities – and especially the quest for happiness – increasingly dominated the *philosophes*' thinking. Such a shift owed much to the rationalising character of the scientific revolution, which was now applied to society and its needs. It was sufficiently broad-fronted an endeavour for the major figures of the French Enlightenment from Montesquieu and Voltaire onwards, to focus on their own individual preoccupations – religious tolerance, legal torture, and so on – without becoming lost to the general cause of enlightenment. Despite efforts to distinguish between 'radical' and 'conservative' variations, this largely holds true for the other enlightenments of the age.

It is no accident, therefore, that the best-known product of the French Enlightenment was not an individual work of sheer intellectual genius, but the *Encyclopedia*, a massive collective enterprise sub-titled as a 'systematic dictionary of the sciences, arts and professions' that represented the totality of human activities. It was conceived in 1750 by Diderot (only recently released from prison for an offending work denying the autonomy of the soul) and d'Alembert as a modern equivalent of Bayle's *Philosophical Dictionary* and Chambers' *Cyclopedia*. Its 17 volumes (plus 11 volumes of plates) and 70,000 articles, to which over 1,500 authors as different in their views as Voltaire, Rousseau, Turgot, and Condillac contributed, were published between 1751 and 1772. The first two volumes of this controversial and critical work were suppressed by the government in 1752, but it survived this potentially terminal setback thanks largely to the complicity of the chief royal censor, Lamoignon de Malesherbes, who personally supported this (and many other related) 'enlightened' publications. Despite real differences of opinion between articles on closely related subjects, an underlying sense of human promise – and the need to liberate it from restraint, superstition, or intolerance – is apparent throughout the successive volumes. The *Encyclopedia* became a Europe-wide bestseller in its successive editions and formats. Its marketing also appears remarkably modern, involving subscriptions by purchasers and booksellers. Within France, clergy and nobles, especially nobles of the robe, purchased some three-quarters of all copies, with relatively few bourgeois subscribers from outside of these educated and leisured classes. The completion and wide diffusion of the Encyclopedia project was, not surprisingly, a genuine encouragement to all *philosophes* seeking a comprehensive understanding of the 'real' world around them in the years preceding the Revolution.

This also suggests that what was emerging was less an explicit programme of changes for state and society than a widening public space for active discussion of the issues of the day. In 1775, Malesherbes, the censor who helped the *Encyclopedia* to escape sudden death in 1752, famously claimed that 'a tribunal independent of all the authorities and whose judgement they all respected', had emerged during recent years. In fact, the 'public sphere', as historians have labelled what Malesherbes was alluding to, had roots stretching back to the seventeenth century, but they were somewhat obscured by the Louis XIV regime's record in 'confiscating' political discussion to itself and its ruling, court-based 'public'. A full separation of private and public spheres was never possible or desirable, as even strong governments needed to justify and solicit support for their policies and actions; weaker governments, as under Louis XV and XVI, could not stem the growing tide of free-wheeling discussion, but in many instances tried to manipulate it. Louis XV's celebrated 'flagellation' speech of 1766 asserting that the 'rights and interests of the nation' were inseparable from his personal sovereignty was delivered as a stinging rebuke to the Paris parlement for not knowing its rightful place. But the fact that it was delivered at all and the language it used suggest how divorced from reality and under challenge the regime had become by then. It is not necessary to think that the increasingly numerous salons, coffee-houses, and masonic lodges were hot-beds of political discussion, let alone of overt opposition or subversion, but it is possible to understand why Malesherbes described France's social and cultural elites – many of whom were government officials – as he did in 1775. Moreover, French involvement in the American revolution extended far beyond military assistance; the American political debates were closely followed by the same French 'public' which was exposed to questions of mounting interest within France – political reform, social change, religious freedom, and so on.

## II

By August 1783, when the Anglo-French treaty of Versailles confirmed American independence from Britain, it seemed that France had recovered spectacularly from its mid-century blues on the European chessboard. The military and especially naval reforms implemented after the disasters of the Seven Years' War enabled it to transport French troops to America and repel the British Navy at critical moments in a conflict (1775–83) that was as much European as American. Although it recovered in 1783 some of the colonies it lost 20 years earlier, American independence was a pyrrhic victory from France's perspective, as it brought few tangible benefits (especially commercial) and hid mounting problems. A mere six years later, it was heading into the unknown, the monarchy's financial and political credit now so exhausted that it was forced to convene the Estates-General for the first time since 1614. How did Revolution steal up like a thief in the night on a country that still presented a brilliant face to the outside world?

It was only in Louis XV's final years (1770–4) that the long decades of political drift abruptly ended with the so-called Maupeou revolution. On becoming principal minister in 1770, Chancellor Maupeou set about restoring royal authority by confronting the increasingly insubordinate parlements. He exiled the Paris magistrates en masse in early 1771, remodelled the parlement, and appointed non-venal, salaried, and revocable magistrates in their place – a novel reform that he then extended to the other parlements. The political shock it provoked was considerable, eliciting widespread criticism of ministerial 'despotism'. It divided opinion, but the reform worked quite satisfactorily until the new king, Louis XVI, decided to ditch it – and Maupeou – in 1774 in his search for political popularity. The damage was done, though, and the following years were dominated by the reverberations of the Maupeou coup.

In political terms, the years 1774 to 1789 can be seen as a sequence of contrasting efforts, led by a succession of leading ministers, to regain political control and effect the reforms needed to re-float the royal finances. The huge additional liabilities accumulated during the recent wars meant that half of the state's revenues were spent on servicing the debt. Turgot, a former provincial intendant, contributor to the *Encylcopédie* and a Physiocrat, attempted to avoid the familiar quick fixes and proposed a wide range of measures, including a universal tax, provincial assemblies, suppressing craft guilds, freeing the grain trade, and so on. Although he won royal support, he only lasted two years (1774–6), and was brought down by a combination of bread riots in towns and the threat his reforms represented to too many vested interests. His more famous successor, the Swiss banker, Necker, was far less ambitious, avoiding anything resembling structural reforms apart from Turgot's idea of restoring provincial assemblies. Necker hit the popularity jackpot in 1781 by publishing his *Compte rendu au roi*, which purported to be a 'balance sheet' of the state's finances. It proved a sensation – and a best-seller which soon shifted over 100,000 copies – since the finances were historically the king's great 'secret'. Despite being doctored somewhat to inflate Necker's own achievements, it revealed the enormous sums spent on the court generally, and especially on pensions to the royal family and courtiers.

Such publicity was unprecedented, and Necker was dismissed shortly after its appearance. But the problems remained. His successor-but-one in charge of the finances, Calonne (1783–7), was an experienced administrator convinced that the government should spend and invest in order to encourage the economic growth that would rescue its finances, but in practice he had to borrow ever larger sums to kick-start his projects. He eventually realised the need for structural changes in government, especially concerning taxes and trade. In early 1787, he convened an assembly of notables – all of them nobles, old and new – in order to circumvent the expected opposition of the parlements to his reforms. Despite being hand-picked, the notables, led by court grandees, proved far more forceful – and duplicitous – than anticipated. Calonne was obliged to reveal to them the true state of the crown's finances, a move that, despite his desperate efforts to mobilise opinion in his favour, only increased the opposition to him from all sides, precipitating his downfall in April 1787. Typically, his chief opponent among the notables, Archbishop Loménie de Brienne, not only succeeded him, but also adopted most of his reforms. He, too, faced similar opposition and when the state's credit collapsed in mid-1788 he had no option but to quit, a mere week after the decision to hold an Estates-General was finally announced. The tenth of its kind since 1559, this state bankruptcy opened up radically new perspectives.

In the decade and a half before 1789, France's governmental, political, and fiscal-economic institutions were opened up for scrutiny – and some for the scrap – in successive attempts at controlled political change from above. Provincial assemblies, for example, were on many agendas, and were mainly intended to introduce taxes (especially on land) payable by all; they were to be controlled by the nobility, as the quid pro quo of *their* acceptance of universal taxes. Such a calculation could – and did – backfire in the febrile political atmosphere of the late 1780s. The expanding agenda of change alarmed many vested interests which, by pulling the strings from behind the scenes, succeeded in blocking the projected reforms, despite approving of some of them in principle! Trapped within the monarchy's long-established 'ways of proceeding' and unable, or unwilling, to mobilise the broader support needed to pursue unwelcome measures, the chronically indecisive Louis XVI's government became increasingly isolated. But as the crisis deepened, so too were its opponents, like the parlements, who criticised its methods as despotic. Just as Calonne had envisaged an assembly of notables to bypass opposition to reform, so the nobility and the parlements played tit-for-tat in reply, insisting that only an Estates-General had the powers to consent to the sweeping reforms that Brienne was now proposing. This was a gamble that Brienne opposed but was unable to prevent. By 1788, normal ministerial government had been seriously dented, which in turn sparked an unprecedented politicisation that extended far beyond high-political circles. Ironically, it obscured certain government measures, such as the restoration of civil rights to Protestants in 1787 or the judicial reforms of 1788 (abolishing torture and other practices), which in any another other context would have been applauded for their 'enlightened' character.

## III

Few of the main players in the faction politics of the 'pre-Revolution' seem to have considered the interests or reaction of the wider population until the elections commenced. But the resurrection of the Estates-General, an archaic institution-event that nobody had any memory of, ensured that the process of politicisation both widened and deepened. As the first of a series of 20 elections or plebiscites during the Revolution, that of 1789 inevitably combined historical precedent and improvisation. Showing its establishment colours, the Paris parlement squandered its remaining political capital by insisting that the three estates – clergy, lords, and commons – remain entirely separate, thus guaranteeing that the clergy and nobility could outvote the commons. Voting by estates no longer quite mapped on to

French society in 1789. It ignored the fact that about 96 per cent of the population belonged to the third estate, yet no obvious or workable alternative was available. A half-break with historical convention, the decision to allow the commons as many deputies as the clergy and nobility together virtually invited the third estate to finish the job once the Estates-General finally met. Elections were often marred by disputes over who was a noble and who was not, while deputies from the discontented lower clergy easily outnumbered their hierarchical superiors or, in some cases, were elected by the third estate. Such friction within individual estates threatened the survival, but also proved crucial to the transformation of the Estates-General in May–June 1789.

Elections also involved the formulation of grievances and aspirations for debate and legislation. The process began in the 'primary' electoral assemblies, where 'model' texts were often circulated to prompt or structure the responses of villagers, lower clergy, or craftsmen in towns. By the time a deputy was finally elected, their demands had become an amalgamated, constituency-wide synthesis, often written up in a more abstract language by local lawyers with a smattering of Enlightenment ideas. These *cahiers* were not a blueprint for revolution, and if anything they looked backwards rather than forwards. But they did identify social targets for reform, such as seigneurial obligations, church tithes, and so on; they sought greater equality over taxation, just as the lower clergy desired a more even distribution of church wealth. Such demands echoed social animosities within or towards social groups, the clergy included. As the 1,200 deputies headed towards Versailles in late April 1789, riot and insurrection were quite independently multiplying across town and country, while censorship of publications had virtually collapsed. In January 1789, the abbé Sieyès's most influential pamphlet, *What is the Third Estate?*, appeared. His answer was extremely simple – it *is* the nation, composed of individuals free and equal under a single law, and in which groups defined by privilege, especially the nobility, could have no place. It too became a best-seller, and its author an influential deputy to the Estates-General.

The Estates-General began in early May 1789 with the third estate repeatedly attempting to persuade nobles and clergy to join it in a single assembly. But opposition from the government and nobility effectively blocked any movement until mid-June, when a trickle of defections by lower-order clerical deputies finally broke the deadlock. Eventually Louis XVI relented and ordered the nobility and clergy to join the self-styled National Assembly where voting by individuals rather than by orders was inevitable. Such clashes only fuelled ever-stronger claims from the third estate that it represented the sovereign nation, explicitly denying that it could be dissolved against its will. The assembly also repudiated older conceptions of representation under which deputies were bound by the precise terms of their individual electoral mandates; with deputies now representing the nation as a whole rather than particular constituents, they were free to think and legislate for France itself.

Such a crucial distinction, the first of many, opened new horizons, and by early July, a committee was established to draft a constitution – hence the name 'Constituent' given to the assembly which sat until September 1791. By early October 1789, it had voted the establishment of a constitutional monarchy, with the separation of powers and a 'suspensive' (rather than absolute) veto for the king over legislation. These moves were triggered by symbolically vital moments of defiance, such as the deputies' Tennis Court oath not to disperse before establishing a new constitution (20 June), the fall of the Bastille prison (14 July), and the return, under popular escort, of the court from Versailles to Paris (5 October). The Assembly itself decamped to Paris a few days later. Meanwhile, a series of municipal revolutions heralded crucial conquests of local power by 'patriots', anchoring political change in the provinces. They began in Paris, whose commune's sense of independence would become a major headache for successive revolutionary governments. No less significant was the 'great fear' that spread like wildfire during mid-1789, especially throughout the countryside. Fear of brigands and noble conspiracy led peasants to attack local landlords, their châteaux and especially 'feudal' title-deeds. Such 'emotions' in turn revived traditional urban anxieties about peasant disorders and the rapid proliferation of a National Guard on the Paris model in order to keep order. These bottom-up actions were not the last during the Revolution to either force or pre-empt initiatives from the centre.

The momentous 'night of 4 August' was one such response: it witnessed a massive, unplanned bonfire of ancient privileges that now seemed insufferable by comparison with modern liberty; noble and clerical deputies competed to renounce seigneurial rights, church tithes, private jurisdictions, *corvées*, venal offices, and so on. But there were some catches, especially where property rights were concerned. Peasants were required to buy out feudal property rights from their landlords. That proved both unworkable and provocative in the following years, especially given the grim economic conditions in rural France in the late 1780s. It was only in 1793 that a more radical regime (the Convention) scrapped 'feudalism' without compensation, a measure that took much of the steam out of continuing peasant discontent. Meanwhile, the sudden and massive sale of church and noble émigré property from 1790 onwards was a decisive step in preventing any return of a full-blown *ancien régime*. Those who acquired such lands had a vested interest in perpetuating these and other revolutionary changes. Despite being the focus for years of agronomy-obsessed elites, the peasantry were still vulnerable to familiar hardships; the transfer of church and noble lands helped the mass of poorer peasants much less than did reduced taxes and the abolition of seigneurial or church dues. Existing tenant farmers benefited rather more, and became the dominant local landowners in many localities. By comparison, the revolutionary upheaval in property did little enough to modernise or increase agricultural output; it consolidated the key structures of peasant agriculture, including old collective rights of use and access, which in turn prevented English-style enclosures and other innovations. Through the 1790s, frequent and acute food shortages undermined attempts to free the grain train. Indeed, it led to drastic measures to cap food prices and force peasants to sell their surpluses, all of which aggravated existing town-country mistrust by the early to mid-1790s.

Meanwhile, political life took off with the emergence of newspapers and political clubs well before mid-1789; the reporting of political debates and pamphleteering generally soared. Within the National Assembly, over 30 committees set to work on specific questions or acted as 'de facto' ministries. By 1793–4, a few key committees (e.g. Public Safety, General Security) were famously the nerve-centre of government itself. Despite continuing fears of Louis XVI's government using military force to suppress such insubordination, the Constituent Assembly quickly launched into an ambitious root-and-branch effort to recast what was probably Europe's most intricate machinery of government, with all its wider social and economic ramifications. While also working on a written constitution, the Assembly rapidly issued, on 26 August 1789, another unprecedented declaration – that of the rights of man and the citizen. It proclaimed equality before the law, the nation as the source of political authority, freedom of expression and religious affiliation, and respect for property. Unlike its English and American predecessors, which were both anchored in English constitutional history, this was more universalist and philosophical in inspiration; legal equality and public utility were among its central motifs. Applying such principles proved to be the most difficult in France's Caribbean colonies, with their large slave population and active slave trade. Slavery was only abolished in early 1794 after a bloody and prolonged slave revolt in Saint-Domingue (the future Haiti). The delay was also due to opposition from planters and their metropolitan trading partners, but also to considerable doubts among French legislators as to whether black slaves should enjoy the same rights as other humans. The abolition of slavery also proved short-lived, as Napoleon brutally restored it in 1802 in the vain hope of preventing the loss of Haiti through either independence (which came about in 1804) or British occupation with planter acquiescence.

Within France, the declaration implied, *inter alia*, a complete reform of the legal system, but that was just the tip of the iceberg. Over the next two years (1789–91) and under the dual banner of national regeneration and homogeneity, historic provinces, church dioceses, and a plethora of judicial, financial, fiscal, and other administrative structures were abolished; in early 1790, 83 new, smaller and more equally sized units, the *départements*, with their own subdivisions (districts and communes), were created to replace them (see Map 6). These fundamental building-blocks of modern France bore the names of mountains, seas, and rivers, so that the memory of old identities could be obliterated. In addition, the sale of office, which had done so much to shape successive generations of France's elites, was abandoned in favour of elections to office at almost every level. Municipal councils and local law-courts were gradually re-designed along similar lines; hitherto dominated by 'venal' officeholders, they were now opened up to bourgeois elites and, by the mid-1790s, even to some members of the popular classes. The notion of liberty as individual and of the nation as a single undifferentiated entity lay behind the drive to suppress forms of privilege or 'particular' status, such as guilds, corporations, religious orders, universities, and so on, that were so central to *ancien-régime* society. The same logic justified the Le Chapelier law of 1791, which outlawed collective petitions on the grounds that no association could have a political existence; it would later become notorious for effectively preventing the formation of trade unions. The criminal law, much criticised by Voltaire and others, was initially reformed by 1791 along Enlightenment lines. Dr Guillotin's new machine was adopted as the most humane instrument of execution. But the codification of civil law, hitherto a patchwork of mind-boggling diversity, inevitably took much longer. Along the way, other momentous changes were effected, such as the reconstruction and disestablishment of the Catholic church, the metric system of weights and measures, and the revolutionary calendar.

The dynamic of these years may be considered a form of cumulative radicalisation, but it did not occur in a political vacuum. Familiar and mundane problems, such as France's spiralling debts, also demanded urgent attention in 1789; the recall then of the popular Necker had failed to restore its creditworthiness. Finally, in late 1789, the National Assembly took a drastic decision to clear the debt-mountain, now bloated by earlier euphoric decisions to reimburse former holders of venal offices, military and civil, and to scrap unpopular taxes like the *gabelle* without identifying alternatives. It was decided to place church property 'at the disposition of the nation' in November 1789, with a view to selling it off; since its tithes had already

**Map 6** *The New France and its* départements, *1790*

been abolished, the state now undertook to pay for religious services, clerical salaries, charitable institutions, and so on. That decision alone placed the church under the unprecedented control of the emerging new regime. The massive sales of church (and later of émigré nobles') property that ensued were tied in to a new experiment with paper money, the *assignats*, which triggered the disaster of the 'great inflation' reminiscent of the Law experiment of 1720. When the *assignats* and their paper successor were finally scrapped in 1797, France once again reverted to metal currency.

The sell-off of church property itself preceded a far more sweeping reorganisation of the Catholic church unilaterally undertaken by the assembly. Full civic rights were granted to Protestants and (initially) some Jews, while the declaration of the rights of man refused to endorse Catholicism as the established religion. In early 1790, monastic and other orders or chapters not engaged in either teaching or charity were suppressed outright for not corresponding to contemporary notions of religious 'utility'. Monastic vows were prohibited as an offence to human liberty, a view broadly shared by the lower clergy. But the civil constitution of the clergy of July 1790 was far more comprehensive: it mapped the church's dioceses and parishes onto the new civil geography of France's *départements* and communes; it required the election, by the laity, of both bishops and parish priests, who were henceforth civil servants paid by the state. Jansenist or reformist influences hostile to features of the old-regime church contributed to both the constitution's gallican format and laity-friendly elements. Attacked for ignoring Rome and the French church itself, the constitution was reluctantly approved by Louis XVI. But it was the imposition on all clergy, from January 1791 onwards, of a specific oath of fidelity to the civil constitution that really ignited the ensuing unrest. The oath split the clergy down the middle, since refusing to take it meant that 'non-jurors' automatically lost their posts. After a long silence that left many clergy and parishioners to shift for themselves, the papacy finally denounced the constitution in April 1791. Thereafter, attitudes quickly hardened. Many clergy who had taken the oath now renounced it; most of the clerical deputies to the Constituent Assembly, even among the lower clergy, did likewise. France sleepwalked into increasingly fractious confrontation not merely between juring and non-juring clergy, but between the lay supporters and opponents of the religious settlement within localities. Town-country antagonisms resurfaced in its wake; 'activists' used force to install or evict clergy; and local variants of civil war multiplied during 1791.

The map of the acceptance and refusal of the new dispensation offers an early glimpse of the geographical differences in modern France not just over church-going and religious practice, but also over their equally enduring political repercussions. Disaffection towards the church and religious practice had already been rising before 1789, especially in cities, but the crisis over the oath revealed – and politicised – it for the first time. Most of the non-juring regions were in the peripheral provinces – Alsace-Lorraine, Picardy-Artois, Normandy-Brittany and the west generally, as well as the south-west from Béarn to the Massif Central; the juring regions were, roughly, in the 'old' central provinces extending from Reims to Bordeaux, Paris to Lyon and the south-east generally. As the non-juring phenomenon spread, a thin-skinned regime not yet used to defiance reacted punitively towards the refractory clergy. It began by depriving them of their offices and then their pension rights; accusing them of personifying 'fanaticism' and 'superstition', it soon added surveillance, suspicion of treason, imprisonment, and deportation. By mid-1793, with rebellion still on the rise in provincial France, such responses mutated into a 'stripping of the altars' and a radical de-christianisation campaign that peaked in early 1794, when the public practice of Catholicism had virtually ceased in most of France.

This campaign owed much to threats, internal and external, now faced by the Revolution, but it would have been unthinkable without the rapid proliferation during the early 1790s of an alternative, secular repertoire of rituals, symbols, and festive activities that competed fiercely with Catholic religious practices for public space; Jacobin political radicalism did the rest. However, the campaign tapered off after July 1794 with the fall of Robespierre, who had briefly tried to replace Catholicism with a cult of the Supreme Being. The first separation of church and state followed in early 1795, when the republic unilaterally repudiated the 'constitutional' church created by the Revolution and its obligations towards it. By then, far larger numbers of clergy (about 30,000) than nobility had emigrated, while almost as many 'juring' priests (22,000 out of 28,000) had abdicated (or married), voluntarily or otherwise, all of which badly affected religious practice. But the 1795 separation allowed the work of restoration, in which laypeople, and especially women, played a major part, tentatively to begin; there was, however, another bout of persecution and de-christianisation from 1797 to 1799, when it was finally curtailed by the coup that brought Napoleon to power. By 1801–2, Napoleon would bring religious peace to France, but the Humpty-Dumpty that was pre-1789 French Catholicism would never be the same again.

## IV

The conflicts sparked by the failure of religious reconstruction overlapped with, and influenced other major developments during the early

Revolution. Large numbers of nobles, led by Louis XVI's brothers, began emigrating as early as summer 1789 and sought foreign assistance to restore the absolute monarchy. The Counter-Revolution was coeval with the Revolution, each one's actions constantly influencing the other's; resistance to the new religious dispensation was but one element of that enduring two-step, even though large numbers of 'refractory' clergy and their supporters were 'anti-revolution' rather than active counter-revolutionaries. Caught in the middle and under popular surveillance within Paris, Louis XVI had reluctantly and passively accepted the Revolution's major innovations. It was his botched attempt in June 1791 to flee the country and join the émigrés – the ill-fated flight to Varennes, near the north-eastern frontier, and his ignominious 'return' under guard to Paris – that did so much to create popular republicanism. Despite that, neither the Constituent nor its successor, the Legislative Assembly (September 1791–September 1792), could bring itself to abolish the monarchy, although war on kings had been declared against Austria and Prussia in April 1792. The new and more radical Convention did so in its very first session (21 September 1792), the first day of Year I of the Republic. Having declared that 'kings are to the moral order what monsters are to nature', it defiantly burned its bridges in January 1793 by having Louis XVI and (later) Marie-Antoinette executed. Regicide made the republic a pariah across Europe, which in turn stimulated extremist politics at home.

While French political life was much affected by such developments, it had also made them possible in the first place. The Revolution emphasised citizenship as a proxy for equality, abolishing titles of address so that people could be called simply 'citizen'. Their political implications proved more difficult to determine. The liberal 1791 constitution distinguished between 'active' and 'passive' citizens. 'Passive' citizens enjoyed legal but not political rights, as many were considered too 'dependent' (servants, women) to be autonomous political actors with a stake in society. 'Active' citizens were men over 25 and paying taxes equivalent to three days of labourers' wages, who could elect local officials and magistrates, but parliamentary deputies only *indirectly*. That distinction was discarded in favour of universal male suffrage for (still indirect) elections to the 1792 Convention. By 1795, 30,000 people were actually elected, each year, to the electoral colleges, out of the 1 million people eligible for office throughout France. The assumption that politics was for men of property left little place in either category for women, despite the advent of divorce and equal inheritance rights, not to mention their activities across the social and political spectrum from salons and local clubs – militant or otherwise – and in food riots or on the barricades. Despite the best efforts of contemporary female political activists, the female iconography of *la Révolution* was not translated into official political practice. Later regimes would tinker endlessly with male suffrage, without making any concessions to women, whose continuing involvement in religious practices only hardened the negative attitudes of town-based ruling elites towards them for a long time. Napoleon's disdain for women 'meddling' in political matters as 'unnatural' was widely shared.

By the fall of the monarchy in mid-1792, the earliest political groupings based loosely on the Parisian clubs – e.g. the Cordeliers, the Jacobins, the Feuillants – had been re-shaped as political groups within the Convention, where the Jacobins and the Girondins were the most prominent. Within most cities, the new administrative 'sections' (voting wards) also became autonomous political societies where committed individuals or groups could wield decisive influence. Socially, they tended to be dominated by artisans and shopkeepers – there was no working-class at this point – but in the 1790s the sections were a real thorn in the side of the authorities; they supported radical measures against 'suspects', while also demanding price-controls and food requisitioning to counteract hoarding or price-rises. As France evolved from a would-be constitutional monarchy to a republic at war with 'despotism', such societies were often the real power within urban areas, and thus indispensable allies to Paris-based governments anxious to impose their rule nation-wide.

The shock of military defeat in mid-1792, raising the prospect of the return of the old regime, was compounded by persistent fears of conspiracy and 'enemies within'. Louis XVI was effectively dethroned by the Parisian 'crowd' (August), while large numbers of prisoners in Paris's jails were massacred as 'suspects' (September). These and subsequent acts were the outcome of 'popular' insurrections which punctuated the Revolution and showed scant respect for elected politicians, especially of the timid, short-lived Legislative Assembly. As already noted, the new Convention declared the republic (Sept 1792), while Louis XVI's execution (Jan 1793) led to an almost pan-European anti-French coalition, whose armies were soon advancing towards Paris. The mass military mobilisation (the *levée en masse*) decreed in August 1793 was designed to produce a new kind of citizen army. But it sparked anti-Jacobin urban revolts in Normandy, Bordeaux, Lyon, and Provence, which were preceded by that of the strongly Catholic west, notably the Vendée region, where a long rural revolt and deliberately brutal repression left scars still un-healed.

Such defiance brought internal political conflicts to a violent head. The hitherto dominant Girondin 'faction' was overwhelmed by their *Montagnard* rivals (June 1793), who relied on the increasingly uncontrollable popular 'sections' and the *sans-culottes* of Paris to gain, and retain, power. Having adopted the most democratic constitution so far, the Convention rapidly suspended it, proclaiming a 'revolutionary' (i.e. emergency) government for the duration of the war; by December 1793, all executive power was devolved to the Convention's committees of Public Safety and General Defence. Decentralised government was now decisively reversed. Local authorities were suspended and 'representatives on mission' despatched to the provinces to enforce the Convention's policies, especially against 'suspects' and refractory clergy, for which they relied heavily on militias (the so-called revolutionary armies) and local Jacobins; revolutionary tribunals proliferated and became increasingly efficient at identifying, sentencing, and executing suspects of all kinds. The ensuing 'reign of terror' escalated until mid-1794, held together by loose coalitions gathered around major political figures such as Robespierre, Danton, and Hébert. Despite, or perhaps because of the ensuing siege mentality, mutual suspicion was rampant within these groups: in early to mid-1794 one Convention leader after another was executed, and their supporters politically eliminated, thus weakening those still standing. Finally, it was military success against the European coalition in June 1794 that emboldened the Convention's moderate majority – and even some former 'terrorists' – to reject the rhetorical and physical excesses (about 15,000 victims of various kinds) of the still-escalating terror. With the execution of Robespierre and his allies in July 1794 began the 'Thermidorian reaction' that set about muzzling the militants and abandoning policies (food-price controls, de-christianisation, and so on) used to obtain their support.

## V

The period separating the dramatic fall of Robespierre from Bonaparte's coup d'état (1794–9) may seem an insignificant hiatus between the twin peaks of the early Revolution and the Napoleonic Empire. 'Thermidor(-ian)' has long been a generic term denoting reactionary closings-down of revolutionary conditions, mostly on behalf of scared middle classes. But the original Thermidor was just as intrinsic to the Revolution as were its glory years, while the Napoleonic odyssey that followed would have been unthinkable without it and its unexpected turns.

The task facing the post-Robespierre Convention was considerable. Economic conditions were worsening (until 1797) and compounded by growing monetary chaos. High, or rising, food prices as well as hostility towards merchants and farmers as hoarders provided a continuing basis for food riots and the political agitation that surfed on them. Consequently, it took the Convention over a year to dismantle the key elements of 'revolutionary' government, price-controls included, and purge those involved, during which the Jacobin clubs were themselves closed down; in return, it faced a number of Paris-based insurrections, which it firmly suppressed by military intervention. The problems of restoring order were far greater than that. Brigandage and lawlessness – overlapping with a widespread 'White Terror' against Jacobins and militants – were a legacy of the provincial revolts and the 'revolutionary' forms of government imposed under the Terror, so much so that the deployment of substantial army units was frequently necessary. But the post-Thermidor political vacuum proved more volatile and unpredictable. It was not resolved by the unloved Convention's decision to give way, in November 1795, to a new kind of regime that was, unwittingly, more likely to register the revival of unwelcome political movements. The Convention devised a new constitution that was less democratic than that of 1793 (but not of 1791), and insisted that two-thirds of its members be re-elected. It was just as well for the new Directory that France's armies were on the offensive against the European coalition.

The Directory, which governed France until Napoleon's coup of 1799, was so-called because the new Constitution confided executive power to five directors, one of whom was to be replaced annually. The new Constitution also innovated by opting for a 'checks and balances' – or rather a 'divide and rule' – approach by creating a two-chamber legislature to restrain the potential excesses of a single chamber; one-third of the deputies were renewable each year. But annual elections soon posed unwelcome problems, despite a very restricted electorate and a numerically minute category of 'electable' citizens. The first five Directors were all regicides, which severely limited the scope for reconciliation with royalists and conservatives generally. Yet the two elections of 1795 and 1797 clearly signalled a significant royalist-conservative upturn, to which the Directory, having secured the required military support in the shape of a young general, Bonaparte, responded with a coup (Sept 1797) annulling many 'unfavourable' elections and purging unwelcome deputies. Increasingly tough anti-émigré and anti-clerical measures followed over the next two years, alienating the Directory from much of the population. While this stemmed the royalist tide, which cruelly lacked a capable leader, it unintentionally sparked a Jacobin recovery, as the 1798 elections indicated. To this the Directory responded with another coup (May 1798), invalidating undesirable results.

By then a pattern of illegality was established in which the Directory, relying now on military rather than popular 'street' support, manipulated electoral politics, but which effectively forfeited it broader support among the electorate. That, and the increasingly widespread use of military forces, facilitated the first great 'modern' military coup, famous as that of 18 Brumaire (9 November) 1799. Its instigator was not a military figure, but one of the Revolution's great survivors and a recently installed Director, the former abbé Sieyès. His aim was to end the 'see-saw' policy of side-lining right and left by strengthening executive power within a revised constitutional framework. Having evicted three fellow-Directors in mid-1799, Sieyès was confident that he could control the military figure finally chosen as his military accomplice, Bonaparte. But the coup was nearly botched, not least by Bonaparte's own precipitation. Military intervention saved the day, thus turning a political coup into a military one, which in turn ensconced Bonaparte, and not Sieyès, as the new strongman. A month later and under a new constitution, a three-man executive was formally installed for a ten-year period, but it was the first consul, Bonaparte, who now held virtually all authority. Henceforth, elections were reduced to submitting lists of candidates to the government, which would decide who would actually serve! The legislature's authority, now spliced up between three bodies (senate, legislative body, and tribunate), was also severely diminished. The new consuls memorably declared 'the Revolution, secure in the principles with which it began, is now over'. But nobody could be certain that the revolving door of political and institutional change opened ten years previously was now firmly locked.

The rise of Napoleon is unthinkable without the wars waged by the Revolution on Europe – or rather its monarchies. Renouncing conquest per se and declaring its intention to liberate peoples held in bondage, the *élan* of the Republic's citizen armies enabled them to overcome initial setbacks and occupy much of Europe from the Netherlands through the Rhineland and Switzerland to Italy, where Napoleon won his early military spurs. Military occupation led either to new *départements* (16 by 1799) being incorporated into France, or to 'sister republics' (six in all) along the eastern borders and under the protection of the revolutionary 'great nation'. Reforms based on those of 1789 and later were introduced with the support of local 'patriots' and Jacobins from Holland to Italy. But different conditions and mentalities made some of these changes so unpopular (e.g. on religion) that they had to be diluted. In several cases, they bred open rebellion, especially in Belgium and southern Italy. On top of that, military occupation meant French armies living off the land and, consequently, increasingly ruthless exploitation.

Within France itself, mass mobilisation after 1792 led to militarisation on an unprecedented scale. Leaving aside the numbers of recruits involved, it was the arbitrary requisitioning of resources and *matériel* that really drove the re-centralisation of government forward. Military service contributed to a far more extensive politicisation of lower-class recruits than was hitherto imaginable. There was also resistance, of course, especially when conscription was formally introduced in 1798; between them, refusals to serve and high desertion rates could generate locally high levels of disorder that often overlapped with political, anti-regime violence.

Bonaparte, as a minor noble from Corsica, owed everything to the Revolution. He could not have risen in the ranks of the old royal army, the massive emigration of whose officers opened up opportunities for young, talented soldiers after 1792; he was, after all, a general by the age of 26. Like other commanders, he could scarcely avoid some involvement in revolutionary politics, either as defender or opponent of the successive regimes. Briefly imprisoned in July 1794 as a Robespierrist, he was appointed commander of the army of the interior in October 1795, only weeks after crushing a royalist rising in Paris, the first of several such interventions by him. In 1799, Sieyès initially picked another general to assist with the planned coup, only for Bonaparte's unexpected return, in a much-hyped but fabricated triumph from Egypt, to change his mind. The unplanned triumph of 'the man on horseback' would lead France in several unexpected directions thereafter. Despite the disastrous *dénouement*, the 'little corporal' remains by far the most celebrated figure in French history.

From the outset, Consul Bonaparte understood the fragility of the power he enjoyed – as the various plots to kill him also indicated – and he proved lucid and decisive in his efforts to fortify it. Regime stabilisation, on which the Directory had already embarked, was the order of the day. It was all the more urgent in 1799 as the European coalition forces were again rapidly advancing on France's frontiers from all directions. Yet the simple fact that the first ever 'national' population census was held in May 1801 suggests that something resembling normality was returning for the 27.3 million people that it recorded. The state of siege in the rebellious western areas was lifted, with an offer of amnesty to rebels there; two years later, in 1802, a similar offer was made to émigrés in return for swearing an oath of loyalty.

Extensive and often long-lasting administrative, fiscal and judicial changes, some already set in train by the Directory, were now implemented. Commenced as long ago as 1793, civil law reform was interrupted several times by regime changes, but was finally completed under Napoleon's active direction. The enormous civil code (renamed code Napoleon in 1806), with its 2,281 articles, was finally published in 1804. Still the foundation of French civil law, it was a landmark in cementing the most fundamental changes of the Revolution, especially those concerning property, contracts, inheritance, and the family. It was only possible because the Revolution had abolished the local customs and privileges that had frustrated earlier attempts at legal codification. The new code maintained individual changes such as secular marriage and divorce. Bonaparte's own misogyny, one shared by many Jacobins, still kept women out of public life and married woman as legal minors under the control of their husbands. Several other codes were completed under Napoleon, but at least two were abandoned, while a planned rural code remained too difficult to implement in a country that was regionally too diverse. As syntheses of the extensive social changes effected by revolution, these law codes were exported, with uneven results, to many French-dominated areas of Europe.

By 1797–8 the Directory had also begun draining the swamp of the state's parlous finances, defaulting on two-thirds of its debt and thus bankrupting many debt-holders. It devised new, mostly indirect taxes (including one on doors and windows), and combined old with new tax-collecting methods. Initially it lacked the personnel and infrastructure to succeed, but the consulate and empire took up the challenge with aggressive gusto, making it a test of bureaucratic effectiveness generally. Those efforts were expanded with the *franc germinal* and the quasi-state *Banque de France*, both in 1803. Such provisions facilitated economic, and especially commercial revival, so that French trade volumes rose again, particularly during periods of peace. Nevertheless, the new regime remained sensitive to food shortages and their potential for trouble, even resorting to secret cartels to manipulate prices and ensure a sufficient grain supply, especially for Paris.

The prefects who dominated French local administration until the 1980s were first introduced in early 1800 as part of Bonaparte's determination to ensure a reliable chain of command reaching down into individual *départements*. The appointment of such key figures was reserved to the first Consul, as was already the case for judges. As exclusively government men, especially in the 16 new *départments* created in Belgium and other eastern acquisitions, the prefects were quite unlike the Revolution's locally elected figures who had to combine central and local loyalties. New *arrondissements* were simultaneously created within *départements* and administered by sub-prefects. They too, like the mayors of the *communes* below them, were all government appointees. At each level, there were councils filled by (appointed) local worthies, which satisfied their desire for inclusion and distinction without giving them much influence in decision-making. Placed under a prefect and a prefect of police, the ever-suspect Paris had already lost its mayor and was sub-divided into 12 *arrondissements*, each with its own mayor. Perhaps the biggest – because previously unknown – test of the new regime was the enforcement of military conscription after 1798. The first two years saw derisory results, but under the post-Brumaire regime military necessity became such that Napoleon gradually raised the annual levy from 30,000 in 1799 to 80,000 from 1806 onwards. It was a complex process to manage, but by 1810 local administrators seem to have mastered it, except that by then it was hitting families, especially peasants, especially hard; levels of refusal to enlist and desertion rose accordingly during Napoleon's last years.

The Napoleonic reconfigurations of authority followed a logic in which the interests of the state trumped what remained of early-revolutionary aspirations to devolved government and citizen participation. Of course, those principles had often been trampled on by successive régimes since 1791, with many election results violated in one way or another, and the holding of office often rendered perilous by sudden political upheavals and purges. Such experiences, spread over a decade, opened the way for a reconstruction of the state on a different basis, that of a well-defined hierarchy. Yet Napoleon himself was no harbinger of the impersonal bureaucratic state: as his positioning of the extended Bonaparte clan made perfectly clear, personal loyalty was vital in making appointments and promotions. He insisted on appointing far more officials than even the most absolute of European rulers ever managed. The internal pacification and political stability of the consulate and empire enabled such methods to become systemic and remain firmly embedded for generations to come.

Other, bigger challenges remained. The combined threat from the second European coalition and local insurrections, especially in southern Italy, brought foreign armies perilously close to France by late 1799. Bonaparte won an arguably regime-saving battle at Marengo in June 1800, and gradually forced the coalition armies into another retreat. Peace followed with Austria in early 1801; that left England isolated, paving the way for a peace treaty in 1802. By now, France had an 'inner' *cordon sanitaire* west of the Rhine from Holland to the Swiss 'Helvetic' republic and into northern-central Italy. But Bonaparte also sought to make peace at home. Unlike the Directory, he understood the urgency of resolving the religious question; unlike the makers of the civil constitution of 1790, he negotiated with the pope rather than ignoring him. Having relaxed measures against refractory clergy, a full-blown concordat, which formally abolished the civil constitution, was agreed with the papacy in May 1801, but not published until Easter 1802. It was one-sided in that a new and heavily 'dependent' Pius VII accepted virtually all the major changes of the Revolution (e.g. the loss of church property and privileges but also civil marriage and divorce) and even that would be no formal re-establishment of Catholicism, merely a recognition that it was 'the religion of the majority of French citizens'. In return, the right to public worship was affirmed. Predictably, the Revolution's prescription of elections of clergy vanished: the first consul nominated all bishops, who in turn appointed all parish priests, a prerogative that their most autocratic predecessors could only have dreamed of. Above all, such a 'modern' hierarchy would ensure that religious affairs were in safe, controllable hands. Despite the concordat explicitly according him the powers of the king of France under the concordat of Bologna (1516), Bonaparte unilaterally added further conditions (the 'organic articles') tying the church ever more tightly to the state, of which the clergy were civil servants.

The great loser in this direct deal cut with the papacy was the historic (and actual) gallican church, whose centuries-old view of its distinctive, autonomous position within Catholicism never recovered. This did not prevent Bonaparte from confiding the administration of the concordat to a Catholic and gallican lawyer, Portalis. Although disliked by the political classes and the army, the concordat was overwhelmingly well received, deflating both anti- and counter-revolutionary affiliations; it reassured (again) those who had purchased church property since 1791. It could not prevent serious conflict between Napoleon and Pius VII (and the increasingly pro-Roman clergy of France) from 1809 onwards, during which Napoleon was excommunicated. By then, the smaller religious denominations (Calvinists, Lutherans, and Jews) were also brought, via separate agreements, under firm state control by Napoleon. It was no accident that, in November 1804, Joseph Bonaparte became grand master of the unified freemasonry of France: its members were required to swear an oath of fidelity to the laws, the government, and Napoleon himself.

From the outset, the authoritarian first consul began squeezing sources of potential opposition hard. There was real opposition to him on many issues (e.g. the imperial title in 1804) within the new legislative chambers, but it was largely eliminated during the successive elections, when pliable candidates were chosen to stand for election. Freedom of (political) expression and assembly generally were promptly restricted, partly by the use of internal passports. Most of the newspapers and similar publications that proliferated during the 1790s were rapidly closed down, especially in Paris; others were sold off to reliable pro-regime owners. The surviving papers knew that they existed under sufferance and close surveillance. By 1810, only four newspapers were published in Paris, exactly the same number as in 1789, while the *départements* were allowed only one title each. A system of ostensibly 'voluntary' pre-censorship of journals and the book trade was imposed in 1806. Given the charged character of recent French history, it is not surprising that many authors exercised self-censorship when addressing, even in fiction, the major subjects of their time. Behind all this operated an increasingly wide-ranging police ministry and spy-network, first established in early 1796 and now presided over by Joseph Fouché, one of the Revolution's most remarkable and treacherous survivors; he and his ministry were mothballed in 1802, but returned with even wider powers in 1804. Having cultivated his own image so assiduously during the 1790s, Bonaparte was never likely to underestimate the need for effective pro-government propaganda, for which he systematically used papers like the *Moniteur*. The arts, as we shall see later, would also be mobilised on a grand scale, especially under the Empire that offered them so many new opportunities. Bonaparte revived the habit, long forgotten by French monarchs, of visiting the provinces.

Bonaparte's repressive measures evinced little or no overt protest, but were accepted by the so-called blocks of granite, the term used to describe the post-revolutionary elites who now dominated provincial France; they were a mixture of bourgeois and former nobles, and based essentially on property ownership. With Bonaparte they finally glimpsed the promised land of stability and order that had consistently eluded previous regimes since 1789. Moreover, the increasingly elaborate – and novel – bureaucracy emerging after 1800 welcomed individuals with experience acquired during or before the Revolution, provided they eschewed political partisanship; given the widespread disillusion with the false dawns of revolutionary politics, that may not have been especially difficult. A re-configured society, which produced no new capitalist or working classes, was painfully emerging from the wreckage of the old regime's privileges, corporations, and special status, but political upheaval had hitherto obstructed its path. The credit for restoring stability and opportunity was banked by the new man of destiny, who was duly made consul for life in 1802, with the right to nominate his successor, before his ultimate consecration as Emperor Napoleon I in 1804. Almost inevitably, a constitutional supplement followed in 1804, reinforcing Napoleon's existing powers considerably, and setting out in some detail the role and rights of the new Bonaparte dynasty. Yet it opened with a declaration that 'the government of the Republic is confided to an Emperor who has taken the title of Emperor of the French'. When, equally inevitably, a plebiscite limited to the question of hereditary rule, confirmed the new regime, a minister congratulated Napoleon on successfully 'bringing the ship of the Republic into port'. Such apparently paradoxical views may prompt scorn in retrospect, but they suggest something of how distant Napoleonic France was from the world before 1789.

## VI

The transition after 1800 from a de facto to a de jure monarchy was gradual and did not radically alter conditions, political or otherwise, within France.

The many efforts already underway to strengthen government, and especially make it more effective (e.g. conscription, tax-collection) on the ground, as Napoleon insisted it should be, continued. Good – and sometimes bumper – harvests kept the threat of inflation and internal disorder well at bay until 1811, the year in which military conscription finally bit hard enough to provoke actual revolt. But the new regime was not limited to fixing problems inherited from the Revolution; it continued to evolve, particularly in response to the huge difficulties posed by warfare on an unprecedented scale, and thus faced new challenges. This dynamic gave it an elusive character that makes undifferentiated verdicts, especially those distinguishing a 'good' consulate from a 'bad' empire, misleading.

Even before Napoleon was crowned emperor in 1804, war had resumed with Britain and the third European coalition. Relatively fleeting during the next decade, peace, as we shall see, seemed little more than a brief interruption of war. One effect of this state of almost permanent mobilisation was a progressive ratcheting-up of the imperial character of the regime. The map of Europe was re-drawn more than once, enabling Napoleon to create satellite kingdoms for his extended family who became princes and kings in far greater numbers than any known dynasty. An element of imperial 'integration' was one outcome of this. Within France itself, a new socio-political hierarchy was in construction, partly because the upstart empire needed to compete with – and rise above – its European rivals. High-sounding titles were devised for the 'court' and its 'households', complemented by equivalent gongs for the empire. Founded in 1802, the legion of honour pre-dated the empire. Some critics feared it heralded a restoration of the pre-1789 world, but Napoleon had few qualms about decorating old-regime figures who actively served the new regime; after all, the old nobility were still the major landowners in most areas of France. Initially intended for about 5,000 people, by 1814 the legion already had a population of about 38,000 individuals, most of them retired military officers. As numbers grew, Napoleon studiously avoided declaring whether they were noble or not, but he did peremptorily reject the idea of ennobling members of the Senate to enable it to become a French House of Lords.

The imperial nobility created in 1808 was far more select. It titles (prince, duke, count, baron, and chevalier) were granted for life to high-ranking civilian and (especially) military figures, but they could be inherited if their heir possessed a *majorat* (entail) of a fixed annual revenue corresponding to the title involved. Some 200 *majorats* were created by 1814, mostly for military commanders, but not a single one of them was based on French soil, since not even Napoleon could re-create hereditary privilege there. Instead, recently confiscated estates in parts of newly conquered

Germany and the former Poland (since 1808 the duchy of Warsaw) were used to grant huge endowments to a combination of Bonaparte family members and marshals. More decisive for the future, however, was Louis XVIII's acceptance of these men in 1814, when he came to the throne, as belonging to the nobility. About three-quarters of them were born commoners, which made Louis XVIII's acceptance an enormous dividend for them. The imperial nobility was, of course, far smaller than its pre-1789 counterpart, but it grew rapidly to around 3,600 members by 1814. This, in turn, seems to have re-assured hitherto detached 'old' nobles about the direction of the Napoleonic regime; it accelerated rather than initiated a trend whereby, after 1808, a growing proportion of old nobles became prefects and other senior officials, within France and the wider empire. By 1814, almost one-quarter of the imperial nobility were themselves 'old' nobles. Long memories and conflicting political affiliations would slow down the integration of the two nobilities thereafter.

Within a modernising perspective of merit, service, and reward, it is worth considering the Napoleonic regime's record in following up the efforts of successive regimes since 1789 to re-make France's educational and cultural infrastructure. The clean-sweep abolition of religious orders (with a few exceptions) in 1790 had a major impact on French society, since the orders had run most of the schools, hospitals, and poor relief generally. Universities, academies, and comparable 'societies' were suppressed in 1793. Coming on top of the sale of church property, such measures left a huge hole in innumerable communities, big and small, at a time when the question of whether the nation's regeneration required it to assume full responsibility for educating its citizens; in theory, instruction was henceforth 'public' (a state monopoly), but that existed only on paper. The Directory provided for 'central' (secondary) schools across France, but little real progress was made on the ground. A few specialised, high-level 'schools' had existed before 1789 to train engineers, botanists, and so on; they were revived in 1794–5, while new 'élite' specialist institutions were added in subsequent years, some of which duly became the well-known *grandes écoles* (the *École polytechnique*, the *École normale supérieure*, the *École des mines*, the *Conservatoire des arts et metiers*) that still exist. But such reconstruction was piecemeal and disjointed, at a time when student numbers had collapsed. Little had come of plans for obligatory primary education, which successive regimes refused to provide free of charge.

After 1800, a full-scale reorganisation along the familiar Napoleonic lines of centralisation and hierarchy followed, focussing essentially on forming the future professionals needed by the new civilian and military establishments. In such a perspective, primary education, which the elites could easily obtain for their children, was left largely to local initiative and financial resources; with no more than 30,000 such schools in existence by 1812, it effectively returned to the hands of the Catholic church, whose parish clergy were also required to teach all pupils the so-called imperial catechism of 1806. Such a title suggests the kind of indoctrination, and especially a personalised loyalty to Napoleon I, that it involved. Most families had even fewer incentives to educate girls, who were doubly disadvantaged by a rigid refusal of mixed classes ('an abuse that cannot be tolerated'), which effectively required separate schools for girls that rarely materialised. And women teachers were banned from teaching boys. Together, such attitudes ensured only severely limited schooling for girls.

The Napoleonic regime focussed essentially on post-primary education, replacing the Directory's *écoles centrales*. In 1802, it created a network of elite *lycées*, which numbered only 37 by 1812. Over one-third of their 6,400 places were reserved for sons of military officers and civil administrators who had 'well served the Republic'; the remainder would be filled by competitive entrance examinations. A denser network of secondary-level colleges, municipal and private, taught the great majority of the 80,000 secondary pupils nationwide. But they could never match the cachet of the increasingly 'militarised' *lycées*, which were expected to effect the *triage* from which the next generation of France's elites would emerge. Above these institutions was the growing network of *grandes écoles*, which increasingly opened the door to high-level government service. Finally, university faculties of letters, law, medicine, and science, were re-constituted, but for generations they remained the poor relations of the new, specialised schools and academies. It was typical of Napoleon that an elaborate, hierarchical institution, the *Université*, complete with its grand master, rectors, and inspectors (many of them ex-clergy) was finally devised in 1808 to administer this newly revamped *instruction publique*.

# VII

Napoleon and war were inseparable until the end. An emperor who owed his status essentially to military success, he was trapped on-stage – and he knew it. A self-styled, modern Caesar or Charlemagne, he admitted that he needed ever more glory, which could only be won in battle. Unlike Europe's other monarchs he could not retire into a civilian role, for fear, *inter alia*, that a more successful commander might one day steal both his thunder and throne. Nevertheless, whatever he thought, he could have had an enduring settlement in Europe. It never came, so that he was frequently absent on lengthy military campaigns across Europe, which inevitably affected the timing and thoroughness of the successive internal policies associated with his rule. During those long absences, France was effectively run by the bureaucrats of the Council of State.

Accounts of Napoleon's campaigns have – and will continue – to fill entire libraries, not least because he epitomised a new blitzkrieg involving vast forces working to precise orders from the top. Between 1805 and 1807, two wars against successive European coalitions brought Napoleon to the pinnacle of his domination of Europe. Austria and Prussia were both humiliated, with both Vienna and Berlin occupied by French troops. The old Holy Roman Empire was first re-designed by Napoleon (1803) and then abolished entirely (1806) to be replaced by a new client-state, the Confederation of the Rhine, from which Prussia and Austria were excluded. A territorially diminished and prostrate Prussia was left to lick its wounds and conduct reforms that would make it capable of resisting France in later years. A more problematic enemy, Russia, lay further afield, whose involvement in the fourth coalition showed formidable it could be. A successful entente with Russia like that negotiated in 1807 (the treaty of Tilsit) would give Napoleon a free hand to deal with the rest of Europe. This fantasy was a critical factor in the disaster to come a few years later.

Simultaneously, but at the other edge of Europe, Portugal, and especially Spain proved a very different – because prolonged – quagmire for the Napoleonic empire. An initially successful military promenade by allied Franco-Spanish forces into Portugal in late 1807 bagged yet another kingdom for the Bonaparte tribe. But very quickly it all turned sour, provoking riots and an internal political crisis within Spain, where a defiant Cortès met in Cadiz, leading political resistance to what had quickly become a French occupation. A novel military term – *guerrilla* – entered the lexicon, while the presence of an English expeditionary force after 1808 encouraged Spanish hit-and-run defiance. Without inflicting the same immediate damage as the failure of Napoleon's invasion of Russia in 1812, the Spanish 'ulcer', as he rightly called it, immobilised substantial French resources down to early 1814. It was also one of the few wars France fought on foreign soil that did not pay for itself.

Napoleon may have said that only war sustained his authority, but it would be mistaken to think that one man's psychology engulfed Europe in ever-widening warfare after 1804. Europe's powers were as mutually suspicious as they were hostile to the upstart emperor, which enabled him to play them off against each for much of the time. But they gradually realised they needed to adapt and borrow as many of the modernising innovations of the Revolution as their anti-Revolution stance, political and social, allowed them. Britain, increasingly Napoleon's most determined opponent, was the least vulnerable of them, especially once French plans to invade from Boulogne foundered by 1805. By then, the conflict was moving to another, more 'systematic' plane with the continental blockade and continental system of 1806. The first entailed economic war with Britain, whose goods would be systematically boycotted by continental Europe. The second was conceived as an economic zone which, by excluding Britain, would enable France to recover economically from its heavy losses, not just of colonies and foreign trade, but also of domestic industrial output, since 1789. Britain and France imposed mutual blockades and tried hard thereafter to prevent neutrals from breaking them, but the post-Trafalgar French navy was simply unable to enforce such a policy, or prevent the British navy from using its superiority to its commercial advantage.

This made Napoleon concentrate on developing the continental *system* within Europe that would make the blockade effective. It was rigged to reserve French markets for French producers but expected French-dominated Europe to become an unprotected 'colonial' market for French goods. This very un-common market, and its complex internal trade rules, offered very little to client-states used to trading with Britain or needing goods from outside the Napoleonic empire. Sealing off loophole areas of Europe became a major concern, as exemplified by draconian customs regulations and, more remarkably, by the curious geography of the 'formal' empire. It led to serious mistakes, such as the final annexation of regions as far apart as the papal states, Holland and northern Westphalia-Hamburg, as well as the ill-fated invasion of Portugal in 1807. The same year a very reluctant Russia was constrained to join the French blockade, despite the damage to its massive exports of raw materials. Not surprisingly, smuggling, profiteering, and fraud were widespread, often with the complicity of high-ranking French military commanders and officials.

By 1810, much of Europe belonged to a shifting 'inner' and 'outer' French empire. As already noted, the lands along France's historic eastern frontiers, from Belgium to Savoy-Piedmont (and further southwards into Italy), were those most enduringly incorporated into France as *départements* (see Map 7). Such stability, and the prospect of its endurance, enabled the legal, social, and other revolutionary changes to be broadly implemented; critically, they also gained the support of the local elites, despite varying degrees of resistance, especially in Belgium and Piedmont. The 'outer' empire of kingdoms and client-states was far more volatile, and routinely susceptible to diplomatic horse-trading. Above all, this kaleidoscopic collection had not existed long enough for major but unpalatable changes (e.g. the abolition of seigneurial lordship resisted by local elites) to become

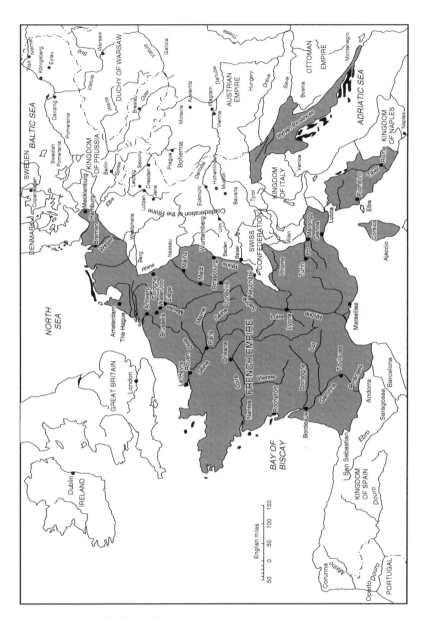

*Map 7* *The Zenith of Napoleonic France, 1811*

irreversible. By contrast, the spoils system which allowed massive plunder of France's conquests by commanders and French officials undermined attempts to endear its 'civilising' rule and its self-consciously 'superior' administrators to local populations. 'Routine' exploitation, in the form of financial and military levies for the grand empire, had the same effects. An increasingly authoritarian centre ('metropolitan' France) imposed self-interested policies, generating discontent that could easily become open unrest if things began to go badly.

The ultimate weakness of the Napoleonic edifice, but also its capacity for reaction, were revealed by the disastrous Russian campaign of 1812, which was provoked in part by Russia's exit in 1810 from the continental blockade against Britain. The vast, 600,000-strong army that invaded Russia was only one-quarter French; the remainder were supplied by annexed *départements* (one-quarter) and client-states or allies (one-half). Fatefully, 200,000 veterans troops were absent, tied down in Spain. Huge numbers died en route, especially during the retreat from Moscow, while desertion rates were also massive from the outset; only 18,000 survivors re-crossed the Russian border with the grand duchy of Warsaw in December 1812. Napoleon had himself rushed back to Paris to mobilise a new grand army to deal with the fall-out from such unheard-of defeat. But 300,000 raw conscripts short of vital military *matériel* could not replace the formidable 'grand army' over-night. As imperial overstretch became ever more evident, states that were recently either allies or neutral began defecting to the anti-Napoleon camp, an unravelling that contributed to his defeat during the enormous 'battle of the nations' at Leipzig (1813). For the first time since the mid-1790s war headed for France itself, and from virtually all sides – Wellington's English from Spain, while the Austrians, Prussians, and Russians poured across the Rhine to news (or rumours) of insurrection as well as of defection by French military commanders. Napoleon's undiminished tactical brilliance won him several time-saving victories along the way, but the relentless force of superior numbers gradually overwhelmed his armies as far as the gates of Paris. Having marched down the Champs Elysées in late March 1814 with apparently no clear idea of what to do next, the tsar of Russia and the king of Prussia were persuaded by Talleyrand – another great survivor of the Revolution – to proclaim the restoration of the Bourbons. Napoleon's former poodle, the Senate, now deposed him and accepted the proposed Bourbon restoration, while Napoleon abdicated unconditionally (6 April 1814) before departing to exile on Elba.

Less than a year later, Napoleon made perhaps the most daring – and briefest – comeback of any major political leader in history. Escaping from Elba and travelling in triumph from near Cannes to Paris (the 'eagle's flight'), he gathered the support, military and civilian, that he needed to scatter the restored but already unpopular and decidedly 'foreign' Bourbons. The famous Hundred Days that followed, during which the warm glow of imperial grandeur promised new dawns, were cut short once the allies recovered their nerve, regrouped their armies, and nailed Napoleon for good at Waterloo in mid-June 1815. This improbable interlude has perplexed many commentators, but it was a crucial episode in creating the Napoleonic myth that would prove so powerful in nineteenth-century France. Having almost completely escaped the destructiveness and exploitation of war across the Rhine and Alps and the atrocities of the Spanish *guerrilla*, metropolitan France was highly susceptible to the Napoleonic myth of grandeur, although experienced politicians, like Talleyrand and Fouché, were conscious of the folly it involved in 1815. In addition, Napoleon now promised to protect France from reactionary émigrés and the return of privilege that many people suddenly feared; such unfamiliar Jacobin-style rhetoric had a widespread and electric effect, especially among former soldiers and the lower classes generally. Napoleon knew that the elites he had done so much to create had abandoned him with few scruples in 1814 and could no longer be trusted. Yet he ultimately showed his true colours by firmly refusing to arm his civilian supporters or lead a popular revolution – a *jacquerie*, as he disdainfully called it – that might take France back to the early 1790s. The gamble failed, and there would be no return from his second place of exile, Saint Helena in the southern Atlantic, where he died in 1821.

## VIII

At its greatest extent, in 1812, the empire's population was approximately 45 million people spread across 134 *départements*. Napoleon's failure (or refusal) to negotiate terms with the European coalition in 1814–15 ensured, *inter alia*, that France's frontiers were now scaled back almost to those of 1789. Avignon, the neighbouring Comtat Venaissin, and Mulhouse did remain French, which meant two *départements* more in 1815 than in 1789. But all other annexed lands, from Belgium to Savoy and Nice, were lost. The country to which the Bourbons and the long-term émigrés returned was a curious mix of the old and the new. Its parliamentary-political institutions may have failed to withstand nearly 15 years of intensifying Napoleonic autocracy, but they did offer a potential framework for the return of the popular sovereignty so unfamiliar to the restored Bourbons, but to which Louis XVIII had to make early concessions. Governance had been radically streamlined along 'rational' territorial and hierarchical lines, and now embraced several fields (e.g. education and poor relief) that were beyond its purview before 1789. Napoleon's bitter conflict with the papacy after the occupation of Rome in 1808 revived gallican sentiments in some quarters, but also helped to trigger, as in the past, royalist stirrings in the west and south. Demographically, the protracted wars, with their repeated levies of conscripts, took their toll, hurting rural society in particular, where foreign travellers remarked on the ubiquity of the elderly and the young, especially female. France was already losing the long-standing demographic primacy that made it so feared across Europe. Its prolonged rivalry with Britain had also cost its commercial sector dearly. Its most thriving colonies were lost, especially the Caribbean islands, precipitating a severe decline in Atlantic trade and the prosperity of its major west-coast ports. France's foreign trade values of 1787 were not reached again until 1826. Partly as a result of the continental blockade, regions like Brittany and Languedoc, historically prosperous from textile production, slid gradually into economic backwardness, while industrial centre of gravity migrated inland towards the Rhône and the north-east.

Such developments, telescoped into a very short timescale, were not necessarily irreversible, but they would set many challenges for nineteenth-century France. By then Napoleon had lived out his last years on Saint Helena, re-writing recent history as an *apologia pro vita sua* and portraying himself as a far-seeing visionary. These memoirs, first published in 1823, were widely read; they were complemented by others – especially military souvenirs – that held up to France an ideal of heroic self-sacrifice in sharp contrast to the self-interest and pusillanimity of venal politicians. The emperor also fascinated the major novelists of the age – Balzac, Stendhal, and Hugo – whose works spread the Napoleon myth more effectively than historical memoirs could. By 1840, when the emperor's remains were buried with great pomp at the Invalides, the myth of Napoleon was about to take on political significance, thanks to the efforts of his nephew and 'heir', the future Napoleon III. Napoleon's fall left a political void that enabled Bonapartism to become a serious political option until the late 1880s, when the Third Republic finally side-lined it.

Napoleon's image was not confined to books. He first emerged during a decade when 'political' painting (as well as caricature) was particularly vibrant. From the outset, the neo-classical style of such painting was perfectly aligned with the oratory and political gestures of revolutionary politicians; the political dramas of the Revolution were perceived as re-enactments of (mostly) Roman precedents, especially where they pitted liberty against tyranny. Jacques-Louis David's paintings of the 1789

Tennis Court Oath or the death of Marat were only the most prominent of the deluge of 'heroic' paintings through which French culture assimilated key moments of Roman history to its own. David's famous portrait of Napoleon crossing the Alps on horseback explicitly shows him following in the footsteps of Hannibal and Charlemagne. David duly became the emperor's court painter, but many others worked to produce visual history designed to teach civic virtue. Architecture followed a similar path, especially with the erection of columns imitating Roman precedents and celebrating the illustrious dead – as was the case of the Arc de Triomphe begun in 1806. Such overkill was always likely to produce responses in the form of caricature, and Napoleon attracted his fair share of it, especially in Britain. Yet arguably the most powerful anti-dote to Napoleon-mania was the disturbing paintings and prints by Goya depicting the repression of Spanish resistance to French rule – works that were considered too dangerous to be made public until the 1860s.

For all his popularity with posterity, Napoleon's iconography needs to be kept in context – as part of the wider legacy of the Revolution. The latter created an enduring repertoire of symbols and a political vocabulary, some of whose elements remained specifically French, while others became universal – 'left' and 'right', 'old regime', 'reactionary', 'counter-revolution', 'thermidor', 'terror', and many others. Its modernity was also evident in its determination to mobilise the arts and literature to draw populations into its embrace and support its aims. For nearly two centuries afterwards, the Revolution would belong to the political present of many Europeans and non-Europeans, especially during times of political upheaval, when it seemed to many a dependable guide towards a better understanding of their own prospects.

## CHRONOLOGY

| | |
|---|---|
| 1762 | Rousseau's *Social contract* |
| 1764 | Jesuits outlawed in France |
| 1766 | Lorraine becomes French |
| 1768 | Corsica purchased from Genoa |
| 1771 | Maupeou reforms |
| 1774 | Death of Louis XV, succeeded by Louis XVI |
| 1777 | The *Journal de Paris* first daily newspaper |
| 1778–83 | French support American colonies revolt against Britain |
| 1784 | Scandal of Beaumarchais's *Marriage of Figaro* |
| 1787–8 | Assemblies of Notables; opposition to attempts at reform |

| | |
|---|---|
| 1789 | Estates-General meet, establishment of National (later Constituent) Assembly; fall of Bastille; abolition of feudal dues and privileges, declaration of rights of man and citizen; church property nationalised. |
| 1790 | Civil constitution of the clergy, followed by oath for clergy; new administrative sub-division of France into 83 *départements*; slave revolt in Haïti |
| 1791 | Papal condemnation of civil constitution; Louis XVI failed flight to Varennes; first constitution promulgated; Le Chapelier law dissolves guilds/unions; Legislative Assembly elected |
| 1792 | War with European powers; revolution of August ends monarchy; new Convention proclaims republic; trial of Louis XVI |
| 1793 | Louis XVI executed; Committee of Public Safety governs France; Vendée and other provinces in revolt; new constitution; *levée en masse* of new armies; law on 'suspects'; revolutionary tribunal; reign of terror; metric system adopted |
| 1794 | Feast of the Supreme Being; military victories; execution of Robespierre; end of 'Terror' and repression of Jacobins; amnesty offered to rebels |
| 1795 | First separation of church and state; new constitution ratified; 'White' terror in south; annexations and territorial gains in Netherlands, Rhineland, and Italy (many lost by 1799); government by five-man Directory |
| 1799 | *Coup d'état* of *Brumaire*, Napoleon Bonaparte heads 'consulate' (until 1804); new constitution |
| 1802 | Bonaparte made consul for life; concordat with Papacy promulgated; amnesty for émigrés; Legion of Honour created |
| 1804 | Civil law code promulgated; Napoleon crowned 'emperor of the French' |
| 1803–5, 1806–9, 1811–14 | Major wars with European powers, invasions of Spain and Russia |
| 1806 | Continental system (economic blockade) against Britain |
| 1808 | *Université* created to control education |
| 1814 | Defeated Napoleon abdicates, exiled to Elba; first Bourbon restoration; 'Charter' proclaimed |
| 1815 | Napoleon returns to France, seizes power during 'Hundred Days'; defeated at Waterloo; second return of Bourbons; France's frontiers of 1790 restored; Congress of Vienna settlement |

# 5 Obstructed Paths

The question of the 'true' impact of the French Revolution – was it economic, social, political, or cultural? – will doubtless continue to exercise historians, but it will not affect its wider significance as a major break in French history. For much of the nineteenth century its legacy was too immediate and divisive for such detached consideration. With some exceptions, such as the ban on associations, its main legal, social, and economic changes were widely accepted, but the threat (or fear) that they might be reversed remained alive during the generation after 1815. This chapter begins by exploring the politics of a society that, despite its profound conservatism, continued to experience revolutionary upheavals that both revived such fears and expectations and generated new political alignments and ideologies.

## I

The difficulty of finding a consensus on what post-Revolutionary society should be was most obvious in the sphere of politics, where it was epitomised by the upheavals, some of them revolutions, which produced five regime changes between 1815 and 1870 alone. Formal political rights belonged to a small minority until mid-century, but political instability and regime-uncertainty concerned a much wider population that was far more politically active, especially locally, than its European counterparts. Not until the 1870s did a republican system finally become acceptable, but only *faute de mieux* and after the search for something more reassuringly monarchical or 'presidential' had failed. Success in shedding the republic's previously debilitating association with Jacobin dictatorship and the accompanying Terror of the 1790s was a crucial factor here. Without it Georges Clemenceau could not have assured the chamber of deputies in 1891 that the Revolution was, whether they liked it or not, a single 'bloc from which nothing can be severed' and that the republic was its sole heir. The republic still had many foes, but it was what divided France the least.

Such an outcome would have seemed inconceivable in mid-1815 with the less than glorious second Bourbon restoration that followed the Hundred Days. Having adroitly declined a constitution prepared by the Napoleonic Senate, Louis XVIII issued his own constitutional charter instead, which attributed his return after a long 'absence' – not an interregnum – to divine providence. The charter was 'granted' unilaterally, not debated or voted. It affirmed full royal executive sovereignty. It also allowed for two legislative chambers, one of which would be elected; the other, the chamber of peers, constituted an element of institutionalised noble privilege. The chambers would vote laws, which could only be initiated by the king, who retained the power to determine their implementation. Yet for all its efforts to revive the past, the charter formally recognised many of the changes of the Revolution, beginning with the all-important sales of church and émigré property. Under the sub-heading of a 'public law of the French' (rather than 'of France'), a series of articles recognised equality before the law and access to military and civilian offices; freedom of conscience and opinion (as well as of publication) was also guaranteed, despite Catholicism being proclaimed as the religion of the state. Nobility, old and new, was also recognised but, with the exception of peers, it conferred no special status or privileges, fiscal or otherwise. Past opinions and voting behaviour were to remain a closed book, while military conscription was abolished outright.

Translating such a delicate balancing act from paper to practice would depend largely on how the restored monarchy and the political class viewed, and acted out, their respective parts. That there was room for conflict became apparent within a month of Napoleon's second abdication in 1815, when the royalist 'ultras' swept the boards in the elections. They were determined to revive an absolute monarchy that was both decentralised and dominated by the aristocracy – a myth if ever there was one! Meanwhile, the chamber of deputies they dominated immediately witnessed heated debates and criticisms of the restored monarchy's 'timidity'. After a year of fractious skirmishing, the 'impossible chamber', as Louis XVIII called it, was dissolved, and the ensuing elections returned a more liberal chamber. This set a pattern of alternating political swings that would recur down to 1830, but which did little to foster the kind of moderation needed to ensconce the new regime. Thus, a relatively liberal ministry governed during the years 1816–21 and again in 1825–7. The 1821 elections, held in the wake of the assassination of the heir-but-one to the throne, produced a second landslide for the ultras, enabling them to dominate politics until 1825 and again in 1829–30, by which time their agenda had reached its most reactionary pitch. Their hand had been strengthened by the accession, in 1824, of Charles X, the 'ultra' brother of Louis XVIII and the last Bourbon king of France. Meanwhile, purges of government officialdom in and after 1815 left many disgruntled individuals in the wilderness. Disaffected minorities, inside and outside of parliament, were resolute enough to weaken the legitimacy of the restoration regime. The latter's own actions, such as rejecting unwelcome election results or promoting a clericalism which returned control over education to the Catholic church, proved just as politically damaging. Indeed, it is telling that Charles X was toppled in July 1830 just when he was planning a coup to re-assert full royal sovereignty, by muzzling the press, imposing pre-publication censorship, and severely shackling an electorate that he manifestly found too liberal.

Such shifting sands reflected endemic conflicts among France's elites, since both voters and deputies in national elections had to be men of both age (40 for deputies, 30 for voters) and substance (taxes of 1,000 francs for deputies, 300 for voters), which produced a tiny electorate of just 90,000 (of whom only 14,000 were eligible) by 1830. No wonder Tocqueville called the French voters a 'little aristocracy' of landed property-owners. Efforts to (re-)fashion the electorate and the elected were hardly new, and harked back to the early days of the Revolution, with its distinction between 'active' and 'passive' citizens. In June 1830, Charles X was planning to reduce to a mere 25,000 the electors who sat in departmental 'colleges'. The July monarchy that followed would preserve such control mechanisms, but it did reduce the age-limit and tax-thresholds, thus almost trebling the electorate to 240,000 by 1846. On the other hand, over two million men were entitled to vote in restored municipal and communal elections after 1831, an incongruity that must have sharpened dissatisfaction with the arrangements for national elections, especially in the poorer *départements*. The radical shift to universal male suffrage made by the republicans in February 1848, which raised the electorate to nearly 10 million, was a European first – one that was retained by Napoleon III who, unusually for his time and in good Bonapartist tradition, saw its potential value to a controlled and plebiscitary, rather than democratic, politics. It was nearly another century before France finally granted the vote to women, which was opposed at least as vehemently on the political left as on the right.

If the rapidity of the Bourbon collapse during the July days of 1830 showed the futility of efforts to restore the world before 1789, it was not merely because so many French people opposed them. Even right-wing political figures after 1815 deprecated both kings and ministers, aired their views very publicly, and sought to strengthen the powers of the chamber of deputies. In doing so, their political culture often undercut their core conservative convictions. With political representation the preserve of prosperous landed 'proprietors' (with a handful of new-style 'bourgeois'), political docility was not easily manufactured or sustained. As a result, a political space unthinkable before the Revolution or under Napoleon was carved out and inherited by the July monarchy after 1830, which would face similar problems with its notables in due course. By 1830, Charles X and the ultras regarded such developments as a 'revolution' that had to be aborted.

However, it was not parliamentary skirmishing that broke the increasingly shrill political impasse, but an unexpected uprising of Paris artisans protesting against high prices and unemployment. Once they took to the streets and erected their barricades, other groups, such as former soldiers and members of the recently disbanded National Guard, joined them. These 'July days' of 1830 *were* a return of earlier historical action, one that would also topple the Orleanist monarchy in 1848. Charles X did not stand and fight this unexpected insurrection, partly because most of France's troops were busy conquering Algiers at that very moment. Instead, his hasty flight into exile enabled the threat of a republic to be avoided and Louis-Philippe of Orleans to be proclaimed, with the support of the liberals, king of *the French*. A new constitution was quickly produced, royal sovereignty curtailed, electoral participation broadened, the National Guard restored, and the Catholic church dis-established – all designed to deflate political unrest and secure wider liberal support for the new regime. The former émigré, Louis-Philippe, was re-packaged as a child of the Revolution, the benefits of which were, therefore, in safe hands.

## II

The reputation of the Orleanist or, to give it its usual sobriquet, the July monarchy is one of selective *laissez-faire* and growing *ennui*. The changes that it implemented in July 1830 were felt to have fixed France's major political dysfunctions, and that it would be misguided to continue tinkering with the regime. Thereafter, the time never seemed right for further reform, even when pressure for change grew in the 1840s. Such *immobilisme* was typified by Louis-Philippe's best-known minister, the historian Guizot, who allegedly replied to demands for a wider electorate by urging people to 'get rich', by which he meant joining the ranks of the higher-rate tax-payers who automatically enjoyed such political rights; political change, in this view, had to be 'organic', and not the consequence of artificial tinkering. The government also dealt harshly with protest, especially from lower-class groups, as highlighted by the reformed National Guard's brutal handling of revolt by Lyon's silk-workers in 1834–5. This in turn prompted tougher press laws and sweeping restrictions on freedom of association (1835), which curbed protest, organised or not, for over a decade. But they also spread disenchantment with the regime. They helped prevent the creation of organised political parties, and left room only for very loose groups associated with prominent individuals. As there was no real room for constructive opposition the regime was subject to little sustained pressure from within. The *ennui* produced by such an environment was best captured by Honoré Daumier's celebrated caricatures of numerous self-satisfied, *embonpoint* figures, from Louis-Philippe himself downwards to politicians, lawyers, officials, and bankers.

Once again, it was a combination of political and social grievances that caught the regime napping in 1848. A campaign of public banquets to demand a moderate extension of the franchise began in mid-1847. This unusual format for political protest – designed to circumvent the laws against free association – quickly caught on and led to several enormous meetings attracting parliamentarians and non-parliamentarians alike. As a subversive force, the banquets may have been limited, but they exposed the isolation of those in power. When the regime finally decided to ban a major banquet in mid-February 1848, the political genie finally escaped its control. Within days – 'the February days' – Louis-Philippe's government lost control of Paris, partly because the National Guard defected to the opposition. Clubs and barricades re-appeared and spread rapidly, as did numerous other revolutionary symbols and gestures. Like Charles X in July 1830, Louis-Philippe abdicated within three days and hurried into exile, but this time there was no neat 'shoe-in' of a royal successor designed to forestall further agitation. Liberal and moderate republicans from the chamber announced a provisional government, while the new self-styled 'radicals' based in the Paris town hall responded by declaring a republic. This echo of the early 1790s kicked off a bloody revolution that would reverberate around Europe during 1848, the 'springtime of the nations'. Elsewhere in Europe, revolutionaries demanded liberal 'national' or political reforms – the sort of regime that had just been overthrown in France – that the post-Napoleonic conservative regimes had long feared; rebels and insurgents looked to France as a beacon, but its bloody convulsions also reflected more specific changes there.

The 'social question' had already been looming since the conflicts and repression of the 1830s. Deteriorating economic conditions in 1845–7 further exacerbated living conditions for artisans, workers, and the poor generally, especially in a city like Paris with its soaring immigrant numbers. That and political rigidity, especially after 1830, fostered the emergence of radical and socialist thought, some of it utopian or religious in character. Until the lid was lifted in 1848, the diffusion of such ideas was limited, dispersed across isolated societies and informal gatherings. It took revolution to uncover an expanding political left, for which republicanism was a common denominator. Declaring a republic was only a *terminus a quo*, as it soon opened up divisions among radicals. The moderate socialist leader and new (de facto) minister, Louis Blanc, obtained the creation of national workshops for the unemployed from a reluctant provisional republican government, but which refused to provide the kind of actual work (rather than conventional poor relief) that Blanc had requested. Yet that and the opening of the ranks of the National Guard to lower-class recruits increasingly worried both the government and liberal republicans, who feared that more such 'social' concessions would follow. An early contest came in the April 1848 elections – the first conducted with universal male suffrage – and the result was a landslide for conservative, monarchist forces, especially in the provinces, where few radicals or socialists were elected. As a result, relations with Blanc and the socialist-radicals soon deteriorated, but it was not until after the June elections that action was finally taken to close down the workshops, which in turn triggered a popular uprising. In reply, the government conferred full emergency powers on General Cavaignac to disarm and regain control of Paris, which he quickly accomplished during the bloodbath of the 'June days' (23–26). The fear and hostility of middle-class and peasant France towards Paris was manifested by the participation of numerous volunteers from several provinces in what had become a civil and class war, whose significance both Marx and Tocqueville would underline, albeit from radically different perspectives.

This outcome confirmed the new republic's conservative direction, which duly became clear in late 1848, with the new constitution (November) and, especially, the election (December) by an overwhelming majority of Louis Napoleon, the emperor's nephew, as president of the republic. A virtual stranger to France, whose name and ideas of what Bonapartism signified had hitherto attracted little attention except jail or exile, the new president seemed to fit almost everyone's bill – order, authority, grandeur. The scale of his victory gave him invaluable political leeway, but numerous points of possible conflict between him, ministers, and an assembly based on male universal suffrage and with many radical deputies, clearly remained. In late 1851, with his and the assembly's mandate about to expire, the assembly testily denied him the right to seek re-election. Having secured the support of the army, he replied with a *coup d'état* ('Operation Rubicon') in December 1851 that the young Karl Marx made famous as *The Eighteenth Brumaire of Louis Napoleon*. Uprisings against the coup followed in several, mostly rural southern and central-eastern, regions, which would figure later among France's most stalwart republican bastions. Their protests were severely repressed and thousands of insurgents jailed or deported; there was relatively little urban lower-class involvement, even in Paris, this time round. But crucially, Louis-Napoleon appealed directly over the heads of the political class to the electorate for its approval of the coup; the result of the plebiscite was even more overwhelming than his election in 1848. A year later, in November 1852, the same method enabled the prince-president to be proclaimed Emperor Napoleon III. Such tactics were as unfamiliar as the notion, hitherto unthinkable, that the popular vote might be conservative rather than radical, though it was consonant with Bonapartist political practice. In an original combination of 'active authority and passive democracy', the Second Empire pioneered 'plebiscitary' politics in which the full apparatus of the state – from prefects to mayors and schoolteachers – was mobilised to obtain the desired outcome.

## III

The Second Empire is conventionally divided into an authoritarian and a liberal phase, with the transition occurring after 1860. But that summary is only indicative of a much more gradual evolution, especially since the formal liberalisation of the regime was delayed until 1870, when it had only months left to live. The Empire's reputation remains that of a pale shadow of the original Napoleonic epic, especially because of its inept attempts to restore France's international prestige and especially its final humiliation by superior Prussian political and military ability in 1870. Its domestic record as a 'modernising' regime may never erase this reputation, but it was both extensive and genuinely impressive, if also unfinished. Its early authoritarian years echoed Napoleon III's own position and background. Since he did not yet know or trust the great majority of the political class, some form of sedentary 'personal rule' resembling that of Louis XIV more than that of the frequently absent Napoleon I was virtually inevitable. Ministers answered to him individually rather than acting as a cabinet government; he had no liking for parliamentary politics or for political parties, even among his own supporters. One upshot of this was a greater reliance on the bureaucracy, central and departmental, with the *conseil d'état*, staffed by lawyers and proto-technocrats, playing a far greater role than any other body in government.

During the 1860s things did begin to change, partly because the emperor's increasing ill-health diminished his activity. The Second Empire was original in that became more liberal towards the end than at the beginning. Economic conditions also improved, making the spectre of hunger politics less threatening than previously. Political life altered incrementally, as a new generation of political figures, inside and outside of government, made their mark. But as memories – and perhaps fears – of 1848 receded, politicians proved less accepting of authoritarian methods. Universal male suffrage did little to alter the identity or behaviour of the elected deputies (Legitimists, Orleanists, Bonapartists, Republicans, and others) who, under the broad banner of 'the party of order', supported the regime for a variety of conflicting motives. Foreign policy choices, especially when they seemed misguided, clearly had domestic impact. Thus, the regime's handling of the 'Roman question' in relation to Italian unification alienated the most vocal and intransigent Catholics, while its free-trade treaty with Britain in 1860 upset protectionist business circles. Even the tightly shackled elected assembly, the *Corps léglislatif*, gradually became more assertive. After 1863 it boasted a modest 'opposition' of 40 deputies, while in 1869 two-fifths of the votes cast favoured opponents, both right and left, of the regime.

Compared to his immediate predecessors in similar situations, Napoleon III proved more flexible in responding to such signals. Not that he was averse to playing off different interests against each other, or seeking popular or liberal support when it suited him. Press censorship was loosened in 1867, after the liberals' Nancy programme had demanded several basic political freedoms. Such momentum was registered in the 1869 elections, which finally persuaded Napoleon III to appoint the liberal, Émile Ollivier, as prime minister. But lack of support from the republicans, who were now biding their time without much prospect of success, prevented significant immediate changes. In April 1870, the Senate approved a broadly liberal political regime, which quickly won the familiar landslide approval in a familiar Bonapartist plebiscite, but the regime fell only months later with many of its projected reforms still on paper.

This suggests that it was not domestic resistance that scuttled the Second Empire a few months later and that it might well have coped with such challenges for several more years. Napoleon III's foreign politics were, as already indicated, less successful and more regime-damaging. Post-Napoleonic Europe down to 1848 kept a wary eye on France to prevent it from disrupting the Vienna settlement of 1815. The quest for empire in North Africa, starting with Algeria in 1830, was thus a second-best option when there was relatively little room for other foreign initiatives. Until Europe's major national unifications were completed in 1870, France remained, in Paul Raynaud's later phrase, 'a giant among pygmies', but one that found exerting its weight highly divisive. The emergence of national movements across Europe after 1848 at a time when France was flying the Bonapartist flag and seeking glory abroad suggested that France's role within the continent's geo-politics would not remain passive forever. But French involvement in the unification of Italy showed how treacherous that terrain was – with radicals and Catholics at loggerheads over which side to support. Old and new political aspirations constantly collided. Territorial gain was not excluded, as Napoleon III's support for Piedmont showed: it brought Savoy and Nice (lost in 1814) into France in 1859–60. The emperor also calculated that supporting German unification in the 1860s, especially if it involved war between Prussia and Austria, would bring France similar acquisitions in the Rhineland. But the wily Bismarck quickly sensed this and successfully kept France out German politics at crucial moments before the showdown of 1870. By then, Napoleon III's reputation had been badly damaged by his highly personal decision to send a French expeditionary force to intervene in the protracted Mexican civil war (1861–7) with a view to establishing a new empire there. Such faraway debacles were, however, dwarfed by events closer to home, when Bismarck deliberately contrived to make France declare war on Prussia (July 1870) over his plans to place a Hohenzollern prince on the Spanish throne. Émile Ollivier's new liberal – in reality, relatively conservative – government was immediately driven off its reforming course, overwhelmed by the general war fever. In a campaign reminiscent of the first Napoleon, it was the Prussians who struck hard and fast, encircling all three French armies in a mere three weeks of fighting; huge numbers of besieged French soldiers surrendered, including Napoleon III himself. At Sedan alone, some 170,000 French soldiers were made prisoner. There was no recovery from such a humiliation, especially as it had been preceded by an unquestioning confidence in victory.

The war might have ended there, but Napoleon III logically declined, as a prisoner of war, to negotiate peace terms with Prussia. Only days later, on 4 September, Parisian crowds and republican deputies led by Léon Gambetta defiantly declared a new Jacobin-sounding republic, established a government of 'national defence', and began recruiting new military forces to confront the invaders. During the winter of 1870–1, the Prussians occupied most of France north of the Loire, and encircled Paris. Now based in Bordeaux, the new but deeply divided French republican government tried, but failed to break the gruelling German siege of the capital and finally sued for peace in January 1871. A truce to permit elections to be held was agreed at Bismarck's insistence, since he needed a legitimate government with which to negotiate the end of the war. A month later, the electors returned a substantial monarchist majority (400 against 150 republicans) that reflected more a desire for peace, internal as much as external, than perhaps for monarchy per se. A government headed by the veteran conservative Adolphe Thiers, who had been a kingmaker as long ago as July 1830, was established to negotiate with the new German empire, which had been proclaimed in January 1871, in the palace of Versailles itself.

The ensuing treaty annexed Alsace and the Moselle region of Lorraine to Germany and imposed a heavy war-indemnity on France, 30 of whose northern and eastern *départements* were to remain occupied by German forces until it was paid. The energetic Thiers rallied the country, paying off the indemnity two years before the deadline of 1875, thus ridding France of its German occupiers; he also began reforms, especially military, to respond to the German threat in the future. But in 1873, he was forced out of office, a victim of new manoeuvres to restore the monarchy. These efforts were themselves torpedoed by their intended beneficiary, the incorrigible Bourbon pretender, Chambord, who would not entertain any compromise with 'mere' politicians. As a result, a republic unwanted by most of its elected politicians and political elites was provisionally preserved until such time as conditions for a restored monarchy materialised. But that time never came, and the new republic's first president, MacMahon, an Orleanist by conviction, concluded that a republic governed by monarchists was the best solution – and he was not alone. What had come to stay was something that was not French and that was entirely unprecedented in French history – namely a unified Germany born on French soil and at France's expense. Moreover, its annexation of Alsace and part of Lorraine located it on the dangerously 'wrong' side of the Rhine, creating a gaping wound and poetic images (e.g. 'the blue line of the Vosges') that would obsess an entire generation down to 1914.

The most enduring memory of the demise of the Second Empire and the Franco-Prussian war was probably the brutal civil war known as the Paris commune. Since the Revolution, relations between the capital and the national authorities, civil or military, during moments of crisis were often such that almost any incident could trigger off an uprising. Confrontation was almost inevitable after the February 1871 election, when Paris voted heavily for radicals and socialists, among them the returning hero, Victor Hugo, but also for Garibaldi and Clemenceau. A month later, clashes with troops seeking to confiscate artillery pieces within the city sparked a massive insurrection and the proclamation of a revolutionary commune, one in which radical political groups, new and old, participated. Mutual provocation, incitement, and revenge killings worsened matters, leading the Thiers government at Versailles to order a full-scale military re-conquest of the city, like that of Cavaignac in June 1848. The German siege of Paris was thus succeeded by a French one, in which provincial hatred of Paris and its 'arrogant' claims to personify France was again a powerful motif. The notorious 'bloody week' of 21–8 May 1871 witnessed the biggest bloodbath of any city in European history, with upwards of 10,000 Parisians killed and perhaps another 10,000 either executed, deported to the colonies, condemned to forced labour, or imprisoned. Only the Saint Bartholomew's Day massacre remotely rivals such savagery. Subsequently, the Commune became the stuff of myth for socialists, communists, and anarchists world-wide as a model of, and a laboratory for revolution; Lenin would call it a festival of the oppressed. As in 1789, it pitted Paris against Versailles (where the Thiers government was now based), exemplifying class hatreds and their political incarnations at their most acute. Its terrible repression showed that the republic had firmly detached itself from neo-Jacobin subversion. As Thiers said at the time, 'the Republic will be conservative or it will not exist'. Similar communes were briefly declared in Le Creusot, Lyon, Narbonne, and Toulouse, but all proved short-lived. Such outcomes helped republicans subsequently to achieve the kind of electoral gains that secured the future of Second Empire's unpredicted successor, the Third Republic. Paris itself was under virtual martial law until 1876, while the government prudently waited until 1879 to return there. Enormous physical damage was done within the city during May 1871, with many of its principal public buildings torched by *communards* trying to slow down the army's progress.

## IV

If post-Napoleonic France found political stability so elusive and its political upheavals were both frequent and (increasingly) violent, it was because they reflected both changes and *blocages* within the country generally. The collapse of its empire in 1814–15 did not make France any less Europe's single greatest power (Russia excepted). It continued to be dominated by its *notables*, aristocratic and bourgeois, who made scant room for outsiders or parvenus, but who were often bitterly divided by their political affiliations. Behind the volatile political façade, less immediately visible but interlocking changes were occurring that would alter that status. The Napoleonic demographic deficit, affecting young males in particular, was quickly made up, but late marriage and growing birth-control practices, due in part to partible inheritance laws, meant that birth-rates declined during every five-year period after 1821. Overall, the population rose from 30.5 million in 1821 to 37.5 in 1871 (the acquisition of Savoy and Nice, and the loss of Alsace-Lorraine complicate the picture). The underlying trend went into reverse from mid-century onwards, just as other European societies were experiencing their strongest rates of population growth. In a century (1811–1911), France dropped from first to fifth place in that European league table. Internally, it was already experiencing the early phases of rural depopulation, via emigration to often-distant towns, a movement that would most affect a wide swathe of *départements* from Ardennes-Champagne to the south-western Landes. Meanwhile, life expectancy at birth only rose modestly between 1817 and 1881 from 39.5 to 42 years, for which high infant mortality rates, poor diet, and living conditions in most French cities were mainly responsible.

The revolutionary land redistribution did not open the road to large-scale capitalist agriculture. Most peasants remained small-holders leasing extra acres or share-cropping and operating in an environment geared largely towards self-subsistence. As late as 1884, over 85% of all holdings were below five hectares (c. 12 acres), which militated against significant productivity gains. In such an environment, credit was both hard to obtain and often usurious, while partible inheritance laws made it difficult to sustain or increase the size of holdings. Consequently, large numbers of peasants needed other non-agricultural skills or seasonal occupations – sometimes involving temporary migration – to keep themselves and their families above water. Thanks in part to the 'putting-out' system of (mainly) textile production, the economic diversity of 'peasant society' remained far greater than usually imagined, and one in which women and children were essential participants. But periods of genuine adversity, like the mid-1840s harvest failures, drove many landless labourers into the cities – or to emigrate abroad to North Africa. By the same token, rural France provided only a limited market for industrial products, for which depressed agricultural prices between 1817 and 1851 were partly responsible. It is hardly surprising, even when allowing for some rhetorical posturing, that so many of those who, from the young Victor Hugo onwards, 'discovered' the various corners of rural France, should have found it so archaic. Rural demographic pressure peaked in 1846, when three-quarters of France's population were peasants of every stripe; by 1886 that proportion had dropped, unspectacularly, to just below two-thirds. However, a declining rural population meant fewer mouths to feed 'on-site', ameliorating conditions for those who remained behind and making greater room for cash crops. Simultaneously, a trend towards direct farming came to involve four out of every five owners of land by 1880, especially in the southern and eastern regions; the corresponding drop in sharecropping and leasing to tenants made for more productive agriculture. That, and access to major new sources of grain (USA, Russia), helped terminate France's centuries-old 'crises of subsistence' forever.

Differences between country and town, rural and urban society, were less clear-cut in France for most of the nineteenth century, precisely because they were not driven by industrialisation of a classic (British) type. For example, political radicalism was as characteristic of large areas of rural

France (especially the Midi and central regions) as of urban populations by 1850 – and would remain so for generations. Since the Revolution, the criterion for a town (*ville*) was 2,000 inhabitants, a threshold that excluded a vast number of small and middling-sized agglomerations that characterised France then. As previously, many towns lived on administrative, commercial, and small-scale textile activities. Consequently, urban France accounted for only 36% of the population before the 1880s. Urban demographic growth remained relatively limited until well after 1850, with the gap between Paris and the major provincial cities further increasing. Lyon and Marseille grew to 230,000 and 200,000 inhabitants respectively by mid-century, while Paris ballooned to some 1.05 million and (thanks to its enlargement in 1860) to 1.9 million by 1872. Underlining the decline of the Atlantic seaboard, both Bordeaux and Nantes actually shrank in size between 1789 and 1836, a decline that would be reversed by new colonial adventures and growing global trade after mid-century. By then, all of France's main cities were expanding, albeit unevenly, with new industrial or commercial centres (Saint-Etienne, Roubaix, and Le Havre) proportionately outstripping their rivals. Such urbanisation sucked in ever more rural immigrants, especially women employed in domestic service with bourgeois and artisan families. But cities often housed their poorest inhabitants in hastily erected, insalubrious shacks, thus making continuing immigration essential to urban survival.

The usual assumptions about the connection between urbanisation and industrialisation in nineteenth-century Europe need to be nuanced where France is concerned. Urban growth, and its vagaries, up to and beyond 1860 were not determined primarily by industrialisation, which differed in subtly important ways to that of Britain in particular. There was no sense in competing head-on with the most advanced sectors of British industry, as many French businesses understood only too well. As we saw, Napoleon I's blockade policies skewed the historical geography of French industry, unintentionally favouring eastern and north-eastern regions. Although the volume of French industrial goods was well below that of Britain, that deficit was offset by their higher quality and value, which ensured ready access to both foreign and domestic markets. This was particularly true of textiles (mostly cotton, woollens, and silk), which constituted one-fifth of France's industrial output until the 1870s and which until then employed as many people as all the other major industries combined. Having long been dispersed and largely rural, textiles gradually – survival *oblige* – adopted first mechanisation and then concentration as pioneered by neighbouring countries. Thus, French cottons proved quite successful, despite Manchester's well-known reputation as the global 'Cottonopolis'. The linen industry avoided making such changes, but sank into decay, as did the regions (especially Brittany) associated with it. Elsewhere, while a cultural reluctance to mass-produce cheap textiles *à l'anglaise* may have affected other French industrial goods, the precocious consumerism of the affluent social groups of Paris and the main cities formed a market for well-produced goods that were the trademark of the artisan craft sector. In any case, for much of the century, protectionist tariffs obviated the need to produce more competitively priced goods, at least for the home market. They did not prevent France from remaining the world's second exporter of manufactured goods until 1870.

The building trade also became a big consumer of credit and employer of labour, thanks largely to Napoleon III's policies. The rebuilding of much of central Paris under the aegis of Baron Haussmann, prefect of Paris (1853–70), was designed to make it a capital worthy of a great empire; the enormous destruction of 1848 and 1871 made the city a vast building-site for a whole generation. The wide criss-crossing boulevards, precisely aligned house façades, street lighting, parks, sewers, and so on – all signalled a new approach to urbanism. Haussmann's critics claimed that he had only moved the city's 'dangerous' industrial districts and their population to the periphery of this 'new' Paris, but they soon returned in 1860, when much of that hitherto *extra-muros* periphery was incorporated into the city. Haussmann's approach to urban transformation was exportable, with Lyon, Toulouse, and Marseille adapting some of its key features, albeit on a more modest scale.

Meanwhile, other heavy industries, such as mining and metallurgy, followed later by chemicals and associated products, had been developing in a more classic 'industrial' format, partly because coal and iron had to be mined or worked by large workforces operating *in situ*. France's relative lack of coal deposits made it unduly dependent on imports that were expensive and required improved transport links. As the major iron and coal deposits were located in the north-eastern area that extended from Picardy to Lorraine, it became France's leading industrial region. Consequently, the German annexation of Alsace and Lorraine in 1871 was a major economic blow to France. For the rest of the century, the map of industrialised France was dominated by a 'greater' north-east (including Paris), with the similarly 'greater' Lyon-Saint-Étienne and Marseille regions as its only real – but far smaller – counterparts.

The geographical unevenness of French industrial development raises many questions. That of communications and transport is both obvious and important, given the country's size and topographical diversity. For major cities like Paris, Lyon, Marseille, and Rouen, good river communications were a historic 'given' that favoured industrial growth, as they had facilitated trade in the past. Canal-building stretched back centuries and was practiced with renewed vigour into the 1830s, when its limitations began to show. Iron deposits in a landlocked location and without a local coal supply, like the Saint-Étienne region, were of little value unless cost-effective transport could be found. Only rail transport could solve the problem, but the building of railways in France did not really commence until the 1840s, a delay that owed much to a disastrous and hugely over-budget canal-building project of the late 1830s and the conflict between the state, its engineers, and the (private) bankers that ensued. In 1842, a map-plan based on the pre-1789 'royal roads' was adopted, but it was only in the 1850s that railway-building really began to accelerate; by 1869 France possessed a recognisably national network that had risen from around 2,000 miles in 1852 to some 10,250 miles. Of course, major non-industrial activities like the wine-trade also benefited from the railways, whose freight-volumes rose six-fold during the same period. But the rail network was, not surprisingly, Paris-centred, and thus not well conceived to improve or develop lateral exchanges. Its first great failure came in 1870 when it delivered French troops on the way to fight the Prussians in the wrong places, notably Paris, producing chaos on a grand scale even before a shot was fired.

This patchiness of French industrialisation also owed something to the financial and banking world of France, which was dominated by the Napoleonic *Banque de France*. It and its shareholders – the precursors of the mythical '200 families' who supposedly governed and owned France – were too closely tied to state finance and borrowing, where yields and dividends were relatively safe, to be tempted by a more creative economic role. Likewise, private banks were slow to develop after the John Law disaster of 1720 and subsequent mishaps; over a century later, they were often closed 'clubs', dominated by family connections and 'old' money. This closed world was one factor militating against the growth of a new middle class. In this sphere, there was little prospect of loans or risk-capital materialising for the benefit of unknown outsiders, although some banks eventually invested in mining and railway development in the 1840s. Most contemporary 'start-ups' had recourse to informal sources of credit, such as local notaries, whose funds were obviously limited, but in most cases probably adequate. In fact, most of the money invested in major projects, such as France's railways before 1850, was English! Closer to the Saint-Simonian gospel of progress and modernisation than the July monarchy, Napoleon III and his government were keen to improve economic conditions. Free-trade treaties were signed with Britain (1860), Prussia (1862), and other countries, even though they were opposed, especially when slumps occurred, in a country strongly inclined to protectionism and with a powerful customs administration. Above all, the regime encouraged the formation of merchant banks such as the *Crédit Lyonnais* or the *Société Générale*. The obstacles to creating joint-stock companies were positively dissuasive until 1867, when a change in the law enabled their numbers quickly to soar. In a family-firm culture historically averse to mergers and conglomerates, explaining the relations between finance and business is a chicken-and-egg problem – was the limited demand for capital determined by small-scale production, or did the limited supply of capital render large-scale production the exception?

Such industrial structures had important implications for industrial relations, not least in ensuring that the emergence of a coherent working class would be slow and uneven. As already noted, where production was small-scale and specialised, artisans (or at least skilled workers) remained indispensable; like artisans elsewhere, they fought to maintain their established position and wages, especially when threatened by mechanisation. Their long traditions of association, epitomised by mutual-aid societies and co-operatives since the 1820s, were adaptable by new categories of workers. But in a world where most migrant workers of rural origin still aimed, often implausibly, to make enough money to return home and acquire land, a fully urbanised, second-generation working-class was genuinely slow to take shape. Nevertheless, fears of such 'dangerous classes' were already well embedded. Both Revolutionary and Napoleonic legislation outlawed association for collective bargaining, strikes included, over wages and conditions of employment; the 1810 penal code provided severe penalties for those found guilty. In particular, French liberalism mirrored the law – and especially the contemporary cult of property – in vigorously rejecting state intervention to curb the rights of owners and employers. In late 1831 and early 1834, major protests by the Lyon silkworkers caught the authorities napping, and required army intervention to restore order; similar protests spread to other cities in the south-east. Worried that such insurrections could attract support from political opponents, especially among the National Guard, the Orleanist government responded in 1835 by toughening legislation over associations and replacing fines with prison sentences for those found guilty. The bitter conflict over the national workshops in 1848 did nothing to mitigate these hostilities, as the bloody uprising of the June days showed. Subsequently, it was Napoleon III who questioned – as in the case of universal suffrage – the view that industrial workers and republicans were natural allies. In this, it probably helped that the Second Empire witnessed relatively few major industrial disputes, possibly because of improved economic conditions. In 1864, the 1791 Chapelier law on associations was replaced by new legislation recognising the right of workers to strike to improve their conditions. This reform appears to have been better received in the Lille and Alsace regions than in the Lyonnais or Paris, while its impact can be measured by the rapid rise in the number of strikes during the following years. Some of the most epic and implacable industrial disputes occurred in places like La Ricamarie (1869) or Le Creusot (1870). The workers at the latter tried to upstage Paris by declaring their own Commune in 1871.

Because of the heterogeneous character of France's industrial workforce – from fully apprenticed artisans to part-time miners-cum-farmers – its degree of organisation was limited until the later nineteenth century, when mechanisation and urbanisation pushed ahead. A wave of strikes in the 1870s and early 1880s finally persuaded the government that deploring the links between workers and socialist politics was not enough, and that if workers could have their own trade-unions, they would cast off such external influences and look to improve their members' lot. The ensuing Waldeck-Rousseau law of March 1884, authorising unions, was voted while a bitter miners' strike was in progress at Anzin, south-east of Lille, and soon rendered famous by Zola's *Germinal*. Such conflicts were potent sharpeners of class consciousness, even where they did not immediately drive up the rate of worker unionisation.

## V

In July 1873 the National Assembly authorised, on the grounds of 'public utility', the building of a Catholic basilica on the slopes of Montmartre. The spectacular Sacré-Coeur was intended as public reparation for the crimes of the Commune, but also, as some contemporary church leaders insisted, for France's wider forfeiture of religion and morality since the Revolution. Such a project – and such sentiments – was not new in the 1870s. First expressed by conservative-monarchists like Joseph de Maistre writing in the 1790s, they were subsequently adopted by people of other backgrounds startled by the bloody events of 1848 and 1871 into defending the 'moral order'. These sentiments were missing among France's Protestant and Jewish minorities, both of whom benefited from the Revolution and feared the possible consequences of a full-blown Catholic restoration. The Protestants, who then numbered about 500,000 and were still settled in the southern regions, naturally felt more relaxed under the Orleanist than the Bourbon regime, but it was not until the anticlerical Third Republic that they felt confident enough to seek careers in politics and the civil service as well as in business. Much the same could be said about the Jewish population, which rose to about 80,000 at mid-century. Their numbers buoyed up by often-poor Ashkenazy emigrés from eastern Europe, French Jewry gradually but massively drifted away from its historic peripheries (Metz and Alsace, Avignon, Bordeaux and Bayonne) towards Paris, where the majority lived by the 1880s. They too benefited from a gradual relaxation of the remaining historic restrictions on them (begun under the Revolution), and sought careers in business, but especially in public service.

In contrast, the revival of Catholicism after 1815, which the building of the Sacré-Coeur epitomised, was not merely political, but had wide social and cultural ramifications. The restored Bourbon monarchy's hatred of the Revolution was beyond doubt, but Louis XVIII's inaugural affirmation of Catholicism as the religion of the state and simultaneous recognition of individual liberty of religion showed how problematic a full religious 'restoration' was. In 1817, the Ultra-dominated chamber rejected a revision of the Napoleonic concordat because it deemed it too favourable to the church and the papacy, thus proving that gallicanism still had some life in it. Other individual measures, such as abolishing divorce, making Sunday a day of rest, and allowing revived religious orders like the Jesuits to open schools, proved a better way to meet Catholic demands post 1815. Charles X rendered the church-state affinity even more conspicuous by appointing the same man, Bishop Frayssinous, minister for ecclesiastical affairs and grand master of the *Université* (the educational system as a whole, and not just universities). Such concessions soon drew criticism, although the expulsion of the Jesuits in 1828, *inter alia*, managed to limit the openly anti-clerical timbre of the 1830 revolution. The new Orleanist monarchy deftly took things a step further, simply recognising Catholicism as the religion of the majority, but was keen to retain the controls enshrined in the Concordat. Church–state relations were henceforth more reserved, but not hostile, the effect of which was to facilitate the revival of Catholicism. For example, a new generation of Catholic intellectuals joined the growing debate on the 'social question', and especially the relations between poverty, urbanisation, and the decline of religious practice. The 1848 revolution was thus less anti-clerical than its 1830 predecessor, but its subsequent violence nudged the church leadership – as well as many of the middle-class – towards the conservative 'party of order'. Above all, Louis-Napoleon's calculated support for the Pope against revolution in Rome in 1849 rallied French Catholics, who became distinctly more pro-Roman as the century advanced. In return for its political support, the Catholic church was permitted, in 1850, to run its own secondary schools, while in 1875 the new Third Republic, still dominated by conservatives and monarchists, went further still, authorising it to open higher education institutions. These decisions, along with that taken in 1873 to build the Sacré-Coeur basilica as a matter of public utility, symbolise the gains for which the church's leadership had fought hard since 1815.

This brief sketch captures only part of the recovery of Catholicism in post-Napoleonic France. The successive regimes insisted on keeping the Concordat since it ensured state control of the church, especially when choosing its leadership, the bishops, who were overwhelmingly Bourbon-legitimist until well past mid-century. The condition of the French church 'on the ground' was far less healthy in 1815. Both dioceses and parishes had been severely reduced in numbers under the Revolution and Napoleon, but the resulting problems were as nothing compared to the collapse in the numbers of serving clergy themselves, especially since the male religious orders had been wiped out completely. Until the re-opening of major and minor seminaries after 1804, the loss of clergy was constant, with no replacements in prospect for those who died, retired, or simply abandoned the cloth. This illustrates how important lay – and especially female – efforts to sustain religious practice could be, and why independently minded laypeople might not always welcome post-1815 clericalism or manifestations of Jansenist moral rigorism. Up to 40% of parishes lacked a parish priest, especially in those areas, like the Paris basin in particular, which had not energetically resisted de-christianisation in the 1790s; such gaps remain unfilled into the 1850s in some cases. Figures like Victor Hugo and Jules Michelet grew up without any religious education, and were not alone. Newly ordained clergy only began to materialise by the mid-1810s, when the total number of diocesan clergy was 36,000, of whom two-fifths were aged over 60; they recovered thereafter to reach 47,000 in 1848 and 56,000 by 1878. Some four thousand new parishes were created between 1848 and 1878. Such round figures are only indicative. They were themselves the product of the peculiar post-revolutionary geography of French Catholicism, which would play an enduring part in French politics and cultural life thereafter, since religious affiliations (or the lack of them) mapped onto numerous other choices (e.g. Dreyfus, Vichy, de Gaulle) down to recent decades. De-christianisation, whose roots reached back before 1789, was most marked in the historic 'centre' stretching from Picardy-Champagne southwards into Burgundy and Provence in the east, and towards Périgord-Guyenne in the west. By contrast, religious practice was most entrenched in the greater 'west' (Brittany, much of Normandy and Vendée), Lorraine-Alsace, and more southern regions from the Franche-Comté to the Basque country. Within such a broad-brush, black-and-white division, innumerable local historic experiences made for a religious map that varied hugely. And, as already suggested, that variation owed much to relations of town and country, gender, and class.

Perhaps the most unexpected but most spectacular novelty down to 1880 was the sustained surge of female religious congregations, which followed from the increased involvement of women in sustaining French Catholicism after the de-christianisation campaign of the 1790s. Unlike their male counterparts, female members of orders and congregations survived the Revolutionary crisis reasonably well, especially those involved in teaching, nursing, and charitable assistance generally. While membership of male orders grew from 10,000 in 1830 to around 30,000 in 1878, that of female congregations rocketed from around 15,000 in 1815 to 30,000 by 1830, 66,000 by 1848 and a staggering 135,000 by 1878. A total of some 200,000 *bonnes soeurs* for the period 1800–80 easily outstripped the combined male clergy, secular and regular, who amounted to 85,000 around 1878. Recruiting between them some 5,000 new members yearly in the 1850s, most of the 400 female congregations were recent and uncloistered, very different from most *ancien-régime* orders in the simplicity of their structures and life-style, and heavily involved in the familiar 'social' activities, especially the teaching of girls that the state or local authorities were unwilling to take on. Their growth peaked by the 1870s, partly because alternative career opportunities were beginning to open up for women. Meanwhile, this 'feminisation of religion' had enabled women from mostly modest backgrounds to take on responsibilities, both onerous and numerous, and not otherwise available to them, especially within marriage. Yet it would be misleading to think that a life of celibacy within often authoritarian communities was the only major outlet for female religiosity before 1880. Alongside the congregations figured numerous 'third orders' and devotional confraternities, which channelled the energies of married women, while often acting as the seed-bed for vocations among girls and young women. The congregations were present above all in the regions of religious fervour, but they were flexible enough to settle in, or send their members to areas where they were needed; some of them became active as missionaries in the developing French colonial empire. Their success was due to a mixture of flexibility and effectiveness – and, of course, the real social needs they met. Such a substantial presence in towns and cities was un-missable, and by the later 1870s it was preoccupying the republican anti-clericals now in power.

The Catholicism of nineteenth-century France was influenced by numerous trends, including its feminisation. It shared some of the contemporary Romantic 'spirit' in its rejection of the rationalist intellectualism of pre-revolutionary religion, and underlined the emotional and spiritual character of Christianity. But even in the wake of the Revolutionary upheaval, shaking off entrenched Jansenist traditions, both theological and moral, was not easy. God the judge was not easily displaced by God the merciful, which meant that certain religious practices, such as frequent communion, did not catch on quickly. For that a new generation of spiritual writers and priests with a different theological training, however limited, was required. The cult of the saints was a key part of that reaction, as it facilitated a personalised spirituality. It was particularly true of devotion to the Virgin Mary, which had already soared before the apparitions at Lourdes (1858) gave it a further boost. Millet's famous *Angelus* of 1859 was a painting eminently of its time. Likewise, devotion to the figure of Christ, seen now as the suffering saviour whose heart overflowed with love for humanity, had flourished well before the decision to build the Sacré-Coeur basilica was taken. In 1861, 17% of all books published in France were religious – a proportion similar to that of the 1780s. The contemporary movement for liturgical revision across France enabled the papacy to support such 'popular' rather than 'elite' religious practices, especially as many of them were of Italian origin. None of this signified a drive towards 'private' religion, as the devotions in question frequently involved collective practices like processions, pilgrimages, novenas, and other festivals – events which were as much social as religious.

But such developments, which characterised the 'peak' of French Catholicism under Napoleon III, could cut across the demands of a revitalised church and the parish clergy emerging from the new-style seminaries. These priests were formed in a tightly controlled and closed environment; they were also under the thumb of bishops who, thanks to Napoleon, wielded far greater authority than their predecessors. Many of these new priests were from peasant and artisan rather than urban backgrounds, with few intellectual pretensions, at least in the early decades after 1800; the model 'bon curé' was to govern his parish in a manner that did not allow for expansive lay autonomy (e.g. self-regulating confraternities). One such priest, Jean-Marie Vianney (1786–1859), the barely literate *curé* of Ars in the rural Lyonnais from 1818 onwards, became a cult figure for converting his religiously detached parishioners into model Catholics. By the early 1830s, Ars had become a place of pilgrimage, and Vianney was duly canonised and declared the patron-saint of parish priests in 1905. Like thousands of other clerics, Protestant pastors included, he energetically attacked 'immoral' activities like swearing, working on Sundays, or drinking, but above all dancing – 'the source of every temptation'. Vianney also encouraged relatively simple devotions that eschewed controversy; above all, he spent countless hours in his confession-box. This new clergy insisted on parishioners taking the sacraments rather than merely attending religious services and, above all, that they confessed their sins and took communion at least once a year at Easter. However, confession and sin – especially but not exclusively, sexual sin – became a major bone of contention, as did the clergy's enduring hostility to birth-control practices. Despite Rome urging discretion and leniency on confessors, it is hard to determine, despite the example of Vianney mentioned above, how positively they responded before mid-century. At any rate, where religious commitment could be fragile, as in towns, such demands often kept people away from the sacraments; if one or more delays in absolution for sins confessed followed, they could ultimately alienate people from religion itself.

While the map of de-christianisation inherited from the Revolution was broadly static, its social contours were less so. The shock of the Revolution cured many of the pre-1789 nobility, especially the emigrés, of Voltairian free-thinking. Their religious commitment undoubtedly helped religious revival within many localities after 1815, but antagonisms between them and the Napoleonic 'notables' kept the latter at arm's length from religion; the same could be said for elements of the better-off peasantry and, as we shall see, the industrial working class. The clericalism that was criticised from the 1820s onwards also helped to perpetuate such cross-class mistrust of the church and its representatives. Such differences were also, as already intimated, a question of gender. Degrees of male religious indifference existed in some regions before 1789, but it accelerated sharply thereafter, to the point where religious practice by men could seem almost an oxymoron. Henceforth, it was only in the most intensely Catholic regions, like Brittany or the Franche-Comté, that male devotion matched its female counterpart. Elsewhere, the gap was widening, which was both cause and consequence of the efforts made by both local clergy, nuns of the new congregations, and catechists to religiously educate women and girls. Yet indifferent middle-class males readily found social and moral arguments to justify their wives and daughters practising their religion, while declining all efforts to grant them political rights.

Catholicism was simultaneously losing a substantial constituency in the towns, where the highest rates of religious ignorance, especially among the younger generations, existed around 1815. The post-Napoleonic church often lacked the means, both human and institutional, to tackle this problem head-on; the choice of preaching missions after 1815 proved a mistake, raising the hackles of non-Catholic liberals and provoking anti-clerical violence in 1830. Moreover, the process of de-christianisation could be a slow and incremental one. The towns that grew most rapidly also tended to have the poorest social infrastructures, and thus fell out of the existing religious safety net. The newer industrial towns – Le Creusot or Mulhouse – were probably worst off in this respect. On the other hand, Marseille was a strongly Catholic and royalist city that developed rapidly in this period, so that between 1850 and the 1870s it switched to democratic and anticlerical politics, as the evidence of declining religious observance, such as the baptism of children or church burial, indicates. In Paris, and especially its most industrial districts, artisans and workers showed themselves to be viscerally anticlerical in both 1848 and especially 1871. Here and elsewhere, the church's leadership was caught napping, largely because it was focussed disproportionately on restoring lost influence and prestige. Its efforts to regain a foothold in education were, as we have seen, increasingly successful between 1833 and 1875, but such gains raised ever more hackles within non-churchgoing circles, while not seriously reducing either illiteracy or religious disaffection among the poorer urban classes.

## VI

The Catholic intellectuals who 'discovered' in the 1830s and 1840s that France had a 'social question' that could not be resolved by classical forms of charitable giving, or who sought to reconcile Catholicism with the consequences of the Revolution, such as political liberalism, were not thinking in isolation. The ideas of figures like Lammenais, Lacordaire, Ozanam, or Montalembert would offer a moral basis for a form of christian socialism, but they were also directed to a broader audience. The Napoleonic regime had shackled ideas and cultural production generally within official channels, so it is scarcely surprising that an intellectual and cultural effervescence characterised the generations that followed it. In their efforts to make sense of a world still in bewildering flux, they only gradually exchanged the rationalist certitudes of the revolutionary generation for the romanticism of Goethe and Walter Scott. Chateaubriand's *Genius of Christianity* of 1802 was a precocious example of such a shift, while France was first introduced after 1814 to German romanticism by Mme de Staël, Necker's daughter. Romanticism was not a purely aesthetic movement since, as we have already seen, it also was exemplified by the emphasis within contemporary religion on its emotional and spiritual sources. Yet the continuing hegemony of classicism delayed the moment when romanticism was powerful enough to inspire poets like Lamartine, painters like Géricault and Delacroix, or historians like Michelet; the fact that many prominent romantics – Chateaubriand, Balzac, and others – were no friends of the Revolution may also have slowed the movement's progress within the intellectual establishment. But Lamartine's election to the French academy in 1829 and Victor Hugo's declaration of 1830 that 'romanticism was liberalism in literature', heralded the golden age of romanticism that would endure until 1848 and beyond. Its triumph was not universal, as architecture remained firmly impervious to non-classical impulses until the neo-Gothic appeared in the 1840s. Within music, the major figure of these years was Berlioz, but his music was far less successful in France than that of foreign composers from Rossini and Chopin to Liszt and Verdi who visited or resided in France. In music, as elsewhere, the cataloguing of 'great names' makes it too easy to forget that in their time now utterly forgotten artists and works were far more popular – from the operettas of Meyerbeer to the paintings of Horace Vernet.

With its cult of emotion and individual self-expression, romanticism rebelled against rules and reason, all of which made it an unstable quantity that could be – and often was – combined with other idioms of artistic expression throughout the century as a whole. Such cross-currents could yield unexpected results. Following the lead of Corot (1796–1875), the Barbizon school of painters of the 1830s combined realism and romanticism in their depictions of nature. In Balzac's vast portrait of contemporary French society, romanticism is irrigated by a heavy dose of social realism that hard-headed readers like Friedrich Engels esteemed, considering it essential material for social commentators and historians. This was in sharp contrast with the history, especially of the Revolution, written by Balzac's direct contemporary, Michelet, which was essentially a poetic, nation-making story of a people powerfully imagined, but which was of limited worth as history. Engels and his collaborator, Karl Marx, were not the only contemporary thinkers to regard France's uncharted political and social evolution as of world-wide importance. The recurrence of revolution in 1830, 1848, and 1871 and the radical changes that it heralded, posed a continuing challenge to social thought. But social concern did not equate to socialism, since some of the responses came from the realm of social philosophy or statistics. The enquiries of the influential proto-sociologist Le Play (1806–82) into the family structures of the working class, both French and European, bridged the gap between academic scrutiny and social reform during the Second Empire. As early as the 1820s, a sequence of more or less utopian social thinkers, who were undoubtedly influenced by the Romantics, also responded to it. Although united in their rejection of the society of their time, with its unjust and irrational distribution of power and wealth, their recipes for a new, just, and harmonious society differed considerably. The transition to such a society posed the most intractable difficulties for them, with recent experience suggesting that violent revolution was unlikely to achieve such results. Liberalism, with its emphasis on individual responsibility, was clearly not a solution, but what kind of alternative was desirable or possible? As we have already seen, a handful of 'social' Catholics like Fréderic Ozanam (1818–53) moved towards a form of christian socialism without abandoning their political conservatism. The earliest exponents of socialist thought – Saint-Simon, Fourier, Proudhon, Cabet – gathered relatively few followers; the latter frequently quarrelled once the founders had disappeared, but their ideas circulated and survived in unpredicted ways. For the most part, they did not envisage a full-scale reconstruction of society, but advocated forms of voluntary association and co-operation more characteristic of independently minded artisans rather than of a factory-working proletariat. Saint-Simon put his trust in science and social progress under a technocratic leadership, but his message was too esoteric and limited for all but a tiny chapel of intellectuals, bankers, and civil servants. Fourier imagined a harmonious relation between capitalists, managers and workers, while dispersed industry and habitat would facilitate self-regulated rather than fully egalitarian communities. Cabet proposed a classless society and common ownership of property, a goal that was to be reached by persuasion and compromise. Cabet's ideas generated most interest, but the violent revolution of 1848 persuaded him to quit France altogether and apply his ideas in America.

By contrast, something approaching a 'real-world' socialism had been developing before 1848, in direct response to the bitter conflicts and hardships since the early 1830s. Louis Blanc, who played a major role in the 1848 revolution in establishing the national workshops, envisaged worker ownership of factories which, once purchased with loans from the government, would be run as co-operatives. But such a project for state-sponsored socialism was hardly realistic in 1848 or later. Rival socialist figures like Auguste Blanqui or Pierre-Joseph Proudhon both advocated more direct and independent action. For Blanqui it should begin by seizing state power in order to redesign society. By contrast, Proudhon, a forerunner of anarchism, was hostile to state power and politics as corrupting, and advocated instead direct action 'on the ground' to achieve a socialist society. Like many others, his socialism was designed for independent artisans and their traditions of mutual aid. His indifference to politics not only hindered the diffusion of his ideas, but helped to keep the 'social' and 'political' Left apart at a time when, in 1864, Napoleon III finally authorised 'coalitions' of workers' and peaceful strikes.

Overall, it appears that the impact of the 1848 revolution was less immediate or decisive than might be imagined within the cultural and intellectual spheres. The romantic muse was weakened by the violence of revolution, but Romanticism's diffuseness prolonged its staying power, so that the realism that would characterise the generation of Baudelaire was slow to gain ground. Elsewhere, an eclectic variety styles, notably that of 'historical' painting, evolved side by side. In making the contemporary rather than the historical world around him his subject matter, the notoriously independent Courbet (1819–77) injected a strong dash of realism and naturalism into mid-century art, as did his contemporary Millet. In particular, Courbet's influence, and that of the Barbizon school generally, was important for what would become known as impressionism. The earliest impressionist works appeared after 1860, especially with Manet's *Dejeuner sur l'herbe* (1863), which was famously 'refused' by the 1863 salon judges. Well before then, the Second Empire had set about 'organising' certain aspects of French artistic life, although without imposing any preferred style of its own. The biennial (annual after 1863) salons of new paintings attracted ever more numerous exhibits. This involved a growing degree of censorship by the contemporary artistic establishment, which in 1863 provoked, with Napoleon III's consent, the anti-salon of the 'refused' paintings, numbering over 600 items. Although such an event suggests growing rejection of official canons, no dominant style emerged until the late 1870s; in previous years, early impressionist works were regularly scorned as unfinished by hostile critics. The two huge, six-month Universal Exhibitions of 1855 and 1867, modelled on that of 1851 in London, stimulated far broader cultural curiosity and exchange, since they included industrial goods and exotic natural products from around the world. Both Exhibitions were organised by Haussmann, whose rebuilding of Paris elicited a range of architectural effects, notably the heavy, monumental 'Second Empire' style, illustrated by the Paris Opera house and the new Louvre, a style which soon migrated to London and Washington. All of this seriously enhanced the status of Paris as Europe's – if not the world's – 'capital of culture'.

Despite the hostility that they often provoked elsewhere in France, especially during moments of revolution, Paris continued to attract and employ a disproportionate percentage of the country's educated elites in virtually every major sphere of activity. Its pull for ambitious and already successful young provincials – from journalists to painters and novelists – far exceeded that of the major regional cities, which they often simply bypassed. In 1876, 55% of all university students were enrolled there. Such imbalances made it all the easier to recycle the myth of the provinces as dreary cultural wastelands, the authors of which were themselves often of provincial origin. Paradoxically, these stereotypes were strongest during the early Third Republic, when provincial politicians were more independent than ever of Paris. Rather than seeking to prove or disprove the veracity of the myth in question, it would be better briefly to consider the cultural resources and capital of *la France profonde* in the days before obligatory, universal education for all.

Educational facilities were thinly spread across France until the late nineteenth century, partly because education itself was a political football throughout. From Napoleon onwards, as we have seen, France's elites largely accepted the Catholic church's involvement in educational activity, especially for girls and at primary level. The Guizot law of 1833 required every commune to have a primary school and pay a teacher, but teachers were for long miserably paid. As attendance was not obligatory, it took a long time for poorer children in both town and country to do so. In 1847, approximately 3.3 million children attended school; by 1867, when free primary schooling for all was introduced, around seven out of ten children did so. In the early 1820s an Italian and a Danish observer maintained that there was a line – the famous Saint-Malo/Geneva line – separating a literate northern and eastern France from an illiterate western and southern France. They both construed the division from statistics on schools, which indicated that 'illiterate' France comprised 54 out of 87 *départements* and 58% of the population. Fifty years later, in his 1877 enquiry into historic literacy rates since Louis XIV's reign based on the capacity of couples to sign their marriage contracts, Louis Maggiolo, a retired French school inspector, confirmed the same divide. He also found that by 1855 nearly three-quarters of urban couples signed their marriage contracts, against just over three-fifths among rural populations. Other disparities continued (women remained less literate than men), but clearly literacy rates were already rising. Undoubtedly, more accurate and comprehensive proxies for literacy could be imagined, but the required historical evidence to test them simply does not exist. Needless to say, such a divide could be – and was – presented under other headings, e.g. a more economically, but also educationally and culturally 'advanced' northern France versus a more 'backward' southern one.

Secondary education was dispensed through a combination of *lycées*, colleges, *pensions*, and minor seminaries, and was reserved for a tiny elite. The numbers attending these institutions before the 1840s were proportionally lower than before 1789. The Falloux law of 1850 succeeded where Guizot had failed in 1835, making it easier, especially for the church, to open confessional (or other independent) secondary schools. Numbers rose as a result to around 150,000 by 1880. Higher education was even more skeletal and dominated by Paris; its numbers (mostly in law and medicine) were infinitesimal, with teaching and degree-granting activities often quite separate. Only perhaps the few *grandes écoles*, essentially for engineers, offered an education that opened doors into the military and administrative elites.

An education did not yet suffice to unlock access for outsiders to the elites, social or otherwise; many desirable positions carried no salary at all. For that, other 'qualities' were required – independent means, good family connections, the right political affiliations. The successive political upheavals encouraged a cronyism that left little room for advancement for unconnected individuals. The social ideal of middle-class France was still that of the 'rentier' who lived off returns from property or other investments, and without exercising a profession. This world of departmental 'notables' was a leisure class that engaged in political and other cultural activities. The *ancien-régime* salons and provincial academies were resurrected under Napoleon, with the former enabling bourgeois or noblewomen to display their social as well as intellectual gifts. But with the political changes of the new century after 1815, salons, especially those of major business figures with political agendas, frequently formed the nucleus of political opposition, notably under the July monarchy. The more formally 'learned' academies were also revived, and from the 1820s onwards, they were flanked by over two hundred new *sociétés savantes*, whose titles and publications indicate the width of their interests – agriculture, industry, the arts and sciences and *belles-lettres*. To take one example: by 1870, Lyon had 15 such societies, of which only four were pre-revolutionary and one Napoleonic; the remaining ten appeared between 1822 and 1870, but were mostly founded in the 1860s; another 15 would follow down to 1898. The *sociétés savantes* held their first national congress in 1833 and their leading light wanted them to become the nucleus of a new, non-Parisian *Institut des provinces*, a concession that no contemporary government proved inclined to make. Most novel in this period, however, was the 'circle', an institution that was exclusively male, non-hierarchical, largely petit-bourgeois in membership, and often dominated by particular professions. More provincial than Parisian, by 1843 there were nearly 2,000 officially registered 'circles', with a substantial nation-wide membership of 122,000; cities like Bordeaux and Lyon had several such clubs, thus satisfying a range of local professional or political preferences. Escaping the domination of the aristocratic salon, the circles mostly used cafés as their meeting-places. They fostered a masculine sociability in which the reading and discussion of the newspapers and journals to which they subscribed often made them political as well as socio-cultural spaces. Such forms of sociability were adaptable to other milieux, notably the freemasons. It is also evident in the workers' associations after 1848, in which politics and self-improvement through education were central.

The fortunes of the press and the publishing world generally reflect these developments. As expected, the successive post-Napoleonic regimes were determined to keep the press under close supervision, especially whenever revolutionary interludes had blown the lid off such control. Penalties and lawsuits could damage newspapers' financial health, sometimes fatally; the financial guarantees required by the 1835 press laws were especially draconian, precipitating the demise of some well-known titles. Not surprisingly, the Second Empire kept a very close eye on newspapers. In the mid-1820s, the 13 dailies published in Paris were distributed to 60,000 subscribers nationwide, among them many reading 'cabinets' which mustered a limited 'hearing' as well as a 'reading' public. When those cabinets later became de facto libraries by allowing members to borrow papers for a modest fee, the impact of the papers was significantly wider. Although ambitious journalists gravitated towards Paris, numerous regional papers like the *Progrès de Lyon* or the *Depêche de Toulouse* became veritable institutions, and, especially under the Third Republic, powerful platforms for local political affiliations. They co-existed with a more archaic world of cheap 'popular' literature supplied for generations by itinerant pedlars. Emile de Girardin's *La Presse* of 1836 was among the first papers available for purchase cheaply and per issue. It also heralded changes that would attract a broader, especially female, readership. It contained business news, advertisements and, as a partial answer to the cost of books, the serialisation of novels by Balzac, Dumas, and many others. Interestingly, Girardin's initial ambition to eschew politics in favour of topics of interest to a wider audience, proved impossible to sustain. It would be mistaken to think that newspapers were only politically driven. Catholic newspapers such as the short-lived and liberal *Avenir* (1830–2) and especially the reactionary *Univers* (after 1840) circulated very widely, as did nearly two hundred variants of the *Religious Weekly* launched during the Second Empire. By the 1860s, the relatively new *Figaro* (1854) and *Petit Journal* (1863) were between them selling about half a million copies daily, figures that would rise further in the next decade. The simultaneous development of railways, especially under the Second Empire, enabled faster circulation, which increased the 'national' coverage at a time when titles, both Parisian and provincial, were still growing in numbers.

## CHRONOLOGY

1818     Foreign troops leave France
1821     Death of Napoleon at Sainte-Hélène
1824     Ultra-reactionary Charles X succeeds Louis XVIII; Right electoral triumph

1829    First volume of Balzac, *La Comédie humaine (les Chouans)*

1830    July Revolution; Louis-Philippe replaces Charles X; French
        conquest of Algiers; Berlioz, *Symphonie fantastique*; Stendhal,
        *Le Rouge et le noir*

1831    Franchise enlarged; National Guard reorganised; revolt in Lyon;
        Victor Hugo, *Notre-Dame de Paris*

1833    Miners on strike at Anzin; Guizot primary-school law

1834    Republican revolts in Paris and Lyon; new anti-association law

1835    Press laws tightened

1842    Plans for railway construction

1847    Political 'banquet' campaign begins

1848    February uprising, 2nd Republic proclaimed, Louis-Philippe
        abdicates; universal suffrage proclaimed, new elections; popular
        revolt of 'June days' repressed; Louis Napoleon elected president

1851    *Coup d'état*; republican insurrections suppressed

1852    Louis Napoleon proclaimed Emperor Napoleon III

1854    Crimean War

1857    Flaubert, *Madame Bovary* (unsuccessfully) and Baudelaire,
        *Les Fleurs du mal* (successfully) condemned for immorality

1860    Nice and Savoy vote to join France

1862    Victor Hugo, *Les Misérables*; Cochinchina a French colony,
        Cambodia a French protectorate (1863)

1869    Liberalisation of laws and government; Suez canal opened;
        Flaubert, *Éducation sentimentale*

1870    Franco-Prussian war; French defeat, Napoleon III abdicates;
        Republic proclaimed; Paris besieged by Prussians

1871    Armistice, German empire founded, Alsace-Lorraine annexed to
        Germany; Paris Commune proclaimed; repression of revolts;
        Thiers president of Republic

# 6  Dangers and Difficulties

*The danger has passed, now the difficulties begin*
*(Gambetta, 1879)*

I

The impact of the upheavals that punctuated French history from the fall of one Napoleon to another is most obvious within the political sphere. Each violent change of regime added to the existing roster of disgruntled, defeated 'parties' biding their time until the moment of their return to power arrived. However, as the early years of the Third Republic show, most of them had to swallow, often reluctantly, compromises with groups they thoroughly disliked in order to stave off the outcomes they feared most. Such behaviour and choices finally made a republic the lowest common denominator, but with so many supporting it *faute de mieux*, political life was also bound to remain deeply fractious, which in turn was exacerbated by the absence of real party-political organisations. Contemporaries were, to use their own vocabulary, acutely aware of the gap between the *pays légal* (the political world) and the *pays réel* (French society), behind which lay the still unresolved and bitterly disputed legacy of the Revolution itself. But political affiliations were closely entangled with many other questions, which meant rival and shifting approaches to subjects like economic development, education, the press, religion, poverty, social protest, and so on. With German unification, France's historic position as Europe's most imposing nation-state, whose past inspired nationalists and radicals across the continent, was rudely challenged. By comparison, Napoleon III's efforts to restore its past imperial glory were chimerical, and ended with France being more effectively surrounded on all sides than at any time in previous centuries. The 'accidental' Third Republic thus inherited a complex and extensive range of challenges, only some of which, as we shall see, were overcome by 1914.

The first of those challenges was existential: it concerned the Republic's own status and future, which were not finally copper-fastened until 1879. During the 1870s several political crises proved to be turning points in a republican direction, but they might just as well have gone the other way.

When the masterly Thiers was trapped into resigning in 1873, he was replaced as president by Marshal MacMahon, a well-known Bourbon monarchist. There was still widespread support, especially from the Catholic church, for MacMahon's un-concealed aim of promptly restoring the monarchy. But the Bourbon pretender Chambord's attachment to pre-1830 monarchy was so rigid as to make even monarchists, MacMahon included, blench. So it was decided in late 1873 to extend the president's term until 1880, in the hope that the monarchy would somehow return before then. However, the relatively rapid disintegration of the pro-monarchy coalition foiled such expectations. This in turn enabled the republicans to register – and preserve – some critical political gains, such as the constitutional laws of the new republic of 1875, which were duly ratified by the elections for a new National Assembly in 1876. However, as these laws were not a coherent constitution, genuine uncertainties persisted, as when the president insisted that governments were answerable to him – and, consequently, that he could dismiss them and dissolve the assembly. But MacMahon effectively lost that argument when he put it to the (electoral) test in mid-1877: the outcome established the republic as parliamentary rather than presidential in character. Equally importantly, republicans now dominated the Senate (upper house) for the first time, proof that they had gained a major foothold among the local elites which dominated that highly conservative institution. It was this patent shift that precipitated, in early 1879, MacMahon's resignation, and with it confirmation of the new politico-constitutional landscape that, with a few exceptions such as the Boulanger affair (1887–9), remained unchallenged thereafter. The 1881 elections saw republican deputies outnumber the conservatives by five to one, a result utterly unthinkable a decade earlier and one which virtually destroyed the political clout of monarchism in its various guises. Henceforth the major political differences would essentially be among republicans who were positioned across the full political spectrum as conservatives, radicals, and socialists. The successive evolutions of the radicals would be a leitmotif of the Third Republic – and later. Republican and strongly anti-clerical, they were 'an extremely contradictory, many-sided, and complicated force' which held the middle ground for generations. At a time when French political parties were mostly electoral alliances, the radicals tended to be socially conservative, with a strong preference for individualism and a limited conception of state intervention. Given they were far from united on a wide range of issues, successive radical centre-right and centre-left groups formed, atrophied, and re-formed over time. With such a history, it not surprising that they were never far from the sources of power within the republic or that a radical party was not formally established until 1901.

By 1880, regime stability had been achieved incrementally. It demon-strated for the first time that a republic was not predestined to descend into violence and, no less crucially, could even govern with moderation. On the other hand, not being able to dissolve the lower chamber and hold new elections meant that henceforth assemblies had to run their full term; political conflicts would be defused by reshuffling ministerial cabinets. The price paid for this was a bewildering turnover-rate of cabinets – nine months being their average duration – that characterised France until 1958. Memories of earlier regimes, especially that of Napoleon III, dissolving chambers and manipulating the electorate remained vivid; the outcome was a strong legislature and a weak executive. Such regular cabinet reshuf-fles seemed a price worth paying for keeping or enticing particular political groups inside the political tent (the practice of *ralliement*); political 'parties' remained flags of convenience, under which ambitious politicians could sail, rather than stable political organisations. Such fluidity could mitigate sudden moments of intense conflict, preventing them from forcing the republic 'out of port' again after 1880. But it soon provoked vehement anti-parliamentary attitudes, which frequent financial scandals involving elected politicians did nothing to deflate.

An early illustration of the new republic's stability came in the crucial years 1880–5, when the so-called moderate republican 'opportunists' gov-erned France. They aimed at embedding republican principles in society, while curbing radical social tendencies in order to rally middle-class sup-port; in approaching such issues, their yardstick was whether an action was 'opportune' or not – hence their nickname. Their leading figure was Jules Ferry, who dominated government from early 1879 to 1885 in eight successive cabinets, which included two spells as president of the council (prime minister in effect). Singularly uncharismatic (unlike his radical rivals Gambetta and Clemenceau) and heartily disliked by left and right, Ferry managed to push through several measures that would entrench republi-canism and show its fidelity to the liberal 'principles of 1789'. Lifting virtu-ally all restrictions on both the right of assembly and the freedom of the press were among the most important of them. In 1884, existing legisla-tion, including the Chapelier law of 1791, was repealed or relaxed in order to facilitate the formation of professional associations – among them trade unions. After over a decade of debate, a major reform of municipalities was also adopted in 1884. It included provision for mayoral elections rather than appointment by prefects, an under-estimated step that ushered in a major feature of modern French politics: the rise of the long-serving mayor who can simultaneously be a parliamentary deputy (the *député-maire*) and a government minister. Regularly criticised, such an accumulation of offices (*cumul des mandats*) allowed politicians with a secure local base to flourish, practise pork-barrel politics to considerable effect, and frequently dominate national politics in an age of loose political alliances. Unintentionally perhaps, the 1884 municipal reform spurred 'political' decentralisation by creating provincial rivals to Paris, which remained the only city without a mayor, appointed or elected, until 1977. Its continuing reputation for being too dangerous excluded *both* of those options. Indeed, Paris was split into 20 municipalities in 1860.

Easily the most confrontational changes of the 1880s concerned the very sensitive terrain of education. Since the Bourbon restoration, the church, as we saw, had gradually reinserted itself into education at all levels, especially for girls, and was determined to defend such hard-fought gains. Equally, nothing could rival education as a recruiter of republican anti-clericals. Indeed, by the 1870s republicans like Gambetta openly declared clericalism to be 'the enemy', because it symbolised everything that was hostile to the Revolution's legacy; the clergy's continuing pressure on parishioners to vote conservatively epitomised, in republican eyes, Catholic aversion to the new republic. By 1880, however, old-fashioned anticlericalism was itself being subsumed into a newer, more positive value-system, that of *laïcité*, which preached the gospel of a lay society with its own moral and cultural compass that was not dependent on religion. Organisations to promote the cause of *laïcité* already existed, and had growing support in republican circles, where freemasons, freethinkers, and advocates of the 'positivist' sciences (of whom Ferry was one) were increasingly prominent. The great evangelist of contemporary *laïcisme*, Ferdinand Buisson (1841–1932), began his career as a liberal Protestant philosopher, but subsequently sought to develop a non-theistic 'lay faith' which would displace christianity altogether. Equally importantly, he was among Ferry's closest advisers from 1879 onwards and the key figure in primary-education administration for decades. Two cultures, two Frances were evolving and were by now on a collision course.

But true to their 'opportunist' tag, the Ferry-dominated governments after 1879 deliberately avoided a full-scale showdown with the church and the papacy over the 1802 Concordat. Ferry believed, as did generations of republican ministers before 1905, that the concordat and its provisions, especially for the payment of salaries to clergy (Protestant and Jewish as well as Catholic), kept the churches on a leash and prevented firebrand clerical figures from attaining positions of influence within them. Instead, he set about dismantling, but only partially, the church's role in education, which also involved an attack on the religious congregations (especially of women) active in schools. Ferry insisted that this was not an attack on religion itself. Similar campaigns were then underway in neighbouring countries, from Belgium to Italy, and especially in Germany with Bismarck's anti-Catholic *Kulturkampf*. Ferry's credo was that primary education must be obligatory, free of charge, and *laïc*, and laws to that effect were passed in 1881–2. The removal of religious symbols like crosses and the discontinuation of catechism classes, were emblematic of the changes involved. Legislated for in 1880, obligatory schooling for girls was more controversial, as the sector was then entirely dominated by church schools, a condition that, according to republicans, kept women in thrall to the clergy and religious obscurantism; by teaching them morality rather than religion, the new schools would make them independent. A major consequence was the eviction from schools, followed in many cases by dissolution, of numerous hitherto 'unauthorised' congregations, male as well as female, that we encountered in the previous chapter. From 1886, the congregations could no longer teach in state schools, whose personnel had henceforth to be lay. Catholic higher education institutions remained untouched, but could no longer award degrees to their graduates.

If these measures provoked less violence than one might expect, it was because the prospect of a better education for children, especially to the age of thirteen, had much popular support. Across France, a massive 'campaign' to equip schools with properly trained teachers and with modern, secular textbooks followed, which produced some of the most indelible images of the country for future generations. From Larousse to Lavisse, rarely have so many intellectuals, philosophers, linguists, geographers, and historians been recruited by ministers, publishers, and editors, in order to re-define a nation's identity – and essentially for its children. In an atmosphere of national regeneration, France's lay, republican teachers – its 'black hussars', as Péguy called them – were mobilised to produce patriots conscious of their obligations towards their *patrie*. One of the greatest best-sellers in French history, the *Tour de France par deux enfants*, first appeared in 1878, and went through 200 editions before 1900 alone, selling eight million copies by 1914. An imaginary voyage by two young orphans from Lorraine – itself a patriotic choice – in search of a lost uncle, its purpose was to glorify the diversity and unity of France. Directing such a massive effort at cultural unification to the youngest cohort of school-attenders made good sense when it is realised that secondary and higher education remained as exclusive as ever. The continuing hegemony of a classics-dominated curriculum ensured relatively low numbers attending secondary schools, with only 128,000 students by 1913, of whom about 53,000 obtained the *baccalauréat*. Over two-thirds of the exiguous university population of 41,000 students took law and medicine degrees. Science and humanities degrees hardly existed at all before the late 1870s, since France's scientists and engineers were educated at the *grandes écoles*. By contrast, technical education and apprenticeships for young workers and overseers were woefully neglected and underfunded.

The republicanisation of France, which was the ultimate objective of the school reforms, extended well beyond government legislation, some of which was only slowly implemented. A few examples from the cascade of smaller changes from 1880 onwards show how extensive and self-conscious that effort was. The first *fête nationale* to be held on 14 July and accompanied by the *Marseillaise* as the national anthem and the *tricolore* as the national flag, was that of 1880. Sunday was also abolished as an obligatory day of rest, while divorce, banned since 1816, was reintroduced in 1884. The centenary of the Revolution was lavishly celebrated in mid-1889 with a huge international exhibition attracting nearly 25 million visitors and marked by the inauguration of Eiffel's tower. Not surprisingly, the republican chamber had already 'de-listed' the still unfinished Sacré-Coeur as an approved project of 'public utility'. Spurred by the municipal reform of 1884, the symbolic landscape of urban and village France was gradually transformed, too, by the building and decoration of town-halls, court-houses, and other public buildings bedecked with republican emblems, statues of Marianne, and so on.

The welcome given to such a neo-classical republican culture like this was, of course, not uniform across France, especially as it made scant concessions to economic, religious, and cultural peculiarities. The Saint-Malo-Geneva 'literacy line' still existed around 1900, despite shifting southwards from Geneva and towards Nice. Although overall literacy levels had risen considerably since Guizot's schools law of 1833, they remained lower in regions west of the line. Teaching in the new Republic's schools was to be exclusively in the French language, which clearly disadvantaged several such regions with their distinctive *patois*. In practice, however, not all teachers were virulently hostile to such differences; some even became enthusiasts for the cultural and linguistic regionalisms typical of Romanticism. Certain regions were also, like parts of Normandy, Brittany, and the west, ones of continuing religious fervour which ignored many of these changes: church schools continued to thrive there while their lay rivals vegetated, deprived of pupils until after World War II. In such places, the rivalry of the *curé* and the schoolteacher that symbolised so many antagonisms under the Third Republic, was to the advantage of the *curé*. French regionalism during these years was more a vehicle for protest against centralisation, negligence, or the dominance of Paris than a catechism of political separatism. This was already noticeable during the Second Empire, which considered decentralisation measures in 1870, when it was too late. By the 1890s, the new extreme right began using regionalism as a stick with which to beat the Revolution and republican centralisation, which, in their eyes, was immeasurably inferior to the pre-1789 benevolent monarchy's acceptance of provincial 'liberties'.

The new republic may have had little to fear from regionalist pressures, especially after the municipal reforms of 1884, but it found it hard to get rid of its own political demons, as a series of crises and scandals from the later 1880s to the mid-1900s demonstrate. The second half of the 1880s was dominated by the extraordinary smoke-and-mirrors saga of General Boulanger. As a reforming and belligerently anti-German war minister – 'General Revenge' he was called – during 1886–7, Boulanger became the darling of the radical republicans. Having then lost his post, he gradually mutated into an 'outsider' and 'victim' who acted as a lightning-rod for contemporary discontent with the political class. By 1888, he was demanding a revision of the constitution and new elections, something which the republicans in power adamantly opposed, because it so obviously evoked dangerous Bonapartist precedents. But Boulanger's triumphant election in 1889 as a deputy for Paris – after his election by other constituencies! – seemed to hasten just that prospect. By now, a wide spectrum of political forces, right and left, viewed him as the man on horseback who would realise their differing visions for a strong France and who would purge the political system. However, when Boulanger unexpectedly refused to storm the Elysée itself, this improbable coalition of opposites suddenly collapsed. Exposed for his links to too many causes, he fled abroad in mid-1889 to avoid being tried for conspiracy and committed suicide.

Conspirators and putchists were not about to disappear from French history, but the Boulangist episode heralded a significant repackaging of nationalist sentiment – which had hitherto been associated with the republic and the left – and shifted it to the political right. In its variously reactionary, xenophobic, and anti-semitic strands, the new-style nationalism would appeal to disaffected groups, from students to shopkeepers, whose 'leagues' became a regular feature of subsequent decades. Such a nationalist turn first became clear with the Dreyfus case in the late 1890s, by which time antagonism towards the political class had been further ramped up by a scandal in 1892 over dealings in shares of the Panama canal project. A sense of crisis was further exacerbated in the early 1890s by a spate of bombings and assassinations conducted by the most ideologically anti-parliamentary movement on the left, the anarchists; but there was little support for their tactics, and they were finally repressed by 1894. From then on, French anarchism veered towards trade union activism of a distinctive and 'direct action' kind.

Anarchism was only a minor element of the continually evolving French political left. By the 1890s socialists of various stripes had become more numerous, but were scarcely more united than the rival political stables. Their recovery after the massive repression of the Commune was gradual, boosted by the amnesty granted its participants in 1879–80. A decade or so later, an inveterate tendency to split into rival formations had produced no fewer than five socialist 'parties', only one of which was orthodox Marxist. In 1893, like the republicans twenty years earlier, the socialists made their first real electoral breakthrough, obtaining forty-nine seats; in 1898, they and the radical-socialists together harvested 131 seats, making them a growing, if not coherent parliamentary force. A year later, the first major case of socialist *ralliement* came with the nomination of the moderate Alexandre Millerand as minister. By then, the socialists had also begun to gain control of cities like Marseille, Limoges, Rennes, and Lille, which gave them substantial and often long-lasting power-bases. On the political right, the monarchists were by now a mere rump with some forty deputies, while a noisy nationalist right, with just ten deputies, first appeared in 1898. One of them, the already well-known anti-semitic journalist and agitator, Édouard Drumont (1844–1917), was elected on an explicitly anti-Jewish ticket for Algiers.

## II

The crises just mentioned, however, were small beer in comparison with the most notorious 'affair' in modern France history – the Dreyfus case. It lasted twelve years (1894–1906) in all, but was at its most politically explosive in 1898–9, in the wake of the novelist Émile Zola's famous article *J'accuse* of January 1898 in the newspaper *Aurore*. Until then, Captain Dreyfus's initial trial and sentencing, in late 1894, to deportation for life to Devil's Island for allegedly passing military secrets to Germany had attracted only limited, intermittent attention from politicians and the public alike, despite evidence gradually emerging that he had been convicted on the basis of forged documents. The Dreyfus family and their supporters' efforts to obtain a retrial and acquittal were obstructed for several years thereafter. Meanwhile, several newspapers competed to blacken Dreyfus as a Jew of Alsatian (and thus 'German') origin and, consequently, a traitor to the army and France – to the benefit of France's worst enemy. Dreyfus and, by extension, Jews in general, were spared no obloquy by Drumont and other anti-semites. Such sentiments capitalised on both recent financial scandals and historical stereotypes of Jews as hard-headed exploiters of others. When, in the wake of Zola's article, the 'affair' really took off in early 1898, the main objective of the anti-Dreyfusards was to show that French politics and state institutions were now under the barely concealed control of Jews, free-masons and related 'enemies', who had together corrupted the republic. With an enemy like Germany nearby, the honour of France's army had to be defended at all costs, and not publicly undermined because of minor peccadilloes such as the methods used to convict Dreyfus. The army in turn relied upon the support of conservative forces, new as well as traditional, to defend it. Thus, in many respects, the Dreyfus case took on a life of its own, separable from the treatment or rights of the man at its centre. Re-tried and found guilty a second time in September 1899, Dreyfus was quickly given a presidential pardon but had to wait until 1906 for his final exoneration. Rarely, even in France, has any 'affair' raised so many wider questions or divided opinion so bitterly and enduringly, despite the fact that many pro-Dreyfus intellectuals and politicians initially considered the case to be of little importance, and even a distraction. The shock to the political world was severe, with a *coup d'état* at times seeming possible. And its legacy was considerable. It included the *League for the Rights of Man* (1898) and the royalist *Action française* (1905), as well as the right-wing *League of patriots* (reformed in 1898) and the *Anti-semitic League* (reformed in 1899), led respectively by the anti-republican putschist and parliamentary deputy, Paul Déroulède, and his occasional associate, Jules Guérin.

A major casualty of the Dreyfus affair was relations between church and state, which had stabilised since the turbulence of the Ferry school reforms in 1880s. Prompted by Cardinal Lavigerie (1825–92), Pope Leo XIII had first urged French Catholics in 1891 to rally to the republic, encouraging more positive forms of social action to remedy the defects of both liberalism and capitalism. Such a call for *ralliement* appealed initially to moderates and even to conservatives worried about the rise of a socialist threat. However, it needed a period of calm and unity of purpose within French Catholicism to gain real momentum, but it got neither. Within a few years the Dreyfus affair clearly showed that Catholic priests and papers, especially the major dailies, *La Croix* or the *Libre Parole*, were among France's most virulent anti-semites. Their attacks were also directed at free-masonry, another *bête noire* of conservative Catholics, who saw it everywhere within the reigning political establishment. Because these papers also denounced the republic, the church was vulnerable to an anti-clerical, republican backlash. Such a prospect emerged especially with the impressive victory of the left coalition (the *bloc des gauches*) in the 1902 elections; by then the *laïcité* of the republic was *the* major factor uniting the left-wing parties in parliament.

The successive Waldeck-Rousseau (June 1899–June 1902) and especially Combes (June 1902–Jan 1905) governments of 'republican defence' – a telling label – both enjoyed unusual longevity by Third Republic standards. They began the task of restoring confidence in the regime by purging the army of compromised or disgruntled elements. By extension, they targeted certain Catholic schools, especially those (like the colleges run by the Jesuits) known to educate future military officers. Beyond them lay the anti-Dreyfus Catholic newspapers and their owners, the powerful Assumptionist congregation. The campaign that culminated in late 1905 with the separation of church and state began with the widely expected suppression of the Assumptionists (1900); it was followed by a 'law concerning associations' (1901), which required religious orders – and indeed, political parties – to apply for authorisation by the government. But the government of Émile Combes, a former theology student who had become one of the most rabid anti-clerical politicians of his time, simply refused to grant such authorisations. And in July 1904, even 'authorised' congregations were banned from teaching, which prompted the closure of some 2,500 schools and the emigration of thousands of members of religious orders. Yet such measures did not make the law separating church and state inevitable. Neither Waldeck-Rousseau nor, for all his rhetoric, Combes really wanted to forego the advantages of the Concordat in controlling the church; it was the radicals in parliament who outflanked both of them along the way, taking Combes' anti-papal outbursts at face value and pushing hard for separation. Indeed, by the time the law was finally debated and adopted (December 1905), Combes was no longer prime minister, but the governing coalition was still intact. Although they too lost their salaries as a result and had initial misgivings over the proposed change of status, Jewish rabbis and Protestant pastors ultimately valued the gains made under republican protection more, and felt less threatened by, the new dispensation than their Catholic counterparts.

The law of separation's statement that 'the republic does not recognise or support (financially) any form of religion' had immediate consequences for hitherto salaried clergy and church property generally. In the short run, it was the inventorying of church property – which in law was considered 'the property of the nation' – in 1906 that provoked the greatest uproar, especially in those regions which had once resisted the Revolution's religious policies. Violence erupted between police and resisters, as it had with the closure of church schools in 1903–4; the prospect of such continuing resistance eventually forced the government to make numerous concessions after 1906. However, it seems that the sale of confiscated church property mostly benefited insiders and politicians. Because the separation was also a unilateral act renouncing a bilateral treaty (the Concordat with the papacy), it had obvious implications for Rome's relations with other countries, although Leo XIII's successor, the highly conservative Pius X (1903–14), would probably have condemned it regardless. He also forbade the creation of the parochial 'religious associations' that were expected to take stewardship of church property henceforth; it was not until 1924 that this major difficulty was overcome under a less intransigent pope. More broadly, the reversal of papal policy since Leo XIII's death in 1903 wreaked havoc on previous attempts at *ralliement*, sowing confusion and division within French Catholicism at a critical time. It was also part of a wider *Kulturkampf* within Catholicism itself. Pius X attacked the dreaded 'modernism' of those Catholic intellectuals and theologians who, across Europe and America, were attempting to re-think religious culture itself in the light of new forms of scholarship and scientific thinking, while also preparing to accept modern social change. Both were anathema to him and fellow conservative Catholics. The two extensive papal condemnations of modernism delivered in 1907 were to leave French Catholic intellectual life badly hamstrung for decades. Because of its scope, this counter-attack hit 'collateral' targets, such as the energetic French *Sillon* movement campaigning for social justice, which was condemned outright in 1910. Despite the earlier encouragement of Leo XIII's *Rerum Novarum* (1893), the *Sillon* and other efforts to develop forms of christian democracy remained deeply suspect, whereas the hyper-nationalist, royalist *Action française*, founded during the crisis in 1905, seemed more in tune with the embattled mind-set of contemporary Catholicism. Finally, with the scrapping of the Concordat came the unexpected prospect of unprecedented papal control over the French church. It was Rome that could now chose and promote the French church's leaders, and thus erode what remained of its gallican independence.

## III

Well before the 1900s, contemporary commentators were acutely aware that while the newly united Germany was powering forward, demographically and industrially, post-1870 France was falling behind its new and fiercest rival. As we have already seen, population growth slowed, with the exception of the strongly Catholic regions. The French middle class was Europe's most Malthusian, the most obvious effect of which was that France only managed a 2.5 million against Germany's 25 million population increase between 1870 and 1914! Mortality rates remained high until vaccination for adults against the major killers – like smallpox – became available around 1900 and later. Growing longevity meant an increasingly inactive population and thus the need, once the economy began to recover during the late 1890s, for foreign immigrants, who represented 3% of the population by 1911. Belgians, Spaniards, and Italians were the most numerous among them and virtually all were unskilled labourers. France's rural population remained relatively high for much longer than in England or Germany, which, of course, facilitated labour-intensive farming but kept living standards and purchasing power there relatively low. The major regions remained faithful to their pasts, with large-scale mechanised agriculture expanding, especially northwards, from the Paris basin, with the small-scale and labour-intensive approach surviving in the west and the Midi. A new ministry of Agriculture was created in 1880 to encourage modern practices, with a specialised bank, the *Crédit Agricole* following in 1894, but the gospel of agrarian improvement was diffused mainly by the co-operatives down to 1914. Indeed, co-operatives played a major part in extending and structuring the politicisation of the peasantry, especially in western and southern regions, where conservative landowners and 'republicans' created rival organisations for that purpose.

From 1873 to 1896, rural France experienced an extended agricultural slump, punctuated by several disastrous harvests, which reduced overall agricultural output by nearly 30%. It was not until 1909 that the output figures of 1869–70 were again reached. During the early years, cheap foreign imports flooded into France, undercutting existing prices-levels and putting small French farmers under severe pressure until protectionist laws, introduced in the mid-1880s, gradually reversed the trend. Above all, phylloxera, a disease caused by aphids that first struck in 1863, was to devastate virtually every French vineyard for over forty years until new resistant vines from America could be planted and come into production. Between 1875 and 1889 alone French wine-production plunged by three-quarters. This hit small *vignerons*, labourers, and the ancillary trades across entire regions particularly hard, since they were the least capable of bearing the loss of earnings or the costs of re-planting the vineyards. The contemporary disappearance of long-standing rural industries, which made many areas de facto mono-cultural, disrupted the historical economic equilibrium of communities as well as traditional town-country relations; it also deprived families, especially women and children, of work and extra income. Some of the most violent protests of the years before 1914 were triggered by the resulting crisis across southern France; it also led to substantial emigration, especially from the Midi to Algeria, and accelerated the existing migration of the younger generations to the towns. The resulting shakeout precluded a return to massive, low-quality viticulture in several regions, which turned instead to dairy farming or fruit and vegetable production for the growing urban markets.

By contrast, France's performance during the 'second' industrial revolution appears more creditable than during the 'first'. It was boosted, from the mid-1890s onwards, by a strong recovery from the long depression and by annual growth-rates of over 5% after 1905. Of course, there was no clean break between the two industrial revolutions after 1870, when France's main industries – textiles, metallurgy, construction – were, for reasons we have already seen, still widely dispersed, mostly in the form of family firms. Further adjustments had to be made after the loss of Alsace and part of Lorraine, a highly developed region with significant mineral deposits that was now in German hands. Gradually, a more recognisably industrial map evolved, featuring major industrial cities like Lille, Mulhouse, and Lyon, but such centres remained thinly spread across that map. The 'second' industrial revolution saw France perform comparatively well when it came to inventing, manufacturing and retailing electrical goods, motor cars, bicycles, and other new items. Its entrenched rivalry with the new Germany was partly responsible for this, even though France was still some way behind Germany and, increasingly, America. Despite that, pre-1914 France was, thanks mainly to Peugeot and Renault, the world's major exporter of cars.

By then, investment in the training of engineers and scientists was paying dividends, although their methods and inventions evoke artisanal workshops rather than the laboratories of modern industry. They certainly helped France to recover from the lean years from 1882 to 1896. That recovery was mitigated somewhat by a return to protectionism in 1885–7 and 1892, which attempted to cushion French agriculture as much as industry, but which made it difficult for French goods to break into foreign markets. Yet since the Second Empire, France had exported such enormous quantities of capital that it ranked second in the world behind Britain under this heading. If that suggests a continuing diffidence among its wealthiest citizens, investors, and banks about their own economy, it also represents the *rentier*'s enduring preference for a risk-free income; the returns, ranging from 22% to 50% by the 1860s, were far higher than what could be expected from domestic industrial investment. Ultimately, France's long-standing reputation for high-quality goods enabled it to retain its niche markets overseas or to find new ones, and to stage an impressive economic comeback, which placed it fourth among the world's economies in the decade or so before 1914. The *belle époque* – the pre-war 'golden age' – with all its glamour and excess, is hard to imagine as the product of hard times.

Comparisons between industrial revolutions and with other countries can easily obscure important domestic developments. If France dropped down the league-table of exporting nations by 1910, it was in part because other forms of work and employment had been emerging in the meantime. The tertiary sector began making its presence seriously felt under the Third Republic, and has never looked back since. Approximately one in four workers were employed in sales and services, as well as the professions and administration, between 1881 and 1906; by 1945 it was one in three – and still rising. Because consumer goods outnumbered other categories of industrial products, administration, sales, and other services grew steadily in importance. Thanks in part to better rail links, this was especially evident with the expansion since the Second Empire of the *grands magasins*, banks, insurance, and other businesses, the biggest of which now had increasingly hierarchical workforces where their predecessors once had a handful of virtually 'domestic' employees.

The role of the state in French economic life during the nineteenth century was a complex but ultimately limited one, in which elements of Colbertism – which some twentieth-century commentators dubbed 'state socialism' – co-habited with British laissez-faire attitudes. During the Second Empire, the state showed signs of moving beyond a legislative and regulatory role, not least because influential civil servants and ministers were themselves influenced by Saint-Simonian (and other) ideas of progress, technocratic leadership, and state economic initiative. But major tensions persisted between 'state' and 'private' interests, leading at times to stalemate over major policy projects. Furthermore, state finances were badly hobbled by a combination of debts inherited from the Second Empire, the German war indemnity of 1870, and the high costs of the Freycinet plan of 1879 to subsidise new railways and related infrastructural improvements. Together they discouraged interventionism by conservative and liberal-republican governments, even had they been so minded. The prolonged economic slump of the 1880s and 1890s was probably an additional deterrent for governments; under heavy pressure to defend interest groups with ties to the main political parties, they were more inclined towards protectionist solutions.

However, the economic role of the state was not defined purely by its policies. Already under the Second Empire, the 'cost of the state' amounted to 10% of France's GDP, rising to about 15% by 1914, nearly twice that of Germany and Britain. Far broader, despite fluctuations over time, than the Anglo-Saxon notion of a 'civil service', the French conception of 'public service' (*fonction publique*) housed a much bigger and more heterogeneous population ranging from civil servants working in ministries to teachers, postmen, *gendarmes*, magistrates and other employees of the state, whose precise status was not always wholly clear. For example, before 1905 the clergy were technically civil servants, but that ceased with the separation of church and state. Excluding the army, the *fonctionnaires* numbered almost 700,000 by 1914 (compared to 5.5 million today), of whom some 130,000 were primary-school teachers. Not all of this workforce, and especially not its women teachers, were well paid, although the status attached to such employment was some compensation, as was the prospect of future promotion. The *fonctionnaires* were widely dispersed across the *départements* and down to local, village level, where they did much to anchor the new republic's presence and values. Like the tertiary sector generally, that societal penetration would increase exponentially during the twentieth century.

## IV

The economic recovery, expanding workforce and gradual rise in living standards that characterised the years of the pre-war *belle époque* were accompanied by some spectacularly violent social conflicts, which were almost certainly exacerbated by successive governments' reluctance to deal with the challenges posed by urbanisation, industrialisation, and lower-class poverty. Because it united the normally fractious republicans, confronting the church over education or 'the separation' was easier – and thus more 'opportune' – than pursuing social reforms that might alienate their conservative republican electorate. Social reform – and especially insurance schemes – was one domain in which the urge to imitate and improve upon German initiatives proved resistible. The political class was still wedded to ideas of mutual aid – as indeed were many artisan-workers themselves – and did not readily accept that republican democracy might entail socio-economic obligations. It was willing to remove restraints on organisation or the right to strike, but blenched at the challenge of providing a financial safety-net for the working classes in times of economic distress. Consequently, employment and welfare measures were regularly kicked into touch from the late 1870s onwards. Between them the highly conservative Senate, which over-represented rural areas and, in some cases, the appeal court (*cour de cassation*) obligingly acted as a guillotine when considering such improvements. The result was that before 1914 the scope of social reforms was at best patchy. This was largely because new-style social provisions, such as insurance in case of industrial accidents regardless of who was to blame, challenged entrenched concepts of fault and responsibility. Politicians and governments were fearful of opening the door for unfamiliar debates and measures. An early ban on children under twelve working came in 1874, while in 1899 the maximum working day for women and children was fixed at ten hours, and that for men at eleven; such a measure had originally been proposed as long ago as 1881, but was endlessly deferred thereafter. A law voted in 1898 to indemnify workers in case of industrial accidents had first been mooted in 1882; but even when it was passed in 1898, payment by employers into the attached insurance fund was left optional. In April 1910 provision was made for retirement and pensions based on contributions from workers and employers, but it was vilified, for different reasons, by both extreme Right and Left. The court of appeal then hobbled it by rejecting the principle of obligatory contributions in certain circumstances, another Rubicon that liberals and conservatives found it excruciatingly hard to cross. Many of these reforms were haphazardly or slowly implemented, as legislation did not of itself change establishment attitudes. Income tax was another *bête noire* of the republicans, but without it ambitious social reforms were simply unaffordable; endlessly rejected by the chamber, it was reluctantly voted in July 1914, only two weeks before the great war began. It is hard to dissent from the view that almost no other industrial state of those years offered so little to its working class.

There were doubtless many reasons for this. The owners of the relatively small-scale and dispersed industrial units considered themselves sovereign like other proprietors, and firmly resisted both external state regulation and worker-inspired restriction. The law was overwhelmingly favourable to them on key questions, which made it all the easier to regard striking workers as rebels or deserters who deserved lock-out and punishment rather than conciliation or concession. For most of the century, the employers (*patronat*) were far better organised and enjoyed more political influence than their workforce. Although strikes were legalised in 1864, the tough laws (especially of 1834–5) against workers' organisation were not scrapped until 1884, with provisions for collective bargaining and arbitration following in 1892. A prolonged period of illegality inevitably prevented open organisation or anything resembling 'normal' relations with the 'social partners' of the working class – employers and the state. The repression of the Paris commune was even more severe in its impact on such relations during the 1870s. Not surprisingly, therefore, conditions were quite different to those of Britain or Germany, leading to the trade unions formed after 1884 exhibiting quite distinctive ambitions and relations to politics. This became clear with the formation, in 1895, of the most enduring federation of trade unions, the *Confédération générale du travail* (CGT), and especially with its Amiens charter of 1906, which declared that its aim was to guide the working class towards the decisive revolutionary moment – the general strike – that would finally emancipate them and transform capitalism into socialism. Such a position was largely inspired by the successive socialist theories since Proudhon, in which Marxist ideas were less decisive than the continuing influence of anarcho-syndicalism. Above all, the CGT was highly suspicious of politics and politicians, and viscerally refused all efforts to subordinate it to any political party or its agenda. Its rhetoric was one of confrontation rather than of compromise with the capitalist enemy, which excluded step-by-step 'reformism' of working-class conditions as an illusion.

But such a purist position was hard to sustain beyond a small cadre of true believers, even with the creation in 1905 of a unified Socialist party (the *Section Française de l'Internationale Ouvrière*, usually abbreviated to SFIO) as the party of class struggle and revolution, and not of 'mere' reform. The fact that only one-tenth of French workers were unionised pre-1914 probably reflected their scepticism about such revolutionary aims, while the CGT's own membership fell off sharply after 1910. Though difficult to articulate publicly, French workers were less averse to tangible improvements in living and working conditions than were their union leaders, which in turn was one reason why most of them preferred local rather than national trade-union federations. In practice, however, CGT leaders found they had to talk to Socialist politicians, and accepted some of the legislation already discussed to improve workers' conditions. Such compromise was a response to the many strikes since the 1880s that never came close to the revolutionary 'general' strike, but which gradually forced governments to respond with more than just force. As the numbers of unions grew and as new sectors – teachers and *fonctionnaires*, for example – demanded the right to unionise, it was not surprising that strikes became more frequent. Their annual number rose steadily from around 200 in the 1890s to over 250 in the early 1900s, with a sharp rise to over 1,000 per year after 1904. While many were wild-cat and short-lived, involving relatively few lost working-days, the strikes infused by a revolutionary spirit of 'direct action' could be prolonged and violent.

That large-scale protest was no monopoly of the urban working-class is evident in the huge 'manifestations' of the wine-growers of 1907. The phylloxera crisis had been recently compounded by bumper harvests and the inflow of cheaper wines from Algeria, which combined to produce a severe collapse in wine prices. In the virtually mono-cultural region of Languedoc, where peasant politicisation was no less advanced than in its urban industrial counterparts, this produced an unprecedented revolt. By the time the protests of April-June 1907 peaked there, the assembled demonstrators, led by a café-owner and a town mayor, numbered over 500,000; municipal administrations resigned in solidarity in many towns, such as

Narbonne and Béziers. Declaring himself 'France's first cop', prime minister Clemenceau did not hesitate to send in the army to restore order, having already done so the previous year against half a million northerners protesting over the death of 1,100 miners in the world's biggest mining disaster at Courières, near Lille. In June 1907, a number of protestors were killed in Narbonne, while a contingent of local soldiers mutinied and refused to fire on the protestors. For their pains, the soldiers were packed off for a tour of garrison duty in a mining town – but situated in central Tunisia! In the meantime, Clemenceau out-manoeuvred the local leaders of a cause with too many divergent interests, and the danger passed. In dealing with domestic unrest, the re-organised Radical republicans, especially under Clemenceau and Briand (1906–11), showed they were more enthusiastically a party of order than of reform.

Among the challenges that the republic's political class was reluctant to grapple with was that of improving the status of women. That status was enshrined in the quasi-biblical *code civil* of 1804, so there was enormous reluctance to alter it. As elsewhere in Europe, it was characterised by conceptions of the family and domestic order as the basis of a stable society, one in which distinct male and female spheres obtained. The more entrenched it became, especially as the core values of bourgeois society from mid-century onwards, the less successive regimes were anxious to undermine or reform it. This was, of course, to ignore the active, indispensable economic roles played by the huge majority of women from peasant and lower-class backgrounds generally, for whom middle-class domesticity and separate spheres were meaningless. And as the century progressed, such work-patterns evolved, especially when rural industry migrated to urban environments, because it gradually made women and men rivals rather than partners in the workplace. Separate spheres of other kinds did exist, as evidenced by the fact that over four-fifths of all domestic servants (numbering about one million in all) by 1900 were women; most of them entered service hoping to accumulate a dowry that would enable them to marry. By 1900, that too was changing, with domestic service in relative decline as a source of female employment. Ever more women now worked in 'industrial' jobs, many of which were no longer in the traditional textile sector that had usually involved working from home or in small workshops. The falling birth-rates noted earlier created further work opportunities, so that the numbers of women in the labour force, especially in manufacturing, jumped from around 1.5 million in the 1870s to over 2.2 million by 1914 (in addition to the one million domestics). Women were much cheaper to hire than men; as few of them were unionised, railways and other businesses snapped them up. The simultaneous growth of business offices, services, and shops in cities, opened up new opportunities for women before the sluice-gates were opened by war in 1914.

The adoption, in the 1880s, of the figure of Marianne, through imagery dating from the 1790s, as the symbol of the new republic was not intended to herald major changes in the condition of women or gender relations within French society. When, for example, divorce was restored in 1884, the grounds for seeking divorce were heavily biased towards husbands. Clemenceau had abandoned his American-born wife, but when he heard of her liaison with another man, he had her arrested and deported from France. Later reforms, such as the reduction of working-hours (1892 and 1900) or maternity leave entitlement (1911) were grudgingly voted; the lack of funding largely undermined the maternity scheme for poorer women. Of course, the school reforms of the Ferry years did open the door to better education, especially with the provision of *lycées* for girls. But the numbers receiving a secondary education before 1914 were tiny, just over 30,000; the *lycée* curriculum for girls was quite explicitly gender-defined, and not at all oriented towards further study or activity outside of the home. The first female law students graduated in 1892 to heckling from male students, while the first woman was admitted to the Paris bar in 1900.

The lack of progress towards political rights for women was due to similar factors. From the 1830s – the age of George Sand and Flora Tristan – France did not lack for outspoken or articulate defenders of women's rights, but the repression that followed women's involvement in both the 1848 revolution and the Commune harmed their cause. However, with the stabilisation of the Third Republic, prospects seemed to improve. Feminist organisations were established, with the support of politicians and intellectuals, but not always with a view to securing the vote for women. As we have already seen, concrete social gains were slow to materialise – and were rarely generous in scope. In this respect, republican politicians replicated Guizot's attitude to political reform in the 1840s – 'the time is not right'. With the long sequence of crises or republican campaigns from 1873 to 1905 attracting virtually all of their attention, the female suffrage and other causes, such as the repeal of the current prostitution laws, would have to wait their turn. The socialists were no more understanding, especially as they largely mothballed their own agenda in order to support the anti-clerical campaign after 1900. Moreover, even pro-feminist republicans remained the prisoners of their anti-clericalism, at the heart of which lay the conviction that women 'belonged' to the church and clergy; any concessions to them would enhance clerical power, not the reverse. The substantial numbers joining Catholic women's organisations either side of 1900 would have powerfully confirmed such an attitude. Of course, the Ferry educational reforms were designed to break that link, but few republicans believed it would yield results overnight. A strongly pro-feminist politician declared in 1888 that the republic would only last six months were women to obtain the vote; twenty years later, in 1907, Clemenceau claimed, even more theatrically, that the female suffrage would drive France back into the Middle Ages. Such statements make it easier to surmise the negative views of so many others and the dearth of support for the pre-war suffragette movement. Legislation to give the vote to women was drafted before 1914, but failed to reach the statute book. The country that had first adopted universal male suffrage remained stubbornly unwilling to extend it to its female citizens, especially in the post-war years.

## V

Fractious relations between governments, business elites, and new social movements were hardly unique to France, but its experience of them suggests how slow – even reluctant – the process of adjustment and resolution was there. It was not because there was a lack of public debate on a wide range of social issues, beginning with demography, family structure, forms of work, and so on. Since mid-century French commentators, from sociologists to economists and engineers, had provided some of the most sophisticated analysis available anywhere in Europe, much of it comparative in scope. Well before 1914, high-ranking scholars like Émile Durkheim, Henri Bergson, Ernest Lavisse and others published informed studies – as distinct from journalism – on the challenges facing France. Like many others after 1870, they were acutely aware of the need to catch up with Germany. Lavisse, who did so much to mobilise historical studies and school textbooks in the cause of patriotism, had resided in Berlin in the early 1870s, specialised in German history, and closely studied its university system's contribution to Germany's contemporary superiority. Once back in France, he became a key figure in promoting educational modernisation, in which he found willing collaborators for nearly forty busy years. Despite the small numbers of higher-education students, the creation of modern multi-faculty universities was first mooted in the mid-1870s but, typically, did not materialise until 1896. The existing *grandes écoles* for engineers – and by extension, administrators – were highly regarded, having already produced some eminent scientists. 'Sciences-Po' was added to the list in 1871 and, although a private institution, it would become the principal launch-pad for careers in government and especially high-level administration until the 1940s. France's most successful business school, the 'HEC'

(Hautes études commerciales), followed in 1881. Within the natural sciences and technology many of the revamped universities successfully created their own 'applied' institutes, initially to train technicians and, later, graduates specialising in subjects closely connected to a major regional economic activity – winemaking (Bordeaux), watchmaking (Besançon), and papermaking (Grenoble). By the 1910s, they were producing almost as many specialist 'engineers' as the *grandes écoles*, a status that some of them would obtain later. Such 'practical' science, connecting scientific research to actual economic needs, had been preached and pioneered by Pasteur at Lille university as long ago as the 1850s. Indeed, the reputation of French science was probably never higher than in the decade before 1914, when it garnered twelve Nobel prizes, a record it never came close to repeating thereafter.

German university methods of combining teaching and research were also adapted post-1870, and the German language itself became an essential requirement for scholarship long before English did. However difficult it was to say so publicly, German contributions to philosophy, philology, and history, to mention just three, became models to follow, especially because of their methodological rigour. All of this was part of a much wider and intense engagement with German high culture that French intellectuals used as a mirror to understand France itself. Some influential intellectuals, from Ernest Renan to Maurice Barrès, disliked what they saw there, and used it decry both the political culture (e.g. the pacifism of the left) and the institutions that had led to France's humiliation and loss of supremacy in Europe. But such introspection, which contributed to the right-wing, anti-republican turn of nationalist sentiment in the 1890s, did not always lead to germanophobia or reduce the more entrenched and probably more widespread anglophobia.

These trends in turn owed something to the trajectories of contemporary intellectual movements, which enabled a revolt against the established rationalist certitudes of 'official' France – political and intellectual – to surface by the 1880s. This was because a new generation of thinkers, European as much as French, were in the process of inventing what would in due course become influential modern disciplines – sociology, anthropology, psychology – in which a 'superficial' rationalist or positivist understanding was jettisoned in the search to re-discover the irrational, subconscious and culture-ingrained drives that governed human nature and behaviour. Because much of the original scholarly work was either on-going or German (Bergson, Nietzsche, Freud), it had not yet been fully absorbed into French thinking before the war, but it was sufficiently domesticated to energise a generation of writers to return to religion, mysticism, tradition, history as the well-springs of human experience. In this 're-orientation of European social thought', the so-called 'generation of 1905' was particularly active in France because it had been mobilised and, above all, divided by the Dreyfus affair. Disgusted by the republican establishment's exploitation of victory for its own ends, many of them adapted views already aired by their 'tutelary deities' (e.g. Bergson, Gide) and took them in a frankly anti-rationalist, nationalist and anti-republican direction. Conversions to Catholicism by Péguy, Claudel, and Maritain announced a revolt against rationalist secularism and a possible revival of religious forces.

It is not hard to see why such efforts at intellectual reorientation could have a wider impact, especially in literature and the arts. France's cultural life had become less and less trammelled by institutionalised political constraints since the 1870s. Indeed, rarely had it been so independent and flourishing as during the long generation before 1914, thanks in part to the republican regime's relaxed stance on press and artistic freedoms. The Second Empire's authoritarian, 'Napoleonic' view of culture as an instrument of state to be activated through established institutions had subsequently been tempered, although the republic retained its role and its resources as France's premier cultural patron. The historic bonds between art and the regime loosened in important respects, with artists increasingly ignoring official traditions like the annual *salons*, organising their own exhibitions, and increasingly selling their works through private art-dealers. And since 'establishment' tastes were invariably slow in adjusting to the rapid evolution of artistic styles during the generation after 1880, a high proportion of their most celebrated paintings were sold abroad. Indeed, a large donation of Impressionist paintings was frostily declined by government officials as late as 1894! This artistic kaleidoscope was, of course, overwhelmingly a Parisian phenomenon, regardless of whether artists themselves preferred to work in Pont-Aven or Arles. The considerable overlap of generations of artists and artistic styles – from Impressionism to Post-Impressionism, Fauvism, Cubism, and Abstract art – drew ever more talented hopefuls, foreign as well as French, to the bohemian districts of Paris, making it the world's unchallenged cultural capital by 1900. The city's status was enhanced by a similar richness and concentration of musical inventiveness, especially in the classical genre, from Gabriel Fauré to Claude Debussy and Maurice Ravel, whose parallel activities as teachers drew growing numbers of students, even from America, to Paris. Such an 'agglomeration' factor made it the obvious place for new avant-gardes (e.g. the Italian Futurists) to pitch their tents. Not all, of course, could make the same impact as Diaghilev's *ballets russes*, especially with Stravinsky's revolutionary *Rite of Spring* (1913).

High-brow art alone did not make Paris what it was by 1900 – a laboratory for the development of cultural activities that would become world-wide in the twentieth century. Early critics decried many of them as decadent or foreign, and thus a threat to French traditions, but economic recovery and growing prosperity during the *belle époque* broadened the 'market' for such novelties. Bourgeois and bohemian Paris came closer than ever. Thus, by 1900, Paris had 300 café-concerts that provided a combination of dance, music, and theatre; they would soon metamorphose into the music-halls that drew large, socially mixed crowds to landmark sites like the Olympia and the Moulin Rouge. As a result, the stars of music hall like Yvette Guilbert, but also from the classical theatre like Sarah Bernhardt, became household names. As for theatre, its menu ranged from Shakespeare, Goethe, and Ibsen to new popular plays like Rostand's *Cyrano de Bergerac*. A French invention, the motion picture had unrivalled novelty value, and attracted growing audiences, especially once mobile projections were replaced by permanent cinemas. Until 1914 French film-making led the world, and could draw on the talents of writers like Anatole France and Edmond Rostand, actors like Sarah Bernhardt, and musicians like Saint-Saëns. Indeed, French westerns were popular even in America, until the war virtually closed down the entire industry in France and handed its leadership role to Hollywood.

To an extent, the growth of such cultural activities reflected social changes that increased opportunities for leisure among different sections of the population. Membership of sports clubs and associations grew sharply before 1914, spurred on by the Olympic games held in Paris (1900) and the annual sensation that was, after 1903, the *Tour de France*. Sport of various kinds, even those involving recent inventions like cars and bicycles, became increasingly common. These new means of circulation helped to expand considerably the scope of existing middle-class leisure travel – including the *voyage de noces* that had taken off in the 1870s – although the vast majority preferred train travel to the major resorts, from Deauville to Biarritz and Nice, not to mention the Alpine winter-stations. Tourism and tourists were among the newest cultural and economic phenomena of these years, stimulating an expanding raft of services such as travel agencies, hotels, restaurants, guidebooks (from the *Guide Joanne* to the *Guides bleus*) and other creature comforts. Before 1914, or even 1945, the 'democratisation' of leisure was more an aspiration than a reality, but decreasing working hours and rising wages made sports accessible to some sections of the working class. And the more sport, travel and tourism attracted the attention of business the more the way was gradually paved for another world record for France – that of the country attracting the most tourists, many of them its own citizens.

The final stage of this present tour de France will be concerned with a quite different but equally authentic product of the distinctive French mix of politics, ideas, and culture in these pre-war decades – the modern intellectual. Few societies have granted intellectuals the same attention or status as France, where complex, love-hate relations between the state, writers, and thinkers, had long existed before 1900. They were exemplified by the careers of *philosophes* such as Voltaire, that semi-permanent exile who declared that he wrote 'in order to act'. The Third Republic's appropriation of the values of the Revolution widened that scope for action, debate, and opinion-forming, but without imagining all of its consequences. In social and geographical terms, the intellectual was primarily a Parisian product, one of many results of the capital's hyper-concentration of cultural institutions, with their often-incestuous connections to government and political life. The explosion of national newspapers, whose numbers rose from thirty-seven dailies around 1870 to seventy by 1910, played a major part in multiplying the number of 'tribunes' available for debate from the 1880s onwards, especially as newspapers were the most common face of the constantly shifting contemporary political 'parties'. Magazines and reviews had a similar effect, attracting smaller but more committed readerships. Newspaper owners were often businessmen who overtly harboured political ambitions, and virtually all major politicians had – and needed to have – their newspapers (e.g. Clemenceau and *L'Aurore*, Jaurès and *l'Humanité*) in order to sustain a political career. This, of course, did not make all journalists or politicians intellectuals, nor unify the opinions or causes either promoted or attacked by intellectuals; that would have been quite unthinkable during the successive crises of the early Third Republic.

The foundational moment of the intellectuals' *engagement* in public life was not just Zola's blistering *J'accuse* in Clemenceau's newspaper, *L'Aurore*, but its publication in subsequent days of lists of signatories to what became known as the 'manifesto of the intellectuals' demanding a revision of Dreyfus's trial. This petitioning was organised mainly by Zola himself, and many of the signatories were explicitly listed as university graduates or students, no doubt as proof of their 'intellectual' credibility. Although the word 'intellectual' had been used a few times before then, the Dreyfus affair gave it much of its contemporary meaning, as its widespread use in the ensuing exchanges showed. The idea that considerations of justice, conscience or morality should prevail over the national interest or the reputation of the army was anathema to anti-Dreyfusards like Maurice Barrès – himself an influential writer, politician, and indeed 'intellectual' – who derided the manifesto's signatories as 'semi-intellectuals'. Equally significantly, battle was almost immediately joined in early 1898 when an anti-Dreyfus letter to the president was published by the right-wing daily, *La Libre Parole*. Other newspapers took sides, and opened their pages to the major writers of the day. Gradually, the repertoire of intellectual interventions as collective rather than individual gestures was taking shape. Petitions were not unknown before 1889, but had been more limited in scope. That launched against Eiffel's 'barbarous tower' in 1887 expressed the views of artists on a subject within their specific sphere of competence, and they sought no wider 'authority' than that. By 1900, such specialist limitations had fallen away, although within literary, musical, and artistic circles, manifestos often became the birth certificate of new movements. The right-wing League of French Patriots owed its origins to a petition against Dreyfusism in late 1898. On the eve of World War I, petitions for and against the extension of military service from two to three years produced intense exchanges, which included street-fights in an increasingly right-wing Latin Quarter.

## VI

'Always think of it, but never mention it' – such was Gambetta's advice on how to deal with France's great 'elephant in the room' problem after 1871, namely the loss of Alsace-Lorraine and the 'sacred' obligation to recover it. But the prospect of a quick recovery was slight, now that France's biggest neighbour unmistakably possessed Europe's most powerful state, army, and economy. Even had it wished to, the stuttering Third Republic had simply too many domestic challenges to attack Germany, least of all without allies. Most of the time French *revanche* was rhetorical posturing but, as the Boulanger affair showed, successive governments needed to exercise vigilance to contain such aspirations. Like Metternich before him, Bismarck effectively kept France under close surveillance from the mid-1860s until his retirement in 1891. When necessary, he willingly contrived war-scares designed to keep France on the back foot, while shepherding it away from European to other theatres of adventure.

Thus confined, France turned elsewhere in search of lost glory and reputation. By 1914, its colonial empire was second only to the British empire in extent if not value. From the Algiers campaign of 1830 to the early 1880s, France gained overseas territories haphazardly and with little continuity of vision or intention. A few scattered and minute ancien-régime colonies (e.g. Martinique, Guyane, Ile Bourbon) had been returned to France in 1814, but were hardly an incentive to renewed empire-building. The 1830 expedition to Algiers was a typical case. Originally a punitive expedition against the city itself, it only later mutated into a conquest of 'Algeria' that by 1848 was incorporated into, and was, in theory, governed as a part of metropolitan France. Although Napoleon III could hardly escape the burden of seeking imperial 'glory', he had no coherent colonial policy worth the name; a few scattered additions were made to the existing collection (e.g. Senegal, Tahiti), but his opportunistic Mexican adventure in the 1860s ended disastrously. The body-blow that was the defeat of 1870 meant that it was not until the 1880s that the republicans, led by Ferry, began again to take colonial expansion seriously; and that in turn was galvanised in part by French participation in the Congress of Berlin (1884), which kick-started the 'scramble for Africa'. French interest in Egypt went back to Napoleon's legendary expedition of 1798, but in both the 1840s and the 1880s its attempts to regain a foothold there were roundly thwarted by Britain. Elsewhere, however, French military intervention engineered 'protectorates' (not always immediately implemented) for Tunisia and Madagascar (1881) and what would become the enormous French Indochina (1881–3). In 1904, a West Africa federation based on Dakar was founded, followed in 1910 by that of Equatorial Africa, based on Brazzaville; between them, these two federations contained a territorially vast collection of twelve individual colonies. The most contentious acquisition of the early 1900s was Morocco, since France's main rival there was Germany.

In both reality and aspiration, French colonial expansion was distinctive, especially from the 1880s onwards. It was presented as different from the British approach, which aimed only, it was alleged, at material and territorial accumulation. On the contrary, France's mission was depicted as a civilising one, embodying the universal principles of 1789, of which the republic was the custodian; native populations would be both assimilated *and* emancipated, so that they could enjoy the fruits of civilisation. By the 1880s, Jules Ferry was, like many of his contemporaries, arguing that 'superior races' had a right and a duty to civilise 'inferior' ones, and that duly became the official doctrine for generations to come. This self-flattering message, which enabled anti-clericals to defend keeping Catholic missionaries in the colonies, was one that Left and Right could, and did, largely share for decades; anticlericalism, as Gambetta deftly put it, was not for export. Its most vocal critics, who initially belonged on the political Right rather than the Left, either doubted the value of having colonies altogether or, more pragmatically, they felt that it distracted France from its real challenge – confronting Germany. But many more came to accept the view that it would contribute to the process of national regeneration and, thus, prepare France to challenge Germany in due course. Clemenceau's objection of 1885, namely that German scholars (*savants*) had used similar racial arguments to proclaim France's 'inferiority' to Germany, was lost on its listeners.

Almost inevitably, there was a significant mismatch between the reality and the rhetoric of French colonial expansion. The extension and governance of this empire was quite haphazard, accurately reflecting the *bricolage* that it actually was. Algeria was French, subject to the Interior ministry, and returned parliamentary deputies in elections, while protectorates like Tunisia, Indochina or Morocco were subject to the Foreign affairs ministry. The remainder – 'mere' colonies – came under the Colonies ministry created in 1894. Imperial expansion was itself primarily the work of a heterogeneous coalition of interested 'parties' – soldiers, explorers, businessmen, intellectuals, to name a few. They constituted what in the 1880s became known as the *parti colonial* – an informal lobby with considerable influence within high political circles. Successive governments were not always interested in colonial matters, which enabled the *parti* to determine the policies to be followed overseas. Even the creation, in 1894, of a ministry for the colonies only seems to have increased the *parti's* grip on colonial policymaking. On the ground, local commanders and administrators enjoyed considerable freedom of action, and the initiatives of certain pro-consuls left governments to face many an awkward *fait accompli*. Despite the establishment of a *grande école* to train colonial administrators in 1889, neither military service nor civilian administration in the colonies attracted the brightest or the most ambitious, which often led to egregious mistreatment of local populations, especially when they protested against colonial rule.

The notion that France's empire was not based on economic calculation had some basis in objective fact. The new colonies brought relatively little wealth to the metropolis, quite the opposite: most of them cost considerable sums to administer and improve. For decades French business interests were not much interested or involved, unlike those of the pre-1789 'first' empire, in which they were key players. Little of the French capital exported before 1914 was destined for the colonies, and it was the government which provided most of the investments – essentially infrastructural in nature – that were made there. At best, the colonies provided certain raw materials for processing and manufacture in metropolitan France, but above all, they became closed markets for finished French goods. Not surprisingly, it was Algeria, with its substantial immigrant population (700,000 by 1914), much of it from southern France, which attracted half of all French colonial financial investment from private sources, and accounted for half of France's trade with its overseas possessions. Algeria, of course, was not technically a colony at all since 1848, but its native population (with the exception of Algerian Jews) was assigned a special 'indigenous' status that belied the formal principles of its integration to metropolitan France.

France's colonial empire was a 'situational' response to its incapacity to avenge the defeat of 1870. Despite its relatively recent history, the huge differences between its various parts, and the reluctance of French people to emigrate to the colonies, the empire gradually took hold in the popular imagination. The fact that the colonial lobby was spread across the political and social elites enabled it to orchestrate a wide range of pro-empire campaigns. The press diffused notions of imperial grandeur from the 1870s onwards, while the numerous geographical societies organised educational 'crusades' to familiarise wider audiences with strange new lands. Hugely popular novelists like Loti, Verne, and Daudet owed their success to the growing demand for such exotic 'education'. The first colonial exhibition was held in Marseille in 1906, and attracted numerous visitors, but all of the Parisian world exhibitions since 1878 had included colonial pavilions. World War I would bring the reality of France's colonial empire far closer than previously.

# VII

European colonial expansion, of which the 'scramble for Africa' was only a part, enabled the major powers to pursue their diverging interests on what seemed relatively safe terrain. However, the metropolitan and colonial worlds could not be kept apart indefinitely, so much so that overseas entanglements played a major part in realigning the major western powers in the decade before 1914. Yet Anglo-French friction in Asia and other parts of Africa since the 1880s, and especially over Egypt, was such that war between the two powers often seemed more likely than common cause against Germany. Bismarck and his successors were only too happy to exploit such friction. It took the vexed question of French policy towards Morocco after 1900 to change that. The *parti colonial* lobby had business and financial interests there and, as with Tunisia two decades previously, it campaigned hard to make Morocco a French protectorate. But Germany also had economic interests there, too, and became convinced that France was deliberately excluding it. It deliberately contrived two incidents in 1905 and 1911 respectively, with a view to forcing France's hand. But German tactics rebounded against it, and at the conferences convened to resolve the ensuing crises, Germany found itself isolated and had to climb down. Significantly, its behaviour led Britain to realise that German naval and colonial ambitions now made it a bigger threat than France, historically its main colonial rival but no longer a real naval threat. The *entente cordiale* of 1904 was the initial outcome, with France finally (and reluctantly) granting

Britain a free hand in Egypt in return for a similar British concession over Morocco. The two Moroccan crises consolidated that outcome, and opened the way for the French protectorate there in 1912. The rather tentative *entente* came on top of an existing French alliance with Russia (1892), whose solidity remained unproven; for years, such alliances were precautionary moves rather than preparations for war.

Domestic politics could not but register the effects of such conflicts and realignments. The Dreyfus affair and the separation of church and state were, as we have seen, moments of visceral internal division, where one side's sacred cause was another's *bête noire*, and where suspicion of putative 'foreign' elements (Dreyfus's alleged 'German' affiliations) or allegiances (Catholics and the papacy) were constantly aired in public. Nor did the political kaleidoscope itself freeze in these years, as is clear from the coming together in 1905, under pressure from the Second International, of France's five existing socialist 'parties' under a single banner as the unified SFIO. The SFIO's membership of the Socialist International ensured substantial contacts with other European socialist movements like the huge German Social Democratic Party, which could not but influence its policies, domestic as well as international. Unification did not put an end to internal differences or groupings, especially those between orthodox Marxist revolutionaries and more 'home-grown' reformist socialists. Under the leadership of the charismatic orator, Jean Jaurès, who found Marxism 'out of date', the SFIO presented itself as a reforming, humanitarian, and peace-seeking party, but not one prepared to 'sell out', as radicals had regularly done hitherto, by joining 'bourgeois governments'. It arrived too late to keep on board socialists like Alexandre Millerand and Aristide Briand, both of whom had already 'rallied' before 1900. By August 1914 the Socialists were the second largest party in the Assembly, but still refused to enter government.

Against this background, fears of war returned, especially in the aftermath of the second Moroccan crisis of 1911, which sparked a nationalistic revival within France. German military superiority remained unmistakable, seriously deterring ministers and *revanchards* alike from taking rhetoric too far. France's continuing demographic deficit was felt as acutely within the military as in industry, keeping its army strength far below that of Germany, which in 1913 was planning to increase its military establishment to 850,000, as against France's 480,000. In response to this, some argued that numbers were not crucial to modern war. In his book of 1911, the *New Army*, Jaurès lauded the value of a new citizen army's *élan patriotique* – clearly echoing the mythical *levée en masse* of 1793 – against technologically superior but downtrodden (meaning German) conscripts. For Jaurès, however, this was a concession. Over the years, his stance had been the pacifist one of the Second International, according to which the working classes could be patriotic, but should keep clear of the bourgeoisie's wars. Officially, the Socialists remained 'not a party of reform, but of class struggle and revolution'. In 1911 and later, Jaurès would only countenance a war of defence, but the Socialists failed to prevent the extension, voted in July 1913, of military service from two to three years. Despite being mercilessly attacked as unpatriotic, the Socialists and their allies actually gained ground in the 1914 elections, albeit just falling short of a majority. What remained uncertain was whether, in the event of war, the Socialists would stand by their pacifist commitments, especially if the German Socialist Party reneged on them.

Few historical subjects have had more ink spilled over them than the question of who or what precipitated Europe into war in 1914. More will certainly follow, despite the discussion no longer being focussed primarily on war-guilt. The French nationalist revival of the early 1910s was not as aggressively anti-German or bellicose as once thought; it was partly directed against the Radical 'establishment' in power. Nor did the failure of efforts to improve diplomatic relations with Germany signal the inevitability of war. In any case, the rapid turnover of French governments during the three years before 1914 made it difficult to pursue consistent policies, especially as the six short-lived foreign ministers mostly lacked the required interest or experience. As already suggested, much of the diplomacy and measures like lengthening military service of these years were precautionary, as the different European powers sought security in numbers and allies. Inevitably, the succession of crises from the Balkans (1908–9, 1912–13) to Morocco (1911) sharpened great-power rivalries, with both France and Germany increasing the length of military service in 1913.

Equally significantly, military preparations accompanied these developments, and were characterised by increasingly precise plans for mobilisation and rapid troop deployment that left virtually no time for hesitation or reconsideration should the dominoes begin to fall. It has been dubbed 'war by timetable', in which railways were intended to play a key part. French military planners were as conscious of the need for speed as their German counterparts, and insisted that in case of war its allies – Russia essentially – should mobilise as quickly as it did, so as to force Germany to defend on two fronts and thus divide its superior forces; if that did not happen, they doubted that France could resist a full-scale German invasion. Like the German Schlieffen plan, the French army's Plan XVII envisaged offensive action, not Jauresian self-defence, in case war was declared; rapid attack was its solution to the problem of France's smaller army and other military inadequacies. But the French high command was again badly wrong-footed by the rapidity of German action in August 1914 and especially its audacious advance through neutral Belgium. Plan XVII, which had made no allowance for the violation of Belgian neutrality, quickly went up in smoke. It gave way to an improvised last-ditch defence on the Marne, with Parisian taxis delivering the troops that would shore up the tottering front, thus sparing Paris a remake of the siege of 1870 and preventing the almost certain collapse of the Third Republic itself.

During the critical weeks following the Sarajevo assassinations in late June 1914, President Poincaré and prime minister René Viviani went on a leisurely state visit to Russia, clearly not expecting a major conflagration. Poincaré, whose Lorrainer origins made him no friend of Germany, impressed on the Russians that standing up firmly to Germany was the best policy, while also urging restraint on them in the Balkans. For that to work France needed the firm alliances that had so far eluded it – hence the state visit. Poincaré's view was already being tested as he and the inexperienced Viviani travelled to and from St Petersburg. Intermittently incommunicado while aboard ship, they had only limited information about, or grasp of, events as they unfolded in France and elsewhere in Europe. Only three days after their return to Paris on 29 July, France began general mobilisation, but it was the assassination of Jaurès on 31 July that triggered the real mood-change. Until that moment, France was convulsed by the murky details of a major political scandal arising from the trial of Mme Caillaux, wife of the Finance minister, who had shot dead the editor of the *Figaro* some months earlier. As the 'guns of August' began firing barely a week later, virtually everyone imagined that a war fought with the weapons of modern industry would resemble the blitzkrieg offensives of Napoleon rather than the static siege warfare of earlier centuries. The *belle époque*, which epitomised the contrast between a modern, cosmopolitan, and urban France and a traditional and rural one, was nearing its end, too, but nobody sensed that either. All but a tiny handful agreed that the war would end before the leaves fell. This belief extended well beyond popular prediction: the crucial decision to finance the coming war by borrowing was based – patently – on an identical assumption.

## CHRONOLOGY

1873   Thiers replaced as president by monarchist, MacMahon; German occupation ends; Rimbaud poems, *Une saison en enfer*; Verne, *Tour du monde en 80 jours*

1874   Impressionist exhibition; Tonkin protectorate

| | |
|---|---|
| 1875 | Constitutional laws for Third Republic; Sacré-Coeur basilica building begins |
| 1877 | Republicans win general elections |
| 1879 | Further Republican electoral gains; President MacMahon resigns; monarchist cause weakened |
| 1880 | 14 July declared national day; amnesty for *Communards*; Tahiti annexed; Sée law on girls' education; Rodin, *Le Penseur* |
| 1881–2 | (Ferry) education laws; liberal press law; Tunisian protectorate; *Ligue des patriotes* founded |
| 1884 | Divorce law reformed; municipal government law, mayors to be elected; trade unions legalised |
| 1885 | Fall of Ferry; parliamentary elections; Zola, *Germinal* |
| 1889 | End of Boulanger crisis (since 1887); Eiffel Tower; Paris World Exhibition |
| 1892 | Méline protectionist tariffs; Panama financial scandal; Franco-Russian military accord |
| 1894 | Dreyfus imprisoned for spying; Debussy, *Prélude à l'après-midi d'un faune* |
| 1895 | Protectorate of Madagascar; CGT (trade union) founded; Lumière opens first cinema |
| 1896 | Albert Jarry, *Ubu roi* |
| 1898 | Émile Zola, *J'Accuse*; beginning of Dreyfus affair; *Ligue des droits de l'homme* and *Action Française* founded; P and M Curie discover radium |
| 1899 | Liberation and pardon for Dreyfus |
| 1900 | First Paris metro line opens |
| 1901 | Law on religious congregations; Radical party launched nation-wide |
| 1903 | First Tour de France cycle race; Marie and Pierre Curie win Nobel Physics prize |
| 1904 | *Entente cordiale* with Britain; relations ended with papacy |
| 1905 | Military service reduced to two years; Moroccan crisis; law separating church and state; SFIO founded |
| 1906 | Dreyfus rehabilitated; labour unrest, strikes, repression (to 1910); Picasso, *Demoiselles d'Avignon* |
| 1907 | revolt of winegrowers in Midi |
| 1911 | Second Moroccan crisis |
| 1912 | French protectorate in Morocco |
| 1913 | Military service increased to three years; Proust, *A la recherche du temps perdu* begins publication; Stravinsky, *Rite of Spring* |
| 1914 | Assassination of Jaurès; outbreak of World War I |

# 7 Two Wars and a Peace

There has never been any doubt in France as to which of the two world wars was the 'great war'. The passage of time has not altered the fact that between 11 November 1918 and 8 May 1945 there is really no competition, as was tacitly admitted by Giscard d'Estaing's abortive attempt in the late 1970s to roll the two dates into one (11 November) for commemorative purposes. Despite its satisfactory outcome, France's participation in the 1939–45 war was brief and largely inglorious by comparison with 1914–18, when it was the key theatre of operations from beginning to end. That experience would dominate public life and popular attitudes for the entire inter-war period, whereas even now the legacy of 1939–45 remains confused and contested. The France that went so unwillingly to war in 1939 was still traumatised by the impact of the great war. This is hardly surprising: the price paid for averting a repeat of the debacle of 1870 in 1914–18 was, by any standards, exceptional.

## I

Several uncertainties about what might happen in the event of war were quickly dispelled in August 1914, reinforcing France's capacity to respond to the crisis. By far the biggest unknown was whether France's allies would stand with it or not. Russia, because of its Balkan commitments, proved the more willing of the two, while Britain dithered until its hand was forced by German actions. France desperately needed the intervention of *both* allies to withstand the expected German invasion, but was not sure that even that would suffice. At home, the Socialists, like their German counterparts, demonstrated their patriotism and voted the war credits, supporting the national consensus that this was a defensive, patriotic war. The CGT's mythical general strike, designed to torpedo capitalist wars, failed to materialise; instead trade-unionists were soon collaborating with the government over war production, working conditions, wages, and so on. The military high command's calculation that about one in eight conscripts would dodge mobilisation was also disproved; the actual figure was tiny – less than one in 60. Recruits joined their units determinedly, but perhaps less joyfully, than elsewhere in Europe, and the mobilisation was completed with few incidents and considerable rapidity. When military insubordination did materialise, it was mainly in 1917 and involved front-line troops rather than *refuseniks* behind the lines. The government's 'B list' of suspects – mostly anti-war trade-unionists or political activists – who were to be arrested in the event of war also proved redundant in 1914. Finally, President Poincaré's appeal for a 'sacred union' of all political forces was well and quickly received. A truce rather than a peace, it suspended the recent conflicts between republicans and Catholics and enabled Catholic politicians to enter government for the first time since the 1870s; it also persuaded the hitherto self-denying Socialists, shaken but in some ways 'legitimated' by the murder of Jaurès, to do likewise. The union only papered over the multiple existing differences, but was decisive in consolidating national unity when it was most needed.

A state of siege was imposed on 2 August 1914 for the duration of the conflict, empowering the army to requisition materials, control the press and police, and impose censorship. A month later, the Chamber devolved powers to rule by decree to the government and even voted a recess *sine die*. This vacation lasted until late December 1914, when the deputies had to be recalled to vote the budget for 1915. Then and later, however, ministers and politicians remained largely excluded from the management of the war itself. The high command, led by chief of staff Joffre, could for once indulge its contempt for politicians and keep them in the dark about key decisions. However, Joffre's downfall in the wake of the hugely costly failures of several military offensives, especially at Verdun and the Somme, finally enabled the politicians to begin wrestling ultimate authority back from the military by mid-1916. This coincided with the gradual unravelling of the 'sacred union' of 1914, which saw new divergences, accompanied by a certain defeatism, gaining ground among the political elite; pacifist ideas were also growing in left-wing circles. Such developments isolated the Socialists and led them openly to break in mid-1917 with the other parties to the union. After a series of increasingly shaky governments, the unexpected appointment in November 1917 of the 76-year old Clemenceau as prime minister was critical because of his implacable determination to win rather than just end the war. With increased conservative backing, the ever maverick, authoritarian 'Tiger' tore into leading political figures, especially the Radical leader Caillaux, who seemed to personify a growing pacifist trend. Indispensable as Clemenceau's stance was towards the final outcome, the decisive victory that France now sought could not have been achieved without the simultaneous arrival of a massive American battlefield force and its huge resources. Until Marshal Foch – Clemenceau's choice – was made generalissimo of the allied armies in early 1918, the French and

English military efforts had been only loosely co-ordinated, which reflected the underlying friction between the commanders and their governments. Making peace and imposing terms on Germany would reveal further rifts within the new triple alliance.

By then, four years of brutal warfare had transformed the map of Europe for good. The initial – and universal – expectation of a rapid outcome was based on a war of movement that actually characterised the opening phase of the war, but that prospect began to fade once the French and British armies halted successive German attempts to outflank them across northern France in late 1914. From the English Channel to the Swiss border, the western front gradually solidified by early 1915. In the static warfare of earlier centuries, one side usually benefited from the shelter of a heavily fortified site. Between 1915 and 1918, however, all sides were exposed in open country to the worst conditions imaginable. Both German and Anglo-French armies engaged in massive assaults on the supposed weak points along heavily fortified enemy lines; both hoped that the use of massed infantry would deliver the decisive breakthrough that would drive their opponents into retreat and disarray. But across the open no-man's land dividing the armies nothing was more vulnerable to the devastating combination of artillery and machine-gun fire (not to mention mustard-gas after early 1915) than unprotected infantry. Defensive warfare held virtually every trump card, especially once elaborate fall-back lines of defence and supply were organised behind the front. If the major French operations of the war, especially around Verdun throughout 1916, produced enormous casualties, it was because German tactics were designed to bleed the French armies white. In such circumstances, trench warfare was an unplanned necessity and became virtually a way of life for millions from 1915 onwards; rotating between front-line and rear-lines, France's infantry, nicknamed the *poilus* (the 'hairy' or 'scruffy' ones), lived in atrocious conditions even when not facing the immediate prospect of going over the top to attack German lines. Such conditions rendered pre-war myths of the glory of combat redundant, but generated a new culture of soldiering that combined endurance and camaraderie, not to mention the will to survive. Whether or not it was in the trenches that France's peasants finally became Frenchmen, there is no underestimating their readiness to bear the brunt of war even in the most extreme conditions. Fighting on French soil with a view to recovering its occupied regions, their sense of defending their *patrie* rarely faltered, despite the hideous price in lives. As already mentioned, mutiny and desertion were remarkably limited. Deserters numbered no more than around 7,000 over four years. When mutinies did occur, especially in April–June 1917, they were moderate in tone, and involved only some 40,000 (out of over 2 million) soldiers on the frontline. The key factor was their loss of confidence in the strategy of their commanders, and especially in Joffre's successor, the wasteful Nivelle; it emerged most clearly in their objections to pointless frontal attacks, but not to defensive postures. Contrary to contemporary insinuations, they were only marginally influenced by pacifist propaganda or news of the Russian revolution; there was no mass desertion or fraternisation with the enemy. Indeed, thanks to a combination of censorship, repression, and ultimate leniency, the Germans only learned of the mutinies after they had ceased, when it was too late to take advantage of them. Pétain, who replaced the short-lived Nivelle as chief of staff in April 1917, realised that by improving conditions (e.g. leave, rotation, rations) and by conserving French forces as far as possible, the *poilus*, whose demands were often supported by their officers, were doggedly ready to fight on. Of the 4,000 soldiers to face military justice in 1917, 629 were condemned to death, but the vast majority obtained presidential pardons; the final number of those executed (43) was actually lower than in 1914–15.

The Russian revolution, which effectively ended the German-Russian war by late 1917, was bad news for France, as it released German forces for their last great offensive in Flanders and Champagne from April to June 1918. The attack came very close to shattering allied lines and brought Paris again within the reach of Germany's long-range guns. But not for the first time, that thrust, which also reached the Marne, proved unsustainable; an exposed and weakened German front line was unable to contain the final allied counter-offensive, for which freshly arrived American forces proved vital, from August 1918 onwards. By early October, Germany, bereft of all its former allies, its forces driven back beyond France's 1914 frontiers, and facing growing internal unrest, finally sought to negotiate terms. The armistice of 11 November paved the way for one of the most contentious post-war settlements of modern times, the treaty of Versailles of mid-1919. Its most draconian contents (German war guilt, substantial war reparations, and occupation of parts of Rhineland Germany) were included at Clemenceau's insistence and clearly echoed those imposed on France in 1871. While France insisted that Germany had to pay reparations, given the massive damage it had inflicted on France, its Anglo-American allies worried not just about whether it could pay, but also over the economic wisdom and wider ramifications of punitive reparations. Beyond that, French demands for guaranteed security implied a permanently weakened neighbour, whereas its allies wanted to see Germany restored to economic health within a revitalised Europe. What emerged was an unsatisfactory compromise that France was simply not strong enough to enforce, as her occupation of the Ruhr region in 1923 amply demonstrated, but whose terms prolonged mistrust among allies during the 1920s. 'Versailles' would in due course become a perfect target for the Nazi propaganda machine.

Meanwhile, the war-time regime formally continued until October 1919. Only then, with German compliance with the Versailles settlement assured, could the 'state of siege' be lifted and demobilisation completed. The experience of war for civilian France depended partly on whether its citizens found themselves under German occupation or not. The ten *départements* behind German lines endured rough, often brutal, treatment from the outset, as well as witnessing the enormous destruction of infrastructure, housing, and agriculture. Their industries, mines, and other facilities were commandeered for the German war effort, and many were deliberately wrecked during the final German retreat in 1918. Workers were deported in large numbers from both occupied France and Belgium to work in factories in Germany; women in particular were targeted for heavy labour in both town and country.

Unoccupied France escaped such exploitation, but the war years did not mean business as usual. Strict censorship meant that information about the war was derived largely from military communiqués and pro-war journalists. War correspondents did not exist, so that French society knew precious little about the world of the trenches. With over 90% of all males between 18 and 46 years mobilised, the 'face' of every local commune was radically altered, producing an unprecedented gulf between the generations and the sexes. Indeed, France drafted the highest percentage of its active male population of any European country for war. This affected rural society most profoundly of all. Peasants were disproportionately mobilised as ordinary infantrymen, since few had the education or skills to become gunners, engineers, or other military specialists. As canon-fodder infantry, they suffered correspondingly huge losses in dead (530,000) and wounded. By comparison, urban recruits working in industry, transport, and other key service sectors fared better; some 500,000 of them were returned from military service to their workplaces during 1915, when it became clear that the war was here to stay and they were indispensable to the war effort behind the lines. On the other hand, certain professions, like schoolteachers, suffered very heavy losses, since as *sous-officiers* (NCOs) they were the most vulnerable of all soldiers.

Women and children were ubiquitous from the outset in the rural workforce, since the war began before the 1914 harvest had commenced; conditions worsened with sustained de-population over the coming years. As a result, the productivity of French agriculture slumped seriously, falling by no less than half between 1913 and 1919. German submarine war against merchant shipping only made matters worse, so that forms of rationing had to be introduced by 1918. Industrial output was some 40% lower by the end of the same period. It was inevitably affected by the German seizure of over half of France's main sources of iron and coal. Such disruption required important adjustments. In particular, much of heavy industry had to relocate from the occupied north-east to other regions, especially around Paris, and to re-develop quickly with a mostly new workforce. While some major industries (e.g. the building trade) vegetated in wartime, the relatively new, war-related sectors (e.g. chemical and engineering) now prospered, with major firms like Renault, Citroën, and others converting their factory floors to armaments production. Metallurgy displaced textiles as the major industry, which in turn facilitated the modernisation of working patterns along American lines. A degree of state-control was gradually established in key war-related sectors, especially where the state had to step in as creditor when the banks were reluctant to make loans; such intervention also promoted the regrouping of production units into cartels which facilitated overall co-ordination of the industries involved. The elements of a command economy that emerged were pragmatic responses to urgent war needs; although mostly disbanded after 1918, they were not to be wholly forgotten in later decades.

It was in the social and financial fields that the price of victory was highest. French military death-rates were proportionately the highest in Europe. Losses were staggering from the outset, and not confined to the 'great battles' of 1916 and later. Eight million soldiers in all, 600,000 of them from the colonies, were mobilised during the war years. Of that total, 1.4 million were killed or lost, compared to 1.7 million for Germany and 725,000 for the UK. Some 200,000 civilian non-combatants also lost their lives. Of the 3 million soldiers wounded, 1.2 million were considered *mutilés de guerre*, mostly unable to work and in need of financial assistance. The agony was prolonged by the more 'democratic' Spanish flu of 1918–19 which scythed down a further 400,000 victims. Such losses were all the greater given the scale of the task of post-war reconstruction. In purely statistical terms, the recovery of Alsace-Lorraine (pop. 1.9 million) partly offset this deficit, but it could do little to plug the gaping holes elsewhere across France. As already noted, anxiety was already considerable before 1914 about declining demography and its social consequences. Now the problem was unavoidable, given the huge number of widows (600,000) and orphans (700,000) by 1918. With over 1 million more adult women than men in France, the prospects of demographic stabilisation, let alone recovery, looked especially dismal; the actual loss of the most active cohorts of the male population would be compounded by a severely reduced next generation of children.

And, of course, the enormous numbers of war-wounded who were still young but incapable of working and entitled to a pension represented a new burden for both families and the state's finances.

Those finances were, at it happened, in parlous shape by 1919, both mirroring and exacerbating the wider economic situation. Less than 30% of the costs of war were met by taxation, a proportion that was higher than for either Britain or Germany. Income tax, although adopted in mid-1914, was only paid from 1916 onwards and generated relatively little funds. War bonds and other forms of borrowing, especially from the US, covered the remainder of the expenditure. Worse still, as that debt rocketed, France's considerable pre-war foreign investments simultaneously went up in smoke, with the major debtor-states, particularly Russia and Turkey, either collapsing altogether or reneging on their obligations; scarcely half of those investments survived the war. Thus Clemenceau's obstinacy in seeking massive reparations from Germany, based on the reconstruction costs of the fifteen *départements* occupied during the war, comes as no surprise, especially as the anti-reparations US firmly refused to cancel France's debts to it. Meanwhile, heavy borrowing led to a massive depreciation of the *franc germinal*, hitherto one of Europe's most stable currencies, although it did recover by 1919 to around half of its pre-war value. The accompanying inflation, especially since 1917, which the agricultural slump aggravated, meant food-price hikes and growing hardship for many civilians. Inevitably, with prices rising by 340% during the war as a whole – but especially in 1917–18 – accusations of profiteering were levelled against farmers and businesses. Worker militancy, evident in the growing number of strikes, was on the rise again. It owed much to the discontent of women factory workers who were invariably paid less than male workers and who were consequently harder hit by price inflation. Until they left government in 1917, the Socialists had worked to obtain better conditions for workers, including obligatory arbitration in disputes with employers that the latter had successfully opposed in the pre-war years. In April 1919, Clemenceau introduced the eight-hour day in order to counter a wave of strikes. By then, France was much closer to full employment than before 1914, but that did not prevent the return of sharp conflicts in the volatile post-war period.

## II

The principal survivor of France's great war was the Third Republic itself; no other regime since that of Napoleon I had weathered such a crisis. The war consolidated the republic to a degree that surprised many, politicians included; it made some pre-war divisions largely redundant, beginning with the biggest of them all. When the post-war Radicals sought to revive the anticlerical laws of 1905 that had been mothballed in 1914 and to extend them to the newly recovered Alsace-Lorraine, the resounding lack of support forced them to abandon the idea altogether. The war-record of French Catholics was irreproachable, and many of them entered parliament and government in a very different political climate after the 1919 elections. Unbeknown to anti-clericals, anticlericalism was no longer a mobilising card. Within a few years, diplomatic relations with Rome were restored and the diocesan associations for the custody of church property that Pius IX had roundly condemned were established. Tensions still existed, with church leaders remaining highly critical of the republican regime's *laïcisme*, especially over schools. Catholic politicians and voters remained heavily conservative in affiliation, and efforts to create forms of christian democracy had only limited success in the inter-war years.

However, the war did not radically change the republican political system itself. Clemenceau's so-called dictatorship, which largely side-lined both parliament and cabinet, was provisional and disappeared with him in early 1920. The 1919 elections produced a parliament two-thirds full of new faces, almost half of them war veterans; the political formations were largely unchanged. A new voting system designed to generate more solid coalitions than hitherto was introduced, and it duly returned the 1919 conservative *Bloc national* and the 1924 Cartel of the Left. But a quirk of the system was that a majority of votes did not automatically translate – often far from it – into a majority of seats in parliament. It also became clear by the mid-1920s that these coalitions were more effective electorally than governmentally: within a year or two of election they tended to disagree and fragment, leading to the familiar outcome of a dizzy turnover of governments. That and a pervasive gravity-pull towards the 'moderate' centre ensured that between 1920 and 1940, the average length of a government was a mere six months; by far the longest and most decisive of them were those led by ex-president Poincaré (Jan 1922–June 1924, July 1926–July 1929). Consequently, a return to the pre-1914 voting system was agreed in 1927, and was implemented during the remaining pre-1939 elections, but without delivering greater political cohesion. Such continuing patterns did little to reduce an aversion to parliamentary democracy, especially in right-wing circles, which criticised its ineffectiveness, irresponsibility, and supposed corruption.

The pre-war galaxies of parties and their sub-sets did not change much either during these years, with the exception of a party that would only come into its own after 1945, the Communist party. Post-war France was not immune to the enthusiasm for revolution generated by the Bolshevik revolution in Russia. Preventing such revolution became a major objective for conservatives and centrists in post-war France, and guaranteed them substantial electoral support. The prospect of revolution also divided the Socialists and trade unions. At the SFIO congress of 1920 at Tours, two-thirds of the delegates voted to join the new Leninist Third International, leaving the Jauresian minority led by Léon Blum to rebuild the Socialist party over the following decade; similar divisions affected the largest trade-union, the CGT. Yet despite its initial advantages, the new PCF long failed to make much headway. Indeed, its bolshevisation on the orders of Moscow actually lost it over two-thirds of its initial membership by 1930. Its increasingly confrontational, not to say sectarian stance towards other left-wing formations, ruled out entering into electoral coalitions, which in turn kept its parliamentary representation small; its deputies represented mainly the 'red suburbs' of Paris and several rural *départements* across central France with a long history of peasant rebellion.

The chief task facing the post-Clemenceau governments was economic reconstruction, which in theory German reparations would pay for. This meant that domestic and foreign policies were inextricably related. But reparations quickly became a highly charged political issue and, from a French perspective, an alibi that enabled the Weimar government to drag its feet over paying. In 1923, Poincaré grasped the nettle and occupied the Ruhr area with the intention of taking rather than waiting for what was owed to France. British and American opposition to this move only encouraged German resistance on the ground, but a negotiated solution emerged in 1924 (the Dawes plan), which included a schedule for future reparation payments and French military withdrawal from the Ruhr. Poincaré thus partly got his way, but France was clearly isolated internationally and its currency vulnerable; that weakness was confirmed by subsequent adjustments, reductions, and moratoria on German reparations. For the remainder of the 1920s, Poincaré's contemporary, the virtually permanent foreign minister, Briand, attempted the alternative approach of conciliating Germany within the framework of collective security associated with the new League of Nations. But there was little natural support for such efforts, and relatively little was achieved before the Nazi regime appeared in early 1933.

During these same years, France's actual reconstruction, which was more or less completed by 1925, was paid for essentially by tax hikes and substantial borrowing (both domestic and foreign), which made an already big debt-mountain even bigger. The result was a sharp fall in the value of the franc and renewed inflation. Poincaré responded with a set of measures nicknamed 'the financial Verdun' of 1924, but its effects were only temporary. The Left cartel governments that followed from 1924 onwards proved unable to master the continuing financial problems; caught between the need to retain Socialist support and to satisfy business interests, they became increasingly unstable. Finally, Poincaré returned to lead a 'national union' government in 1926 and promptly set about cutting budgetary deficits, for which he raised taxes. In 1928 the franc was fixed at 20% of its 1914 value – a drastic measure that earned it the nickname of the Poincaré *franc*. Such medicine hit France's numerous savers extremely hard, but it restored the state's credit, repatriated funds recently invested abroad, and boosted French exports. Moreover, Poincaré's timing also helped the conservatives to win the 1928 elections. By boosting confidence, political as well as economic, these measures prolonged the post-war revival and postponed France's rendezvous with the great depression. Having recovered strongly after 1919, industrial production remained at a high level, as did foreign trade, well into 1930, both helped by a solid currency. The internal market soaked up much of the output of consumer goods, sparing France for a time the problems facing other, especially more industrialised nations with greater exposure to international markets. Unemployment remained low, partly because of the post-war demographic deficit, with immigrants filling many of the resultant gaps. It was in such an upbeat context that the decision to build the expensive but ill-fated Maginot line was taken.

In certain respects, the post-war reconstruction looked backward rather than forward, for which a price would be paid during the subsequent depression. The rebuilding of damaged industries was conceived as a matter of straightforward restoration rather than of modernisation or merging for future global competition. This was especially so for older industries where small-scale units and conservative attitudes to investment dominated. In the newer automobile, chemical, and electrical sectors, conglomerates and *sociétés mixtes* proved more forward-looking; having been stimulated during the war, such 'cartels' appealed to government and, especially, to business interests wishing to protect markets and control prices. But most of the state control and initiatives of the war years were closed down by 1921; the liberal-conservative establishment had little interest in maintaining permanent or systematic forms of *dirigisme*, which would have to wait for another generation.

In addition, the fact that the urban population finally overtook its rural counterpart in the 1931 census did little to alter the self-image of France as rural and agricultural – especially when 'urban' extends to populations of just 2,000 people. Agriculture still accounted for the largest occupational group (36%), and outside of the Paris basin and north-east, the vast majority of holdings remained small, even marginal. It is thus no surprise that across a range of staple crops during the mid-1930s, French agricultural productivity figured last in comparison with ten other European economies. Plans for technical and financial assistance to modernise agriculture were devised by both experts and parliamentarians, but they failed to attract the sustained attention of the Radical (i.e. moderate) politicians who owed so many of their seats to rural voters. With the ensuing depression came falling agricultural prices, and thus little prospect of major change.

Other unfinished business commanded even less attention. With the return of peace, the role of women in French society had become less easy to ignore. Their experience of autonomy in their workplaces and households during the war was, as elsewhere in Europe, unprecedented. In a country with as many dead and walking-wounded as France, a return to the status quo ante 1914 was improbable, even if many thought it desirable. By now the great majority of women's associations, even those of Catholic and conservative leanings, believed it was time to grant the right to vote for women: their record on the home-front since 1914 surely entitled them to the status of full citizens. The Chamber of deputies concurred overwhelmingly in May 1919, although one-third of the deputies were absent or abstained. Not for the last time, the real hurdle was ratification by the Senate, and many politicians expected – and probably secretly wished – that it would reject the bill. Under little pressure, the upper house finally condescended to debate the issue in late 1922, only to kick it into touch where, despite subsequent efforts at revival, it effectively remained thereafter. Not even a 488-to-1 resolution by the chamber in 1936 in favour of the vote made any difference. If this heavily symbolic Rubicon was not yet to be crossed, at least several elements of the legal subordination of wives to husbands enshrined in the Code Napoleon were abolished in 1938.

What was certainly on politicians' minds after 1918 was how to restore France's enormous population deficit. Immigration plugged many gaps but was viewed purely as a temporary stopgap, which only a rise in birth-rates could remedy. But it was far easier to vote measures against abortion (which Vichy would later make a capital offence), forbid information on birth control, or slap an extra tax on males and females over the age of 30 without children, than it was to achieve actual demographic recovery. None of them prevented a birth-rate that was Europe's lowest since the 1920s from falling *below* the death-rate during the mid-1930s. Despite much discussion and some private initiatives, more positive incentives failed to emerge. Only with the family code of July 1939 was a comprehensive pronatalist scheme promulgated, granting financial allowances to women with two or more children who remained at home to raise them. As with income tax in 1914, its timing was unfortunate and its implementation would have to wait until after 1945.

France's equivalent to the 'roaring twenties' was the hardly less evocative *années folles* ('crazy years'), a label that is strongly suggestive of the social and cultural churn they generated. To many in France these years seemed like a return, in spirit if not in substance, to the *belle époque*. The continuities were visible in that the most important artistic, literary, and intellectual figures of the pre-war period were still active. The differences would gradually emerge in new movements, intellectual and artistic, while the sharpness of those differences would be intensified by the unusually big gap between the pre- and post-war generations, something that became especially apparent during the 1930s.

Inter-war Paris remained Europe's premier cultural melting pot. Its cosmopolitanism was reinforced by emigrés escaping from new regimes in Russia, Italy, Germany, and Spain, but also by its attractiveness to no less exotic figures like Joyce or Hemmingway. Montmartre, the historic capital of 'Bohemia', acquired a rival in Montparnasse, where many of the new generation congregated. Of the new and recent cultural movements, Surrealism represented the most radical rejection of traditional ideas of reason, human progress and, more broadly, everything that bourgeois culture represented. Growing out of, and rejecting Dadaism, it gradually took shape under the leadership of André Breton, whose Surrealist manifesto of 1924 advocated an art centred on the unconscious and the automatic. Then and later, the movement attracted a wide spectrum of intellectuals and artists, from poets (Eluard, Aragon), writers (Artaud, Breton, Cocteau), film-makers (Clair, Buñuel), and painters (Dali, Miró), many of whom collaborated in each other's work. But under Breton, Surrealism was not a tolerant, broad church, and it noisily rejected the Fauvists, Cubists, and Abstraction. Hardly surprisingly for intellectuals who deliberately sought to subvert 'normal' ideas, the Surrealists' politics were themselves theatrically turbulent, especially in their relations with the Communist party, which Breton and his closest associates joined in 1927. Many of them boisterously left it later, especially during the crises of the 1930s (Spanish civil war, Moscow trials), refusing to accept Breton's own 'dictatorial' behaviour. The Surrealists were far too diverse and fractious to be 'representative' of the French avant-garde. Yet their efforts to align art, ideas, and political commitment prefigured many of the key dilemmas of the more troubled 1930s.

Viewed from the consumption rather than the creative or intellectual end of the cultural spectrum, the return of peace in 1918 witnessed an intensification of earlier developments. This was helped by social changes, such as the shorter working day and week for industrial employees, which the reforms of the Popular Front would take further still, especially by introducing workers' rights to paid holidays. Increased leisure-time and rising wages also generated greater demand for a range of cultural and sporting activities. Pre-war overtures towards more mixed, demotic cultural forms in music, cinema, and theatre gained ground, especially with the growing influence of America. Of course, the familiar world of newspapers remained well inhabited, with 175 regional dailies still appearing in 1938. Of the biggest-selling Parisian titles some, like the *Petit Parisien* and *Paris-Soir*, were relatively new, selling three-quarters of their print-run in the provinces. The numerous weeklies were often mouthpieces of specific political tendencies, but they also covered cultural and related developments. By the late 1930s, a new competitor emerged, the magazine, beginning with *Marie Claire*, *Confidences*, and the illustrated *Match* (later *Paris-Match*). A far more revolutionary competitor made great strides during these years. In 1927, France had about 600,000 registered radios, by 1939, 5.2 million – equivalent to one for almost every two households. Stations were both private and state-owned. As a purveyor of news, radio challenged the existing press, especially as it gradually came to enhance the coverage of current events. But it was the broadcasting of music, theatre (both popular or highbrow), and sports that set radio apart. As a medium for making French people out of provincials, it proved far superior to the previous vehicles (road and rail, education, military service) because it brought France to their doorsteps rather than vice-versa.

Post-1918 France also resumed its passion for the cinema, despite having fallen behind the US during the war years. The switch from silent to talking films after 1928 further enhanced American domination, but French production of full-length films rose from 130 in 1922 to 170 in 1937. By 1938, when 250 million cinema-tickets were sold, the medium had overtaken rather than destroyed theatre and music-hall (which boasted enduring favourites like Rossi, Trenet, and Chevalier) and now claimed over 70% of all box-office receipts. Cinema was not all 'mere' entertainment, as documentaries or current-events 'shorts' made by Pathé or Gaumont were also shown. It was also during these years, and especially the 1930s, that an enduring French tradition of making films of serious political or moral content was forged, thanks to a generation of original directors like Jean Renoir, Marcel Carné, Jean Cocteau, and René Clair, whose personal political convictions inspired their best work. With them, cinema both echoed and contributed to the wider debates, and especially divisions, about the country's condition. As on previous occasions, the 1937 World Exhibition in Paris showcased the host nation and city's wealth in the arts and technology, and left a legacy of landmark buildings such as the *Palais de Chaillot* and the *Grand* and *Petit Palais*. But the two most notable pavilions of 1937 were those of Nazi Germany and the Soviet Union, their fortress-like exteriors reflecting the implacable rivalry of two rival systems.

## III

Depression finally hit France by early 1932, just when it seemed such a fate had been avoided. Its immediate trigger, the devaluation of sterling in September 1931, quickly eroded France's previous advantage in foreign trade, exposing it more than previously to the realities of the international slump. Ironically, only a few months earlier the *Banque de France*, thanks to its huge gold holdings, had been lending heavily to both Britain and Germany. Factors that had hitherto protected France, such as a fixed currency, now aggravated matters. Starting late, the depression followed a long timetable peculiar to France that, thanks to the rigours of German occupation after 1940, remained mired in depression until 1945, whereas the other major economies had begun to recover by 1935.

France compounded its problems after 1932 by refusing to join Britain and the US in leaving the gold standard, and by pursuing orthodox deflationist policies, cutting deficits and wages while raising transport and other costs. This response sucked demand out of the economy, while failing to balance the budget or align French with foreign prices. With exports increasingly expensive, the government's response was to erect a protectionist tariff-wall, a common tactic worldwide after 1929. At home, cartels were encouraged to agree on production volumes and prices as a convenient way of protecting domestic output. Although state interventionism grew during these years, it was ad hoc in character; it was far removed from economic planning and, if anything, it reduced competition even further. One consequence was that, increasingly, France had to fall back on its colonies, both as a source of raw materials and as markets for finished exports. By comparison with 1929, industrial production dropped by a quarter by the mid-1930s; agricultural prices slumped even more heavily, partly because of over-production, which hit incomes in rural France especially hard. Only devaluation was likely to reverse such trends, but the successive 1930s governments were committed to fiscal orthodoxy, and especially to a stable currency and balanced budget. By the time France finally quit the gold standard and devalued in September 1936, several years had been lost; its economic problems were now engulfed in social and political turmoil that included a wide spectrum of disgruntled parties.

One reason why options to deal with economic crisis were limited was that the May 1932 elections produced a substantial majority for the Left (and left-leaning Radicals), dominated numerically by the Socialists. But the latter would still not form or join a government, and during the next two years the Radicals, led by Edouard Herriot, proved unable to produce stable governments; all of them collapsed because of Socialist opposition to more austerity in dealing with economic problems. There was no Poincaré now to command respect and fix what was broken. Worse still, such paralysis was badly timed, as it allowed the frustrations of numerous social groups that considered themselves victims of economic recession to fester. Such *immobilisme* further undermined the reputation of France's elected politicians at a time when organised and mostly right-wing groups were increasingly taking politics onto the street. As we have already seen, 'alternative' political leagues had existed since the 1890s and were still growing in numbers and in membership, especially in the early 1930s. The older leagues, such as the royalist *Action Française* and the League of Patriots, were established institutions by now – with their newspapers, annual congresses, house-intellectuals, and so on. But newer organisations, such as the *Croix de Feu* of 1928 (with about 100,000 members by 1932), *Solidarité Française* (about 30,000 members), or the *Jeunes patriotes*, ate aggressively into their territory by the early 1930s, attracting *anciens combattants*, students, and some disillusioned left-wing militants into their ranks.

Such a proliferation of street-focussed groups was hardly unusual in inter-war Europe, but historians disagree sharply over whether these French groups should be considered fascist, with the requisite authoritarian ideology marked by anti-Bolshevism and aiming at a one-party state led by a dictator. Given the fluidity of the notion of 'fascism', it is probably pointless to seek a simple 'yes' or 'no' definition of groups whose actions and expectations adjusted to changing situations. Several of their leaders and rank-and-file were formerly Communists or from the political left; others were conservatives and Catholics; some were racist and anti-semites, others not. What they opposed is often more evident than what they represented, and for many the real moment of truth only came with France's defeat in 1940. There is no disputing that most were hostile to the Republic, whose decadence they all denounced; their hatred focussed especially on the cliques – Jews, freemasons, and other *métèques* (aliens) – who, they alleged, manipulated and corrupted it from behind the scenes.

The expansion of such groups, their parades in uniform, their provocative gestures – all contributed to the confrontational environment of the 1930s, in which political scandals easily became a catalyst to direct action. The Stavisky affair of early 1934 provided the classic ingredients: a Jewish swindler who had corrupted politicians, newspapers, and the police, and who successfully avoided trial for years on end, before being found dead in highly suspicious circumstances in January 1934. A succession of revelations, arrests, and ministerial resignations brought the various groups of both right and left onto the streets, culminating in the violent clashes of 6 and 9 February, when an invasion of the Chamber was narrowly prevented by the police, but at the cost of 17 dead and over 2,300 wounded on 6 February alone. The Daladier government fell overnight, the first time a riot had such an outcome. Suddenly, it seemed that the political system was vulnerable to a paramilitary *coup d'état*, although that had not been the intention of the leagues. The intensity of the shock was visible in the first responses to it. A new conservative government of 'national unity' was quickly formed. Within days, the Communists, on the Comintern's orders, began dropping their long-standing hostility not merely to the Socialists as 'social fascists' but even to the Radicals, and agreed to join an 'anti-fascist' coalition. Within a year, such an alliance, the *Rassemblement populaire*, was hammered out, with a moderate programme of economic reforms inspired more by Roosevelt's New Deal that by socialist theory. Inaugurated with a huge demonstration on 14 July 1935, the *Rassemblement* became the basis for the Popular Front that triumphed in the May 1936 elections.

## IV

The Popular Front (June 1936–April/November 1938) remains one of twentieth-century France's most mythic moments – rather like 1848 for the nineteenth – seeming to bring a 'new' republic and a more just social system suddenly within reach. Only months earlier, in March 1936, a similarly broad Popular Front was elected in Spain, and its accession anticipated events in France by sparking off widespread social movements, both rural and urban. For the first time ever, France's Socialists (but not its Communists) were prepared to enter government, and Léon Blum formed a ministry that included three women as under-secretaries of state despite the continuing lack of the franchise for women. The depression was biting hard by then, as previous governments had been crippled by a lack of political will to agree on, or apply effective remedies. The Popular Front, as its name suggests, was as much about atmosphere and expectation as about concrete policies. It was far less radical than later myths suggested, but its supporters were more so. Thousands of largely spontaneous strikes involving the occupation of factories by workers – which made lock-outs and other strike-breaking tactics of the Clemenceau era unusable – began even before the Blum government took office, culminating with that of the huge Renault car factory by its 30,000 workers. They opened the way to social concessions that had seemed inaccessible for so long. The 'Matignon agreements' were hammered out in early June 1936 during negotiations between unions and employers under the government's auspices (itself a landmark). Maurice Thorez, the Communist leader who a few months earlier had promised a revolutionary conquest of power by the working class, now demanded, and rapidly obtained, the termination of the strikes; more startlingly, he also preached a new gospel of social collaboration with peasants and middle-class employees. The unionisation of workers rocketed five-fold during these early weeks, suggesting that the working-class was coming on board.

The core of the Matignon agreements was a 40-hour, five-day working week, collective bargaining between workers and employers, trade-union representation in firms with more than ten employees, a rise in wages of up to 15%, and two weeks' paid holidays per year. For later generations, these were the foundational *acquis sociaux* – social rights that were no longer negotiable and that should be extended wherever possible. As part of the Blum government's broader strategy for economic recovery, these measures were intended to soak up excess capacity and increase demand. Plans for public works, agricultural subsidies, and bonds to attract small investors were also announced, as was extending the age of compulsory schooling. Anticipating resistance from employers and conservatives generally, the government placed the *Banque de France* under state control, nationalised armaments production, and created a wheat office and a national railway system, the SNCF. Having promised during the elections to support the *franc*, it was soon forced to devalue it in September 1936 (and again in 1937), a move that did produce an economic spurt in the following months. Nevertheless, it indicated that Popular Front policies were already in trouble, especially as price rises soon eroded the salary increases. By early 1937, faced with rising inflation and budgetary difficulties, Blum effectively put the Front's (moderate) reforms on hold, which meant that its reformist momentum was lost. A year later, the political coalition that had made the Front possible had, like so many before it, fallen apart. A hostile, conservative-leaning government led by the Radical, Daladier, took its place and rolled back many of the Front's reforms. By then, thousands had taken holidays, helped by cheap railway travel, and seen the sea for the first time, all of which in turn stimulated the further growth of leisure and sports facilities. The Front went out with a whimper, having briefly united the Left and raised enduring hopes for a better quality of life among those who had experienced it.

The Popular Front's difficulties were due partly to the fact that it could not simply ignore conventional politics. At home, its very existence enraged the political right, and the extreme right most of all. It moved swiftly against the leagues whose activities had made the Front possible in the first place, dissolving several of them in June 1936. The *Croix de Feu* was immediately resurrected as the conservative *Parti Socialiste Français*; it abjured street-politics for the republican ballot-box and had the largest membership of any political party by 1939. Almost simultaneously, the *Parti Populaire Français* was founded by the ex-Communist, Jacques Doriot, and attracted disillusioned or excluded figures from the Left. While no guarantee of domestic harmony, such moves steadied the ship and prevented a repeat of the 1934 riots.

The growing international tensions proved far more challenging, and not merely for the Popular Front. Having come to power just a year after the retirement of Briand the conciliator (Jan 1932), Hitler set about wrecking what remained of the Versailles settlement and accelerating German rearmament. He then re-occupied the demilitarised Rhineland (March 1936) in the face of both Anglo-American indifference and inaction by France and the League of Nations. Such inaction further dented French credibility and encouraged a *sauve-qui-peut* response among its post-war allies, especially across east-central Europe. Well before 1936, French conservative nationalists had lambasted the political and military establishments for their indecision and open squabbles over how to counter the threat from Nazi Germany. The decision of early 1931 to build a defensive Maginot line from Switzerland to Luxemburg only was presented as evidence of France's peaceful intentions, but for its allies that signified that direct French intervention to support them in case of danger was unlikely. At home, the slow pace of military modernisation was perceived by many as leaving the armed forces with antiquated hardware and correspondingly limited tactical options.

The dominant military doctrine, developed primarily by Pétain, remained one of defence. Such a posture chimed well with the 'never again' or outright pacifist attitudes towards war that developed strongly in the inter-war years. Numerous intellectuals, teachers, trade-unionists, and other opinion-formers were active pacifists, although the rise of fascism and the Spanish civil war forced many of them to rethink their positions. But the nearer war with the most fascist and dangerous of all enemies loomed, the less prominent pacifist sentiments became. Nevertheless, there was enormous pressure for peace to be given every chance of success. Thus popular responses to the Munich agreements were highly positive, only to alter considerably within months. Where Chamberlain returned to London proclaiming 'peace in our time', Daladier, surprised by the huge crowds that welcomed him at Le Bourget, could only retort, 'what idiots'. By 1940, a fearful country knew it might well be Hitler's next target and increasingly accepted that war might be no longer avoidable.

Entering office only months after Hitler's triumphant re-occupation of the Rhineland, the Popular Front was keen to oppose fascism abroad as well as at home. A hefty and sustained increase in spending on re-armament followed, so much so that the government faced a major dilemma: how to finance *both* social reforms and re-armament. Following the two objectives simultaneously precipitated further budgetary overruns, capital flight, and pressure on the currency at a time of unusually difficult financial conditions. The ensuing clinch forced a suspension of the reforms in early 1937, as the need to catch up with German and Italian military expansion saw France spend far more on guns than on butter. In addition, the Spanish civil war, which became the most 'popular' anti-fascist cause of the 1930s, coincided with the Front's years in power. In the event, its dismal failure, along with that of other democracies, to support the legitimate Spanish Republic – and *its* Popular Front – against the Falangist revolt did it extensive reputational damage, especially since both Germany and Italy openly supported and equipped the rebels. Blum's strict non-intervention policy could hardly reassure those who worried about how France might react if Nazi Germany attacked them.

Since re-occupying the Rhineland in March 1936, Hitler had remained relatively un-troublesome, focussing mainly on quickening German re-armament. The *Anschluss* with Austria in March 1938 heralded a new surge of activity, culminating in the Munich agreement of Sept 1938 that enabled him to dismember Czechoslovakia. The humiliation that such appeasement heaped on France and Britain was all the worse as they had initially, it seemed, foiled Hitler's designs on Czechoslovakia. But their continuing mutual mistrust came to his rescue. Britain's Chamberlain was prepared to defend France but feared anything resembling a blank-cheque in support of French policies across Europe. France under Daladier was seeking to defend its eastern allies, of which Czechoslovakia was one, that were essential to its efforts to constrain German expansion, yet it allowed Britain to take the initiative and appease Hitler. The same inability to checkmate Hitler applied to his next target, Poland, another historical French ally and protégé. When Stalin, tired of French vacillation, finally preferred a deal with Hitler (the Nazi-Soviet 'non-aggression pact' of August 1939), the door was immediately opened for a German-Russian partition of Poland, which took only three weeks to complete. Such blistering success now left France and Britain, having declared war against Germany on 3 September, with the prospect of facing the undivided force of German military power. German offers of peace in October 1939 were turned down, so the state of war continued. Despite that, France and Britain did little more than mobilise their forces and station them defensively along the anticipated line of Germany's westward advance once Poland had been wiped off the map. Even when Germany occupied Denmark in April 1940, they did not budge. The 'phoney war' lasted nine months until 10 May 1940 when German forces first smashed through, or outflanked, the allies' defensive lines, as they had in 1870, 1914, and 1918, only this time to finish the job as comprehensively as in 1870.

This disaster has produced a whole library of answers to the question, 'what was wrong with France in 1940'? Writing during 1940, Marc Bloch, who was both a historian and a reserve officer, labelled it the 'strange defeat', with the high command as the principal, but not the only, culprit. Pétain, the 'hero of Verdun', vehemently denied that it was the army's fault, pinning blame on the politicians and French society generally. Charles de Gaulle excoriated the military, beginning with Pétain himself; but he added that only a battle had been lost, and that the struggle to come would vindicate the character of the 'true' France. Then and later, as we shall see, personal and political agendas underpinned the widespread retrospection concerning these years.

In fact, the expenditure on French re-armament since 1936 meant that it had as many divisions, almost as many aircraft, and actually more naval forces and tanks than Germany by 1940. But the two opponents developed radically different views of how they should be deployed. France had the 'wrong' kind of airpower and most of it was not even located in metropolitan France in 1940, while its tanks were thinly dispersed as back-up for conventional infantry operations. Colonel de Gaulle was a rare French advocate of concentrated, tank-led *blitzkrieg*, but his ideas were largely ignored until it was too late. France's high command was still fighting the previous war, unable or unwilling to switch to more offensive tactics but also making few plans for military survival in the immediate short-term.

## V

In the event, the rout of 1940 was staggering because it was more than merely military. Once they had had been sliced through like butter and then encircled, France's static-defensive infantry divisions were rounded up in huge numbers within six weeks. This is not to imply that they gave up without a fight. In numerous individual encounters they fought fiercely and inflicted heavy casualties on German forces. They were out-thought rather than out-fought. Of the 1.8 million troops taken prisoner, over half would remain in the camps until 1945; by comparison, 'only' 50,000 soldiers were killed in 1940. Bad as the debacle was, it was in turn dwarfed by the social upheaval that accompanied defeat, as over 8 million civilians from the northern regions, terrified by either personal experience or stories of German brutality towards civilians in 1914–18, precipitately headed south-wards. Civilians and masses of defeated soldiers jammed the roads, where they were routinely strafed by a Luftwaffe intent on crippling 'normal' military mobility. As the German armies advanced inexorably, they found cities like Lille, Rouen, Troyes, Chartres, not to mention small towns and villages, virtually emptied of their populations. In Versailles, a town-hall notice read: 'Evacuation order – the *mairie* requests everyone to flee'. Little more encouragement was needed; as in the past, the government itself promptly left Paris for Bordeaux. With the Germans initially banning fugitives from returning home without permission, huge numbers of people faced severe problems of dislocation, employment, and subsistence.

Where the Polish, Belgian, and Dutch governments fled abroad to fight on rather than sign terms with Hitler, Pétain openly sued for an armistice on 16 June, a day after his promotion from deputy to full prime minister. Daladier, along with a few fellow-ministers and deputies fled to Morocco, possibly to establish a government-in-exile, but they were arrested on arrival at Casablanca the day before the armistice was signed (21/22 June), repatriated, and accused of treasonable behaviour by Pétain. There was no chance whatever of a re-run of the 'sacred union' of 1914. Since then, political divergences had deepened as well as widened, with supporters and enemies of both Nazism and Bolshevism now complicating earlier align-ments. Consequently, political realism – or defeatism – took its course, championed now, ironically, by Pétain, the 'hero of Verdun' who had begun advocating capitulation only a week after the German invasion began. His age and unparalleled reputation re-assured the population that he would protect them, but he also had a right-wing agenda that was not yet widely familiar. The new driving force was his deputy, Pierre Laval, a former social-ist, pacifist, and prime minister with many political scores to settle; above all, he was convinced that France must now imitate the successful totalitar-ian regimes. On 10 July 1940, he cajoled and manipulated the deputies and senators assembled in the Grand Casino of Vichy into voting 'full powers' to Pétain by a majority of 569 to 80 with 20 abstentions. At Laval's insistence, the Third Republic was formally abolished, replaced by a somewhat non-descript 'French state' that, pending a promised new constitution, pledged to 'guarantee the rights of work, the family and the *patrie*'. In fact, there would be no parliament, parties, deputies – or even a new constitution – to impede the new authoritarian government, whose hostility, and that of its staunchest supporters, to the Republic and everything it symbolised was visceral. De Gaulle's famous 'appeal of 18 June' was the only public act of defiance against capitulation, but it was scarcely known at the time.

This outcome probably exceeded German expectations, as a defiant government-in-exile determined to fight on would have rendered the task of governing metropolitan France much more problematic. De Gaulle would attempt to fill that role, but as he lacked any recognisable basis to claim it, his task proved a long and tortuous one. Meanwhile, Hitler granted the Pétain government relatively lenient terms, while also enjoying the luxury of carving up France in a novel fashion (see Map 8). The regions north of the Loire and west of a line from Tours to the Spanish frontier near Saint-Jean-de-Luz were subject to military occupation; these were the richer parts of France, and the ones that Hitler needed most in his conflict with Britain. The remaining regions, embracing south-central France broadly speaking, were left to a compliant French government under Pétain. But everywhere French civil servants, police and other familiar institutions could continue to function as usual, even within occupied France where, of course, they were under close German control. To that quite considerable extent, the core of the French state survived defeat intact, cutting directly across the new regime's desire for counter-revolution. As in 1870, Alsace-Lorraine was annexed to Germany and subjected to a grim combination of repression and nazification. The carve-up was completed by a 'forbidden' strip of territory from Switzerland to the Channel, some of which was governed from German-occupied Brussels.

The costs of German military occupation were also to be paid by France – and they were not modest, despite the limited scale of German military and civilian officialdom based in France. Deliberately inflated, they were set initially at 400 million francs *per day*, equivalent to over half of the government's revenues. Increased to 500 millions when the Germans occupied the hitherto unoccupied Vichy zone in November 1942, and then to 700 millions after D-Day, those sums were paid punctually until August 1944, by which date they totalled the astronomical sum of 860 billion *francs*. Heavy as these and other German terms were, they probably felt tolerable when the alternatives – especially direct military government everywhere – were considered. The new Vichy regime had some semblance of autonomy that enabled it to rebut charges of being a mere vassal-state of Germany. At his encounter with Hitler in October 1940, Pétain promised to collaborate with Germany, though not to join it militarily in the war against Britain. That suited the still-victorious Hitler perfectly, as he had no intention of treating

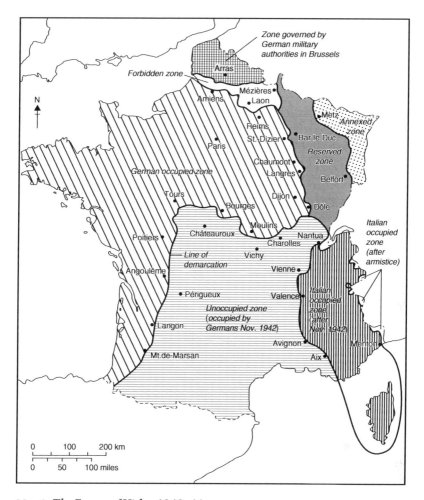

*Map 8  The France of Vichy, 1940–44*

France as a partner. The fall of France freed him to prepare war on his real enemy, the Soviet Union. However, once Hitler discovered, like Napoleon before him, the military quagmire that was Russia, German demands on France would quickly escalate, producing by 1942 several knock-on consequences that would prove increasingly divisive.

Vichy – both the place and the regime – remains a byword, like its Norwegian counterpart Quisling, for capitulation and collaboration in the negative, dishonourable sense. However, it was not stable or consistent throughout its four-year existence; its location on the authoritarian right of the political spectrum did not prevent continuous factional in-fighting resembling that of the Republic it replaced. In 1940–2, Pétain wanted to be – and to be seen as – the active head of government, so he rapidly discarded Laval and his immediate successor. By 1942 that would change, as German pressure increased inexorably, well before the occupation of the unoccupied 'Vichy' part of France that November. In April 1942, the Germans forced Pétain to recall Laval, who was henceforth 'head of government', with Pétain himself reduced to 'head of state'. 'Laval II' was even more anxious to impose himself, which led to increasing collaboration with, and even anticipation of German demands in order to maintain a modicum of political initiative.

The Vichy 'ideology', as personified and expressed by Pétain, was a return to the 'eternal France' of conservative thought; its trinity of 'work, family, country' was intended to replace the much-disliked, un-historic republican abstractions of 'liberty, fraternity, and equality'. The *maréchal* proclaimed a 'national revolution' that was designed to renew or recover the 'true' (i.e. rural and peasant) France rather than to revolutionise it. But Vichy France was still dominated by Third Republic politicians and officials, whose behaviour and attitudes made them the most unlikely revolutionaries. Moreover, the small-scale governing apparatus around Pétain, housed in spa-town Vichy's many hotels, displayed none of the youthful energy of fascist regimes elsewhere. Indeed, before 1942–3, the most ideologically 'fascist' elements of the French right were – and felt – unwelcome in 'Vichy-land'. They much preferred Paris, where they could consort with, and be funded by the German administration. The latter also tightly controlled intellectual and artistic life, from newspapers to theatre, and thus drew a large number of French intellectuals – many of them would-be politicians – into collaborationist or at least very ambivalent relations with the Nazis. Vichy, in contrast, was well buttoned-up, preferring the traditional socio-political pillars such as the church, the army, bureaucracy, and business. But with Laval II that would ineluctably change. The pressures on his government made the participation of the most committed collaborationist groups seem indispensable and desirable by 1942–3. By comparison, Vichy's efforts, especially in and after 1941, to attract young, modernising technocrats into its service were a sideshow, albeit one with a very bright future after 1944. It briefly seemed possible, within a less sclerotic political environment than that of inter-war France, to modernise its economy and institutions. But here, too, timing was beyond everyone's control: the technocrats' plans and blueprints hardly got off the drawing-board before the Liberation.

Subject to partial and then full German occupation, the population of France almost universally accepted the strange defeat of 1940, seeing few prospects of its undoing until at least 1943. The increasing number of restrictions on mobility and activity made the challenge of 'making do' more difficult for many. The familiar demographic deficit was now compounded by the loss of at least 1.5 million prisoners of war who remained either in camps or working on farms or factories in Germany until 1945. As in 1914–18, such a massive additional loss most affected an agricultural sector that was still under-mechanised and heavily dependent on manual labour. The fall in agricultural productivity during the war varied from one staple crop to another, but was commonly somewhere between 20% and 50%. As if that was not enough, German food requisitions and purchases diminished the available food supply by a further 15%.

Partial rationing, introduced in September 1939, became total a year later. Peasants could at least engage in self-subsistence, but urban populations were less capable of doing so, even when they had access to empty land or cabbage plots. A grey and black market developed, and dependency on such sources of food became a way of life – a 'culture' even – for many people. Town-dwellers with rural connections, family or otherwise, were better positioned than most to get by. But urban wages fell by a quarter between 1938 and 1943, making it more difficult to afford the black-market prices for basic necessities. Nutritional levels in France during these years were exceptionally low which, among other things, seriously reduced the productivity of industrial workers. Those willing to work in Germany were at least better fed.

The 'dark years', as these are often called, differed from previous 'hard times'. Most obviously, they were the result of comprehensive military defeat and occupation, which produced widespread resignation to the new status quo. But France was not Poland or Russia and the Germans knew full well they had to behave differently there. Early relations between German troops and officials and French people were less hostile than is usually imagined, as both sides tried to work out a *modus vivendi*. The results varied widely from place to place, as different terms for acceptable degrees of fraternisation with the occupier were also improvised; those deemed to have gone too far, especially young women, could be shunned, criticised and, as happened to many at the liberation in 1944, beaten up or even summarily executed. The number of German officials and police resident in post-1940 France was so small that normal law-and-order administration simply had to be left to French officials; there was no purge of town-halls and local government, and ordinary French citizens had little contact with the German occupier. Yet the resulting triangular relationship generated all kinds of ambiguities and dilemmas, which people negotiated as best they could. Rather than a nation painted in black (collaborators) or white (resisters), the majority of French people belonged to a very large grey 'middle' intent on using their wits to lessen the burdens of occupation and scarcity.

The environment of Franco-German co-habitation was itself unstable, mainly because of Germany's failure to defeat Soviet Russia. By 1942, increased German demands for both foodstuffs and manpower; the escalation of persecution of Jews and other groups; the growth of armed resistance; the German occupation of the unoccupied zone – all inevitably affected Franco-German relations, though without necessarily producing incidents or reprisals in every locality. They pushed the Vichy regime itself into a more overtly 'collaborationist' posture than previously. Symptomatic of this shift was the German-driven return, as already noted, of Laval as head of government in April 1942. More pro-German than previously, he was now overtly contemptuous of the Pétainist moonshine of 'national revolution'. As problems mounted and resistance activities spread, Laval II's Vichy attracted several prominent fascist figures into key roles. Pétain's view of 'collaboration' signified limited inter-state co-operation which did not have to be pro-German in inspiration; that of Jacques Doriot, Marcel Déat, Joseph Darnand, and others was viscerally ideological, boosted by their frequentation of German Nazis in Paris. Whereas Vichy's first *commissaire* for Jewish affairs, Xavier Vallat, was anti-German, he was replaced, again at German insistence, in early 1942 by the rabidly collaborationist Darquier de Pellepoix. As opposition to Vichy grew, the extremists responded by organising and deploying new armed units, the notoriously thuggish *Milice*. By late 1943, again with German support, extremists had gained further ground, becoming ministers in Laval's government.

The treatment of France's Jews illustrates the trajectory of the Vichy regime's collaboration with Nazi Germany. In the post-1945 generation, it suited most French people to believe that the persecution of 'outsiders', especially Jews, by the Vichy regime was, like many other policies, conducted on German orders, which simply could not be evaded. But that politically convenient myth was subsequently shattered by abundant evidence to the contrary. Instinctive dislike of immigrants and foreigners was a well-known right-wing prejudice long before 1940. In fact, the pre-war Daladier government had already rounded up many immigrants, especially from Spain or Germany, in holding camps; Vichy then handed many of them back to their governments, while extending its own hit-list of undesirables to include freemasons, Communists, and Jews. The speed with which such measures were taken is also worth emphasising. Within a month after the armistice, a commission began reviewing the citizenship of people naturalised since 1927, investigating about 500,000 cases. Some 15,000 people were deprived of their French nationality; about half of them, in turn, were Jews, overwhelmingly from abroad.

The regime was not yet ready to intern French-born Jews, because so many belonged to the middle and professional classes. Yet the *statut des Juifs* law of 3 October 1940, promulgated without any German pressure, showed that Vichy was preparing to exclude Jews from certain professions. The revised *statut* of mid-1941, which allowed Jews either no or only limited access to the major middle-class professions and businesses, showed which direction Vichy policy was taking. Simultaneously, a census of the Jewish population of the unoccupied zone was ordered. Vichy also began to 'aryanise' Jewish businesses, something the Germans had commenced earlier in Occupied France. After the Wannsee conference had decided upon the 'final solution' in January 1942, some 75,000 Jews in all – from a total population of around 330,000 – were deported to the extermination camps in Germany, where relatively few survived. Some Jews escaped deportation thanks to their own networks, financial resources, and help from non-Jews, although prejudice and fear ensured that such 'kindness of strangers' was in relatively short supply. The zeal displayed by the French commissariat for Jewish affairs, a haven for some exceptionally unpleasant anti-semites, in identifying, rounding up, and deporting Jews surprised even their German counterparts, who were more accustomed to the foot-dragging of Vichy officials. The attitudes and actions of the French authorities towards Jews varied from place to place. In Paris, for example, it was mostly foreign Jews who were deported, but in the Loire valley, the local prefects did not spare French Jews and claimed that no Jews were left in the region by late 1942.

The ramping-up during 1942–3 of German demands for labour and resources represented a very different challenge. Vichy had earlier encouraged volunteers to work in Germany in the hope of bringing prisoners of war back to France. But the results were mediocre, which led to direct German demands for 250,000 workers for 1942, and a further 500,000 for 1943. Typically and after trying an unsuccessful scheme of its own, Vichy undertook in early 1943 to organise the new *Service de Travail Obligatoire* (STO) rather than surrender control of it to the Germans; it was modelled on the now-mothballed system of military recruitment. The STO proved enormously damaging to Vichy, since it mainly affected the more naturally pro-régime rural population, whereas skilled workers, especially if employed in industries deemed essential to the German war-effort, could obtain exemption from such service. Soon enough, STO dodging-rates began rising, with many draftees simply disappearing into the 'bush' (*maquis*); and as those rates rose, Vichy responded with 'muscular' methods to round up the *réfractaires* (draft-dodgers) and punish the local people hiding and protecting them. As the *réfractaires'* numbers grew, especially in the more inaccessible regions, they were subject to regular manhunts by German troops and French *milices*. For most of them, refusing the STO was, as with military service in earlier generations, a non-political act; but inevitably, such refusals politicised and led some of them to join resistance groups that, by 1943, had certainly increased and multiplied.

Between them the shock defeat of 1940, the failure to establish a government-in-exile, and the reassuring presence of Pétain at the helm ensured that resistance, popular or organised, to German domination was slow to emerge. The Communist party, which figured prominently in the subsequent Resistance, initially had its hands tied by the 1939 Nazi-Soviet pact, which had provoked its dissolution in France and the imprisonment of many of its members. De Gaulle's 'appeal' of June 1940 only reached a few ears outside of the French emigrés in Britain and made few immediate converts. Early resistance was a steep learning process and was rarely of the armed kind; it mostly involved individuals disillusioned with Vichy gradually coming together to share their discontent and, in due course, using clandestine printing presses to forge identity papers, diffuse papers, tracts or posters, and so on. Initially, this was less dangerous in town than in country, especially in the Unoccupied zone, where the Vichy government was not yet actively pursuing protesters. Resistance grew in a slow and uncoordinated manner, with women often playing a major role in an environment where the attention of the authorities focussed instinctively on the activities of adult males. Indeed, it was such activity that persuaded the conservative de Gaulle to bow to pressure from within the Resistance and finally to grant the suffrage to women in 1944.

By 1942 numerous organised groups existed whose acronyms, political affiliations, and alliances recall the political tapestry of the Third Republic. With the Nazi invasion of Russia in mid-1941, the Communists returned to the fold. But their underlying motives were widely suspect to other groups, thus making co-operation between them as difficult as it was for their collaborationist enemies in Vichy. The former prefect-turned-resistant, Jean Moulin, worked tirelessly to unite the various movements under the umbrella of the CNR (Conseil National de la Résistance) by early 1943, with de Gaulle as the recognised leader of the French resistance. Moulin's fate – tortured to death by the Gestapo – is a reminder of how dangerous resistance could be, as the Germans, energetically supported by the Vichy *Milice*, were adept at infiltrating groups and 'turning' those caught into double-agents.

As already noted, not all deserters (nicknamed *maquisards*) from the STO were politically committed, but that changed incrementally during 1943–4, making some of the most inaccessible regions of rural France major points of resistance muster. And as the geographical scale and the numbers involved in the Resistance grew, so did their activities, which involved, among others, intelligence-gathering, helping allied airmen to escape, disruption of communications, sabotage, and assassination. Inevitably, the last of these activities tended to alienate local communities, which knew only too well the kind of reprisals – hostage-taking and mass-shootings – that German occupying forces unfailingly inflicted on them. Yet as the moment of liberation in 1944 came closer, the more numerous and better supported the resister-*maquisards* became. Once the Allied invasion of June 1944 began to roll German forces back, the resistance swarmed across virtually every region, but even then their *active* members and capacity were limited. When some of them decided, in June–July 1944, to abandon hit-and-run tactics for direct encounters with German forces, as occurred in Brittany, Auvergne, and the Vercors plateau, the results were disastrous.

De Gaulle would later claim that France was a country of 40 million resisters and that Paris was liberated by its own citizens. Both statements were 'politically necessary' myths designed for post-liberation consumption, against which a later generation of historians would launch a counter-claim that there were as many pro-Vichy collaborators as there were resisters. That de Gaulle could march triumphantly down the Champs-Elysées at all on 24 August 1944 was due to his enormous persistence and self-belief, which helped him to minimise and to some extent overcome faction within the Resistance. Churchill's early support for him was critical, but it did not prevent numerous clashes with the prickly and gesture-sensitive general thereafter. While de Gaulle's military skills remained largely untested, his political antennae were exceptional. He set about imposing his leadership of 'Free France', initially by rallying support in the un-occupied French colonies, especially in North and West Africa, where significant French military forces remained mobilised after 1940. It was his hard-won success over a series of military rivals, especially in Algeria, that gave him real pre-eminence within the Resistance; without it, he would have made little impression on the Anglo-American allies who – the Americans in particular – long preferred rival figures such as Darlan and Giraud to de Gaulle. Kept uninformed of the precise date set for D-Day, he transformed the main resistance organisation into a provisional government in Algiers only days before it began. Within a week after the invasion, he made sure he was in Bayeux, the first French city to be liberated; he did the same elsewhere to widespread popular acclaim, proclaiming the illegitimacy of Vichy and preparing the ground for national renewal. The political capital that he accumulated proved vital in forcing the hand of the Allies; his rapid despatch of hand-picked *commissaires de la République* to the liberated areas enabled him to thwart Allied plans to subject France to military administration. The sooner France could be rendered self-governing under civilian rule, especially after such a long occupation, the easier it would be to avoid a possibly bloody civil war and return to normal conditions. For the same reason, de Gaulle ordered the dissolution and integration of the resistance units into the reconstituted regular army, to prevent them maintaining their autonomy or causing potential trouble.

France was conquered in just six weeks in 1940, but its liberation from German forces was more arduous. A second Allied landing in Provence in August 1944 helped by advancing rapidly up the Rhône valley. Although German forces were not finally driven out until March 1945, all but the Vosges-Alsace region was liberated by mid-September 1944. A week earlier, de Gaulle formed a government of national unity, but it had serious difficulties in restoring order, as elements of the resistance were unwilling to hang up their boots and leave politics to Paris. In numerous places, improvised purges and score-settling threatened law and order. Occurring in roughly two stages – the spontaneous and the officially organised – these purges involved some 10,000 executions (of which only 1,500 were formally legal) and 50,000 'degradations' stripping those condemned of certain civic rights. Pierre Laval was executed, while Pétain himself was condemned to death, but escaped with life imprisonment and degradation. The mass of France's administrative civilian and military apparatus survived intact. Some major culprits did slip away, escaping notice or obtaining discreet protection in 1944, only to be brought to book by French justice, often reluctantly, decades later. Their trials re-opened painful memories, but for the great majority of French people they revealed the frequently un-glorious realities of life under occupation.

## CHRONOLOGY

1914   Battle of Marne halts German invasion; stabilisation of front in
       North-East
1916   Battles of Verdun, Somme
1917   Battle of *Chemin des dames*; mutinies in armed forces; Pétain
       military commander of French forces; Clemenceau prime minister
1918   Anglo-American-French armies repulse German offensives;
       Germany accepts armistice; Right wins legislative elections
1919   Treaty of Versailles; France regains Alsace-Lorraine; Germany
       agrees to reparations

1920    SFIO split, majority join breakaway Communist party (PCF)

1922    Female suffrage accepted by Assembly, rejected by Senate

1923    France occupies Ruhr region

1924    Left cartel wins elections; Dawes plan for reparations; France recognises Soviet Union; Surrealist manifesto

1926    Moroccan revolt repressed

1928    Right wins elections; France rejoins gold standard

1931    Colonial exhibition in Paris; economic recession hits France

1932    Céline, *Voyage au bout de la nuit*; first number of *Esprit*

1933    Hitler comes to power; Air France created; Malraux, *La Condition humaine*

1934    Stavisky affair; political riots, fall of government; left-wing coalition begins to form

1936    Action française dissolved; electoral victory of Popular Front coalition; social protests/strikes, Matignon agreement on social reforms; Spanish civil war

1937    Blum government halts reforms, resigns, returns; Paris World Exhibition; Renoir, *La grande illusion*

1938    SNCF created; Popular Front government falls; measures to intern foreign immigrants; Munich agreement

1939    France recognises Franco regime; war with Germany; Communist party dissolved, deputies arrested

1940    German invasion; defeat of French armies; armistice, collapse of government; France divided into 'occupied' and 'non-occupied' zones; Pétain voted 'full powers' as head of new 'Vichy' regime; Third Republic suppressed; De Gaulle urges resistance; first anti-Jewish laws

1941    Early acts of resistance, which Communists join; first internments of Jews

1942    Pro-German Pierre Laval head of Vichy government; deportation of Jews; Germans occupy previously 'un-occupied' zone

1943    *Service de travail obligatoire* (STO); National Resistance Council (CNR); de Gaulle leader of unified resistance movements

1944    Provisional government under de Gaulle; Allied landings and liberation; purges and retaliation against collaborators; Christian Democrat MRP founded; first number of *Le Monde*

# 8 The *Trente glorieuses* and After

## I

During the victory promenade on the Champs-Elysées in August 1944, de Gaulle famously refused a call to 'proclaim the Republic'. He rejected such a *pronunciamento* on the grounds that the Republic had never been abolished and Vichy was merely an illegitimate parenthesis that could now be closed. For all its consistency and political necessity, this stance could not resolve the practical problems at hand. There was widespread support for political changes that would remedy the Third Republic's long-acknowledged defects. De Gaulle himself was known to favour a much stronger executive within the political system. The rapidity with which he closed down potential rivals (resistance councils, military groups, and so on) to state institutions in 1944 was designed both to prevent civil strife and accelerate orderly political change. An unusually elaborate political consultation followed and was only completed in November 1946. French voters, who included women for the first time, went to the polls no fewer than eight times during 1945–6, before a new constitution and republic – the fourth – were finalised and became operational in January 1947.

By then, de Gaulle, the would-be strongman of post-war France, had thrown in the towel, at odds with the drift towards a regime that, in its final constitutional iteration, surpassed even the Third Republic's enthronement of parliament over government. Fears that de Gaulle had Bonapartist or Boulangist leanings towards dictatorship, as suggested by his ambition to lead a single anti-party 'movement of *rassemblement*', certainly contributed to this outcome. So, too, did fears of the Communist party, by now France's biggest party. De Gaulle was not alone in suspecting the Communists of deliberately 'using' the constitutional vacuum to establish a Soviet-style 'people's democracy' in France, and they in turn played a major part in his departure. In fact, Stalin had directed the party to respect normal politics rather than seize power or provoke revolution in France; its task, he insisted, was to support the interests of international communism against its new enemy, American imperialism.

That hard-fought tussle apart, the new Republic faced fewer overt obstacles or uncertainties than its predecessor had in the 1870s. Due to the discredit of the pre-1940 right-wing political elite, the three main parties after 1944 (PCF, SFIO, and MRP) all belonged to the political left and centre-left; their combined majority sufficed to establish stability during the crucial early years. The MRP (*Mouvement républicain populaire*) was the first Christian Democrat party to achieve a political breakthrough in France. Its early success showed that the clerical-versus-anticlerical alignments of the previous republic were redundant. Within a few years, however, and preceding the full onset of the Cold War, a very different kind of outcast replaced the Catholics – the Communist party. In early 1947, its participation in government threatened to leave it damagingly 'offside' in the war of the classes, as a result of which the party chose to support a wave of strikes against austerity policies and rampant inflation. The ensuing dismissal of its ministers in May 1947 effectively ended the tri-partite consensus that had obtained since 1944 and signalled the onset of Cold War politics. Despite their consistently high election scores thereafter, the Communists were kept out of government for over a generation – until 1981. This long exclusion made any coalition of left-wing forces impossible until the 'common programme' with the Socialists of 1972. In 1947, a Gaullist party, the RPF (*Rassemblement du peuple français*), was founded and soon made substantial electoral gains, mainly at the expense of the Christian Democrats, but de Gaulle himself remained the proverbial 'elephant in the room' for the rest of the Fourth Republic.

It was thus by default that the political forces of the middle-ground – the Third Force, as it was called – came to dominate the Fourth Republic. The new regime effectively faced down the violent strikes and protests 1947–8 led by the Communist-dominated CGT (Conféderation générale du travail), which also nudged it towards the political centre. The rapid turn-over of ministries familiar from the previous republic continued unabated down to 1958, even if reshuffles disguised considerable stability at the personal level. It was not until the mid-1950s, however, that the political system, increasingly dominated by the provincial 'notables' of the centre-right, began to suffer creeping paralysis in facing the challenges arising mainly, but not exclusively, from the dilemmas of decolonisation. At least it proved much more willing than its pre-war predecessor to pursue social and economic changes that were in tune with post-war experiences elsewhere across Europe.

## II

Political rebuilding was not the only challenge facing post-war France. Materially and economically, it was much worse off than in 1918. Intensive, country-wide Allied bombardment had destroyed a massive range of key production, transport, and communication facilities, especially in 1944. The occupying Germans had ruthlessly fleeced its economy without investing in it. Both agriculture and industry were now producing only about half of their already mediocre 1938 output.

Modernisation was overdue, but there was no prospect of German reparations to pay for it in 1945. Hitherto the preserve of authoritarian regimes of right and left, economic planning now seemed a better option than leaving things to businesses themselves. Vichy's limited experiments with planning had whetted the appetite among some politicians and younger technocrats for a more systematic approach, which also figured among the war-time National Resistance Council's agenda. Before that, however, the provisional government of the Liberation had the luxury of doing something that would have been nigh-on impossible in normal times: the nationalisation of a range of key economic actors, some of whom, like Renault, were vulnerable for having collaborated rather too eagerly with Vichy and the Germans. In 1945–6, the major banks – beginning with the previously private *Banque de France* itself – and insurance companies became state-owned, thus giving the state unprecedented leverage over the financial sector. Mines, manufactures, transport, gas, and electricity companies followed suit, some of them now amalgamated into unified state monopolies. The state ended up owning more utilities and businesses than any western counterpart, post-war Britain included. This was not the 'popular' nationalisation or collectivist economy imagined by many workers and trade unions, some of whom expressed their disappointment during the massive strikes of 1947.

In late 1945, a general *commissariat* for 'indicative' planning – France was not Soviet Russia – logically followed such un-primitive accumulation. Work commenced in 1946 on the first plan, led by an experienced international businessman with few utopian fixations, Jean Monnet who, with Robert Schuman, would become the major promoter of European economic co-operation. Almost simultaneously, France obtained desperately needed conventional loans from Canada and the US, which were subsequently dwarfed by the Marshall Plan grants of 1948–51, of which France was the second largest beneficiary after Britain. De Gaulle was not alone in being wary of the US's motives – in this case, its determination to penetrate European markets – but as the Cold War took shape, France's economic dependency on America was inescapable. At any rate, the well-timed Marshall aid was critical not just in enabling Monnet's 1947–52 plan (the first of ten down to 1992) to invest heavily in transport, energy, iron and steel, but also in facilitating wider economic exchanges and, in due course, promoting closer ties between western European economies. By 1949, pre-war production levels had been overtaken, and subsequent plans could shift their focus from mere recovery to more long-term economic strategy and social needs (e.g. schools and hospitals in the 1954 and 1962 plans). Planning alone did not produce growth during these years, especially in the 1960s: the creation of the Common Market provided the kind of manageable competition that supported modernisation efforts. The ensuing economic growth, ranging between 4 to 6% a year, enabled the long period from 1945 to 1973 to be dubbed 'the thirty glorious years' (*les trente glorieuses*).

Such labelling came after the event, in the late 1970s, by which time France had metamorphosed from the 'productivist' society that was demanded in 1945 into a modern consumer society. Perhaps the best illustration of such a revival comes from a sphere familiar for its lack of good news – demography. By 1945 the perspective was similar to, albeit less severe than in 1918: the overall toll of World War Two on France stood at 600,000 dead, with over a million prisoners of war sequestrated for five years in Germany, all of which worsened future demographic prospects. The early social reforms of the Liberation years built upon the pro-natalist ideas of the pre-war years, and offered financial incentives to *familles nombreuses* (i.e. three children and over). Along with declining death rates, especially among children, and growing life-expectancy for both sexes, they helped to reverse France's long-standing Malthusian record, and triggered a baby-boom whose beginnings have been traced back to 1942. The population rose from 40.5 million in 1946 to 46.5 in 1962 and 52.6 by 1972, when birth-rates had already begun to slow down. From the 1950s onwards a growing flood of immigrant workers helped to sustain these unusually high rates of population growth.

These developments created needs and opportunities (e.g. more housing and schools) but contributed before that to increased demand within the economy. Economic growth rates were equally impressive during these years, averaging 4.9% annually during the 1950s, and then rising to 7.6% during 1959–73, when unemployment fell to an all-time low of around 1.5%. Such a record owed much to France's revival as an exporting economy, which was facilitated in part by often-hefty devaluations of the *franc* and by the advent of the new Common Market just when its colonial markets were shrinking. The major negative feature of the period was rampant inflation, which endured through into the oil-price shock of the early 1970s. Nevertheless, Harold Macmillan's quip, 'you never had it so good', arguably applied more to 1960s France than to Britain, whose growth rates were more consistently sluggish.

In 1944–5, the scope of reconstruction extended well beyond economics. By then, a strong desire for a revised state-society compact, one in which the state would take on a more pro-active role in promoting social justice and democracy, had emerged from the combined impact of two successive regime failures, memories of the Popular Front, and Resistance thinking about social and moral renewal. In the new *état-providence* (welfare state), state intervention was set to become a philosophy, not an occasional event; and such a long-delayed 'turn' provided the state with an opportunity to rebuild its legitimacy. France had, as we have seen, much ground to make up in the social sphere, and it helped that the otherwise conservative Gaullists were not averse to such efforts after 1945. The state now had the means to extend its reach beyond economic and territorial (or infrastructural) objectives.

To begin with, the social reforms of the Popular Front were quickly restored. An ambitious social security system, based on family and maternity allowances, unemployment protection, and pensions, followed by other measures such as a minimum wage (the future SMIG), was launched in 1945–6. Funded by obligatory contributions from employers and employees, the new schemes also provided for effective participation by elected representatives of the employees in managing the various insurance funds; it was an act of democratisation that mirrored their new rights to representation on works' councils and management boards of firms with more than 50 employees. It positioned France's trade-unions – suppressed under Vichy, restored in 1944, and now boasting record membership figures – within an elaborate system designed to loosen company owners' long-standing grip on industrial relations. Not everything could, or did, get equal attention during these years. One chronic problem was poor housing, which would worsen with the inflow of immigrant workers for many years after it was publicly denounced by the celebrated *abbé* Pierre in 1954.

During the 'invisible revolution' of the *trente glorieuses* French society was in a greater state of flux than perhaps at any time since 1789. Ever-increasing numbers of young people left the land in search of careers in both the secondary and tertiary sectors, reducing the total numbers engaged in agriculture from 5 million in 1954 to 2 million (or a mere 7.5% of the workforce) by 1975. The accompanying transformation of agriculture is often seen in terms of a transition 'from peasants to farmers' whose business-like outlook and activities replaced a supposedly quasi-subsistence agriculture. Vichy's much-trumpeted rural revolution had brought few benefits to rural France and was then discredited by its politics. Yet until the early 1960s, the post-war story was one of patchy agricultural progress due to limited specialisation and modernisation. From the early 1960s, that changed sharply, with a younger and better-educated generation of forward-looking farmers. They also dominated the farmers' unions, formed cooperative associations, and gained political clout. Mechanised and specialist agriculture was now encouraged, with the *Crédit Agricole* and other banks lubricating the process of change. Where the 1950s had witnessed demonstrations and disruption by angry farmers, the 1960s saw the Common Market's Common Agriculture Policy (CAP) undergird agricultural prices to the benefit of the large and middling landholders. Henceforth, smallholdings declined sharply, facilitating the growth of larger and more productive units focussing increasingly on particular crops. Overproduction and unsalable surpluses became more common, bringing their own sources of discontent to rural France. But the overall result was surprisingly positive: by the early 1980s, France had Europe's biggest agricultural sector, which was heavily mechanised, and was second only to the US as an exporter of agricultural produce.

One major side-effect was a sharp decline in 'village' France, which lost not merely its small farmers but also its labourers, artisans, and shopkeepers. The loss of schools was no less marked, as was the virtual disappearance of parish clergy, even from those regions that were historically strongly Catholic. Town and country became less and less distinct, but the traffic was one-way. The society-wide growth of leisure-related activities would diminish that divide even further, with the motor-car gradually enabling town-based people gradually to re-populate the countryside.

The major social change of these years was the emergence of a much broader urban middle class, in which new-style professionals greatly outnumbered the older bourgeoisie of property-owners and *rentiers*. The post-war welfare state became France's biggest employer and saw a huge increase in the number of civil servants in the widest sense. The *grandes écoles* now came into their own, led by the newly-founded *École nationale d'administration* (ENA, 1946). Their graduates monopolised all senior positions in both the state bureaucracy and the newly-nationalised business sector, crossing over from one to the other – and indeed into politics – with all the ease of the pre-destined. Below them lay an ever-widening tier of lesser mortals, the middle managers (*cadres moyens*). At the lower end, the ranks of the *fonctionnaires* were swelled by more administrators, teachers, and medical personnel than ever. By the mid-1970s, this 'tertiary' services sector accounted for half of all French people in employment. If individual elements of the Third Republic's presence in village France, such as schools and post-offices, were beginning to disappear by then, the 'sociological' presence of the state in general was stronger than ever. As this middle class grew in numbers and prosperity, their aspirations for better housing, white goods, cars, vacations, but also education for their offspring, sustained an increasingly consumer-driven economy.

By contrast, the working class, involved mainly in industry and the building trade, represented a fluctuating one-third of those in employment. Long-standing French aversion to factory work, but also owners' preferences for immigrant labour because of their lack of militancy, meant that a high proportion of about one in six industrial workers by 1975 continued to originate from former colonies of the Maghreb and West Africa. After Algerian independence in 1962, large numbers of them, especially the European settlers, the *pieds noirs*, came to settle in France *en famille*, in contrast to many earlier immigrant workers. Portuguese and Spaniards, but relatively few Italians, Belgians and Poles, continued to join their ranks. Increasingly, however, many workers were native 'immigrants' from elsewhere in France. Most of these workers were unskilled, low-paid and often badly housed in the various *bidonvilles*, the ancestors of the more recent *banlieues*.

The Communist party sought above all to act as the exclusive guardian of the workers' cause, and did so by dominating the largest post-war union, the newly reconstituted CGT. But the bitter 1947 strikes produced a first split in the CGT, when *Force Ouvrière* broke away, with covert CIA financial help; other unions, one of them of Catholic inspiration, the CFTC (Conféferation française de travailleurs chrétiens), later CFDT (Conféderation française démocratique du travail), also dented but did not really challenge the CGT's dominance. While all unions sought to recruit members among newly arrived workers, especially immigrants, French unionisation rates (22% of the workforce in 1970 and still falling) remained low by German or British standards. Yet the 1944–5 reforms gave the unions seats on company boards and a role in collective bargaining. The 1950s and 1960s all experienced major strikes, of which that of 1968 was the largest in French history, as workers demanded their share of the economic boom of these years.

The invisible revolution of these years had its losers, too. In the mid-1950s, Pierre Poujade led a coalition of such groups – artisans, peasants, independents, the older middle classes who felt left abandoned in the brave new modernity then championed by the Fourth Republic's best-remembered politician, Pierre Mendès-France. Although the movement, which flourished mostly south of the Saint-Malo-Geneva line, peaked in the 1956 elections, the sources of *poujadisme* did not vanish in subsequent decades; they provided an anti-Parisian and anti-technocratic language for later protests against modernisation (e.g. supermarkets) and its social effects. Its contents were also open to 'recuperation' by right-wing political groups like the Front National, whose founder, Jean-Marie Le Pen, was first elected a Poujadist deputy in 1956. The repertoire of French 'contestation' remained a wide one, and protests by farmers, hauliers, and other interests against prices (too low for some, too high for others), often in the form of wild-cat blockades of ports or motorways, have been common coin over the past half-century.

## III

De Gaulle's insistence in 1944–5 that France belonged among the victors was designed to cancel out the defeat of 1940. Above all, it meant that France remained a great power, entitled to be a co-occupier of defeated Germany and permanent member of the new United Nations' Security Council. Occupying and partitioning Germany did not resolve the German problem, however. Despite the onset of the Cold War and the formation of NATO (North Atlantic Treaty Organization) to counter the threat of Communism, post-Liberation France was, like post-1918 France, often at loggerheads with its Anglo-American allies over Germany. Divided and de-legitimated as Germany was, its future divided French opinion for at least a decade. Europeanists like Monnet and Schuman sought novel solutions, and pressed for the creation of a European Coal and Steel Community (ECSC) that would pool precious resources among member states. Intended as a precursor of other forms of association and integration, the ECSC was inaugurated in 1952. It had the signal advantage of enabling France to keep a close eye on the Ruhr and Germany generally. By contrast, the idea of a European Defence Community (EDC), also proposed by Monnet in 1950, proved a genuine hornet's nest. Its purpose was to spoil American demands, prompted by the Korean war and problems elsewhere, to re-arm West Germany. This was anathema to France, so the government sought a way around it by creating a European military force that would contain, among others, German soldiers: Germans, but not Germany, would be re-armed. Nevertheless, after four years of debate and fierce attacks by Gaullists and Communists alike, the Assembly declined to ratify it in 1954. Coming at a moment when France was facing military humiliation in Indochina, the rejection served to reinforce NATO. However, the EDF had unintended pedagogical value, opening the way towards a more accept-able forms of association – economic rather than military – that in 1959 would become the Common Market under the Treaty of Rome (1957). This fitted much better, as we have already seen, with the economic recov-ery and modernisation then under way in France, while offering welcome protection to French agriculture. The return of de Gaulle to power in 1958 heralded, though not immediately, a more combative French policy towards Anglo-American domination, one in which French leadership in Europe, either alone or with Germany, was a key aspiration. Better relations with the Communist bloc, a separate French nuclear deterrent, withdrawal from NATO's military (but not political) structure, vetoing Britain's accession to the Common Market because Britain was, for de Gaulle, an American Trojan horse – these were the principal elements in France's search for an early 'third way' in European politics, one that would enhance France's 'grandeur'. However, when American policies, especially over Vietnam, were being heavily criticised worldwide during the 1960s, de Gaulle failed to persuade West Germany (or Britain) to join him in defying US hegemony. In any case, he fully shared the strong anti-Communist sentiments of most French people, and understood France's ultimate need for American protection. His policy of grandeur was primarily for internal French consumption, but few of his successors could rival his ability to articulate it.

Despite these blind alleys and set-backs, post-war France, buoyed up by its growing prosperity, fared much better within Europe than overseas, where it would pay a high price for not registering how hostile the brave new world of 1945 – America, the Soviet Union, and the United Nations – were towards European colonialism. France had done little to reward its colonies for their military contributions in 1914–18, and dealt harshly with the early independence movements during the inter-war years. As we saw, de Gaulle and his wartime resistance rivals rightly viewed the colonies, and especially North and West Africa, as invaluable – because the only – springboards from which to defy Nazi Germany and Vichy. With the Liberation came another potential moment of reckoning. However, despite vague promises to acknowledge the new realities, de Gaulle's obsession with France's great-power status, which virtually all politicians shared, implied redesigning rather than dismantling its colonial empire. What emerged was the concept of a 'French Union' that figured in the Fourth Republic's constitution of 1946. Events would soon show that it was mostly window-dressing. It extended the laws and rights of the French republic to its overseas citizens, but gave their local assemblies few real powers of action and made no mention of possible independence.

From the perspective of colonial societies and their incipient independence movements, France's record in World War II, both at home and in its colonies, was that of a humiliated imperial power. This alone sufficed to make re-imposing the status quo ante with only minimal modifications unacceptable to adversaries of colonialism. There was not long to wait for a response. A revolt in Madagascar was brutally repressed in 1947, using methods that would be endlessly repeated in Algeria a decade later. The Communist Vietminh had already declared Vietnam an independent republic in September 1945, only weeks after Japan's surrender. France engaged in desultory negotiations until armed revolt broke out there in 1946. Financed by the US, which feared the rise of Communism in Asia before, and especially after China became communist in 1949, France would fight a debilitating eight-year war against the Vietminh's guerrilla forces until it was compelled to negotiate at Geneva in 1954. Defeat and surrender at Dien Bien Phu, also in 1954, was France's final humiliation in Indochina, but this war had attracted scant interest in France until then. Because Vietnam had few French settlers and the war there was fought exclusively by the professional army, it impinged very little on French society and opinion, with the exception of some precocious anti-colonial groups.

However, the Indochina war did not remain un-noticed in France's other colonies, and its outcome soon encouraged their independence movements to press their case even harder. The French political establishment was too shaken and too divided by then to resist, and between 1954 and 1960 virtually all of its 'newer' colonies gained independence, beginning with Morocco and Tunisia and including Madagascar. The oldest colonies in the Caribbean were by then better integrated as overseas *départements*, while the Pacific colonies would not begin to make waves until the 1970s.

That left Algeria, the non-colony and the Ulster of France. Its long road to independence in 1962 was particularly distinctive and left painful memories rivalled only by those of the Occupation. The rhetoric of Algeria's 'French-ness' hid a multitude of anomalies and inconsistencies, especially the denial to its Arab population of the political, legal, and other rights enjoyed by its European settlers. Its nationalist movements were gerrymandered out of the local political assemblies over the years, and their modest 'home rule' demands were simply ignored. As early as May 1945, an uprising around Constantine spread across the coastal region, the repression of which involved perhaps some 10,000 casualties – an early taste of things to come. Moves towards independence in neighbouring Tunisia and Morocco in 1954 were bound to galvanise Algeria's nationalists into action. Only three months after France finally accepted an independent Vietnam, the Algerian National Liberation Front (FLN) formally declared independence and began its campaign with the 'red Halloween' atrocities of November 1954. The ensuing conflict, 'a savage war of peace', as it has been called, was not conventional warfare, but continued as it began, with bombings, assassinations, ambushes, and summary executions, some of which spread to the French mainland. Not even French success in the notorious 'battle of Algiers' of 1957 could stop the spiral of violence. By the time Algerian independence finally arrived in 1962, it had claimed perhaps 300,000 lives, 25,000 of them of French soldiers; more deaths would follow independence itself. It also produced the largest migration in French history, as over one million European *pieds noirs*, many of them Jews or of non-French origins, fled the continuing massacres in Algeria to settle in France during mid-1962. Arab Algerians who had worked with the French army or administration (the *harkis*) also left in large numbers to avoid the vicious retribution awaiting those who stayed.

There were several mutually reinforcing reasons, beyond mere geographical proximity, why the impact of the Algerian war on France, then and subsequently, was far greater than that of Indochina. After a century of substantial European settlement and politico-administrative integration, in which the *pieds noirs* consciously distinguished themselves from native Algerians by insisting on their 'French-ness', the idea that Algeria was part of France had taken root. As such, Algeria was the beacon of France's civilising mission, a belief held as much by the Left as by the Right, which made changing attitudes painful. Secondly, some 1.2 million young French conscripts performed their military service there from 1956 onwards, witnessing or participating in a brutal struggle with the FLN and the civilian population that supported it; many were disgusted or radicalised by the experience, which they disseminated in their correspondence or on their return to France. Thirdly, French intellectuals, whether members of the Communist party, fellow-travellers or committed Catholics, played a major role in criticising 'a war with no name' – its aims and methods, and especially the use of torture; a minority went further still and acted as a support network for the FLN. Unlike Britain or Italy, France was the only leading European state to have *both* colonies and a powerful and vocal Left whose ideological hostility to colonialism steadily increased. As a result, 'Algeria' was the apogee of the politicised public intellectual in France. Petition and counter-petition denouncing or defending France's policies attracted long lists of signatories. The most famous was 'the manifesto of the 121' of 1960 which called for 'the right to insubordination in Algeria'. By contrast, the state-controlled radio and television were prevented from reporting 'unwelcome' news. The 'usual suspects' on the political left, such as Sartre, Beauvoir, and many now-forgotten luminaries, wrote or signed petitions denouncing the successive governments' betrayal of the Republic's core principles. As during the Dreyfus affair, the army's 'honour' was again at stake, but that was now pitted against the 'infamy' of France practicing and condoning torture. Such terms of confrontation hit many a raw nerve, and comparisons with the Gestapo's use of torture against the Resistance raised the burning question of how the victims could, or had, themselves become the persecutors.

The biggest casualty of the Algerian crisis was the Fourth Republic itself, whose successive cabinets proved unequal to the challenge after Mendès-France, who had made peace over Vietnam in 1954, was ejected the following year. The political parties were, with the exception of the 'excluded' PCF, too fractured internally to sustain a government for long. Algeria was not the only source of political strife in these years, but by 1957–8 the 'events' there (the word 'war' was studiously avoided) produced an internal 'Franco-French' conflict parallel to that emerging in Algeria itself. A huge demonstration in Algiers in May 1958 saw the army openly support the *pieds noirs* in their determination not to be sacrificed on the Parisian altar of decolonising expediency, even though an independent Algeria was not yet in prospect. The army, which was desperate to avoid another Dien Bien Phu and which effectively ruled Algeria, simultaneously established a 'committee of public safety'; its leaders appealed to de Gaulle to speak out on the crisis. A thinly veiled appeal for a *coup d'état* in order to save French Algeria, such insurrectionist provocation, replete with echoes of 1793, was unfamiliar since the days of Boulanger. De Gaulle declined this new invitation to a *pro-nunciamento*, while declaring himself willing to return to office by 'normal' process. Nobody wanted to re-enact Pétain's investiture 'with full powers' of July 1940, although de Gaulle was granted 'exceptional' powers for six months. 'The general' thus became the last prime minister of the Fourth Republic, despite his unchanged views on the need for strong (presidential) government. His acceptance of office indicated that significant change was now on the cards, and within a few months, he obtained massive approval of a draft constitution for a new (the Fifth) Republic, of which he was elected president in December 1958. An insurrectionary moment produced a peaceful transfer of power and a new regime, not exactly the *coup d'état* that François Mitterrand would frequently accuse de Gaulle of contriving. It was not until 1962, however, that de Gaulle was elected president by direct universal suffrage, as have his successors ever since. That and the Gaullist landslide in the ensuing parliamentary elections was the second coming of the Fifth Republic, whose legitimacy was now firmly consolidated. The fact that the Algerian crisis had been resolved by then was equally decisive for its survival.

The intervening years brought France to the brink of civil war, which the new Gaullist regime struggled hard to prevent. The Algerian crisis, which peaked in 1961–2, was increasingly characterised by pro-'French Algeria' violence on both sides of the Mediterranean, and by fears and rumours of a full-scale military revolt. A generals' putsch in Algiers itself failed to take hold in April 1961, but the threat of its spreading to France sufficed to bring out tanks to protect the National Assembly in Paris. The new and soon notorious Secret Army Organisation (OAS), which would attempt to assassinate de Gaulle himself, advocated a settlers' rebellion and secession in Algeria. The heightened prospect of civil war appears finally to have persuaded de Gaulle to abandon the prevarication and studiously ambiguous language he had used hitherto on Algeria's future. Opting for Algerian independence led to (resumed) negotiations with the FLN and the Evian agreements that followed were confirmed by a landslide vote in April 1962. 'Algeria' had divided friends and allies like nothing else since 1940, or perhaps the Dreyfus affair, but the Fifth Republic was as anxious to 'forget' this traumatic episode as the Fourth had been with Vichy. Yet despite there being so many disaffected *pied noir* immigrants on French soil by 1962, the war's aftermath proved less turbulent than had it occurred under the Fourth Republic. A combination of a new Republic, de Gaulle's policy of national 'grandeur', economic prosperity and social change were largely responsible for that.

## IV

De Gaulle's re-election as president for a second seven-year term in 1965 involved a run-off round against François Mitterrand; two years later, the Gaullists won the legislative elections, but with the tiniest of majorities – one. Both outcomes showed that the age of landslide scores and Gaullist invincibility was not inevitable, and that political normality, at least as expressed by tactical second-round voting habits, had returned. Nor had the Gaullist party that had been resurrected in 1958 absorbed France's other conservative or centrist forces, where anti-gaullism still had many outlets. A Gaullist-led alliance entitled the 'Action Committee for the Fifth Republic' fought the 1967 elections, but that was no guarantee of subsequent cohesiveness; during and after de Gaulle's presidency, a number of centrist, liberal parties survived and gradually regained ground. They remained broadly distinct, despite the constant and confusing re-naming of these parties – the Gaullists most of all! On the left, the tightly disciplined Communists easily remained the largest single formation, still polling well over 20% in successive elections. But their servility towards Moscow, especially in the wake of the Soviet invasions of Hungary (1956) and Czechoslovakia (1968), gradually damaged them, as the visceral mutual hostility between them and the 'younger' Left in May 1968 openly demonstrated. Until the creation of the Socialist Party in 1970, the non-Communist Left was far more fragmented. With a habit of participating in government after 1945, the SFIO had been losing ground, despite depending increasingly on support from outside the working class. It was no friend or ally of the Communists, and leaders like Guy Mollet were rabidly anti-Communist. Even after the Common Programme of 1972, Socialists and Communists were rivals rather than genuine allies.

The post-1958 political 'system' was designed to fit de Gaulle's own preferences, for which it was much criticised. However, its performance after his final departure in 1969 shows that it was much more flexible than previously imagined. Having survived the unprecedented events of May 1968, the first major test came when François Mitterrand, the republic's most persistent critic since 1958, became president in a peaceful, even euphoric, transition from Right to Left in 1981; such an 'alternance' was repeated in subsequent decades, disproving predictions of political gridlock. Moreover, in 1986, Mitterrand found himself 'co-habiting' with a government of 'opposition' political parties led by the Gaullist, Jacques Chirac; the 'co-habitation' experience was repeated twice in the 1990s and thus ceased to be exceptional. Indeed, Mitterrand himself became the Republic's longest-serving president without ever attempting serious changes to its architecture. The key political levers, especially concerning European, foreign and defence matters, remained firmly in the president's and not the legislature's or ministry's hands. This was a major alteration, to which both the political and governing institutions had to adjust after 1958; all political roads led to the Elysée palace and its staff of presidential advisers and specialists. The National Assembly's capacity to overthrow cabinets was also severely restricted, and whenever the two players were at loggerheads, the government could still impose its will by special 'decree' powers. The president chose the prime minister and could dissolve the assembly.

Having jettisoned key elements of the political system since the 1870s, it is not surprising that the Fifth Republic has often been tagged a 'presidential monarchy', the model for which was de Gaulle himself. His tactic of announcing major decisions, especially in moments of crisis, in televised press conferences was both novel and effective. By speaking directly to the nation over the heads of politicians and other (selfish) interests, he further enhanced his status. His use of referendums, which the political class deeply disliked, had the same effect until he unnecessarily went one too far in 1969. His successors extended his recourse to the media, but could never quite match the inimitable style of 'the general', the title (judging by street-names at least) by which he is most remembered.

It is fair to say that the real beneficiary of the economic planning and policy of the Fourth Republic was its successor, which began life on firm economic foundations, especially after Algerian independence. Growth-rates now reached an all-time high, and would continue into the early

1970s. The early baby-boomers were entering their teens, and the new-found prosperity enabled the state, via its successive 'plans', to provide improved educational resources for them. Increasingly, university education (or its equivalent) was necessary to meet the demands of a society in which the service sectors, public and private, now employed three out of five adults in work. Peasant France may have been disappearing, but the industrial working class were still growing in numbers and feeling the benefits of economic growth in rising wages, better conditions, shorter hours, and longer holidays. Large numbers of immigrant workers from the Maghreb and Portugal fared far less well, suffering especially from poor housing conditions.

Women were more numerous than ever in the workforce, and in proportions much higher than among France's neighbours for the time. The 1946 constitution affirmed that no distinction be made on gender grounds for state employments, but for most of the following three decades women tended to be employed in perceived 'female' positions or sectors, as evidenced by the posts occupied by women in government, and were paid less. Gaining entrance to elite institutions like the *École Polytechnique*, the *Académie Française* or the *Collège de France* would have to wait until the 1970s and later. Despite as many girls as boys obtaining the *baccalauréat* by 1965, when female student numbers at university were also rising sharply, it remained difficult for them to enter the major professions (especially law and medicine); teaching was still regarded as their most suitable destination, though university posts remained very hard to obtain. Breaking that mould also took time elsewhere, even in 'modern' fields like the media, where for many years women were decorative announcers rather than programme hosts or animators.

Thus, despite the growing 'visibility' of women, and that at a time when many were having three children, social reality and formal rights were slow to align. For example, it was not until 1965 that married women were finally permitted to take employment and open a bank account without their husbands' explicit authorisation. Taking encouragement from, *inter alia*, Simone de Beauvoir's *Second Sex* (1949), which affirmed that women were made, not born, a determined post-war feminist movement took root but faced stiff opposition. Many of its activists, and especially de Beauvoir, were politically left-wing, participating with other intellectuals in the successive 'campaigns' (e.g. Algeria) of the 1950s and 1960s. That in turn drew wider support for feminist campaigns in a society still deeply reluctant to make the concessions they demanded. The 'events' of 1968 blew off many accumulated cobwebs, and opened up far greater space for campaigning activism. In a country still reacting against so-called Malthusian demography, change came painfully slowly. Unofficial advice centres for family planning had opened in 1956, but contraception was not legalised until 1967; despite the new law's limitations, fierce opposition to it continued, preventing its full implementation until 1972. 'Illegitimate' children finally acquired equal rights in 1972. The greatest taboo, however, was abortion. The campaign for it involved some spectacular interventions by its activists; the most provocative was the 1971 'manifesto of the 343' – many of them household names – confessing (falsely in some cases) to have had an abortion. Such determined militancy eventually paid off, aided by one or two *causes célèbres*. When 1975 was declared the 'year of the woman' in France, Simone Veil was minister of health and Françoise Giroud secretary of state (junior minister) for the 'female condition'. The year was inaugurated with a law allowing abortion, followed by another instituting divorce by mutual consent which, for once, mainly benefited women.

## V

Feminist activism was only one of several movements refracting the social and cultural developments experienced by the post-war generation, and in which the personal and the political were becoming famously entangled. The events of May 1968, which de Gaulle declared at the time to be incomprehensible (*insaisissable*), lifted the lid off the still crusty surface of French society and enabled unfamiliar tendencies to crawl out from underneath it. 'May 68' came as a bolt from the blue: it did not occur, as in the past, during a time of hardship or want, let alone military collapse. Instead, as a journalist famously put it some weeks earlier, 'France was bored' (*la France s'ennuie*), an assertion which suggested an element of frivolity, even psycho-drama, in this revolution *manquée*. Never before had student discontent, which initially appeared to have minimal explicitly political content, provoked such upheaval, which in part accounts for de Gaulle's – and others' perplexity in dealing with it. 'Les jeunes', an imprecise category that included students, were an unfamiliar, new generation whose culture and tastes had previously been confined to magazines, radio or television programmes, and pop music. Now they clamoured for recognition and autonomy, and their most sarcastic and quotable slogans (e.g. 'be reasonable, demand the impossible') also signalled a generational revolt against their elders. Rival student political groups had existed since Dreyfus and been critical of French policies in Algeria; some of the older student leaders of 1968 had either served in Algeria, joined the Communist party for a time, or pursued Maoist, Trotskyite or other libertarian visions of revolution before 1968. The initial protests over university conditions were virtually un-political, while the revolutions represented by their tutelary deities – Che Guevara, Mao Zedong, Ho Chi Minh – had little obvious applicability to the France of 1968 or later. Such intellectual heterodoxies put May '68 on a collision course with the firmly institutionalised Communist party, which was determined not to lose its grip on the French working class or exchange the material gains of economic growth for a make-believe revolution championed by deluded young bourgeois afflicted by a false social consciousness. In reply, the more left-wing students were, the more they despised the party's Stalinism and conservative behaviour.

The differences emerged most clearly during the second phase of May 1968, when huge wild-cat strikes and 1936-style occupations broke out within big industrial plants like Renault and spread like wildfire to other sectors. What to some appeared like the onset of revolution was to the PCF and the CGT an opportunity to obtain wage-rises and better conditions for workers. Negotiations with the government over these issues produced agreement in virtually a single session; despite the CGT being soon outflanked by worker militancy on many factory floors, the 'Grenelle agreements' held and the wave of strikes soon receded. De Gaulle recovered from a brief loss of nerve and obtained support in a massive march by supporters down the Champs-Elysées. He called new elections for late June, which gave his UDR (*Union pour la défense de la République*) party an absolute majority in the new Assembly; the Left parties lost heavily and could only lick their wounds. The new government set about reorganising the university system and, more surprisingly, planning for regionalisation. The political crisis seemed over, until de Gaulle announced a referendum on regionalisation in February 1969. All those groups (which included previous political allies) anxious to see the back of de Gaulle queued up to oppose the referendum, so that when he demanded a 'yes' vote as his condition for remaining in office, the voters called his bluff two months later. He immediately left office, as was his wont. He died in late 1970, insisting on being buried in his own pantheon, Colombey-les-Deux-Églises. By then Georges Pompidou, a former prime minister who had done most to resolve the crisis of May '68, had succeeded him as president, only to die in office in April 1974. His successor, the former finance minister, Giscard d'Estaing, became the Fifth Republic's first non-Gaullist president.

By the later 1960s, as May '68 made clear, it was de Gaulle rather than the Fifth Republic that was the political problem. His rejection by the 1969 referendum echoes the fate of Clemenceau in 1920 – a collective wish to escape from too many years of rule by a dominant individual. But since May '68 was three crises rolled into one, resolving the political one did not banish the others. Subsequent years were marked by bitter individual strikes (e.g. Lip in Besançon, 1973), but which failed to spread nationwide despite generating much support and polemic. Likewise, student occupations and demonstrations became almost routine, especially in Paris, but were not usually sparked by university or school-related problems; equally regularly, they involved skirmishes between the police forces and groups of *gauchistes* bent on demonstrating the repressive brutality of capitalism and the need for revolution; injuries and occasional deaths of protestors led to further confrontations. As during the 1920–30s, the 'street' was again the theatre of collective political action, especially for anti-imperialist causes like Vietnam. It was not 'mere' theatre, however, but was capable of triggering political crises that regularly caught governments off-guard since then.

A new political culture, replete with its rituals, slogans, posters, and tracts, but not confined to students or *les jeunes*, was another major legacy of 1968. The latter gave a real fillip to movements already in gestation (sexual liberation, ecology, or *tiers-mondisme*) as well as to pacifism and regionalism. For the Left as a whole, Marxism was still the basic idiom for political analysis and discussion. The Communist party's rebarbative Marxism-Leninism had already prompted many post-war exegetes to rethink Marxism in the light of the 'young' humanistic Marx's writings in particular; they also tried to connect it to more recent intellectual movements such as existentialism or structuralism. A new generation of intellectual gurus, epitomised by the psychoanalyst Jacques Lacan and the philosopher-historian Michel Foucault, appeared during the 1960s to accompany, challenge, and replace the generation of Sartre and Raymond Aron. They would be joined later, especially during the 1980s, by a more diffuse galaxy of thinkers, for some of whom Marxism itself, and not just Communism, was a recipe, not for liberation, but for totalitarian repression.

By then a series of wider social and cultural shifts was contributing, at least indirectly, to a gradual deflation in the pontifical standing of the French intellectual. The surge in post-war prosperity ultimately produced consumerist life-styles and media innovation that dovetailed into a new landscape of cultural supply and demand. In a country as attached as France to the printed word, a modern visual culture evolved in stages. If newspapers and politics were inseparable, party-political connections became much looser. The most celebrated French daily, *Le Monde*, was founded in late 1944 at de Gaulle's request, but remained steadfastly independent and went on to become the voice of high-brow, middle-class modernity. *Libération*, the irreverent and at times iconoclastic left-wing daily founded by Sartre and friends, has survived several near-death experiences since its first number in April 1973. The much older *Figaro* and

*L'Humanité* continued to serve their respective conservative and communist camps. Special-interest papers like *L'Équipe* (sport) rivalled, if not outsold, most dailies. Apart from these titles, national papers fared increasingly less well than regional papers, whose print-runs remained remarkably high. Weekly magazines (e.g. *L'Express, Le Point,* or *Le Nouvel Observateur*) with significant political or cultural content also flourished, possibly because week-end newspapers remained, by comparison with the dailies, seriously under-developed. Illustrated magazines oriented to leisure and life-styles entered a new era by the 1960s, boosted by the growth of radio and television, while newspapers had to adapt as they tried to gain – or retain – readers. Women's magazines, from *Elle* (1945) and the re-vamped *Marie Claire* (1954) onwards, were even more numerous, but faced the ire of feminists by 1970 for their role in preserving gender stereotypes.

Post-war French cinema audiences were exposed to trans-Atlantic films as never before, largely because of direct pressure from Washington. The government responded by generously subsidising both French film-making and cinemas. That response was crucial in enabling a brilliant pre- and post-war generation of film directors to turn out a distinctively French stream of films that obtained international recognition. It continued – even grew – with the appeal of the 'new wave' cinema during the 1960s, when films by Godard, Rohmer, Truffaut, and others extended French cinema's reputation for exploring social and moral issues. Some of these productions, espe-cially in the 1970s, also dealt with sensitive political subjects like Vichy or Algeria, and generated fierce debate; a few films proved too sensitive to be shown at the time and only made their debut later on television.

Inevitably, television became the cinema's main rival, especially during the 1960s, when it increasingly became one of the household 'must-haves'. Only 13% of households had a television in 1960, but by 1980 it had risen to 90%, well ahead of washing-machines, telephones, or cars. Television was a single state-owned monopoly (the RTF, then ORTF (*Office de radio-diffusion-télévision française*)) until 1974, when it was broken up into seven non-competitive organisations; partial privatisation had to wait until 1981. With just two channels, its programmes were at least culturally unifying, despite the range of genres and subjects they provided. Entertainment dominated their schedules, with live screening of football matches or the Tour de France becoming popular highlights. However, 'real-life' political events, especially if controversial like May '68, were far more sensitive. For years, state control of the media meant formal appearances by de Gaulle or other ministers to explain government policies, as occurred during the Algerian crisis and in May '68. As channels multiplied in the 1970s, more provision was made for interviews and debates, book chat-shows, and other 'tribunes' on current issues (and not just political ones). All of this gave some French intellectuals far more 'visibility' than the printed word, let alone the Anglo-American media, would ever have provided. The price for being a 'media intellectual' was a certain 'dumbing-down' or the relegation of such engagements to dedicated channels or non-primetime programmes.

The *jeunes* who came of age in 1968 belonged to a generation which increasingly benefited from a secondary and higher education. Secondary-school pupil numbers rose from 1.5 to nearly 5 million between 1956 and 1972, with a corresponding growth in *baccalauréat* success year-on-year. This was due largely to the creation of secondary 'colleges' alongside the highly selective *lycées*. University education waited longer to be taken seriously. Before 1968, relatively few new (or expanded) universities were established, despite student numbers quadrupling from around 140,000 in 1950 to 570,000 by 1968. Discontent at the lack of basic amenities was common, and at the new university at Nanterre, which became the eye of the May '68 storm, it erupted as early as March 1967. One major outcome of May '68 was a reform of university studies and the creation of a large number of new universities. Their teething troubles were equally numerous and kept student militancy alive for years to come. The historic *grandes écoles* continued unperturbed by such anxieties, their numbers expanding with the addition of new creations, especially business schools, whose graduates were in ever-greater demand. Middle-class families much preferred such a cursus (and its entrance-exam 'cramming') for their offspring, which had the effect of increasing specialist at the expense of generalist education. The hegemony of the expert, as defined by his or her higher education, was consolidated by the 1970s. It left little prospect of substantial professional promotion to those without quite specific educational qualifications, and favoured social groups with the right cultural capital to negotiate the passage into – and beyond – the *grandes écoles*. By the same token, French universities and their mass of students, lacking the support of the country's elites, faced more acute questions over the value of their courses and degrees than their European counterparts. The decline of the generalist intellectual may have been another consequence of such a turn towards the specialisation of education and interests.

## VI

By early 1974 Georges Pompidou had died of leukemia and Giscard d'Estaing, an independent centrist who had been de Gaulle's and then Pompidou's finance minister, was elected president. The post-de Gaulle

Republic enjoyed several exceptional years of grace, during which France's economic performance outstripped West Germany's. Pompidou could thus strut the European political stage and generously accept the UK's entrance into an enlarged Common Market, while remaining no less insistent than de Gaulle that he favoured a Europe of nation-states. Elsewhere, however, his touch was less sure and his anti-American gestures were less effective than those of de Gaulle. The Pompidou years witnessed further modernisation of the country's infrastructure, pushing ahead with badly needed motorways, new fast railways (the Paris RER, the future TGV), and airports like Roissy. Existing amenities, especially telecommunications, were upgraded during these years. Some of the urban modernisation of these years, especially under Pompidou, was far less felicitous, badly disfiguring the centres of Paris, Montpellier and Lyon among others; the construction of lifeless and poorly serviced dormitory suburbs (the *grands ensembles*) continued unabated, storing up problems for later decades.

Things changed seriously after the Arab-Israeli war of October 1973, when the mainly Arab oil-producing countries' cartel, OPEC (Organization of the Petroleum Exporting Countries), ratcheted up oil prices by 400%. France was not on the blacklist of pro-Israeli countries to which OPEC refused to export oil, but that was little consolation as the world economy, in which France was now far more embedded than ever, faced major recession. As already noted, France had long had high rates of inflation, which hit a record 15.2% in 1974 before dropping below 10% in 1976, but high inflation had hitherto been counterbalanced by impressive growth-rates and rising incomes. Now, growth plummeted to 1% and minus 0.3% in 1974 and 1975 respectively, recovering to a modest overall average of 2.8% for the period 1973 to 1979, which actually put France ahead of the US and the main EEC (European Economic Community)/OECD (Organisation for Economic Co-operation and Development) countries during these years. Investment fell but unemployment, previously modest in scope, jumped from 500,000 to 1 million in 1974–5 alone, and reached 2 million by 1981. By then, the second oil crisis, that of 1979, was, although less severe, another body blow; it sent inflation back into double figures and heralded low growth figures that would endure until well into the 1980s.

By the mid-1970s, the *trente glorieuses* had definitely given way to the age of stagflation (high unemployment and high inflation), whose manifestations perplexed economists and politicians world-wide. It took time for them to grasp that the familiar corrective techniques for dealing with short-term, cyclical down-turns were ineffective. The standard Keynesian recipe of boosting public demand no longer seemed to work, but there was no consensus on the best alternative. These difficulties came to dominate – but not immediately – the agenda of the post-Pompidou governments, forcing them to scrap or delay parts of their electoral agenda. For example, Giscard d'Estaing, who was elected by a tiny majority over François Mitterrand in May 1974, came into office with plans for 'an advanced liberal society'. Reforms implemented soon afterwards included authorising abortion, easier divorce, voting rights at eighteen for *les jeunes*, breaking up the state-broadcaster (the ORTF), and streamlining secondary education. Such acts, which had willing support from the Left, suggested a novel readiness to align political action with the social change of recent decades. But it was quickly curtailed as economic conditions deteriorated, with declining investment and rising unemployment. It led, in mid-1976, to the noisy resignation as prime minister of Jacques Chirac, leader of the Gaullist party whose support Giscard badly needed to govern. Chirac's successor, Raymond Barre, an economist and technocrat rather than a career politician, simultaneously served as finance-cum-economics minister.

This change signalled new priorities. Barre reversed Chirac's consumption-oriented policies by adopting austerity and then liberalisation measures – wage-restraint, additional taxes, budget-balancing, and so on – all designed to make France live within its means, restore the huge balance of trade deficit caused mainly by the cost of oil imports, and re-launch investment and productivity. The Gaullist party, which was reorganised by Chirac in his own likeness, were not Barre's only critics. The 1972 Union of the Left brought together the newly constituted Socialist party of 1971(PS) and the Communists (plus the much smaller Left-Radicals). By 1976, their predictably hostile response to austerity policies began paying dividends in the opinion polls and local elections. But the Union's efforts to update the 1972 programme for the parliamentary elections of March 1978 led to major dissensions. The Communists realised that Mitterrand's Socialists were its main beneficiaries, and retreated into a hard-line position. Such hara-kiri enabled Giscard's UDF (*Union pour la démocatie française*) and the Gaullist RPR to obtain a comfortable but far from harmonious majority in 1978. Raymond Barre continued with his policy of economic stabilisation, which seemed to be working until the second oil crisis struck in 1979, raising oil prices by 300% and sending growth plummeting to virtually zero by 1981.

Despite the ensuing economic gloom, the Left seemed too fragmented to prevent Giscard d'Estaing from winning a second presidential term in the 1981 elections. The shock that ensued was all the greater for that. At his third attempt and by a modest margin, Mitterrand finally made it into the Elysée, and immediately consolidated that triumph with a Socialist landslide in the ensuing parliamentary elections. Chirac's positively tepid endorsement of Giscard deprived him of key votes in the run-off, whereas Mitterrand successfully presented his 110 propositions (mostly taken from the Common Programme) while differentiating them – and himself – from the Communists, whose electoral performance was their weakest since 1936. Consequently, on both ends of the political spectrum people felt re-assured enough to vote tactically, or simply abstain, in the run-off. Of course, such choices punished the Right's failures to deal effectively with economic problems during Giscard's presidency; they also confirmed the underlying leftward drift of French society post-1968.

## VII

Mitterrand's victory was that of a serial survivor and opportunist who carried little ideological baggage and who was often referred to as 'the Florentine', an allusion to Machiavelli and his political maxims. However, his and the Socialists' double victory of 1981 generated enormous euphoria akin to a 'second coming' – this time of the Popular Front. The advent of a full-blown socialist government so feared by the Right passed off without the mythical seizure of power by the Communists, whose political capital had clearly shrunk over the years. With perhaps the biggest mandate for change in modern French history, the new government included, albeit in secondary ministries, several Communists and Left-Radicals. Anxious to capitalise on its post-election 'honeymoon' and in the spirit of the Popular Front, it set about reversing Giscard and Barre's policies and applying Mitterrand's electoral agenda. It introduced wide-ranging changes, such as reforming the penal system, ending the state's grip on the media by partial privatisation, abolishing the death penalty, and decriminalising homosexuality. More expected were the 'Auroux laws' seeking to introduce at least some democracy into the workplace, as well as a tax on the rich. Equally significant, despite its real limitations, was the first attempt since de Gaulle's aborted efforts of 1968–9 to de-centralise the administration, with the creation of 'regions' enjoying wide powers of action. Indeed, so many reforms were tabled in 1981 that there were soon calls for a pause!

As many of the Socialists' objectives needed substantial financing, the nationalisation of numerous industrial and banking concerns soon followed; as in 1944–5, the purpose was to help the new government, still wedded to broadly Keynesian methods, to pilot France towards economic revival. It was to be stimulated by increasing both consumption and employment, which in turn would be facilitated by social measures such as shorter working weeks without salary loss, longer vacations, retirement at 60, a rise in the minimum wage (the SMIC) and other social benefits. A half-million new jobs were created in the public sector. All of this proved expensive and sharply increased the public debt, but without producing a compensating economic surge or improving underlying employment figures. Not even three devaluations of the *franc* could halt the broad surge in the public debt, trade deficit, unemployment, and inflation. In late 1981 and early 1982, with its options now severely reduced, austerity and inflation-control were embraced; both prices and salaries were frozen, but without producing the hoped-for turnaround. The government was deeply divided over what to do next, but by early 1983 the champions of 'rigour' (a term now openly used) led by finance minister Jacques Delors, a future president of the European Commission, had persuaded Mitterrand to abandon independent action within France and remain within the European and international framework. The spectacle of a socialist government espousing, however discreetly, economic liberalisation was deeply unsettling in a country as receptive towards anti-capitalist rhetoric as France had been since 1968. Plans for cutting public-sector spending, and especially for scaling down major but loss-making 'historic' industries, like mining, steelmaking, and ship-building, were only swallowed by the unions because generous funds were provided for the re-conversion and re-skilling of their workforces. Of the western economies during the early 1980s, France was already the odd one out. Its neighbours and competitors had conservative governments (under Reagan, Thatcher, and Kohl) that were ideologically committed to economic liberalism, financial rigour, and belt-tightening policies, which seemed more effective at this juncture; the Keynesian projections of the Common Programme, even in attenuated form, now seemed to belong to another age, that of the *trente glorieuses*.

By 1984, when the Communists refused to continue in office, the worst effects of the economic crisis were receding; the economic climate after the mid-1980s would be less severe. Yet it was the continuing high rate of unemployment that remained most evident. De-industrialisation produced bitter protest, nowhere more so than in the great north-eastern region of the Lille and Lorraine coal and steel basin, but also at Le Creusot and Saint-Nazaire where historic industrial concerns were facing unsustainable losses. The biggest single protest against the Mitterrand regime's policies of these years was not over economic matters, however. It concerned 'private' (i.e. primarily Catholic) schools, which the Common Programme wished to see 'nationalised'. The conflict, which heralded the arrival of 'issue' politics, to which we shall return later, spread across two years and became a stick with which to beat the government and re-mobilise the Right after the battering of 1981. To many people, the proposed school changes seemed a throwback to the superannuated politics of the Third Republic, while the Socialists were accused of attacking 'liberty' itself. Although the government's proposals were both moderate and conciliatory, it was forced to back down in 1984 by massive opposition that extended well beyond the Catholic constituency. Two years later, in late 1986, a similarly huge mobilisation against university reforms had the same outcome: the new government led by Jacques Chirac was caught off guard and had to withdraw its plans. By then local and European elections were already registering a significant resurgence of the Right, with Jean-Marie Le Pen's Front National polling almost as well in 1984 as the Communists, whose decline was beginning to affect their traditional power-bases in industrial urban centres and the working class.

The parliamentary elections of 1986, which were dominated by problems of unemployment and insecurity – these were years of frequent bombings and assassinations – duly confirmed the decline of the governing Socialists. Much of the political debate before and during the elections focused on what might follow a conservative victory. The outcome was itself unprecedented for the Fifth Republic, namely an experiment in political 'co-habitation' between a Socialist president and a right-wing government based on the new parliamentary majority led by Chirac. Both sides had an interest in making co-habitation work at a time when the outcomes of virtually biennial elections, whether local, regional, legislative, presidential, or European, were increasingly shaping policy and political calculation. Indeed, the first Mitterrand-Chirac co-habitation was itself programmed to end by 1988, when presidential elections were due. Both men expected – and were expected – to be the candidates of the rival camps, so in the intervening two years Chirac attempted to burnish his pro-market credentials by reversing the Socialist nationalisations of 1981 (and some of 1944!) and by a more general liberalising of the economy. But although popular with investors, the economic impact of these changes was limited by the tight election deadline, while the stock-market crash of 1987 had more dramatic, if short-term, effects. Thus, when Chirac faced Mitterrand in the 1988 elections, he came off second-best. Mitterrand's campaign for a 'united France' was a far cry from 1981, and by increasing his margin of victory it enabled him to dissolve the Assembly and seek a new parliamentary majority.

The Socialists duly won the largest number of seats, but fell narrowly short of a clear majority. This outcome was reflected in the make-up of the new government led by Michel Rocard until 1991. The able Rocard was a long-term political rival of Mitterrand within the Left, and his cabinet, the biggest in French history, was itself a microcosm of co-habitation, as it included a wide range of ministers who were either non-socialists or with no party affiliation at all. However, five years later, in 1993, the Right won the legislative elections by a landslide, ensuring that the last years of Mitterrand's presidency would be ones of renewed co-habitation, which was by then appearing like a 'normal' option. The electorate had found a way of conveying to France's politicians the message that the 'miracle' of 1981 was not repeatable, and that 'alternations' were now part of normal politics. At another level, it also suggests the slow demise of a long-standing revolutionary conviction, in which only major changes to political institutions (with or without a corresponding social revolution) could fix the nation's problems. With the Communists in free-fall and losing voters in droves to the Front National, and the Socialists chastened by their disappointed expectations, the way now seemed open for more pragmatic take on the scope of political action and government capacity.

# VIII

It may be pedestrian to say that de Gaulle's legacy could not be ignored by his successors, but it was especially true where the wider world-stage was concerned. Having one's own nuclear deterrent made it both inescapable and possible. With some exceptions in the Indian and Pacific Oceans, France's colonial empire was history by the 1960s, but de-colonisation was decidedly limited in scope. Militarily, diplomatically, and culturally, French 'boots on the ground' remained a prominent feature of its relations with its former colonies, especially in Africa. Its economic interests, especially in mining and other raw materials, were a major factor here, with France invariably the principal beneficiary of co-operation or aid agreements with its African partner-states. Such relations, which became a jealously guarded preserve of successive presidents from de Gaulle onwards, were vulnerable to political upheavals in some of these new states. French military interventions, which were not always well judged or well received, propped up many a despotic or fragile regime. In an anti- and post-colonial environment, such dependency, epitomised by France's role as the *gendarme* of *Françafrique*, evoked strong criticism, especially when it produced scandals, as it regularly did. Above all, it was attacked for perpetuating a new form of imperialism under the flag of a shared culture and language entitled *Francophonie*.

By the mid-1960s, de Gaulle had famously frozen the institutions of the EEC, but on becoming president in 1969, Pompidou almost immediately abandoned this particular legacy. Actually proposing the addition of new member-states, he insisted on the positive knock-on benefits of Europe for the French economy. The germanophile Giscard d'Estaing was even more pro-European and his close relations with West German chancellor, Helmut

Schmidt, facilitated moves for greater integration. An informal Council of Europe began regular meetings in 1974, but the idea of an elected European parliament had to wait until 1979, when it was heavily criticised by Chirac and the gaullists as too federalist and 'Atlanticist' to be in France's best interests. Giscard saw in 'Europe' a valuable ally in countering the economic effects of the successive oil crises of the 1970s, even though attempts to create a workable European Monetary System (EMS) were less than smooth or successful.

By the 1980s it was the fate of Eastern Europe that demanded attention, as it sought to escape from under the post-1968 Soviet icecap. The détente apparently achieved by East-West and intra-European diplomacy during the 1970s faded as Cold War tensions were revived, especially by the Soviet invasion of Afghanistan in late 1979, and by the massive build-up of nuclear weapons on both sides of the iron curtain. Eastern Europe's struggles had implications for internal French politics. Many of the most entrenched myths about 'real socialism' were exposed during the 1970s, but neither then nor later was the PCF, unlike its Italian and other counterparts, ready to abandon its servitude towards Moscow or tolerate a degree of internal dissent. The ultimate success and subsequent contagion of the Polish 'Solidarity' movement was warmly welcomed in France, which had many historic ties with Poland. The exception here was the PCF, for which the experience was all the more excruciating as Solidarity was spearheaded by industrial workers from Gdansk to Nova Huta, and directed against a Communist regime turned military dictatorship. Yet few foresaw the general collapse of European communism until the fall of the Berlin wall. Since his election in 1981, Mitterrand had pursued a policy of diminishing the power of the US and the USSR in order to end the Cold War, largely by encouraging integration, stability, and peace within Europe. By 1985–6, this produced, among other things, the idea of a Single European Market, due to take effect in 1992, with the promise of a full-scale European Union to follow. When, with less than enthusiastic French support, a reunited Germany became a reality in 1991, the only available cure for French worries about a new German hegemon bestriding Europe was to lock Germany even tighter into a united Europe. With that purpose in mind, the Schengen Convention of 1990 and Maastricht treaty of December 1991, with its promise of closer political union, a common currency, and a European central bank by 1999, were finalised. But Maastricht, which introduced a single European market, was only adopted by the narrowest of margins in the referendum of September 1992, mainly because many voters, 12 million of whom abstained, viewed it as a surrender of French sovereignty.

The capacity of François Mitterrand to tack and turn was as consummate – and as important – in external as in internal politics during these crucial years. From 1990–1 onwards, he was increasingly willing to leave the business and the brickbats of domestic government to his prime ministers, the last of whom, Eduard Balladur, headed a conservative government of 'co-habitation' from 1993 to 1995. Like Pompidou during his last years, Mitterrand was in failing health by 1992, when his cancer, a long-kept secret, was finally divulged. His second term was characterised by his continuing search for a legacy via his 'great projects' (all of them Parisian) which culminated in the Louvre pyramid (1988) and the new national library (1995). Despite his tense relationship with Mitterrand, Michel Rocard's relatively long spell (1988–91) as prime minister was important, the lack of an assured majority in the Assembly notwithstanding. He quickly opened the way to independence for Nouvelle-Calédonie, which had been a theatre of gruesome incidents in recent years. Fully aware that 1988 was not 1981, Rocard stuck inflexibly to the path of financial rigour and international competitiveness, while respecting the election promise neither to nationalise nor privatise businesses (the 'ni-ni' policy). Equally, though, he understood better than most of his contemporaries the need to rebuild social cohesion; the resumption of economic growth in the late 1980s gave him sufficient leeway to introduce the *revenu minimum d'insertion* (RMI) in late 1988. To be paid for by a new tax on the wealthy, the RMI was a social-welfare benefit for those without work but not entitled to unemployment relief; the condition for receiving it was to engage in the process of social re-insertion (i.e. work), as its name suggested. A million people more than expected proved entitled to collect it, even though the under-25s, the most vulnerable to unemployment, were excluded from it. This was, of course, a reminder that unemployment had not disappeared. Indeed, by early 1993, it reached a record 3 million people, over 10% of the active workforce. Such a statistic suggests growing problems, and the massive strikes of 1988 and, to a lesser extent, of late 1989 were an earlier manifestation of it. In attempting to stem the snowballing of such strikes, the government found itself having to find new financial resources to placate some of the protestors in order to regain control of events. Jean d'Ormesson, a Gaullist journalist, asked what the purpose of the Left could be when it could not guarantee social order.

Overall, the picture changed relatively little under Rocard's successors, Edith Cresson and Pierre Bérégovoy. Both applied liberal economic policies enthusiastically, and for a time the French state became the leading source of job losses! Inflation fell as a result, but not unemployment. With time, it became less and less obvious what separated Left from Right where economic affairs were concerned, not least because many key levers of policy continued to be surrendered to Brussels and international bodies like the IMF. The government of Eduard Balladur (1993–5), which did have a huge parliamentary majority, showed there was at least one difference: the Right would privatise state assets. It certainly needed to at this juncture, as the economy had fallen back into recession; privatisations would fund in part fiscal concessions to businesses in the hope that the latter would rebound and kick-start growth again. The advent of the single European market in 1993 reduced government ability to pick and choose which measures to use, and obliged it to conform to European norms instead. Resentments fed into social discontent, which continued to be widely dispersed, from school-goers to farmers and railway employees, in 1993–4. The inexorable rise, as it seemed, of unemployment during these years, was part of a wider problem which conventional attitudes and methods were now less capable of coping with. It was part of a new social reality – *précarité* or 'fragility' – of which structural job-insecurity, which was already on the rise, was an intrinsic part. This new world of the 'excluded' – the unemployed, the never employed, or the unemployable – was comprised of people of different ages, genders, professions, and social backgrounds, and who had fallen through the *état-providence*'s safety net. Some 'activists' like the comedian 'Coluche' with his 'restaurants of the heart' (soup kitchens) and the already widely known abbé Pierre, had raised the alarm during the 1980s, but its social implications were not widely appreciated until the 1990s.

A major, and not unrelated fracture in French society also surfaced during the 1980s, one that proved equally difficult to deal with, though for other reasons. Until the 1930s, as we have seen, France's immigrants came overwhelmingly from neighbouring countries, but that changed during the 1950s: it was now Portuguese, Algerians, Spaniards, and Moroccans – and in that order – who were the most numerous, working mainly in the major urban and industrial regions. Algerians poured in after independence in 1962. By 1975, immigrants numbered nearly 3.5 million and comprised 6.5% of the population; in 1990 it was 3.6 million and 7%, a proportion that has only dropped modestly since then. By the 1990s, new immigrants from Asia and francophone West Africa were topping the list.

For as long as they were single males who did not envisage permanent settlement in France, immigrant workers were both welcome and unproblematic, especially during the prosperous *trente glorieuses*. With the arrival of economic recession in the mid-1970s, it became clear that 'settlement' immigration had already been replacing 'work' immigration; whole families had been settling in France, where they were increasingly considered a burden on local communities (schools, health services, etc.).

With recession came rising unemployment and competition for jobs, so in 1978 the Giscard government offered immigrants financial incentives to return home, but relatively few, most of them Portuguese and Spaniards, responded positively. Thereafter, the problem evolved into one of how to integrate immigrants, especially the Arabs among them, who lived mostly on the margins of society in the *bidonvilles* and other hastily built *cités* with limited facilities for education and leisure. Clandestine immigration, especially from North Africa, continued in spite of efforts to close it down, leading to large numbers of immigrants without papers facing possible expulsion. Shortly after Mitterrand's election in 1981, some 132,000 cases were examined, but the problem of the *sans papiers* did not vanish; in 1997, 142,000 requests for legalisation were considered, almost half of which were rejected. With governments vacillating in how to deal with immigration (assistance to those willing to return home was reinstated in 1984), it increasingly became a subject of heated public debate. Activist groups like *SOS-Racisme* were formed to defend immigrants and their value to France against attack, especially from Le Pen's Front National, which began gaining ground in the early 1980s thanks to his astute exploitation of popular fear and xenophobia. Le Pen, whose original 'constituency' was disgruntled small businesses and artisans, was a major beneficiary of the decline of the PCF, many of whose historic working-class supporters – and their municipal councils – began moving from Left to Right politically.

To the new Right, Arab and Muslim immigrants were culturally beyond assimilation, replacing the similarly 'alien' Jews for an earlier extreme Right. In late 1989, an apparently banal incident sparked massive polemic over precisely this sensitive question. Three Muslim girls were excluded from their local school for refusing to remove their headscarves. For those who considered this a religious gesture, it was also an act of defiance towards French *laïcité*, which forbade religious symbols in state schools; the magistrates of the *conseil d'état* agreed and banned 'ostentatious' religious symbols from classrooms. The conflict over Catholic schools a few years previously had, as we saw, mobilised the 'lay' and 'religious' camps within French society, but that was an old 'hexagonal' dispute in which most of the passions of earlier generations had cooled; it did not herald a broad revival of Catholic religious practice or militancy. The headscarf affair raised new hackles because it cut right across the assimilationist assumptions of French republicanism that, in its imperial-colonial heyday, made no concessions to 'inferior' peoples or cultures. Now the question of religious (and cultural) difference was being posed within France itself, but not in the historical terms familiar since the Revolution. Nor was it an abstract issue, since it concerned real-life communities in which such cultural difference was embedded.

The headscarf conflict arose at a time when a second generation of French Muslims of (mainly) Arab descent were reaching maturity – and the two phenomena were connected. Familiar only with France, many young French Arabs felt second-class citizens there. Quasi-segregation in the *cités* and peripheral urban districts was aggravated by poor educational (and other) facilities, not to mention antagonistic relations with the authorities, especially the police. Local 'incidents' could spark violent riots, especially in the 1990s and 2000s. On the other hand, there simultaneously developed a hybrid popular culture in music, language, and comedy that was distinctive, but which the mainstream media, more concerned during these decades with categorising Arabs as aliens and dangerous, were slow to adopt and diffuse until the 1990s. The first wave of Islamic militancy in Algeria during the 1990s threatened to spill over into France, but the violence it unleashed was, with a few exceptions, confined to Algeria itself. Indeed, the 1990s saw both sides of the coin, with successful black and 'beur' (slang for Arabs) comedians and, especially, footballers enjoying film-star notoriety, but with localised rather than nation-wide riots in the 'hot' suburbs of Lyon and Rouen as its flipside. Against such a backdrop, France's first-ever victory in the 1998 football World Cup was hailed as a triumph, evidence that a multi-racial *black-blanc-beur* fraternity – the linguistic mix was deliberate – was a model for what could be achieved under the *tricolore*.

## CHRONOLOGY

1945    Nationalisations of businesses and banks; *commissariat* for economic planning; women vote for first time; Pétain death sentence (commuted); de Gaulle head of provisional government; referendum formally ends Third Republic; *Les Temps modernes* (Sartre, Beauvoir, and others)

1946    De Gaulle resigns; new constitution for Fourth Republic; *Union Française* of metropolitan France and colonies; first American loans negotiated; first Monnet plan; war in Indochina

1947    Communist ministers dismissed; widespread strikes; Marshall aid accepted; revolt in Madagascar; population census at 40.5 million; Gaullist RPF founded

1949    NATO pact signed; *Paris-Match* first number; de Beauvoir, *The Second Sex*

1952    European coal and steel community (ECSC) signed; François Mauriac Nobel Prize for Literature

1954    Vietnam War ends, Algerian rebellion begins; European Defence
        Community (EDC) rejected; Françoise Sagan, *Bonjour tristesse*
1956    Morocco and Tunisia independent; Franco-British raid on Suez
        canal
1957    Treaty of Rome; Camus Nobel Prize for Literature
1958    Algiers military coup; de Gaulle heads last Fourth Republic
        government; new constitution for Fifth Republic; de Gaulle first
        president
1959    *Salut les copains* radio programme; Truffaut, *Les 400 coups*; Resnais,
        *Hiroshima mon amour*
1961    Referendum on Algerian independence; failed generals' putsch in
        Algeria; Arab protestors killed in Paris; first album of Goscinny,
        *Astérix le Gaulois*
1962    Algerian independence
1963    De Gaulle rejects British entry into Common Market, vetoes
        European integration
1964    Sartre refuses Nobel Prize for Literature; *Nouvel Observateur*
        founded
1966    France withdraws from NATO military command
1968    The 'events of May', protests and strikes; Grenelle agreements with
        trade unions; Gaullists win legislative elections
1969    De Gaulle resigns after losing referendum, Georges Pompidou new
        president; Jean-Pierre Melville, *L'Armée des ombres*; Eric Rohmer,
        *Ma nuit chez Maude*; Paris-region RER inaugurated; *Concorde's* first
        flight
1970    De Gaulle dies; first feminist demonstration
1971    *Chagrin et la Pitié* film on Vichy; new Socialist party founded,
        François Mitterrand leader; campaign for abortion launched
1972    PS and PCF negotiate 'common programme'; Front National
        founded
1973    First oil crisis; *Libération* appears; Solzhenitsyn, *Gulag Archipelago*
        published in Paris
1974    Death of Pompidou, Giscard d'Estaing succeeds as president; Louis
        Malle, *Lacombe Lucien*; Roissy-Charles de Gaulle airport opens
1975    Law to allow abortion voted; conflict in Corsica
1977    Jacques Chirac first ever (elected) mayor of Paris; union of the Left
        collapses; Pompidou Centre opens
1978    Liberal party (UDF) founded; *Amoco Cadiz* disaster
1979    Second oil crisis; first European parliament elections
1980    *Le dernier métro* (film by Truffaut); *Médecins du monde* founded;
        death of Sartre

1981    Mitterrand defeats Giscard in presidential elections; Left coalition in government; first TGV train, Paris-Lyon

1982    Law on decentralisation, nationalisations; liberalisation of media

1983    U-turn from spending to austerity; decriminalisation of homosexuality

1984    Communists quit government; Green party and *SOS-Racisme* founded; first volume of *Lieux de mémoire*

1985    Successful protests in favour of Catholic schools; violent clashes in Nouvelle Calédonie; Claude Lanzmann's *Shoah* screened; Greenpeace's *Rainbow Warrior* sunk by French agents; *Restos du coeur* inaugurated

1986    Single European Act ratified; first 'co-habitation' after Centre-Right win legislative elections, Jacques Chirac prime minister; protests over school/university reform; Musée d'Orsay opens

1987    Trial of Klaus Barbie; world stock exchange crash

1988    Mitterrand re-elected president; Left win legislative elections, Michel Rocard prime minister

1989    Louvre 'pyramid' inaugurated; fall of Berlin Wall; affair of the head-scarf (*foulard*); Jean-Luc Besson, *Le grand bleu*

1990    Schengen agreement for free circulation with European Union; German re-unification

1991    Edith Cresson first woman prime minister

1992    Euro-Disney opens; Maastricht Treaty on European Union ratified; *Arte*, Franco-German TV station launched

1993    Single European Market begins; Right-wing landslide in legislative elections; new 'co-habitation' arrangement; reform of nationality code; 3 million unemployed; EU formally begins

1994    Channel tunnel opens

# Epilogue

When Jacques Chirac finally made it to the Elysée in the 1995 presidential elections, he was emulating his long-time rival and predecessor, Mitterrand, who had also been elected at his third attempt; and like Mitterrand, he went on to serve a second term, though one of five rather than, as hitherto, seven years. Both presidents benefited from having the biggest, best structured, and most disciplined parties at their disposal. In order to distance himself from the Mitterrand regime, Chirac campaigned energetically on the theme of France as a fractured society needing reform. Such a strategy was risky because the promises he made were bound to raise popular expectations almost in inverse proportion to their lack of specific detail. Crucially, the need for belt-tightening in order to meet the Maastricht criteria in preparation for the arrival in 1999 of the new currency, the euro, soon clashed with, and then took precedence over, reform. Very quickly, individual plans (e.g. reform the social security system, reduce budget deficits) and particular actions (e.g. against illegal immigrants) made the government led by Alain Juppé extremely unpopular. Within just six months, the biggest wave of strikes and protests since 1968 crippled the country and dominated public life for weeks (Nov.–Dec. 1995). In early 1997, Chirac finally concluded that only early parliamentary elections could extricate the government from creeping paralysis and deliver a renewed mandate for reform. To widespread surprise, however, the electorate refused to comply, returning a thin but absolute majority for the Left that wiped out its catastrophic result of 1993 and paved the way for the longest co-habitation regime to date. Moreover, the Socialist Lionel Jospin, Chirac's defeated rival in the 1995 presidential elections, led the new government. That defeat avenged, the Left could now set aside the president's domestic agenda to pursue one of its own. It would remain comfortably in office from 1997 until 2002.

In fact, with the economy performing much better during the late 1990s and unemployment rates falling slightly, the Jospin-Chirac co-habitation worked relatively smoothly for several years. Jospin, whose approach was dubbed 'social-liberalism', declared in 1997, more in regret than in triumph, that 'the state cannot do everything'. Not averse to the fiscal restraint that the 1997 European 'stability and growth' pact demanded, Jospin used funds derived from the privatisation of state-owned businesses to alleviate some of the consequences of economic liberalisation. The Maastricht criteria were duly fulfilled and the euro was introduced without difficulty in 1999. However, implementing the much-disputed 35-hour working week after it became law in 1998–9 did cause much friction, both politically (within the Left itself) and economically (with businesses). Designed to produce more jobs, it failed to achieve its primary objective. The introduction in 2001 of a universal health insurance (the CMU) met similar criticism from business and conservative interests, but its broad popularity overcame such opposition.

Only on his re-election in 2002 did Chirac regain the political initiative, aided by a conservative majority and government that itself held office until 2007. This government's internal fractures were barely concealed, with the hyperactive Nicholas Sarkozy, whose history of defying Chirac would continue, ruffling many feathers with his controversially 'tough' public order and security policies as Interior Minister. There was serious opposition on other fronts, too. The long overdue reform of the chronically indebted social security system, which had been dropped due to the protests of late 1995, was now revived. This time, the combination of a president and government of the same political stripe enabled François Fillon, later prime minister under Sarkozy, to push through, in 2003, the reform of the complex and expensive pensions system, mainly by demanding more years of contributions. This long-unlikely success, achieved despite massive street protests, restored, temporarily at least, the reputation of the Right for 'can-do' government. Its comfortable parliamentary majority allowed it to continue deregulation, reduce both taxes on business and the number of civil servants, and tighten unemployment benefits as part of France's transition from 'welfare to workfare'. A combination of austerity measures and Sarkozy's abrasive approach to policing the *banlieues* and immigrant integration provoked further major protests in 2005 and early 2006.

Nicolas Sarkozy's one-term presidency (2007–12) was the shortest under the Fifth Republic. It was dominated by the financial crash of 2008 and its consequences across Europe. By then, the French state no longer controlled the principal levers of the economy, but the crisis proved how indispensable the state was in containing financial bubbles. Although the BNP Paribas bank was the first in Europe to sound the alarm as early as August 2007, France's financial institutions were structurally sound and, with the exception of the BNP Paribas and the Société Générale, were relatively un-exposed to the American property-market meltdown. New plans for 'economic modernisation' (i.e. liberalisation) were introduced in 2008, but fell short of international expectations, especially as the budget deficit soared well above the European ceiling of 3% of GDP. Consequently, the main economic indicators, especially on employment, trade and GDP, remained 'offside' into the early 2010s, when France suffered the humiliation of losing its 'triple-A' credit-rating. In relative terms, its economic competitiveness had been declining, with its labour laws, high taxes, and social contributions still widely viewed as diminishing its attractiveness to investors. This in turn hit its export-oriented industrial base, leading to knock-on trade deficits. It also kept unemployment levels stubbornly high, especially among the long-term unemployed, whose numbers have increased by over 50% since 2008.

In order to remain competitive, some of France's biggest firms (e.g. Renault, Michelin) had since the late 1990s been moving much of their production to eastern Europe or overseas, where labour costs were far lower. President Sarkozy was himself an instinctive economic liberal, although prepared to defend individual national interests where they collided with liberal economic logic. For a brief time after his election in 2007 he seemed to promise a return to *dirigisme* and job-creation within the state sector as a solution. That particular prospect was soon erased and belt-tightening became, at German insistence, the order of the day across Europe. Sarkozy's substantial tax concessions to business and the well-off 'wealth-creators' at a time of austerity and deficit-reductions earned him the unwelcome sobriquet of 'president of the rich', which almost certainly contributed, alongside various other *faux pas*, to his failure to obtain re-election in 2012. Variously dubbed a *pompier-pyromane* (a firebug-cum-firefighter) and a 'reality-show' politician, his 'bling' style was widely considered ill-suited to his office. With some critics declaring his presidency an 'ego-cracy', his impetuosity and hyperactivity had proved divisive long before he lost the Elysée to the distinctly un-charismatic François Hollande.

It is also possible that the shorter presidential term of five years has substantially altered the political style of the French presidents – especially of those seeking re-election. Both Sarkozy and Hollande have been more visibly hands-on as de facto heads of government rather than heads of state (albeit retaining considerable 'reserved' powers), which downgrades prime ministers to a junior role and makes presidents increasingly responsible for – and thus vulnerable to – government policy failures. Politics as a near-permanent media spectacle, with 'communication' specialists playing the role of choreographers, has certainly grown in the past decade, particularly under Sarkozy. A president who is deemed too divisive (Sarkozy) or ineffective (Hollande) thus risks the wrath of the electorate in ways previously reserved for the political parties. Above all, the holding of presidential and legislative elections in quick succession, combined with an electoral system with two rounds of voting, encourages candidates who survive into the second round to make sometimes extravagant promises, especially in order to attract citizens who voted for rival parties in the first round. The rapidity with which u-turns over such election promises have had to be made since the 1980s has contributed substantially to popular scepticism towards the political process itself.

## II

Viewed in a longer perspective, France's recent history, especially with the regular succession and cohabitation of the major political 'families' in power, confirms that the Fifth Republic itself has come safely into port. That has led some commentators to wonder if such adjustments do not amount to a de facto Sixth Republic. But this alteration is only one facet of a more complex picture. None of the huge protests of the 1990s or 2000s remotely resembled the kind of threat posed by the monarchists of the 1870s or the anti-Republic leagues of the 1930s. The process of decentralisation may not have turned France into a German-style federal state, but it was considered sufficiently important for Article 1 of the 2003 constitutional reform to declare that 'the organisation of the Republic is decentralised'. Regional and 'territorial' communities (mostly large cities and their wider conurbations) have emerged to a degree unthinkable until recently, and are now the primary point of contact between the population and the state. In some respects, the central state's grip has loosened sufficiently for it to exchange its long-standing role of universal micro-manager for that of the regulator of a layered, nation-wide governance process. The practice of co-habitation blurred the locus of governmental legitimacy, which tended to rest with the president or the parliamentary majority, depending on which of them enjoyed the most recent electoral endorsement. The reduction of the presidential term to five years in 2002 was intended to resolve this problem, and there has been no co-habitation since then. What remains is the frequency of elections, from local to European, whose often 'contrary' results have repeatedly weakened the will of governments to pursue policies deemed unpopular and have encouraged a tendency to reshuffle governments or defer action until the next election.

More significant, however, are the signs that the historical relations of politics and French society – what one historian has called 'the republican eco-system' – have shifted in recent years. The electorate remains capable of voting, as it did massively against Le Pen in the 2002 presidential run-off, when there was a perceived threat to the republican consensus. A

Left and a Right have continued to exist, and between them the Socialists and the post-gaullist RPR (UMP since 2002) usually take the lion's share of the popular vote. But with the virtual disappearance of the Communist party, the historic content of the Left-Right divide has clearly diminished, election-time rhetoric notwithstanding. The conversion to economic liberalism, first of the neo-gaullists under Chirac during the 1970s, and then, more surprisingly, of the Socialists after 1983, paved the way for this, while the successive bouts of political co-habitation have almost inevitably generated greater Left-Right convergence, especially on economic and financial questions. This has left the historical commitment of *both* sides to modernisation and social justice to operate within ever-decreasing circles, which has in turn tempted their dissidents, especially on the Left, to form breakaway parties. European Union rules on deficits and economic competitiveness, often devised by French civil servants, have caused much conflict, especially under Sarkozy, and have often been broken, but overall they have gradually reined in old habits of spending one's way out of trouble, by devaluing the currency or printing money if necessary.

The major result has been a widening gap between the political classes and the population broadly conceived. Turnouts in elections have fallen steadily, suggesting popular apathy. But this would be misleading, because participation is invariably high in presidential elections and on other occasions when it was considered crucial to vote. It is 'Europe' which best illustrates this problem, now that it is as much an internal as an external entity. European elections have witnessed very high and still-rising levels of abstention – from 38% in 1979 to 50% in 1999 and 59% in 2014. An opinion poll of 2012 found that only 44% of those questioned on Europe considered it a positive development, which makes it perhaps easier to understand why the Front National topped to poll in the 2014 European elections. Whenever the elites and the media have openly supported European changes or policies, the electorate has regularly taken it as a cue to vote against them. The single biggest demonstration of this came in 2005, when there was a 69% turnout to reject the European constitution, despite its being drafted by a committee led by Giscard d'Estaing! This was hardly political apathy or indifference – rather a protest against a Union perceived as too narrowly financial and economic in outlook and lacking a compensatory social or welfare component that would appeal to its citizens.

The unpopularity of Europe, even before its handling of the financial crash of 2008–9 damaged it further, was emphatically not confined to France. For some time now, Europe has also been closely identified with a major element in the rise of disaffection towards the French establishment. As we have already seen, the term *précarité* is widely used to describe the social malaise of the past 25 years. French unemployment, whose statistics are increasingly complex, officially remained over 10% in 2010, but in reality it was probably higher; in the most 'difficult' *banlieues* of the Paris region and other major cities, it can be up to twice or three times that percentage. Unemployment is only part of the story, however, since *précarité* is shorthand for the reverse of the post-war French social model. Under pressure to compete effectively in a neo-liberal world driven by market forces, conditions of employment have been gradually loosened since the 1980s, with temporary fixed contracts (the *CDD* or equivalents) becoming ever more common. Between 1982 and 2010, the proportion of working people on CDD (Contrat de durée déterminée) rose gradually from 5% to 13%, while in 2010 itself, as many as 80% of all new jobs – some of them in the public sector – involved such contracts. Criticism of successive governments, both Left and Right, has focussed on the wider social damage inflicted by such policies on families, communities, and individuals themselves. The spectre of joblessness, *déclassement* or poverty no longer hovers solely over the lower classes or the elderly, as in the past, but has spread to the professional middle-classes in the now dominant service sector. In the past generation, it has made young people and the long-term unemployed, especially from immigrant communities, the most vulnerable groups within French society.

The rise of *précarité* and its scattergun effects have been a major factor in the gap between the elites and the population. *Précarité* was also viewed an extension of the problem of insecurity on which Le Pen's Front National had long campaigned and which brought it much popular support. So far, however, the Front National's populist xenophobia and hostility to the political establishment (which it denounces as 'all corrupt', *tous pourris*) renders it too untouchable to be a 'party of government'. Yet that did not prevent it from gaining a powerful stranglehold on Right wing militancy generally, with its electoral performances enabling it to hoover up new protest(er)s from the extreme Right. Le Pen's own exploit of knocking out Jospin in the first round of presidential voting in 2002 caused a sensation, and although it has not been repeated, it revived the party's appeal. As already noted, its stance is one of hostility to the establishment in general and 'Europe', which represents everything the Front detests most – open borders, free movement of people, and reduced national sovereignty. Unthinkable until recently, the fact that in 2014 the Front had the largest number of French deputies elected to the European parliament shows the degree of political disenchantment with Europe. Since Marine Le Pen became the Front's leader, the more offensive features of her father's behaviour (anti-Semitism, the defence of French Algeria) have been quietly dropped, replaced by an insistence that the Front stands firmly with those most affected by adverse social and economic changes. In contrast, the Green Party (*les Verts*) has not absorbed newcomer movements on the Left, where the landscape produced by the proliferation of social causes with distinctive agendas has been, as we shall see presently, more luxuriant.

The question of immigration and nationality has continued to loom large and polarise opinion, not least because developments in the wider world – e.g. the 'war on terror' or the 'Arab spring' – impinge directly on attitudes within France. The triumph of a multi-racial and multi-cultural France with the victory in the 1998 World football cup proved to be less conclusive than many imagined at the time. Indeed, only three years later the outcome of another sporting event – the first ever France-Algeria football match played in Paris – came as a cold shower. The Algerian, or Algerian-born supporters heckled when the *Marseillaise* was played and later invaded the pitch, forcing the match to be abandoned. Such behaviour was manna from heaven for the Front National, which had long considered immigrants from Muslim societies as beyond assimilation into French culture; only repatriation could solve the problem. On the Left, *SOS-Racisme* has tried to combat such positions, while smaller associations, mostly local, have fought to improve conditions for immigrant communities in the toughest *banlieues*. Here, too, the tendency was for grassroots self-organisations to stay clear of institutionalised trade unions and protect their autonomy, even when supported or financed by state bodies.

The radical Islamist movements that emerged in the wake of the Afghanistan and Iraq wars created real dilemmas in France, especially as the country's post-colonial role as the *gendarme* of French Africa has regularly involved potentially contentious military intervention in several countries there. As successively minister of the Interior and president for most of the decade from 2002 to 2012, Sarkozy regularly prioritised security concerns and encouraged confrontational policing ahead of measures that would have lessened the sense of alienation felt in immigrant communities. For many immigrants – or their descendants – who felt themselves unwanted, second-class French citizens the temptation to embrace the trend towards islamisation, culturally and religiously if not necessarily politically, grew apace. But it has been less massive than the propaganda of the Front National about France being inundated by aliens that were beyond integrating, would like people to believe. Indeed, it became clear that the major disturbances of 2005 in the larger cities owed little to Islam, whose religious leaders in France failed to exercise any influence over those involved in the clashes with the forces of order. On the other hand, the established republican culture, shared equally by Left and Right, continues to have no less difficulty in requiring anything less than full integration of its immigrants. With the Front National prompt to denounce concessions here, the room for manoeuvre has been far less than in countries willing to practise multiculturalism. A revised ban on all but 'discreet' religious symbols in schools (2004), followed by one on the full veiling of women in public spaces (2010), makes this clear. In this context, the purpose of Sarkozy's evocation of France's Christian civilisation and its traditions was not hard to decipher. Likewise, recent re-affirmations of *laïcité* have been directed at Islam rather than its original target during the Third Republic, Catholicism.

## III

Recent decades, especially since the 1990s, have also witnessed the emergence and embedding of other social movements, often of a single-issue kind, which have been part of the drift away from inherited politics. There were older models to follow, but much to be invented. The Green party (les *Verts*) and spin-off ecology movements first made their mark in the 1970s, since when they have usually been loosely attached, despite their own fears of political entrapment, to what became known by the late 1990s as the *gauche plurielle* (a 'rainbow Left'). By the 1990s, too, the *Verts* were significant enough for their leading figures to be enticed, Third-Republic style, into successive governments – evidence that their cause now deserved serious attention. Other ecological groups eschewed political affiliations, left or right, and were frequently in open conflict with ministers and technocrats because of their objections to 'modernisation' projects (nuclear power stations, new airports, intensive agriculture etc.) that they considered environmentally dangerous or undesirable. Some earlier campaigns, such as that of Larzac (1971–81), were epoch-making, attracting contrarians of many stripes and forming militants who would later pioneer, either side of 2000, anti-globalisation and associated movements, such as the world-wide ATTAC (Association pour la taxation des transactions financières et pour l'action citoyenne), in which French activists played a major role. Like many other ginger groups, they were un-afraid of civil disobedience and hostile to entrenched 'the-state-knows-best' attitudes.

Feminism had led the way, as have seen, especially in the 1970s, when it made its most spectacular gains. Thereafter its campaigns were frequently focussed on gender relations, and especially on gender parity in politics, business, and work generally. Such a record made it a model that others could follow, in particular those involved in another gender movement, the struggle for gay rights. It became public with a 'gay pride' march in the early 1980s, only a few years before the AIDS crisis seemed to shatter hopes of change. When the movement regained momentum in the 1990s, it had the support of activist groups like SOS-*Racisme*, the Greens and the *Mouvement des citoyens*. This enabled it to resist opposition from the Catholic church and conservative France generally and pave the way for the opaquely titled *pacte civil de solidarité* (PACS) of 1999, which conferred legal status and other normal rights on homosexual unions. It was not until 2012–13, after a heated campaign characterised by huge demonstrations for and against, that gay marriage – or, more accurately, 'marriage for all' – was voted.

This protracted campaign surprised many outsiders who considered France to be highly tolerant of its sexual minorities, but that misses the point, which was that, within the country's established political culture, rights, whether sexual or not, should be available equally to all. Playing the 'universal' card ('marriage *for all*') rather than the 'difference' card of a particular community, could still be decisive in France. In campaigns of this kind, the key to success also seems to be the capacity to trigger a response of solidarity among other comparable, activist movements. When that solidarity is effectively tapped into, it has brought huge crowds onto the streets, and thus obliged the media and the politicians take them seriously.

Some commentators have viewed the successes of the single-issue movements as proof of a healthy civil society bubbling away under the hard crust of the official *res publica*. If so, they seem to have done relatively little to improve the overall morale of French society since, as one French historian recently put it, 'France is faring better than the French themselves'. It attracts more tourists than any other country in the world, their numbers rising steadily from 61.5 to 83 million between 1996 and 2012 and contributing around 7% to its GDP. Few visitors could fail to be impressed by the modernity of its communications and transport infrastructures, or the quality of its health system, to name just two world-beating achievements. Easily the single largest item in the state budget is education and research, which by the 1990s had well outstripped expenditure on the economy. With nine Nobel Prizes since 2005 (not to mention an impressive run of Field's Medal winners in mathematics), France has rediscovered the kind of high intellectual distinction that it exhibited during the first decade of these prizes. A generation of high-profile *engagé* scholars from Jacques Lacan to Michel Foucault and Jacques Derrida have enabled a transatlantic hybrid – dubbed 'French theory' by some because 'recycled' in the US for global consumption – to set the terms and the language for debate within the humanities and social sciences. Finally, while second only to Germany within Europe, France ranks much higher than it in world politics, despite abandoning de Gaulle's route to grandeur. Indeed, Sarkozy cultivated US friendship and completed France's return to NATO's

(North Atlantic Treaty Organization) military command in 2009 the better to strut the world stage.

In both their experience and attitudes, France's elites have never been more European or 'global', increasingly responsive to the challenges and opportunities of a wider world. But that does not endear them to the wider population, for whom Europe and globalisation have seemed inseparable since the neo-liberal 'turn' of the European Union a generation ago. In early 2014, an opinion poll found that 85% of those interviewed thought that France was in decline, a sentiment that is often expressed in terms of France 'descending' to what are supposed to be the lower standards of Anglo-Saxon societies. An obsession with decline has, as we have already seen, repeatedly surfaced in modern France, usually in the wake of military defeat. During the Third Republic and after, the reasons given for decline tended to be relatively specific – demographic, intellectual, or military – but the contemporary malaise has elicited fewer convincing, because less tangible, explanations. In a country whose politicians and intellectuals formed a far tighter continuum than anywhere else in Europe, the successors of Sartre and Aron no longer managed to emulate their forerunners, either as critics or supporters of the political establishment of the day. But this may have less to do with diminished intellectual ability on their part than with the evolution of the French media towards greater autonomy – and even to a more critical stance towards the republican establishment. With the exception of a maverick like the *Canard Enchaîné*, and, more recently, *Médiapart*, France long lacked an investigative press that would not merely challenge the government-élites 'club' but would also pursue skulduggery and wrongdoing in high places. As this changes, and as scoops and scandals encompass figures like Chirac and Sarkozy, the sense of decay may well increase rather than the opposite.

For the present, however, pessimism about the future seems to reflect a sense that the 'French model' of a distinctive chemistry that bonds polity, society, and culture, has been forfeited for a mess of Euro-pottage, and that the accompanying surrender of national sovereignty has left France incapable of reversing that loss. The implicit post-war compact for extensive modernisation – which only the state could deliver – and a generous social-welfare system, has been under immense strain for a generation now. *Both* sides of that equation have become extremely expensive, but while the state has done well in finding European funds for infrastructure and other big projects, their counterpart, the social benefits – essentially healthcare, conditions of employment, and pensions – have increasingly become an ideological battleground. When politicians and governments talk of 'reform' they usually mean cutbacks in provision, to which the response of civil society has usually been more 'solidarist' than external observers might expect.

This is true even when the proposed reforms concern only a small number of professions whose particular benefits (the so-called *régimes spéciaux*) now appear seriously out of line with the general norm. When the professions in question (e.g. freelancers in the entertainment world) invariably defend their corner under the banner of *acquis sociaux* (social gains), they tap into a wider, more potent sentiment of universal concern: it may be our turn today, but tomorrow it will be yours if you fail to support us. Such solidarity has frequently frustrated governments intent on limited, specific reforms.

The modern history of France shows that under conditions of political tranquillity, incremental change can be hard to come by, and that major change rarely occurs without unforeseen upheaval. A generation ago, Raymond Aron suggested that 'this apparently tranquil people is still dangerous', but despite – or perhaps because of – his lifelong immersion in the French political-intellectual world, he resisted the temptation to predict how or when popular dissatisfaction might manifest itself.

## CHRONOLOGY

1995    Chirac president; strikes against austerity measures; new National Library inaugurated; *La Haine*, film by Matthieu Kassovitz

1996    Death of François Mitterrand; end of compulsory military service; anti-immigration laws strengthened

1997    Left coalition victory in snap legislative elections; new co-habitation, Socialist Lionel Jospin prime minister; Maurice Papon trial for role in Jewish deportations by Vichy; European stability pact agreed

1998    Legislation for 35-hour working week; France world football champion

1999    Homosexual couples obtain legal recognition (PaCS); population reaches 60 million

2002    Euro replaces franc; Chirac re-elected president; centre-right UMP wins legislative elections; end of 'co-habitation' government; public-sector strikes over government privatisation plans

2003    Devolution of powers to regions and departments becomes constitutional; protests against reforms to pension system; summer heat wave triggers high death-rate

2004    UMP lose regional elections; Nicholas Sarkozy president of UMP; last French coal-mine closes

2005    Public sector strikes against reforms; European constitution rejected in referendum; riots follow electrocution of youths fleeing police

2006    Proposed youth employment law (CPE (*Contrat première embauche*)) withdrawn after successful protests

2007    Nicolas Sarkozy elected president; UMP wins parliamentary elections with reduced majority; protests against pay cuts, jobs losses, and reform of pension benefits

2008    Lisbon Treaty on reform of European Union ratified; global financial crisis; *Bienvenu chez les ch'tis* major box-office success

2009    France rejoins NATO military command

2010    Spending cuts to reduce deficit announced; UMP loses control of 21 out of 22 regions in elections; protests against raising retirement age to 62

2011    Ban on face veil comes into force; austerity measures to reduce public deficit; sharp rise in unemployment

2012    France loses triple AAA credit-rating from Standard & Poor's; Socialist François Hollande beats Nicolas Sarkozy in presidential election; Jean-Marc Ayrault prime minister

# Bibliography

France has consistently challenged historians to write both general and specialised scholarly works on its past. The resulting bibliography in English alone is impressive in range and volume. The translation into English, in full or in part, of some French series of general histories attests to the subject's enduring interest for English-language readers. But while single-volume accounts of French history abound in French, their English-language counterparts are remarkably few. What follows is a tiny selection of the best and most accessible works in English for each chapter, prefaced by a short general section of works that are cross-period, thematic, and topical in their scope. The abundance of accessible and high-quality works does, however, vary from one period to another.

## GENERAL

*The Cambridge History of Modern France*, 11 volumes, Cambridge, 1983–93 (*CHMF*, translation of the Le Seuil 16-vol. *Histoire de la France contemporaine*):

Vovelle, Michel, *The Fall of the Monarchy 1788–92*, 1984

Bouloiseau, Marc, *The French Revolution 1792–1794*, 1983

Woronoff, Denis, *The Thermidorian Reaction and the Directory 1794–1799*, 1983

Bergeron, Louis, *France under Napoleon*, 1983

Jardin, André and Tudesq, André-Jean, *Restoration and Reaction 1815–1848*, 1988

Plessis, Alain, *The Rise and Fall of the Second Empire 1852–1871*, 1985

Mayeur, Jean-Marie and Rebérioux, Madeleine, *The Third Republic from Its Origins to the Great War 1871–1914*, 1984

Bernard, Philippe and Dubief, Henri, *The Decline of the Third Republic 1914–1938*, 1985

Azéma, Jean-Pierre, *From Munich to Liberation 1938–1944*, 1984

Rioux, Jean-Pierre, *The Fourth Republic 1944–1958*, 1987

Berstein, Serge, *The Republic of de Gaulle 1958–1969*, 1993

*History of France*, 5 volumes, Oxford, 1991–96 (*Blackwell HF*, English translation of the Hachette *Histoire de France*):

  Duby, Georges, *France in the Middle Ages 987–1460*, 1991

  Le Roy Ladurie, Emmanuel, *The French Royal State 1460–1610*, 1994

  ——, *The Ancien Regime 1610–1774*, 1996

  Furet, François, *Revolutionary France 1770–1880*, 1992

  Agulhon, Maurice, *The French Republic 1879–1992*, 1993

*The New Cambridge Medieval History* [*NCMedH*] vols 1–7, Cambridge 1995–2005 (useful chapters in each volume on France until ca 1500)

*The Short Oxford History of France*, ed. William Doyle, 6 volumes, Oxford, 2001–03 (*SOHF*, covers period from 900 to 2002):

  Bull, Marcus, *France in the Central Middle Ages*, 2002

  Potter, David, *France in the Later Middle Ages*, 2002

  Holt, Mack P, *Renaissance and Reformation France*, 2002

  Doyle, William, *Old Regime France*, 2001

  Crook, Malcolm, *Revolutionary France*, 2002

  Macmillan, James, *Modern France*, 2003

Collins, James B, *From Tribes to Nations: The Making of France 500–1799*, Toronto, 2002

Jones, Colin, *The Cambridge Illustrated History of France*, Cambridge, 1994

Price, Roger, *A Concise History of France*, Cambridge 1993, 3rd ed., 2014

Alexander, Martin, ed., *France since Napoleon*, London, 1999

Schwartz, Vanessa R, *Modern France, A very Short Introduction*, Oxford, 2011

Wright, Gordon, *France in Modern Times*, 3rd ed., New York, 1991

Zeldin, Theodore, *France 1848–1945*, 2 vols, Oxford, 1972–1977

Farr, James R, *The Work of France: Labor and Culture in Early Modern Times 1300–1800*, New York, 2008

Foley, Susan K, *Women in France since 1789*, London, 2004

Gildea, Robert, *The Past in French History*, New Haven, 1994

Hazareesingh, Sudhir, *Political Traditions in Modern France*, Oxford, 1994

Higonnet, Patrice, *Paris, Capital of the World*, Cambridge, Mass., 2002

Jones, Colin, *Paris, the Biography of a City*, London, 2004

Nora, Pierre, ed., *Realms of Memory*, 3 vols, New York, 1996–8

Rémond, René, *The Right Wing in France from 1815 to de Gaulle*, Philadelphia, 1966

Robb, Graham, *The Discovery of France: A Historical Geography from the Revolution to the First World War*, London, 2007

Sahlins, *Boundaries*: *The Making of France and Spain in the Pyrenees*, Berkeley, Calif., 1989

——, *Unnaturally French: Foreign Citizens in the Old Regime and After*, Ithaca, 2004

Tilly, Charles, *The Contentious French. Four Centuries of Popular Struggle*, Cambridge, Mass., 1986

Tombs, Isabelle and Robert, *That Sweet Enemy. The History of a Love-Hate Relationship*, London, 2006

# 1   CAPETIAN BEGINNINGS

In addition to Bull, *France in Central Middle Ages* (*SOHF*); Duby, *France in Middle Ages* (*Blackwell HF*) and *NCMedH*:

Bradbury, Jim, *Philip Augustus, King of France 1180–1223*, London, 1997

——, *The Capetians*, London, 2007

Cheyette, Frederic L, *Ermengard of Narbonne and the World of the Troubadours*, Ithaca, 2001

Duby, Georges, *The Three Orders: Feudal Society Imagined*, Chicago 1980

——, *The Age of the Cathedrals: Art and Society 980–1420*, Chicago, 1981

——, *The Legend of Bouvines, War, Religion and Culture in the Middle Ages*, Berkeley, Calif., 1990

——, *France in the Middle Ages 987–1460*, Oxford, 1991 (Blackwell HF)

Dunbabin, Jean, *France in the Making 843–1180*, 2nd ed., London, 2000

Fossier, Robert, *The Axe and the Oath. Ordinary Life in the Middle Ages*, Princeton, 2010

Geary, Patrick, *Before France and Germany: The Creation and Transformation of the Merovingian World*, Oxford, 1988

Hallam, Elizabeth, *Capetian France 987–1328*, London, 1980

James, Edward, *The Origins of France, from Clovis to the Capetians*, London, 1982

Le Roy Ladurie, Emmanuel, *Montaillou: Cathars and Catholics in a French Village*, London, 1978

McKitterick, Rosamund, *The Frankish Kingdoms and the Carolingians 751–987*, London 1983

Paterson, L M, *The World of the Troubadours. Medieval Occitan Society c 1100–1300*, Cambridge, 1993

Strayer, Joseph R, *The Reign of Philip the Fair*, Princeton, 1980.

Wei, Ian P, *Intellectual Culture in Medieval Paris: Theologians and the University c 1100 to 1330*, Cambridge, 2012


# 2   A SOCIETY AND POLITY IN CRISIS AND RECOVERY

In addition to *NCMedH*; Duby, *France in the Middle Ages*; Farr, *Work of France*; Fossier, *Axe and Oath*; Ladurie, *Royal French State*; Potter, *France in Later Middle Ages*:

Allmand, C. T., *The Hundred Years' War: England and France at War*, Cambridge, 1988

Beaune, Colette, *The Birth of an Ideology: Myths and Symbols in Late Medieval France*, Berkeley, Calif., 1991

Blunt, Anthony, *Art and Architecture in France 1500–1700*, Harmonsworth, 1957

Curry, Ann, *The Hundred Years' War*, London, 2nd ed., Basingstoke, 2003

Huppert, George, *Les bourgeois gentilshommes*, Chicago, 1977

——, *The Public Schools of Renaissance France*, Urbana, Ill., 1984

——, *The Style of Paris. Renaissance Origins of the French Enlightenment*, Bloomington, 1999

Knecht, Robert, *Renaissance Warrior and Patron. The Reign of Francis I*, Cambridge, 1994

——, *The Rise and Fall of Renaissance France 1483–1610*, London, 1996

——, *The Valois Kings of France 1328–1589*, London, 2001

——, *The French Renaissance court*, New Haven, 2008

Lewis, P S, *Later Medieval France*, Oxford, 1968

Potter, David, *A History of France 1460–1560: The Emergence of a Nation-state*, London, 1995

Le Roy Ladurie, Emmanuel, *The French Peasantry 1450–1660*, Oxford, 1987

Small, Graeme, *Late Medieval France*, Basingstoke, 2009

Thomson, David, *Renaissance Paris: Architecture and Growth 1475–1600*, Berkeley, Calif., 1984

Verger, Jacques, *Men of Learning in Europe at the End of the Middle Ages*, Notre Dame, 2000

Zerner, Henri, *Renaissance Art in France: The Invention of Classicism*, Paris, 2003

## 3   THE *ANCIEN RÉGIME* IN THE MAKING

In addition to Blunt, *Art and Architecture*; Doyle, *Old Regime France* (*SOHF*); Farr, *Work of France*; Holt, *Renaissance and Reformation France* (*SOHF*); Knecht, *Rise and Fall*; Le Roy Ladurie, *French Royal State* (*Blackwell HF*) and *French Peasantry*:

Beik, William, *A Social and Cultural History of Early Modern France*, Cambridge, 2009

Benedict, Philip, ed., *Cities and Social Change in Early Modern France*, London, 1989

Bercé, Yves-Marie, *The Birth of Absolutism. A History of France 1598–1661*, Basingstoke, 1995

———, *History of Peasant Revolts: The Social Origins of Rebellion in Early Modern France*, Cambridge 1990

Bergin, Joseph, *Church, Society and Religious Change in France 1580–1730*, New Haven, 2009

———, *The Politics of Religion in Early Modern France*, New Haven, 2014

Bohanan, Donna, *Crown and Nobility in Early Modern France*, Basingstoke, 2001

Briggs, Robin, *Early Modern France 1560–1715*, Oxford, 1976

———, *Communities of Belief: Cultural and Social Tensions in Early Modern France*, Oxford 1989

Burke, Peter, *The Fabrication of Louis XIV*, New Haven, 1992

Collins, James B, *The State in Early Modern France*, 2nd ed., Cambridge, 2009

Doyle, William, ed., *The Oxford Handbook of the Ancien Regime*, Oxford, 2012

Gibson, Wendy, *Women in Seventeenth-century France*, London, 1989

Goodman, Dena, *The Republic of Letters: A Cultural History of the French Enlightenment*, Ithaca, NY, 1994

Greengrass, Mark, *The French Reformation*, Oxford, 1987

———, *France in the Age of Henry IV: The Struggle for Stability*, 2nd ed., London, 1995

Holt, Mack P, *The French Wars of Religion 1562–1629*, Cambridge, 1995

Hufton, Olwen, *The Prospect before Her: A History of Women in Western Europe 1500–1800*, London, 1996

Kettering, Sharon, *Patrons, Brokers and Clients in Seventeenth-century France*, Oxford, 1986

——, *French Society 1598–1715*, Harlow, 2001

Knecht, Robert, *Richelieu*, London, 1991

——, *Catherine de Medici*, London, 1998

——, *The French Civil Wars*, London, 2000

Le Roy Ladurie, Emmanuel, *The Peasants of Languedoc*, Urbana, Ill., 1974

——, *The Ancien Régime 1610–1774*, Oxford, 1996 (*Blackwell HF*)

Jones, Colin, *The Great Nation 1715–1799*, London, 2002

Lossky, Andrew, *Louis XIV and the French Monarchy*, New Brunswick, N.J., 1994

Lynn, John, *The Wars of Louis XIV*, London, 1999

McCluskey, Phil, *Absolute Monarchy on the Frontiers. Louis XIV's Military Occupations of Lorraine and Savoy*, Manchester, 2013

Parker, David, *The Making of French Absolutism*, London, 1983

Pritchard, James, *In Search of Empire: the French in the Americas 1670–1730*, Cambridge, 2004

Rapley, Elizabeth, *Dévotes: Women and the Church in Seventeenth-century France*, Montreal, 1990

Ranum, Orest, *Paris in the Age of Absolutism*, 2nd ed., University Park, Penn., 2002

Sturdy, David, *Louis XIV*, Basingstoke, 1998

——, *Richelieu and Mazarin*, Basingstoke, 2004

## 4    FROM ENLIGHTENMENT TO EMPIRE

In addition to Crook, *Revolutionary France* (*SOHF*); Doyle, *Old Regime France* (*SOHF*); Furet, *Revolutionary France* (*Blackwell HF*); Jones, *Great Nation*:

Andress, David, *The French Revolution and the People*, London, 2004

Aston, Nigel, *Religion and Revolution in France*, 1780–1804, Basingstoke, 2000

Bell, David, *The Cult of the Nation in France: Inventing Nationalism 1680–1800*, Cambridge, Mass., 2001

Bergeron, Louis, *France under Napoleon*, Cambridge, 1983

Bosher, John F, *The French Revolution*, London, 1989

Broers, Michael, *Europe under Napoleon*, London, 1996

Chartier, Roger, *The Cultural Origins of the French Revolution*, Durham, N.C., 1991

Crook, Malcolm, *Napoleon Comes to Power: Democracy and Dictatorship in Revolutionary France 1795–1804*, Cardiff, 1998

Darnton, Robert, *The Literary Underground of the Old Regime*, Cambridge, Mass., 1982

Doyle, William, *Origins of the French Revolution*, Oxford, 1980

——, *The Oxford History of the French Revolution*, Oxford, 1989

——, *The French Revolution, A very Short Introduction*, Oxford, 2001

——, *Aristocracy and its Enemies in the Age of Revolution*, Oxford, 2009

Ellis, Geoffrey, *Napoleon*, 2nd ed., London, 2000

——, *The Napoleonic Empire*, 2nd ed., Basingstoke, 2003

Farge, Arlette, *Subversive Words. Public Opinion in Eighteenth-century France*, University Park, Penn., 1994

Forrest, Alan, *The French Revolution*, Oxford, 1995

——, *Paris, the Provinces and the French Revolution*, London, 2004

——, *The Legacy of the French Revolutionary Wars: The Nation-in-arms in French Republican Memory*, Cambridge, 2009

——, *Napoleon*, 2012

Furet, François, *Interpreting the French Revolution*, Cambridge, 1981

Garrioch, David, *The Formation of the Parisian Bourgeoisie 1690–1830*, Cambridge, Mass., 1996

——, *The Making of Revolutionary Paris*, Los Angeles, 2002

Hardman, John, *Louis XVI*, London 1993

Hufton, Olwen, *The Poor of Eighteenth-century France*, Oxford, 1974

——, *Women and the Limits of Citizenship in the French Revolution*, Toronto, 1992

Jones, Peter, *The Peasantry in the French Revolution*, Cambridge, 1989

——, *Reform and Revolution in France: The Politics of Transition 1774–1791*, Cambridge, 1995

Kates, Gary, ed., *The French Revolution, Recent Debates and New Controversies*, London, 1998

Kennedy, Emmet, *A Cultural History of the French Revolution*, New Haven, 1989

Landes, Joan B, *Women and the Public Sphere in the Age of the French Revolution*, Ithaca, NY, 1988

Lyons, Martyn, *Napoleon and the Legacy of the French Revolution*, London, 1994

Maza, Sarah, *The Myth of the French Bourgeoisie: An Essay on the Social Imaginary 1750–1850*, Cambridge, Mass., 2003

McPhee, Peter, *A Social History of France 1789–1914*, 2nd ed., Basingstoke, 2004

Roche, Daniel, *France in the Enlightenment*, Cambridge, Mass., 1998

Sutherland, D M G, *France 1789–1815, Revolution and Counter-Revolution*, London, 1985

Tackett, Timothy, *Religion, Revolution and Regional Culture in Eighteenth-century France*, Princeton, 1986

Van Kley, Dale K, *The Religious Origins of the French* Revolution, New Haven, 1996

Vovelle, Michel, *The Revolution against the Church*, Oxford 1991

Woloch, Isser, *Napoleon and his Collaborators. The Making of a Dictatorship*, New York, 2001

——, *The New Regime. Transformations of the French Civic Order 1789–1820s*, New York, 1994

Woolf, Stuart, *Napoleon's Integration of Europe*, London, 1991

## 5    OBSTRUCTED PATHS

In addition to Alexander, *France since Napoleon*; Crook, *Revolutionary France (SOHF)*; Furet, *Revolutionary France (Blackwell HF)*; McPhee, *Social History of France*:

Agulhon, Maurice, *The Republican Experiment 1848–1852*, Cambridge, 1983 *(CHMF)*

Aldrich, Richard, *Greater France: A History of French Overseas Expansion*, Basingstoke, 1996

Charle, Christophe, *Social History of France in the Nineteenth Century*, Oxford, 1994

Gibson, Ralph, *A Social History of French Catholicism 1789–1914*, London, 1989

Gildea, Robert, *Children of the Revolution 1799–1914*, London, 2008

Harris, Ruth, *Lourdes: Body and Spirit in the Secular Age*, London, 1999

Hazareesingh, Sudhir, *The Legend of Napoleon*, London, 2004

――, *From Subject to Citizen, the Second Empire and the Emergence of French Democracy*, Princeton, 1998

Jardin, André and Tudesq, André-Jean, *Restoration and Reaction 1815–1848*, Cambridge, 1988 (*CHMF*)

Macmillan, James, *Napoleon III*, London, 1991

Magraw, Roger, *France 1800–1914, a Social History*, London, 2002

Pilbeam, Pamela, *1830, Revolution in France*, Basingstoke, 1991

――, *Republicanism in Nineteenth-century France 1814–1871*, Basingstoke, 1995

Plessis, Alain, *The Rise and Fall of the Second Empire 1852–1871*, Cambridge, 1985 (*CHMF*)

Price, Roger, *The French Second Empire, an Anatomy of Political Power*, Cambridge, 2001

Rapport, Michael, *1848, Year of Revolutions*, London, 2010

Robb, Graham, *Victor Hugo*, London, 1997

Sutcliffe, Anthony, *Paris, an Architectural History*, New Haven, 1993

Tombs, Robert, *France 1815–1914*, London, 1997

――, *The War against Paris 1871*, Cambridge, 1981

## 6   DANGERS AND DIFFICULTIES

In addition to Alexander, *France since Napoleon*; Charle, *Social History*; Crook, ed., *Revolutionary France* (*SOHF*); Gildea, *Children of the Revolution*; Macmillan, *Modern France* (*SOHF*); Magraw, *France 1800–1914*; McPhee, *Social History of France*; Tombs, *France 1815–1914*:

Agulhon, Maurice, *The French Republic 1879–1992*, Oxford, 1992 (*Blackwell HF*)

Alice Conklin et al., *France and Its Empire since 1870*, Oxford, 2010

Larkin, Maurice, *Church and State after the Dreyfus Affair*, London 1974

――, *Religion, Politics and Preferment in France since 1890: The* belle époque *and its Legacy*, Cambridge, 1995

Lyons, Martin, *Readers and Society in Nineteenth-century France*, Basingstoke, 2001

Macmillan, James, *Twentieth-century France. Politics and Society in France*, 2nd ed., London, 1992

Magraw, Roger, *A History of the French Working Class*, 2 vols, Oxford, 1992

Mayeur, Jean-Marie and Rebérioux, Madeleine, *The Third Republic from Its Origins to the Great War 1871–1914*, Cambridge, 1984 (*CHMF*)

McManners, John, *Church and State in France 1870–1914*, London, 1972

Painter, George D, *Marcel Proust*, 2 vols, London, 1959

Passmore, Kevin, *The Right in France from the Third Republic to Vichy*, Oxford, 2013

Rearick, Charles, *Pleasures of the* belle époque: *Entertainment and Festivity in Turn-of-the-century France*, New Haven, 1985

Shorter, Edward and Tilly, Charles, *Strikes in France 1830–1968*, Cambridge, Mass., 1974

Sowerwine, Charles, *France since 1870. Culture, Politics and Society*, Basingstoke, 2001

Smith, Timothy B, *Creating the Welfare State in France 1890–1930*, Montreal, 2003

Weber, Eugen, *Peasants into Frenchmen. The Modernization of Rural France 1870–1914*, London, 1979

## 7    TWO WARS AND A PEACE

In addition to Alexander, *France since Napoleon*; Conklin, *France and Empire since 1870*; Macmillan, *Modern France* (SOHF); Macmillan, *Twentieth-century France*; Sowerwine, *France since 1870*:

Adamthwaite, *Grandeur and Misery. France's Bid for Power in Europe 1914–1940*, London 1995

Andrew, Christopher, and Kanya-Forstner, A S, *France Overseas: The Great War and the Climax of French Imperial Expansion*, London, 1981

Azéma, Jean-Pierre, *From Munich to Liberation 1938–1944*, Cambridge, 1984 (*CMHF*)

Becker, Jean-Jacques, *The Great War and the French People*, London, 1986

Bell, Philip M H, *France and Britain: Entente and Estrangement 1900–1940*, London, 1996

Bernard, Philippe and Dubief, Henri, *The Decline of the Third Republic 1914–1938*, Cambridge, 1985 (*CHMF*)

Burrin, Philippe, *France under the Germans: Collaboration and Compromise*, New York, 1996

Conklin, Alice, *A Mission to Civilise: The Republican Idea of Empire in France and West Africa 1895–1930*, Stanford, Calif., 1997

Evans, Martin, ed., *Empire and Culture. The French Experience 1830–1940*, Basingstoke, 2004

Gildea, Robert, *Marianne in Chains. In Search of the German Occupation of France 1940–45*, Oxford, 2002

Hélias, Pierre-Jakèz, *The Horse of Pride: Life in a Breton Village*, New Haven, 1974

Jackson, Julian, *The Popular Front in France: Defending Democracy 1934–38*, Cambridge, 1988

——, *France, the Dark Years 1940–1944*, Oxford, 2001

——, *The Fall of France. The Nazi Invasion of 1940*, Oxford, 2003

Kedward, Rod, *La Vie en bleu. France and the French since 1900*, London, 2005

Keiger, John F V, *Raymond Poincaré*, Cambridge, 1997

Kuisel, Richard, *Capitalism and the State in modern France*, Cambridge, 1981

Larkin, Maurice, *France since the Popular Front*, London, 1996

Milward, Alan, *The New Order and the French Economy*, Oxford, 1970

Paxton, Robert, *Vichy France, Old Guard and New Order 1940–1944*, New York, 1972

Rearick, Charles, *The French in Love and War: Popular Culture in the Era of the World Wars*, New Haven, 1997

Reynolds, Sian, *France between the Wars: Gender and Politics*, London, 1996

Vinen, Richard, *France 1934–1970*, Basingstoke, 1996

——, *The Unfree French. Life under the Occupation*, London, 2006

Weber, Eugen, *The Hollow Years. France in the 1930s*, London, 1995

## 8   THE *TRENTE GLORIEUSES* AND AFTER & EPILOGUE

In addition to Alexander, *France since Napoleon*; Conklin, *France and Empire since 1870*; Kedward, *La Vie en bleu*; Larkin, *France since the Popular Front*; Macmillan, ed., *Modern France* (SOHF); Macmillan, *Twentieth-century France*; Sowerwine, *France since 1870*; Vinen, *France 1934–70*:

Ageron, Charles-R, *Modern Algeria, a History from 1830 to the Present*, London, 1991

Ardagh, John, *France in the New Century: Portrait of a Changing Society*, London, 2000

Atkin, Nicholas, *The Fifth French Republic*, London, 2005

Berstein, Serge, *The Republic of de Gaulle 1958–1969*, Cambridge, 1993 (*CHMF*)

Chadwick, Kay, ed., *Catholicism, Politics and Society in Twentieth-century France*, Liverpool, 2000

Gildea, Robert, *France since 1945*, 2nd ed., Oxford, 2002

Hazareesingh, Sudhir, *In the Shadow of the General. Modern France and the Myth of de Gaulle*, Oxford, 2012

Horne, Alistair, *A Savage War of Peace. Algeria 1954–1962*, London, 1991

Jackson, Julian et al., eds, *May '68. Rethinking France's Lost Revolution*, Basingstoke, 2011

Keiger, John V F, *France and the World since 1970*, London, 2001

Kuisel, Richard F, *Capitalism and the State in Modern France. Renovation and Economic Management in the Twentieth Century*, Cambridge, 1981

Noiriel, Gerard, *The French Melting Pot. Immigration, Citizenship and National Identity*, Minneapolis, 1996

Nord, Phillip, *France's New Deal, from the Thirties to the Post-war Era*, Princeton, 2012

Rioux, Jean-Pierre, *The Fourth Republic 1944–1958*, Cambridge, 1987 (*CHMF*)

Rousso, Henry, *The Vichy Syndrome: History and Memory in France since 1944*, Cambridge, Mass., 1991

Shennan, Andrew, *De Gaulle*, London, 1993

Wall, Irwin M, *The United States and the Making of Post-war France 1945–54*, Cambridge, 1991

Weil, Patrick, *How to Be French. Nationality in the Making since 1789*, Durham, N.C., 2009

Wylie, Lawrence, *Village in the Vaucluse*, 2nd ed., New York, 1964

# Index

48337243R00184

Printed in Poland
by Amazon Fulfillment
Poland Sp. z o.o., Wrocław